C000185610

THE ROYAL TOMBS
OF ANCIENT EGYPT

To the memories of:

Edwin C. Brock (1946–2015), Otto J. Schaden (1937–2015)
and Nabil Swelim (1935–2015)

THE ROYAL TOMBS
OF ANCIENT EGYPT

Aidan Dodson

First published in Great Britain in 2016 by
PEN & SWORD ARCHAEOLOGY
an imprint of
Pen and Sword Books Ltd
47 Church Street
Barnsley
South Yorkshire S70 2AS

Copyright © Aidan Mark Dodson, 2016

ISBN 978 1 47382 159 0

The right of Aidan Mark Dodson to be identified as the
author of work has been asserted by him in accordance
with the Copyright, Designs and Patents Act 1988.

A CIP record for this book is available from the British Library

All rights reserved. No part of this book may be reproduced or transmitted
in any formor by any means, electronic or mechanical including photocopying,
recording or by any information storage and retrieval
system, without permission from the Publisher in writing.

Printed and bound in England
by CPI Group (UK) Ltd, Croydon, CR0 4YY

Typeset in Times New Roman by
CHIC GRAPHICS

Pen & Sword Books Ltd incorporates the imprints of
Pen & Sword Archaeology, Atlas, Aviation, Battleground, Discovery,
Family History, History, Maritime, Military, Naval, Politics, Railways,
Select, Social History, Transport, True Crime, Claymore Press,
Frontline Books, Leo Cooper, Praetorian Press, Remember When,
Seaforth Publishing and Wharncliffe.

For a complete list of Pen and Sword titles please contact
Pen and Sword Books Limited
47 Church Street, Barnsley, South Yorkshire, S70 2AS, England
E-mail: enquiries@pen-and-sword.co.uk
Website: www.pen-and-sword.co.uk

Contents

Preface

The tombs of the kings of Egypt include some of the most iconic sepulchres of all time, and very many books – of distinctly variable quality – have been published on various groupings or aspects of them. Indeed, the present writer has issued a volume on the pyramids and another on the tombs that followed them. However, none ever seems to have attempted to provide coverage of all such monuments, from the earliest times down to the end of paganism, including both native rulers, buried in Egypt, and those of foreign monarchs, buried abroad. The present volume is an attempt to fill this gap, and as such includes descriptions, images, discussions and references for not only such tombs as the pyramids and those in the Valley of the Kings, but also the funerary monuments of the kings of Persia (who formed the Twenty-seventh and Thirty-first Egyptian Dynasties) and the mausolea of the Roman emperors, who continued to claim pharaonic dignity down to the end of the third century AD. It also provides data on the tombs of the families of the kings as Egypt, an aspect of the Egyptian funerary world that is rarely covered, with the exception of a few 'star' tombs, for example that of Nefertiry, wife of Rameses II.

Aside from providing the full story of the Egyptian royal tomb, the opportunity has been taken to include the results of the very latest fieldwork in Egypt, which has revealed a whole hitherto-unsuspected royal cemetery at Abydos, a tomb full of members of the royal family in the Valley of the Kings, and the tombs of more family members in a remote valley at Western Thebes. As very much work-in-progress, it is possible that some of the initial conclusions reported here (some from the excavators' oral presentations at conferences, in particular the 2015 annual meeting of the American Research Centre in Egypt in Houston and the 'Abusir and Saqqara in the Year 2015' conference in Prague) may change from the position when the manuscript for the present book was submitted in the autumn of 2015.

In writing a book such as this, one inevitably falls into the debt of many people; in particular, I would like to thank Felix Arnold, Andrew Chugg, Caterin Johansson, Piers Litherland, Dawn McCormack, Alireza Moftakhori, Leire Olabarria, Hourig Sourouzian, Joe Wegner, Kent Weeks and Magdy Abu-Hamid Ali for all their help, as well as others who have allowed me to visit their work, discussed finds, provided images or assisted in a wide range of ways. In doing so, I must pay tribute to Edwin Brock and Otto Schaden, two of my oldest friends in Egyptology, who died shortly after the manuscript was completed and to whom this book is dedicated. Much of their careers were devoted to the Valley of the Kings, Ted in particular for his work on the study and reconstruction of the royal sarcophagi, Otto to the clearance and study of the tombs of Ay and Amenmeses, also finding the first 'new' tomb there since Tutankhamun's – KV63, perhaps the embalming cache of that tomb. Also taken from us during the same fatal autumn was Nabil Swelim, another old friend, in this case in the study of pyramids, among whose distinctions was the rediscovery of the Brick Pyramid at Abu Rowash, 'hidden in plain sight' for many decades.

I would also like to thank my principal partners in tomb and temple visiting over the years, my wife Dyan Hilton and my dear friend Salima Ikram, for their company and insights. I am also indebted to Martin Davies and Reg Clark for proofreading the manuscript (and providing photographs!), but all surviving errors of typography, fact and/or judgement remain, of course, my own responsibility.

Department of Archaeology & Anthropology
March 2016
University of Bristol

Abbreviations and Conventions

BM	British Museum, London, UK.
EMC	Egyptian Museum, Cairo, Egypt.
G	Giza monument number.
KHM	Kunsthistorisches Museum, Vienna, Austria
KV	Valley of the Kings tomb number.
L	Pyramid number assigned by Richard Lepsius.
Louvre	Musée du Louvre, Paris, France.
MMA	Metropolitan Museum of Art, New York.
NMS	National Museums Scotland, Edinburgh, UK.
NRT	Tanis royal cemetery tomb number.
Ny Carlsberg	Ny Carlsberg Glyptotek, Copenhagen, Denmark.
QV	Valley of the Queens tomb number.
TA	Tell el-Amarna tomb number.
TT	Theban Tomb number.
UPMAA	University of Pennsylvania Museum of Archaeology and Anthropology, Philadelphia, PA, USA.
WV	Western Valley of the Kings tomb number.

Renderings of Egyptian names are intended as far as possible to preserve the original consonantal structure of the original written Egyptian, rather than any hypothetical ancient pronunciation. Persons of the same name are distinguished by roman numerals (upper case for kings and certain other senior figures; lower case for others) or letters, according to a basic system that has been developing within Egyptology since the 1970s (see Dodson and Hilton 2004: 39). This is not wholly internally coherent, as it is desirable to preserve some long-standing designations for avoidance of confusion.

When giving bibliography for monuments, for reasons of brevity references are generally restricted to Porter and Moss (various dates) and substantive publications that have appeared after the publication of the relevant Porter and Moss volume.

Introduction

The Egyptian tomb was at its heart a magical machine for aiding the journey of a dead person from this world to the next, and keeping them nourished in the beyond. To fulfil this role, it ideally comprised two distinct elements, the burial chamber in which the body would lie for eternity, and an offering place where food and drink could be placed by the living for the benefit of the dead, or which could generate such nourishment by means of written spells and often painted or carved depictions.

The most elaborate examples of such machines were of course generally those of the rulers of the country, and also often differed from contemporary non-royal norms both architecturally and in such matters as the choice of texts and representations, the latter reflecting the different posthumous destiny envisaged for the already-divine king. There was also significant change across the three millennia of pharaonic history as features appeared, transformed, disappeared, reappeared in different forms, and typical ownership changed. Thus, the pyramid appeared above royal tombs at the beginning of the Third Dynasty, disappeared during the First Intermediate Period, was reintroduced by the Twelfth Dynasty and then ceased to be employed by kings at early in the Eighteenth Dynasty – at which point it became a regular feature of private tombs. It was then adopted by the Nubian kings of the Twenty-fifth Dynasty, to remain the usual royal tomb-monument until the end of the Kushite monarchy around AD 350.

Similar shifts in employment are to be found in the texts placed in the substructures of the tombs, with the Pyramid Texts of the later Old Kingdom later becoming usable by private individuals, and spawning the primarily-private Coffin Texts and Book of the Dead. Then, in the New Kingdom, the Book of *Amduat* and its derivatives (the 'books of the underworld'), focussing on the nocturnal voyage of sun-god, were introduced as purely-kingly confections,[1] with marginal supplements from the Book of the Dead. However, during the Third Intermediate Period the books of the underworld became universally available, while parts of the Book of the Dead never previously employed for kings began to be used in royal tombs. The significance of such shifts has been much debated, a theory that the adoption of the Coffin Texts by private individuals marked a fundamental change in their potential to attain eternal life (the 'democratisation of the afterlife') becoming all but canonical. However, the late Harold Hays's comprehensive demolition of this long-held idea[2] means that a rather more nuanced explanation needs to be found (which is, however, beyond the scope of the present work). On the other hand, the appearance of the Book of Dead motif of the judgement of the dead, featuring the king, during the Twenty-second Dynasty (pp. 110-11) may well be a reflection of the diminution in the status of the king that can be seen in many aspects of the history of the later Third Intermediate Period.

The following pages thus navigate through these changes and developments, including descriptions, plans and photographs of, together with published references to, all significant funerary monuments belonging to those claiming kingship over Egypt. They also provide more summary descriptions and discussions of the burial places of their immediate families, whose nature also changed significantly over time, ranging from burials inside the king's tomb to independent structures of considerable size. Maps of principal cemeteries are also included, since the locations of tombs within the landscape and relative to one another can give important data on a range of factors, including in some cases dating where this is not made clear by inscribed material or architectural factors. They also indicate the way in which the elements making up an individual's funerary monument can be widely distributed across the landscape, both contiguously, as in the case of Old and Middle Kingdom pyramids, and also quite independently, as in the case of the tombs and memorial temples of the New Kingdom and tombs and enclosures of the Early Dynastic Period. The book is thus intended to provide a wholistic view of this long series of mortuary structures, both great and small, the former including those that continue to be considered wonders of the world.

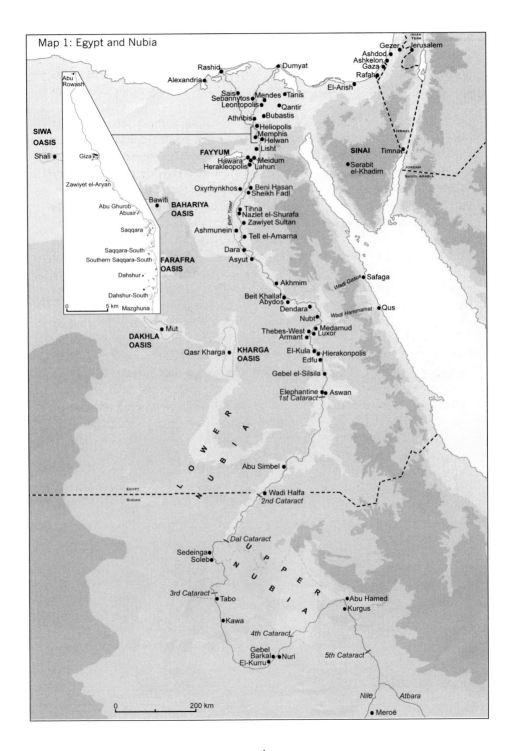

Map 1: Egypt and Nubia

SIWA
OASIS
Shali

Abu
Rowash

Giza

Zawiyet el-Aryan

Bawiti
Abu Ghurob
Abusir
Saqqara

Saqqara-South
Southern Saqqara-South

Dahshur

Dahshur-South

Mazghuna

BAHARIYA
OASIS

FARAFRA
OASIS

0   5 km

Rashid   Dumyat
Alexandria
                                        Sais
                                Sebannytos   Mendes   Tanis
                                Leontopolis   Qantir
                                Athribis   Bubastis
                                        Heliopolis
                                        Memphis
                                        Helwan
                                        Lisht
FAYYUM
        Hawara   Meidum
Herakleopolis   Lahun

Oxyrhynkhos   Beni Hasan
                            Sheikh Fadl

                    Tihna
                Nazlet el-Shurafa
                Zawiyet Sultan
Ashmunein   Tell el-Amarna

Dara
Asyut

El-Arish

Gezer   Jerusalem
Ashdod
Ashkelon
Gaza
Rafah

ISRAEL

SINAI   Timna
        Serabit
        el-Khadim

JORDAN
SAUDI ARABIA

Bahr Yusef

Mut

DAKHLA
OASIS

Qasr Kharga

KHARGA
OASIS

Akhmim   Wadi Gasus   Safaga

Beit Khallaf
        Abydos
                Dendara
                        Nubt   Wadi Hammamat   Qus
                Thebes-West   Medamud
                Armant   Luxor
                El-Kula   Hierakonpolis
                Edfu
        Gebel el-Silsila

Elephantine   Aswan
1st Cataract

L
O
W
E
R

N
U
B
I
A

Abu Simbel

EGYPT
SUDAN

Wadi Halfa
2nd Cataract

Dal Cataract

Sedeinga
Soleb

U
P
P
E
R

N
U
B
I
A

3rd Cataract   Tabo

Kawa

Abu Hamed
Kurgus

4th Cataract

Gebel
Barkal   Nuri   5th Cataract
El-Kurru

0   200 km

Nile   Atbara

Meroë

xi

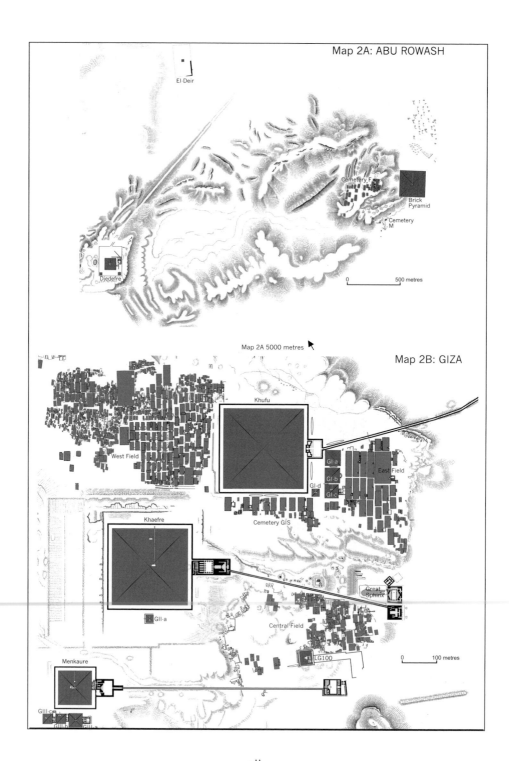

Map 2A: ABU ROWASH

El-Deir

Cemetery F

Brick
Pyramid

Cemetery
M

Djedefre

0   500 metres

Map 2A 5000 metres

Map 2B: GIZA

Khufu

West Field

GI-a

GI-b

GI-d   GI-c

East Field

Cemetery GIS

Khaefre

GII-a

Great
Sphinx

Central Field

LG100

Menkaure

0   100 metres

GIII-c

GIII-b   GIII-a

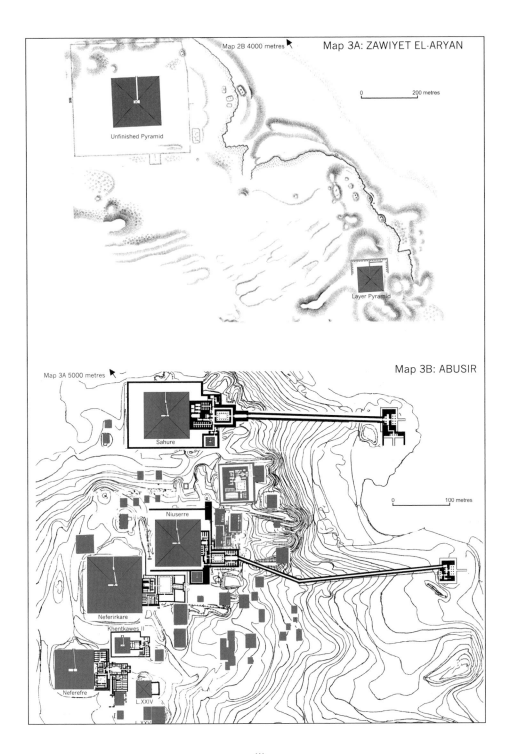

Map 3A: ZAWIYET EL-ARYAN

Map 2B 4000 metres

0   200 metres

Unfinished Pyramid

Layer Pyramid

Map 3B: ABUSIR

Map 3A 5000 metres

0   100 metres

Sahure

Niuserre

Neferirkare

Khentkawes II

Neferefre

L.XXIV

xiii

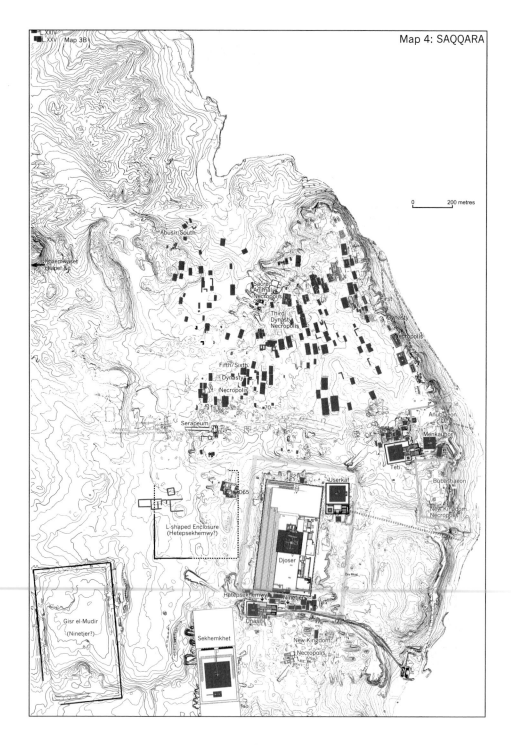

Map 4: SAQQARA

0   200 metres

Abusir South

Ptahemwaset
Chapel &

Sacred
Animals
Necropolis

Third
Dynasty
Necropolis

First
Dynasty
Necropolis

Fifth/Sixth
Dynasty
Necropolis

70

Anubieon

Serapeum

Menkauhor

Teti

3065

Userkaf

Bubastieon

L-shaped Enclosure
(Hetepsekhemwy?)

New Kingdom
Necropolis

Djoser

Dry Moat

Gisr el-Mudir

(Ninetjer?)

Hetepsekhemwy   Ninetjer

Unas

Sekhemkhet

New Kingdom
Necropolis

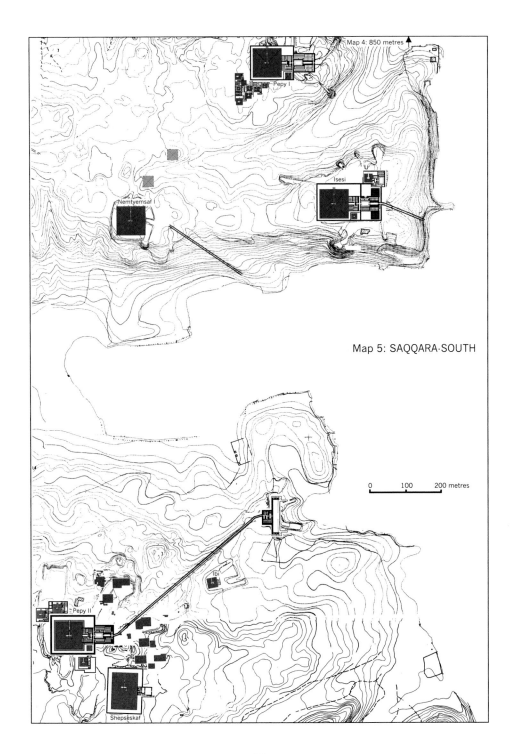

Map 5: SAQQARA·SOUTH

Map 4: 850 metres

Pepy I

Isesi

Nemtyemsaf I

0   100   200 metres

Ibi

Pepy II

Shepseskaf

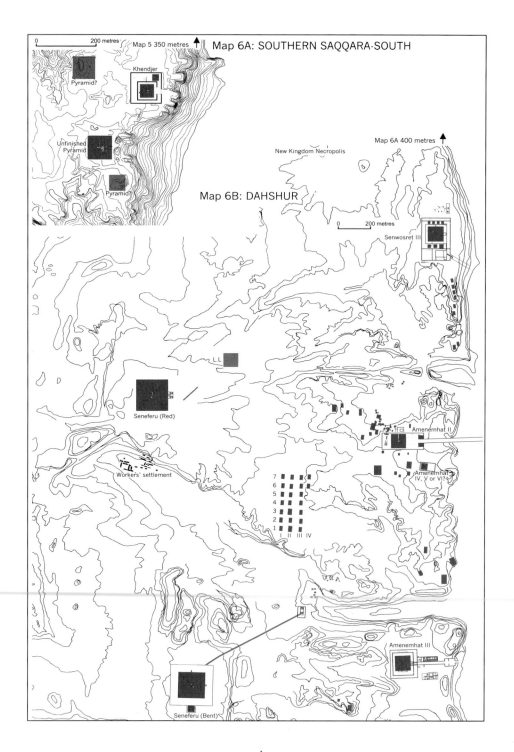

Map 6A: SOUTHERN SAQQARA-SOUTH

0   200 metres   Map 5 350 metres ↑

Pyramid?

Khendjer

Unfinished Pyramid

Map 6A 400 metres ↑

New Kingdom Necropolis

Map 6B: DAHSHUR

Pyramid?

0   200 metres

Senwosret III

L.L.

Seneferu (Red)

Workers' settlement

Amenemhat II

Amenemhat IV, V or VI?

7
6
5
4
3
2
1
  I II III IV

Amenemhat III

Seneferu (Bent)

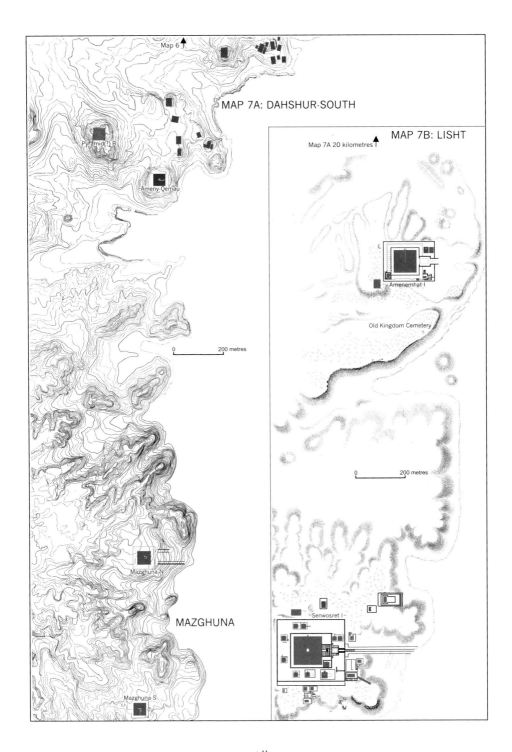

MAP 7A: DAHSHUR-SOUTH

Map 6

Pyramid(?) B

Ameny-Qemau

0   200 metres

MAP 7B: LISHT

Map 7A 20 kilometres

Amenemhat I

Old Kingdom Cemetery

0   200 metres

Mazghuna-N

MAZGHUNA

Senwosret I

Mazghuna-S

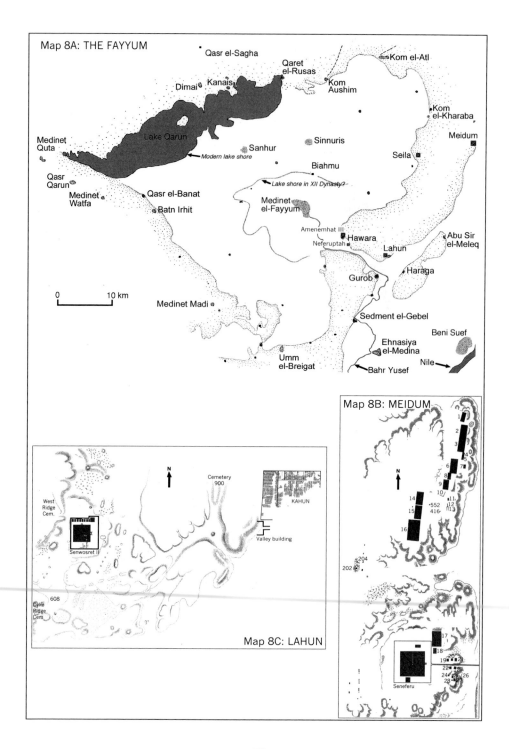

Map 8A: THE FAYYUM

Qasr el-Sagha
Qaret el-Rusas
Kom el-Atl
Dimai
Kanais
Kom Aushim
Kom el-Kharaba
Lake Qarun
Sinnuris
Meidum
Medinet Quta
Sanhur
Seila
Biahmu
Modern lake shore
Qasr Qarun
Qasr el-Banat
Lake shore in XII Dynasty?
Medinet Watfa
Batn Irhit
Medinet el-Fayyum
Amenemhat III
Hawara
Abu Sir el-Meleq
Neferuptah
Lahun
0   10 km
Haraga
Gurob
Medinet Madi
Sedment el-Gebel
Beni Suef
Ehnasiya el-Medina
Umm el-Breigat
Nile
Bahr Yusef

Map 8B: MEIDUM

N

1
2
3
6
8
14   11
552   12
15   416   13
16

204
202

Map 8C: LAHUN

N

Cemetery 900

West Ridge Cem.

KAHUN

Senwosret II

Valley building

Dyke Ridge Cem.   608

17
18
19
22
24   25/26
28
Seneferu

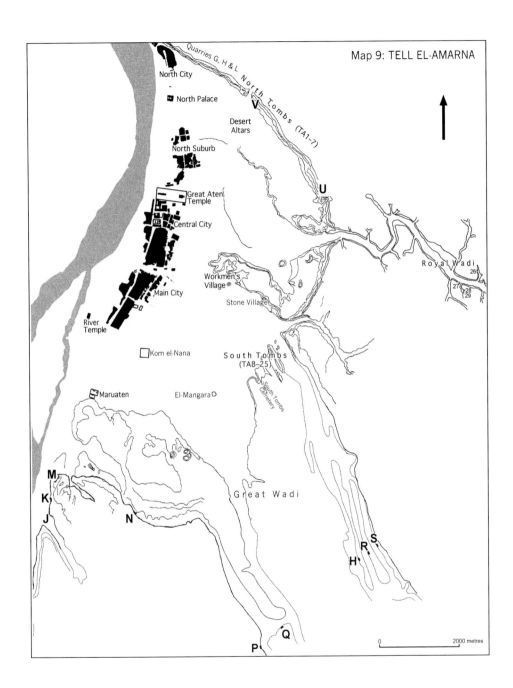

Map 9: TELL EL·AMARNA

North City

Quarries G, H & L

North Palace

North Tombs (TA1–7)

V

Desert
Altars

North Suburb

U

Great Aten
Temple

Central City

Royal Wadi
26

27 28
29

Workmen's
Village

Stone Village

Main City

River
Temple

Kom el-Nana

South Tombs
(TA8–25)

South Tombs
Cemetery

Maruaten

El-Mangara

M

K

J

N

Great Wadi

R S

H

Q

P

0   2000 metres

xix

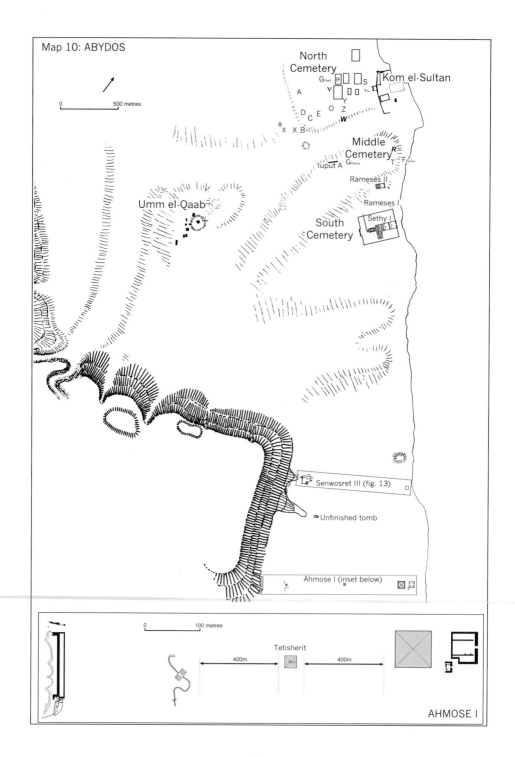

Map 10: ABYDOS

0   500 metres

North Cemetery

G Peet

μ

ν

S

Kom el-Sultan

A

O

Y

D

C

E

Z

W

φ

χ

X

B

Middle Cemetery

G Petrie

R

T

F Ayrton

Iuput A

Rameses II

Rameses I

South Cemetery

Sethy I

Umm el-Qaab

Senwosret III (fig. 13)

Unfinished tomb

Ahmose I (inset below)

0   100 metres

Tetisherit

400m

400m

AHMOSE I

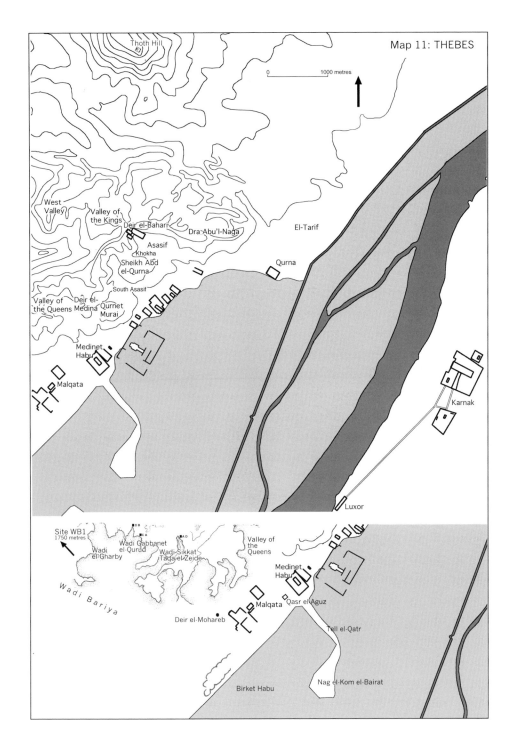

Map 11: THEBES

0   1000 metres

Thoth Hill

El-Tarif

West Valley

Valley of the Kings

Deir el-Bahari

Dra Abu'l-Naga

Asasif

Khokha

Sheikh Abd el-Qurna

Qurna

South Asasif

Valley of the Queens

Deir el-Medina

Qurnet Murai

Medinet Habu

Malqata

Karnak

Luxor

Site WB1 1750 metres

Wadi el-Gharby

Wadi Gabbanet el-Qurud

Wadi Sikkat Taqa el-Zeide

Valley of the Queens

Medinet Habu

Wadi Bariya

Malqata

Qasr el-Aguz

Deir el-Mohareb

Tell el-Qatr

Birket Habu

Nag el-Kom el-Bairat

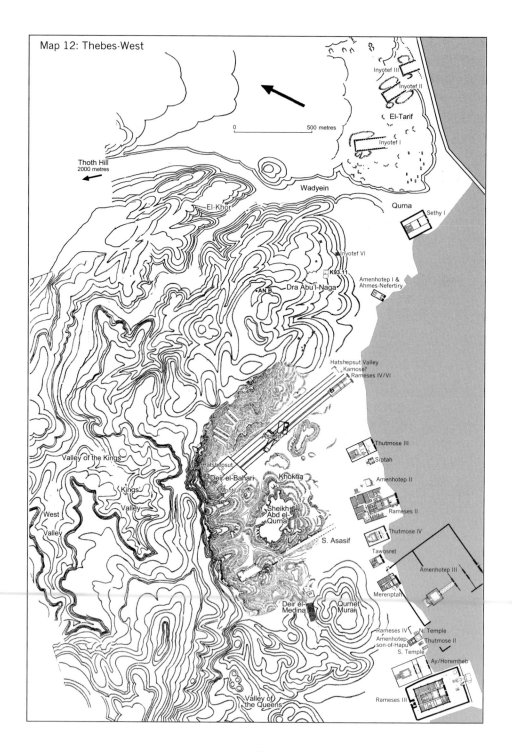

Map 12: Thebes-West

0 ————————— 500 metres

Inyotef III
Inyotef II
El-Tarif
Inyotef I

Thoth Hill
2000 metres

Wadyein

Qurna

El-Khor

Sethy I

Inyotef VI

K93.11

Amenhotep I &
Ahmes-Nefertiry

AN.B

Dra Abu'l-Naga

Hatshepsut Valley
Karnose?
Rameses IV/VI

Asasif

Thutmose III

Valley of the Kings

Siptah

Hatshepsut

Amenhotep II

Deir el-Bahari
Montuhotep II

Khokha

Rameses II

Kings'
Valley

Thutmose IV

Sheikh
Abd el-
Qurna

Tawosret

West
Valley

S. Asasif

Amenhotep III

Merenptah

Deir el-
Medina

Qurnet
Murai

Rameses IV
Amenhotep,
son-of-Hapu
S. Temple

N. Temple
Thutmose II

Valley of
the Queens

Ay/Horemheb

Rameses III

xxii

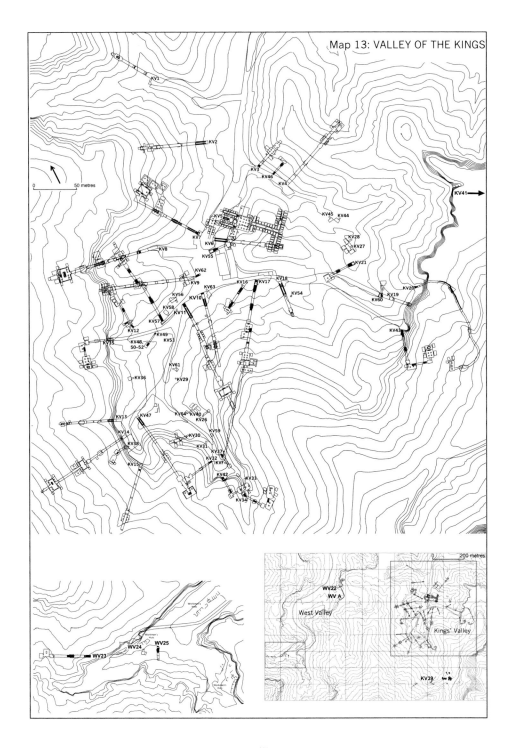

Map 13: VALLEY OF THE KINGS

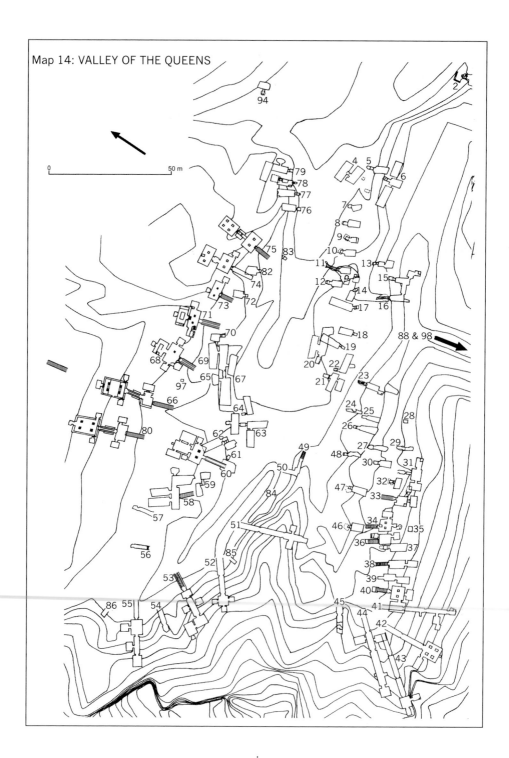

Map 14: VALLEY OF THE QUEENS

0   50 m

Chapter 1

In the Beginning

The first royal tombs

Until the latter part of the fourth millennium BC, Egyptian burial places were generally simple graves cut into the desert surface and marked by little more than low mounds of sand or gravel. In such graves, a flexed corpse was laid on its side, facing east, surrounded by various possessions. Graves of the Badarian and Naqada I cultures in Upper Egypt were generally oval or circular, with the body placed in a foetal pose, often wrapped in goat skins or mats and facing east, with the head to the south. Funerary equipment is largely restricted to pottery vessels, together with some examples of ivory and bone combs, slate palettes and perhaps pottery figurines. By Naqada II, the design of the grave became more rectangular, with more plentiful and standardised funerary equipment. The orientation of the body was also generally reversed to face west, which was in historic times the location of the home of the dead; the head remained at the south end. The graves were sometimes elaborated with wooden linings and roofs, while some very high-status examples were lined with brick and divided into two compartments by a wall.

Amongst these is the first known decorated tomb in Egypt, Hierakonpolis 100.[1] The mud-brick walls of the tomb were covered with a layer of mud plaster and then by a coat of yellow ochre. Only one wall was wholly covered with decoration, although hints of decorated areas survived on the other walls at the time of discovery. The scenes contained elements of what later became part of the Egyptian iconographic canon, such as hunting, smiting enemies and a series of bound prisoners. The apparently unique nature of the decoration suggests a particularly high status owner, and as such the tomb could be seen as one of the very earliest 'royal' tombs in the country.

Hierakonpolis appears to have been the focus for the grouping of southern Egyptian polities that seem to have begun to coalesce around 3300 BC into what would ultimately become the united kingdom of Egypt. Some of its later chieftains constructed a cemetery of brick-lined tombs 2 km to the west of tomb 100, up the Wadi Abu'l-Suffian, which had already been used as a cemetery in Naqada I times.[2] The tombs here were considerably larger than earlier examples and occupied areas of between 9 and 22 m^2. One tomb, number 23 of Naqada IIa/b date, was particularly large and preserved traces of a superstructure of wood and reeds (pl. Ia). It is possible that other such superstructures existed, although they have not survived.

Tombs with very similar substructures were constructed in Cemetery U at Abydos (fig. 1). They formed part of the Umm el-Qaab cemetery, which lay in front of a valley leading back into the western hills (pl. Ib, map 10), and was first used in Naqada I-IIa times, with elite tombs beginning in Naqada IId2 and running through until historic times. These were almost certainly the tombs of the men whose immediate descendants would unite the country for the first time.

The succeeding Naqada III culture saw a more general elaboration of burial places, the rectangular form now becoming standard. There was also far greater distinction between the sepulchres of the highest status individuals and those of lesser folk. One of the most impressive of the former was U-j at Umm el-Qaab (pl. IIa),[3] constructionally identical with Hierakonpolis 100, although far larger, with a dozen rooms, the result of at least two phases of construction, which added additional storerooms to an original core of a burial chamber and surrounding cavities. It was the direct ancestor of a whole series of similar tombs built there by the kings of the First Dynasty, the first rulers of the whole country. Its precise date remains a matter for some debate, particularly over whether its apparent owner, 'Scorpion', is identical with a king of that name who owned a mace-head found at Hierakonpolis and is datable directly before the unification of Egypt around 3000 BC, or an earlier homonym.

The Umm el-Qaab spread southwestward over time, with the sepulchres of kings of the Early Dynastic Period at its furthest extension. The first of these lay in Cemetery B, just beyond Cemetery U, and included two tombs that appear to date to the period just before the unification. One, apparently belonging to a king named Irihor (B0/1/2),[4] comprised three pits in the desert gravel, of which one (B2) was lined with brick, with a wood and mud-brick roof. Another, apparently of Ka (B7/9), was similar but was made up of only two pits.[5]

The First Dynasty

The sepulchres constructed following the unification continue the pre-existing construction philosophy for such structures, brick-lined cuttings in the desert gravel. They were roofed with wood beams, but the structure above this is unclear. One or more layers of mud brick lay above the roof, but the form of the actual superstructure remains unclear, given the almost total lack of preservation above the level of the substructure walls. However, a few traces suggest a sand-tumulus directly above the wooden roofs of the

2

substructure in at least some cases, with the whole tomb covered with a mound of gravel, perhaps defined by brick retaining walls, although no actual remains have been identified.[6]

The tomb of Narmer (B17/18),[7] probably the principal historical prototype for Menes, the traditional unifier of Egypt, was a modest structure, comprising what was originally two separate pits, but had become a single cavity when the dividing wall between them collapsed; a thin brick dividing wall was then added as a repair.

Three pits (B10/15/19), with brick linings between 1.5 and 2.1 m thick comprised the tomb of Hor-Aha (pl. IIb),[8] roofed with two to five layers of mud-bricks, laid on matting and supported by wooden beams. Chamber B15 served as the burial chamber, the three chambers covering an area of 12 by 9 m, apparently covered by sand mound 40 by 16 m. A series of subsidiary graves lay northeast of the main tomb, those closest to the king's tomb probably belonging to members of his family (see p. 6).

Hor-Aha's complex at Umm el-Qaab was supplemented by a group of three brick enclosures, all dated to the reign by sealings, some 2 km to the northeast, overlooking the cultivation (see fig. 1).[9] It is possible that Narmer may have also built an enclosure in the area, part of a wall having been found still further northeast.[10] The largest of Hor-Aha's enclosures included key features that would recur in later examples, in particular a complex entrance at the southern end of the east wall, with a brick-built multi-room structure just inside. There were at least four – probably originally six – subsidiary graves outside the enclosure, while on the northwest side were a pair of much smaller enclosures (perhaps attributable to his wives?).

These structures stand at the beginning of a sequence of such 'remote' enclosures that were built down to the end of the Early Dynastic Period, with some (but not all) of the Umm el-Qaab kings' tombs matched with an enclosure (pl. IIIa).[11] All appear to have had entrances at the southernmost end of the east face – the location of the offering place in contemporary and later private mastabas – and another at the eastern end of the north face – in the direction of the Kom el-Sultan, the site of the city temples. They were clearly part of the kings' broader funerary complex, at least some housing a small brick chapel and perhaps a number of wooden/other plant-material structures (albeit not fixed into the ground, given the lack of any surviving post-holes), the possible form of the latter being perhaps indicated by the skeuomorphic stone structures in Abydos enclosures' lineal descendant, the Step Pyramid complex of the beginning of the Third Dynasty (p. 12).

While seal-impressions from some enclosures indication significant ritual usage, each enclosure was demolished prior to the completion of the enclosure of the succeeding king, with walls tumbled inwards onto a specially-laid layer of clean sand. They thus seem to have been employed on a time-limited basis, perhaps for a defined period of time following a king's death or interment.

The tomb of Djer (O – pl. IIIb)[12] marked a significant change in the structure of recent royal tombs (although reminiscent in many ways of U-j). Rather than a series of separate adjacent pits, a single large cavity was sunk in the desert and lined with brick nearly 3 m thick. Along all sides but the south, a series of stub-walls was built, creating storerooms. The remaining area of the tomb was then enclosed with wooden partitions to define the burial chamber itself. The tomb was modified during the Middle Kingdom, when it was converted into the symbolic tomb of Osiris, an entrance stairway being added at the south end, together with a recumbent figure of the god, datable to the Thirteenth Dynasty.[13]

The tomb is the first from which any trace of an offering place survives (although any other superstructure has entirely vanished). While nothing has been recorded in situ, a stela bearing the king's name and closely resembling others from later reigns found on site found its way to the Egyptian Museum, Cairo (pl. IVa). Later examples certainly came in pairs and seem to have stood together on the eastern side of the tomb as a focus for the dead king's cult. Bearing the king's Horus-name, such pairs are known from royal offering places down to the early Fourth Dynasty at least. Compared to the tomb of Hor-Aha, the number of subsidiary burials was greatly increased (to over 300) and rearranged in geometric blocks, principally to the north and west of the king's tomb itself, each equipped with a small stela, indicating that the owners were members of the royal household. Questions remain over whether some or all of these graves were occupied at the time of the king's own interment, and thus represent human sacrifices (cf. p. 6).[14]

His remote enclosure (now almost entirely vanished) covered some six times the area of the largest of Hor-Aha's examples, and was surrounded by 269 subsidiary graves. The similarly-denuded enclosure of Djer's successor, Djet, was slightly smaller, and had only 154 subsidiary graves. This reduction in numbers is also seen adjacent to that king's actual tomb, where only 175 subsidiary graves are to be found.

The sepulchre of Djet (Z)[15] was very similar to that of his predecessor, Djer, but again slightly smaller. Traces survived showing that the substructure had been topped by a mound that lay entirely below the surface of the ground was perhaps a representation of the primeval mound; it seems likely that this was a feature of other First Dynasty royal tombs as well.[16] The limestone stelae (pl. IVb) were particularly fine, as compared with those coming before and after. Djet's widow, Meryetneith, seems to have served as regent during the minority of her son, Den, and as a ruler of the country had a tomb at Umm

4

el-Qaab (Y).[17] This had only a single line of subsidiary graves on ea
totalling forty-one, but the basic concept of the tomb followed th
preceding kings – a central burial chamber, surrounded by storerooms. The
remote enclosure also followed the usual pattern, but again with a greatly
reduced number of graves (seventy-nine).

A major design-innovation is to be seen in the tomb of Den himself.
Previous tombs had no means of access except through their roofs; thus final
structural completion was not possible until after the burial. However, the
tomb of Den (T)[18] incorporated a 29 m-long stairway, running under the
tomb's subsidiary graves and (lost) superstructure, giving access to the burial
chamber via a door closed after the burial with brick blocking and a wooden
portcullis. Stairways were also introduced around the same time into private
tombs.[19]

The internal layout of tomb T also varied from earlier examples, store-
rooms being placed entirely outside the burial chamber structure to the south,
and apparently only accessible from above, while a stair-accessed complex
in the southeast corner was possibly a shrine. The brick walls of the wood-
lined burial chamber were 4m thick, while the room was paved with
rough-dressed granite – the first use of stone in the structure of a royal tomb,
although a limestone chamber-lining had been used in a private tomb of the
previous reign.[20] The tomb featured significantly less subsidiary graves than
those of the preceding kings' tombs – around 130 – reflecting a trend that
continued until the end of the dynasty. Den's remote enclosure has not been
positively identified, although it may be one of two anonymous examples,
the so-called 'Donkey Enclosure' (named after the burials made in front of it
at the time of construction), directly behind those of Hor-Aha, or the 'Western
Mastaba', directly southeast of that of Djer. Associated with it is a series of
fourteen wooden boats, placed within individual brick 'tombs' that lie directly
to the southwest.[21] Boats were also associated with other tombs of the Early
Dynastic Period,[22] and would later form parts of royal tomb complexes from
the Fourth Dynasty onwards, but their purpose remains moot, and they appear
to be absent from all intervening royal tombs. Possibly in favour of Den's
ownership of the Western Mastaba the fact that it lacks any subsidiary graves,
human or animal.

The remaining kings of the dynasty also lack identifiable remote
enclosures, but in any case continued to have tombs at Umm el-Qaab. In the
tomb of Anedjib (X),[23] a much shorter stairway was employed than in that of
Den, terminating in a wooden portcullis.[24] The burial chamber was half the
size of that of the preceding tomb, and had a separate storeroom to the west,
apparently accessible only from above. The number of subsidiary graves fell
to sixty-four, although this rose to seventy-five under Semerkhet, whose tomb

(U)[25] was also much simpler than the monuments of the middle of the dynasty. His tomb had but a single room, accessed by a slope terminating in a wood and brick blocking; a stub-wall in the east may indicate storage niches. The subsidiary graves were constructed directly against the exterior of the lining of the burial chamber.

Tomb Q, of the last king of the dynasty, Qaa (pl. IVc),[26] was a rather more elaborate structure, the most important features including two pairs of store-rooms opening off the descending stairway, which terminated in a limestone portcullis. This combination of lateral store rooms opening from the main access route into the tomb and stone portcullis blocks would be key elements of the following generations of royal tomb-substructures
In this structure, only twenty-seven subsidiary compartments surrounded the tomb; while most were certainly subsidiary graves, a few may have rather functioned as storerooms for the king's tomb itself.

Royal family tombs of the First Dynasty
Very little is known of the royal family's burial arrangements in Early Dynastic times.[27] At the very beginning of the First Dynasty Neithhotep, wife of Hor-Aha, had at Naqada a large panelled brick mastaba.[28] Its interior was divided into square storage compartments, with a massive set of three tomb-chambers in the middle. Similar tombs exist at Saqqara, differing mainly in the fact that the burial chambers were sunk into the ground for greater security.[29] While apparently principally the tombs of the nobility, some members of the royal family may have been buried there.[30] For example, vases from tomb S3507 belonged to Herneith, probably a wife of Den, making it possible that it was her sepulchre. Other fragments giving a queen's title came from tomb S3035, dated to Den's reign.

At Umm el-Qaab, a cemetery of smaller sepulchres lies directly south of the tomb of Hor-Aha, of which the largest two are directly adjacent to the king's tomb. The northern, B14, contained items naming the king and Benerib, thus making it likely that it was her tomb, with the adjacent B6 probably also a queenly sepulchre (pl. IVd).

In the tomb of Djer were found apparently female human remains, including a skull, suggesting that this king's principal wife may have shared his sepulchre. Other consorts were buried in some of the small tombs that surrounded the royal tombs. It remains uncertain whether some or all were occupied at the time of the king's death, and if so whether the tomb's occupants were killed or committed suicide to accompany the king to the next world. These small tombs were equipped with stelae giving the names and titles of the deceased, and amongst those with far more humble titles are a number with contemporary royal wives' designations. One (Nakhtneith) was found in the complex of Djer, with three in the subsidiary tombs of Den.

The Second Dynasty

The advent of the Second Dynasty led to an important change in royal burial arrangements, with its founder, Hotepsekhemwy, abandoning Umm el-Qaab in favour of Saqqara, over 300 km to the north, overlooking the national capital at Memphis, according to tradition established following the unification of the country (pl. Va). Rather than constructing a tomb in the neighbourhood of the existing First Dynasty private cemetery at the site, he chose a location nearly two kilometres to the southwest, in an area apparently without earlier occupation. This could be seen either as a conscious distancing from the monuments of the previous dynasty or/and a reflection of the non-royal nature of the old Early Dynastic necropolis: interestingly enough, private tombs continued to be built in the latter area through the Second Dynasty, and into the Third. On the other hand, a new private necropolis was established to the south of the location chosen for the royal tomb.[31]

These new Second Dynasty necropoleis lay at the end of the wide wadi that extended from the northeastern edge of the Saqqara cemetery, and which would be one of its principal processional approaches through to Ptolemaic times (cf. map 4).[32] The substructure of Hetepsekhemwy's tomb[33] was unlike any of those at Abydos, being largely tunnelled in the bedrock, with an axial corridor and flanking store-rooms, an approach also employed for some Saqqara private tombs of the dynasty (fig. 2a).[34] In the king's case, there were at least 120 storerooms, all around 2 m high, the whole substructure finally covering an area of some 122 x 48 m. The tomb had originally been intended to be considerably smaller than in its final form, the main axis being extended northwards – in some four principal stages – as an open trench and subsequently roofed-over with limestone blocks back to the foot of the ultimate descending stair (pl. Vb).[35] This section was blocked by a series of four portcullises, lowered from the surface, the last of which blocked the doorway into the inner wholly rock-cut section of the tomb.

Nothing of the tomb's superstructure is known, all traces having been obliterated when the Fifth Dynasty funerary complex of Unas was erected on the site,[36] leaving the ancient royal tomb's substructure partly under the inner part of Unas's mortuary temple and partly under the east face of his pyramid. However, Hetepsekhemwy's tomb lay in a precinct separated from the rest of the cemetery on the north side by a deep and wide trench that was cut from west to east across the plateau (pl. VIa). This was later subsumed into the 'dry moat' that surrounded the Third Dynasty Step Pyramid, but its position relative to the tomb of Hetepsekhemwy and the sepulchre of the king's second successor Ninetjer makes its original authorship clear.[37]

Ninetjer's tomb was cut 140 m due east of that of Hotepsekhemwy, its entrance likewise close to the edge of the cutting, and comprising a main corridor, blocked by two portcullises, flanked with storerooms (fig. 2b).[38] However, in contrast to the regular layout of the earlier tomb, the galleries curved in various directions, the plan further complicated by later additions when the sepulchre became a general catacomb in the Late Period, although intrusive burials have been found going back to at least the New Kingdom. The main corridor was 33m long, curving towards the west, and descending rapidly into the bedrock to reach the burial chamber, the substructure occupying an area of 3,850 m², around a third less than that of Hetep-sekhemwy.

The access-route from the northeast is flanked by two very large rectangular enclosures that seem to have been the equivalents of the remote enclosures found at Abydos (fig. 3).[39] Of these two enclosures, the northern one (known as the 'L-shaped Enclosure' from the superior preservation of its south-west quadrant) possessed defining embankments that were composed of desert sand and gravel, with brick and limestone traces, of which 140 m of the southern end of the west wall survives, together with probably 200 m of the south wall.[40] Its full extent remains unclear,[41] but the southern wall may have extended as far east as the point where a north-south extension of the east-west rock cutting begins.

The southern enclosure, known as the *Gisr el-Mudir*, was of different construction.[42] Covering an area of some 25 hectares, its 15 m thick walls comprised a mixed filling within pairs of walls of limestone blocks, still standing in places to a height of over 3 m. Their building technique is relatively primitive, while some pottery from the site has been dated to the Second/Third Dynasty. A prepared pavement extended at least 25m from the wall inside the enclosure, but no trace of any structure at the centre has been identified.[43] Given the lack of limestone walls in the construction of the perimeter of the L-shaped Enclosure, it is likely to have been the earlier of the two monuments, and thus probably to be attributed to the burial complex of Hotepsekhemwy. On this basis, the structurally-later *Gisr el-Mudir* should probably be attributed to the other known royal Saqqara tomb-owner of the dynasty, Ninetjer.[44]

Given the presence of the tombs of Hetepsekhemwy and Ninetjer at Saqqara, the question arises as to whether other Second Dynasty kings were buried there, in particular Reneb, who reigned between these two rulers. A stela of Reneb, of the same type as those found marking the offering places of the Abydene royal tombs, was allegedly found at Mit Rahina (Memphis),[45] suggesting his tomb lay nearby at Saqqara. The funerary priesthoods of two later Second Dynasty kings, Sened and Peribsen, are mentioned in the

Saqqara tomb of a Fourth Dynasty notable, Shery,[46] but while at first sight suggesting that the kings might have been buried near him, Peribsen is known to have been buried at Abydos (see below), indicating that this might not necessarily be the case.

No trace of a tomb attributable to either Reneb or Sened has been identified at Saqqara,[47] although one suggestion has been that a series of galleries under the western part of the Step Pyramid enclosure might represent the overbuilt remains of a Second Dynasty royal tomb.[48] Certainly, there are close similarities between these passages and rooms and those of Hetepsekhemwy and Ninetjer, with the principal entrance at the north end of their long, rectangular superstructure. Their location is certainly not inconsistent with being part of the same cemetery, the southern extremity of the structure being only 55 m due north of the entrance to Hetepsekhemwy's tomb. A further set of galleries under the northern part of the temenos of the Step Pyramid could also represent a Second Dynasty royal tomb overbuilt by Djoser.[49] However, none of these complexes has preserved any indication of its having been used for an original Second Dynasty interment.

As already noted, the sepulchre of Shery's second king, Peribsen, was found in the ancient royal cemetery at Umm el-Qaab (tomb P – fig. 2c; pl. VIb).[50] It was wholly unlike the tunnelled tombs of the earlier kings of the Second Dynasty, and followed the basic concept of First Dynasty royal tombs, built of brick, sunk in a pit in the desert surface. The burial chamber was surrounded by a series of well-stocked storerooms, the whole structure having a corridor running between it and the outer retaining-walls of the tomb. The two stelae that marked the offering-place were of granite (pl. VIIa), following the pattern seen with Reneb's surviving stela.

The associated monumental enclosure (known as the 'Middle Fort') lay adjacent to the First Dynasty examples, compared with which it had a more elaborate north gate and lacked subsidiary burials.[51] Its walls had been dismantled in the same way as earlier ones, but enough survives to show that it had been decorated with typical Early Dynastic panelling, with gateways in the south-east and north-east corners and containing a small brick building that appears to have been a chapel of some kind. The lower part of the enclosure's walls was painted red, as was a strip around the interior of the southeast gate.

Peribsen's name-serekh was in his inscriptions topped with the figure of the god Seth, rather than the usual Horus-raptor. In later Egyptian mythology, the two gods are depicted as opponents, extensive texts in Horus' great Ptolemaic temple at Edfu giving graphic accounts of the war that took place between the two gods and their followers.[52] With this in mind, it was long ago hyphesised that these much later texts constitute a poeticised record of a real civil war that raged in Egypt, and that the key figure in this conflict was 'the Seth' Peribsen.[53]

That something had happened under (or just before) Peribsen is suggested by the resumption, after a fairly long gap, of royal burial at Umm el-Qaab by that king. A breakdown in national unity is also suggested by the presence of a brick enclosure akin to those at Abydos at Hierakonpolis (pl. VIIb),[54] possibly suggesting the presence of an Early Dynastic royal tomb there.[55] The royal name found associated with the enclosure is that of Khasekhem, a ruler whose positioning towards the end of the Second Dynasty is clear, as is his association with Hierakonpolis, whence come most of his monuments. Since all earlier historic kings had either been buried at Umm el-Qaab or Saqqara, the construction of this royal funerary monument here was presumably because of the non-availability of any more northerly necropolis.

That his reign marked a phase of civil war is indicated by a number of sources, which suggest that he controlled the south in the face of an opponent or opponents in the north. However, it would seem unlikely that Khasekhem's enemy was Peribsen, as the latter was clearly considered a legitimate king by later generations. This would suggest that the civil war might have been between Peribsen's successor(s) and Khasekhem (and perhaps a predecessor of the latter). Whatever the turn of events, the period of conflict seems to have been brought to a close by victory being granted to Khasekhem, who then changed his name to Khasekhemwy, his *serekh* uniquely surmounted by both Horus and Seth, as a symbol of reconciliation. Following victory, the king's putative Hierakonpolis funerary monument would then have been abandoned in favour of a tomb further north. However, rather than returning to the Saqqara burial place of the earliest kings of the dynasty, Khasekhemwy built his new tomb at Umm el-Qaab, together with a funerary enclosure alongside those of the First Dynasty kings.

Khasekhemwy's Abydene monuments are the biggest of their respective types there. The underground tomb (V – fig. 2d; pl. VIIIa)[56] was, as usual, constructed in a pit and composed of mud-brick, albeit with a stone burial chamber. However, its ultimate form is wholly different from that of earlier Abydene royal sepulchres, being no less than 68 m long by 12 m wide. On the other hand, it occupies an area only 15% of that of the Saqqara tomb of Hetepsekhemwy, and then only after a number of extensions.

The tomb centred on a limestone burial chamber, the earliest of its kind known in a royal tomb, although such a feature had appeared in private tombs since the middle of the First Dynasty.[57] Initially it had a single row of brick store-chambers on the east and west, plus a greater number on the north. However, a series of rebuildings added further rooms on the north, a new group of ten on the south bringing the total number of rooms to fifty. Finally, two pairs of rooms were added on each side of the access-ramp at the southern end of the tomb. Two skeletons lay in a contracted pose to the east of the burial chamber, presumably representing the last-known manifestations of the custom of burying retainers with the king, which had surrounded the nearby First Dynasty royal tombs and funerary enclosures with hundreds of interments.

Khasekhemwy's funerary enclosure, known today as the *Shunet el-Zebib*, is by far the best-preserved of its genre at Abydos (pl. IIIa),[58] with its panelled walls still standing nearly 11 m above the desert surface. It was also a much more massive structure than earlier examples, with a further outer wall enclosing the main panelled structure, and it remains unclear whether its survival was owing to it being the last such enclosure built at Abydos, or whether it was intended to be, unlike earlier examples, intended for long-term usage. As in previous enclosures, it housed a small brick chapel, but much of the interior of the enclosure was reused as a cemetery for sacred ibises in Late and Ptolemaic times, thus obliterating any other original features.

Royal family tombs of the Second Dynasty

The royal cemeteries of the Second Dynasty are little explored, and only four royal offspring are known from funerary remains. The Princesses Shepsetipet and Syhefernerer were buried at Saqqara, the former possibly in S3477, near which tomb her stela was found. This sepulchre was a fairly small, niched brick mastaba within the noble necropolis of the previous dynasty, found intact and containing a celebrated funerary meal.[59] A shallow cutting led to a large burial chamber, on the western side of which was a pit in which the coffin had been placed. Syhefernerer was buried in a small tomb nearby (S2146E), a modest chamber 2m below ground, approached by a staircase.[60]

Three other royal offspring of the dynasty were buried across the river at Helwan, a huge necropolis of the Archaic Period. Khnemetptah was buried in tomb 175 H8, with a shallow shaft, and chambers on the north and west, the latter being the burial chamber; Satba's tomb 1241 H9 and Nysuheqat's 964 H8 were also very simple.[61]

It is possible that the vast tomb K1 at Beit Khallaf (pl. VIIIb)[62] was that of Queen Nymaathap, given the presence of her name on a number of seal-impressions there, alongside some of Djoser, members of the court, and even Peribsen. The tomb is a mastaba, with a substructure of standard Second/early Third Dynasty design of an axial corridor descending from the roof of the mastaba, including portcullises lowered from the roof of the mastaba, but on an exceptionally large scale. The building is some 85 m long, 45 m wide and 8 m high, and incorporates one of the earliest brick arches known.

Chapter 2

The Old Kingdom

The Third Dynasty
At the end of the Second Dynasty, the basic form of the royal tomb had been set for some four centuries as a burial structure, supplemented by a rectangular enclosure some distance away. With the beginning of the Third Dynasty, however, there occurred a major conceptual and technological leap forward, which included the erection of the first known pyramid, the precursor of a series that would only come to a final end nearly three thousand years later.

Khasekhemwy was succeeded by a ruler known to history as Djoser (although during his lifetime as Netjerkhet),[1] the builder of the Step Pyramid at Saqqara (L.XXXII: fig. 4a; pl. IXa).[2] Conceptually, this monument combined in one monument the previously-separate burial-place and monumental enclosure. The enclosure followed the basic model seen at the *Shunet el-Zebib*, with a panelled exterior and a principal entrance at the southern end of the east wall. This led via an elaborate colonnade to an open courtyard, containing elements associated with the ritual run that formed part of the royal jubilee (*ḥb-sd*) ceremonies. A complex of shrines in the adjacent '*ḥb-sd* Court' was also associated with these activities (pl. IXb), while many of the other structures within the pyramid enclosure also seem to belong to jubilee or coronation ceremonies. Most of these buildings were solid dummies, and imitated construction in plant materials, suggesting that their prototypes may have been temporary structures of such, erected within the Early Dynastic enclosures of Abydos and Saqqara.

Taking the former elements together with the presence in the subterranean portions of the the complex of reliefs of the king taking part in *ḥb-sd* ceremonies (q.v.), it seems possible that the jubilee ceremonies (which were intended to refresh the vitality of an aging king) may have formed a basis for the conception of the dead king's revivification at this point in Egyptian history. Given the clear affinities between the Step Pyramid complex and the enclosures associated with earlier royal tombs, it may be that these were also intended as the venues for a posthumous *ḥb-sd*. Unfortunately, the lack of any textual material relating to the king's posthumous destiny prior to the appearance of the Pyramid Texts at the end of the Fifth Dynasty makes any assessment of the beliefs potentially underlying the earliest royal funerary monuments problematic.

It is possible that the Step Pyramid enclosure was originally laid out somewhat smaller than was ultimately the case, with a somewhat simpler layout, and was only later extended to the north and west to achieve its final form.[3] The area occupied by the enclosure was ultimately separated from the surrounding plateau by cuttings on all four sides (see map 4), the southwestern section being taken over from works accompanying the building of the Second Dynasty royal funerary monuments in that area (see pp. 7-8). This part of the 'dry moat' is split on the south side, suggesting that the ancient approach to the entrance to the complex was past the Second Dynasty enclosures, then along the northern fronts of the Second Dynasty royal tombs themselves and finally on to the wide terrace on the east front of the Step Pyramid enclosure, as defined by the eastern arm of the 'dry moat'.

The Step Pyramid itself (for its dimensions, and those of other Old and Middle Kingdom kingly funerary monuments, see table 1) was constructed in the centre of the enclosure. It was begun as a low square structure, which was then enlarged into a four-stepped pyramid, and then into the final six-stepped rectangular monument (pl. Xa). Although the core was built of limestone quarried nearby, this was faced with much finer stone from the Tura quarries on the opposite side of the Nile. This pattern of stone-use continued in all subsequent stone-built pyramids, Tura limestone casings continuing even when pyramid-cores switched to mud-brick.

A temple built against the north face of the pyramid, but entered from the east, followed a plan known (in private tombs) since the First Dynasty, and included a statue of the king, enclosed in a windowless room known as a *serdab*. A mastaba was built into the south enclosure wall (dubbed the South Tomb), with chambers mirroring those of the pyramid, but on a smaller scale. It was found empty and no clue as to its purpose exists, but it seems to be the direct ancestor of the later subsidiary pyramids – also lacking in any firm indication of their purpose.[4]

The entrance to the tomb-chambers lay within the temple. These centred on a burial chamber constructed at the bottom of a vertical shaft. In the substructure's final form, the royal mummy was to be placed in a cavity in a structure of granite blocks, entered via a hole in the roof, blocked by a piece of stone similar to a sink plug, above which was apparently a limestone chamber at the end of the passage that descended from the entrance in the temple; the plug seems to have been concealed under a stone pavement.[5] A series of galleries surrounded the burial chamber, some decorated with blue faience plaques, others also with reliefs of the king running the *ḥb-sd* course (pl. Xb) – apparently the first and last time a king would be shown in his tomb until the New Kingdom.

The earliest explorers found parts of one or more mummies within the pyramid – clearly intrusives of Late Period or later date, with a number of portions of a body found in the burial chamber in the 1930s. The date of the latter remains uncertain since, although their context suggests that they ought to belong to the king, radiocarbon determinations have thrown doubt on this.[6] Otherwise, non-architectural material recovered from the pyramid itself has been limited to a wooden box with the king's name.

The Step Pyramid's union of the burial place with the complete cult complex was to continue until the beginning of the New Kingdom, although with many changes and developments during that period of a thousand years. That development during the rest of the Third Dynasty is on occasion difficult to trace with confidence, since the historical sequence of its kings is uncertain and in part derived from the perceived developmental order of its monuments.

Possibly the next royal funerary monument to be constructed was El-Deir at Abu Rowash,[7] a 20 m-square brick massif, built upon a knoll of rock, and still 4 m high in 1902, within a brick enclosure, some 280 x 150 m (fig. 4b), from which some early Old Kingdom pottery was recovered (the site had been extensively overbuilt down to Coptic times). The scale and form of the monument – particularly its combination of a central monument with a rectangular enclosure – strongly suggest that it was a royal tomb subsequent to Djoser. As for its owner, he may have been Sanakhte, apparently with the personal name Nebka, who is to be dated to the dynasty and is otherwise lacking a tomb: his names appear in the mastaba K2 at Beit Khallaf,[8] but the form of this tomb is inconsistent with being a king's monument. Unfortunately, El-Deir has been largely destroyed by irrigation schemes in the area, and apparently not examined since 1931.

Certainly to be dated after Djoser, in particular owing to its use of distinctly larger limestone blocks in its construction, reflecting the trend that is seen during the Third to Fourth Dynasties, is an unfinished step pyramid to the southwest of the Step Pyramid (fig. 4c; pl. XIa),[9]. Owned by Sekhemkhet, who seems to have had the personal name Djoserti (found on a label recovered from the substructure), the pyramid, in contrast to that of Djoser, square; however, it had risen to less than the height of its first step (of an intended seven) when abandoned.

The large panelled enclosure had been enlarged at least once before being abandoned, and had what was presumably intended to be a ritual mastaba tomb in its southern part. This had, however, been used for the burial of a 2-year old child, probably during the Third Dynasty. The entrance to the pyramid itself lay in the centre of the north face, the approach ramp cutting through the terrace upon which the mortuary temple would have been built. Interestingly, two attempts had been made to cut the subterranean corridors. The first had been abandoned after 10m; the floor of the ramp was then raised and a new cutting begun, which formed the definitive entrance passage, leading to a burial chamber under the centre of the pyramid. A long 'U'-shaped corridor, with 132 small storage chambers, was accessed by a passage from close to the pyramid entrance, holding many stone vessels, amongst which were the seal impressions that bore the name of the pyramid's owner. Beyond the doorway leading to the storerooms, a vertical shaft penetrated up through the superstructure, perhaps intended for a portcullis-slab of a kind common in tombs of the period.

The roughly hewn burial chamber contained an alabaster sarcophagus of unique form, with a sliding panel at one end sealed with plaster, and the remains of what was interpreted as a funerary wreath on top (pl. XIb).[10] This was the first freestanding stone sarcophagus to be used in a king's burial – and the last until the reign of Khufu.[11] Unfortunately, the sarcophagus proved to be empty, with no trace of a body anywhere in the pyramid.

The unusual store-galleries seen in Sekhemkhet's pyramid are otherwise found only in the Layer Pyramid at Zawiyet el-Aryan (L.XIV: map 3A; fig. 4d),[12] attributed to Khaba on the basis of inscribed bowls found in a nearby tomb. Significantly smaller than that of Sekhemkhet, the Layer Pyramid lies on the edge of a steep incline from the desert down to the edge of the fields, a rather different location from those of earlier monuments and one unsuitable for the kind of rectangular enclosure found around them. It may thus be at this point that the first major shift in the architecture of the pyramid-complex occurred, with a much less elaborate cult installation centred on the east side, and some form of ramp leading down to the edge of the desert. Here have been noted blocks that might have formed part of a valley building. Such an arrangement might explain its hitherto novel position on the very edge of the desert, with perhaps an as yet untraced causeway leading down to it.

Compared with Sekhemkhet's pyramid, the store galleries have storerooms on one side only, but demonstrate a number of advances. The latter's store galleries had been approached via an awkward passage that doubled back on the entrance gallery, which would have made access difficult. In the Layer Pyramid, the entrance ramp was turned through 90 degrees so that at its bottom a right turn would lead direct to the store-rooms, and a left-hand one to the burial chamber. This basic conception was maintained through a number of modifications, all apparently intended to place the burial chamber still deeper underground. This may have been a result of poor quality rock. Whatever the reason, galleries at two successive levels were abandoned before the final burial chamber was cut – and apparently left unused.

The final royal funerary monument that should probably be placed in the Third Dynasty is the Brick Pyramid at Abu Rowash (L.I: map 2A; fig. 4e; pl. XIIa).[13] Today, all that survives is a massive natural rock-knoll something over a kilometre south of El-Deir, with trenches that once allowed the keying-in of a mud-brick pyramid, the remains of which survived into the 1840s, but were subsequently quarried for use as fertiliser.

High up on the north side, a passageway descends to an entirely rock-cut burial chamber; if projected to the surface of the pyramid itself, this will have placed the entrance itself some 25m above the ground, in marked contrast with the ground-level entrances of all earlier royal tombs. This method of chamber-construction is not found in pyramids after the early Fourth Dynasty, while a high entrance is also a feature of that dynasty. As all early Fourth Dynasty kings have known tombs, the Brick Pyramid's owner must be placed late in the Third Dynasty, with the most likely candidate the dynasty's final ruler, Huni.

The most plausible reconstruction of the former brickwork would make the monument a step pyramid, some 215 m square. This would make it by far the biggest pyramid yet begun, and the fourth largest pyramid of all time, although reverting to brick (as had done El-Deir)[14] – a material not to be used again for a pyramid until the Middle Kingdom. The pyramid seems, however, never to have been finished, and by the end of the Old Kingdom enough of the rock core was exposed to allow the construction of tombs cut into it. The distant memory of a giant brick pyramid of the Old Kingdom may lie behind the Greek historian Herodotus' story of Asychis, 'the successor of Mykerinos (Menkaure), who ..., wishing to go one better than his predecessors, built a pyramid of brick to commemorate his reign, and on it cut an inscription in stone to the following effect: "Do not compare me to my disadvantage with the stone pyramids. I surpass them as far as does Zeus [the Greek 'translation' of the Egyptian god, Amun] the other gods. They pushed a pole to the bottom of a lake, and the mud that stuck on it they collected and made into bricks. That is how they built me."'

Royal family tombs of the Third Dynasty

Burials of at least a few of Djoser's family were made in some of a series of eleven shafts, originally cut outside the eastern face of the first square monument, partially running under the king's own subterranean complex, but then covered by the final pyramid.[15] Galleries I–V were panelled with wood and functioned as tombs, at least six alabaster sarcophagi once having been present, one of them containing the remains of a gilded plywood coffin and the skeleton of a young female. VI–XI were unlined and employed for storage, VI and VII containing the remains of around 40,000 assorted stone vessels. Also, under the northern end of the pyramid enclosure were a number of galleries that might have been intended as royal family tombs.[16]

As already noted, wooden coffin and skeleton of a two-year-old boy was found in the subsidiary tomb of the unfinished pyramid of Sekhemkhet at Saqqara.[17] Their significance is, however, uncertain, particularly as such subsidiary tombs are not otherwise known to have been used for actual interment but seem to have fulfilled some ritual role. Perhaps a son of the king had died suddenly, and this represents an emergency arrangement; unfortunately no clear evidence exists.

The Fourth Dynasty

The Fourth Dynasty marks the last part of the experimental phase of pyramid design and construction. During the dynasty's one and a quarter centuries, pyramids not only reached and passed their zenith in terms of size and quality of building, but also established the principles of the 'standard' pyramid complex, which was still to be found as late as the Twelfth Dynasty, eight centuries later.

The dynastic founder, Seneferu, was to build no fewer than three full-size pyramids, and was responsible for one, if not seven, smaller ones of uncertain purpose. Of the full-size monuments, the earliest was a step pyramid at Meidum (L.LXV: map 8B; fig.5a; pl. XIIb).[18] This is by far the southernmost of all the major pyramids of the Old Kingdom, close to the entrance of the Fayyum. The most credible explanation for its presence so far from the capital at Memphis may be that it was built near a country residence of the king.

In contrast to the wholly or largely tunnelled substructures of Third Dynasty pyramids, the chambers of the Meidum pyramid were largely built within the structure of the pyramid, only the lowest part of the descending passage and the following horizontal section being constructed in a cutting in the rock. The actual burial chamber, entered from below, was entirely built inside the core of the pyramid, with a distinctive corbelled roof, a type of structure typical of the reigns of Seneferu and his successor, Khufu (pl. XIIIa, XVa, XVIIa). Corbelled cavities, to relieve pressure on flat roofs, were constructed above the antechambers and the lower part of the descending corridor. No sarcophagus was included. A subsidiary pyramid, now destroyed, stood opposite the middle of the south face of the main pyramid, superseding the subsidiary mastabas seen at the pyramids of Djoser and Sekhemkhet; no trace of a secondary tomb has been identified at the other Third Dynasty royal tombs.

The superstructure was begun as a seven-stepped structure, which was then enlarged and converted to an eight-stepped one (never finished as such). Finally, probably after a hiatus in construction (see below), it was converted into a true pyramid. Later stone robbery caused the collapse of some of the outer layers of the upper part, leaving the true pyramid intact at the bottom, together with a tower-like structure that preserves the fifth and sixth steps of the eight-stepped version. The reason for the change to a true pyramid has been much debated, but the most generally posited suggestion is that the true pyramid was a solar symbol, representing the sun's rays striking down from the sky. This fits well with the prominence of the sun cult during the remaining part of the Old Kingdom, and it is likely that in addition to any benefits that would accrue from being buried under such a manifestation of the sun there was some conception of the rays providing a 'ramp' to the heavens.

Presumably from the outset the complex was equipped with what is the earliest surviving causeway (although see p. 15 for the possibility that such an element was introduced earlier).[19] Certainly, in the complex's final form, a causeway ran from a gate in the enclosure wall down to the edge of the cultivation, where any remains of a valley building would seem to lie below the modern water table. The final mortuary temple, contemporary with the third phase of the pyramid, comprised an offering place flanked by a pair of never-inscribed stelae, approached via a pair of vestibules, the whole a development of the arrangements at the Bent Pyramid at Dahshur.

Built from the outset as a true pyramid, it is unclear whether the Bent Pyramid (L.LVI: map 6B; fig. 5b; pl. XIIIc)[20] was begun in parallel with work on the stepped phase of the Meidum pyramid or whether it was begun as its replacement. A feature of step pyramids had been inward-sloping masonry, with the blocks laid at right angles to the slope of the face of the pyramid. This practice was continued with the new pyramid. Part way through the pyramid's construction it appears that structural problems manifested themselves in the substructure. This led to the angle – and so supercumbent weight – of the upper part of the pyramid being reduced, creating its distinctive shape and modern name, the Bent Pyramid; this part was built in horizontal courses, as were all later pyramids.

A subsidiary pyramid (L.LVII) lay south of the main pyramid, with a chapel to its east, with a pair of stelae bearing the king's image and names (pl. XIIIb). A similar mortuary temple was built on the east side of the main pyramid (pl. XIVa), the causeway leading to the valley building leaving from the northeast corner of the enclosure. The valley building – the earliest surviving example – lay at the top of a wadi leading down to the desert edge. It was extensively decorated with reliefs and statuary.[21]

The Bent Pyramid's original substructure was similar to that of the

Meidum pyramid, with the exception that the shaft leading up to the burial chamber was replaced by a steep staircase. However, a unique additional set of corridors and chamber, approached from the west, was built within the pyramid masonry itself, equipped with unusual diagonally-sliding portcullises and apparently added following structural failures within the original complex, evidenced by significant cracking. No stone sarcophagus was included in either the Meidum or Bent pyramids.

It is possible that the conversion of the Meidum pyramid to a true pyramid – using horizontal courses of masonry – was begun as an insurance after structural problems manifested themselves at the Bent Pyramid. However, both the replanning of the Bent Pyramid and the recasting of the Meidum pyramid were evidently regarded as sub-optimal, as yet a third pyramid was commissioned, some 2 km to the north of the Bent Pyramid.[22] The so-called Red Pyramid (L.XLIX: fig. 5c; pl. XIVb) was built entirely at the lower angle of the upper part of the Bent Pyramid. A rather more elaborate mortuary temple than those of the previous two pyramids was provided, but a proper causeway seems never to have been constructed. The form of the valley building remains unknown, although possible parts were noticed during the nineteenth century. Likewise, no subsidiary pyramid has been identified, although the pyramidion (capstone) of such a monument – too steeply angled for the Red Pyramid itself – has been discovered.

The substructure of the Red Pyramid was built at ground level entirely within the body of the pyramid. It comprised three spectacular corbelled rooms (pl. XVa), the third entered from high up in the wall of the second, clearly for concealment. The floor of the third chamber is now represented by an irregular cavity, and it is possible that a sarcophagus made up of a number of blocks had been built into the floor; fragments of a mummy, probably that of the king, were found in the pyramid.

Seven small step pyramids, apparently devoid of any chambers, appear to date to the end of the Third or the beginning of the Fourth Dynasty. One, at Elephantine (pl. XVb),[23] has been dated to the reign of Huni by the discovery of his name nearby, and another, at Seila, near Meidum,[24] to that of Seneferu by an inscribed altar, statue and stelae in its chapel. The five others[25] are therefore likely to belong to one or other of these reigns, but their purpose remains wholly obscure.

Seneferu's successor, Khufu, shifted the location of the royal cemetery northwards to Giza (map 2B; pl. XVIa), where he built what was to be the largest of all pyramids, the so-called Great Pyramid (L.IV: fig. 5d; pl. XVIb).[26] As laid out by Khufu, his Giza necropolis differed significantly from earlier royal cemeteries in that it placed the tombs of the nobility and royal family (see below) directly adjacent to the king's tomb, rather than at a distance from. In addition, these subsidiary cemeteries were laid out on a formal gridded plan, with the cores of the constituent mastabas constructed by the central authority before allocation to and completion by their final owners. This kind of integrated necropolis was not repeated by any subsequent king, although the concept of royal family and senior nobility being buried close to their king would continue.

As for Khufu's own tomb, the pyramid had the now-standard mortuary temple on its east side, a structure significantly more elaborate than any of those of his father; it had been decorated in relief, but only scattered fragments can now be identified.[27] Directly south of this lay the subsidiary pyramid. This was a change from the previous location of the subsidiary tomb opposite the south face of the main pyramid; during the remainder of the dynasty its position would vary from reign to reign, before finally coming to rest back in Khufu's position early in the Fifth Dynasty. A causeway led from the mortuary temple toward the valley building, some elements of which have been detected under modern buildings below the desert escarpment.[28] A number of boat pits were constructed on the south and east sides of the pyramid, two still containing wooden boats when investigated in modern times.[29]

The pyramid's substructure seems to have been constructed in three phases.[30] First, a rock-cut descending passage was built, leading to what was intended to be the first of a series of chambers deep under the centre of the pyramid. This seems to have been abandoned when it was desired to include a stone sarcophagus in the burial, the passages being too low and narrow to introduce such a piece. An ascending corridor was thus added, apparently cutting through extant masonry, giving access to the so-called Queen's Chamber. This could have received the sarcophagus before its walls were built, but plans seem to have changed again. The chamber is interesting, in that it replaces the corbelled roof with a new pointed type, which is subsequently standard for such rooms.

To allow plug-blocks to be slid down the ascending passage after the burial, a corbelled room had been begun, beyond the entrance to the passage leading into the Queen's Chamber, to store the blocks. A shaft was also built to allow workmen to exit down to the descending passage after releasing them. The corbelled room was then apparently greatly extended to become the Grand Gallery (pl. XVIIa), to give access to the final burial chamber – the King's Chamber – approached via an antechamber with portcullis slabs. Above the King's Chamber was built a series of relieving chambers, while both it and Queen's Chamber both had narrow (20 cm square) channels angled upwards from their north and south walls, apparently aimed at the stars. Since such features are not found in any other pyramid, they may be a result of the shift to an elevated burial chamber – a feature unique to the Great Pyramid – whose ascending access passage lacked the direct 'sight-line' to the heavens implicit in other pyramids' descending access-passage.

These channels from the King's Chamber – wrongly dubbed 'air shafts' – continue to the exterior of the pyramid, but at least one of those of the Queen's Chamber terminates within the body of the pyramid, probably the result of the chamber's supersession as the burial chamber, the terminations corresponding to the level reached by the pyramid at the time of the plan change. The King's Chamber still contains a rectangular granite sarcophagus, the earliest of its kind in a royal tomb (pl. XVIIb); such hardstone containers would subsequently be standard for the vast majority of such sepulchres.

A novel oval-shaped sarcophagus was adopted in what seem to have been the next two pyramids to be built. That of Djedefre at Abu Rowash (L.II: map 2A; fig. 6a; pl. XVIIIa)[31] was certainly that of Khufu's direct successor. His pyramid was built in a truly spectacular location, on a mountain top with views north into the Delta, and south to at least as far as Dahshur. The relatively modest size of the pyramid, relative to the immediately preceding monuments, would thus have been more than offset by its visibility, its base lying some 20 m higher than the Giza plateau. The structure is now very badly ruined, only the native rock core, plus a little masonry, being visible. However, these remains indicate that a large proportion of the pyramid casing was of polished granite.

The mortuary temple lay on the east side, and was partly constructed in brick, suggesting the king's premature death. Extensive remains of sculpture have been recovered, hinting that it was adorned with statuary to a degree not found in previous royal mortuary temples. A boat pit was constructed directly south of the temple. The causeway led, uniquely, from the north side of the complex, to allow it to follow a 1.5 km natural ridge for the descent; this probably explains why much of the mortuary temple lay adjacent to the northern part of the east face. The valley building at the bottom has never been excavated, but must have lain close to the Third Dynasty El-Deir. What seems to have been the subsidiary pyramid lay in the southwest corner of the enclosure, an unusual position otherwise found only at the slightly later Giza pyramid of Menkaure.

The substructure (now almost entirely destroyed) was built in a very deep T-shaped cutting (pl. XVIIIb), which placed the burial chamber far below the pyramid base. While only a fragment of what seems to have been the oval sarcophagus appears to have survived, a complete example of such a monument has been found in the Unfinished Pyramid at Zawiyet el-Aryan (L.XIII: map 3A; fig. 6b; pl. XIXa).[32] Nothing more than the T-shaped cutting for the substructure and some marking-out of the site seems to have been achieved before work on this monument was abandoned, the only indications of its ownership being quarry-marks that seem to name a king Nebkare Seth?ka. Although early scholars placed the structure in the Third Dynasty, its close similarity to the corresponding part of Djedefre's monument makes it clear that it is a Fourth Dynasty monument. The fact that deep placement of the burial chamber was abandoned by the time of Khaefre makes it most likely that the Unfinished Pyramid belonged to an otherwise-unattested direct successor of Djedefre, perhaps his eldest son Setka.

The next king, Khaefre, returned to Giza for the construction of his tomb, known today as the Second Pyramid (L.VIII: fig. 6c; pl. XIXb).[33] This monument, the second largest pyramid in Egypt, has an angle of elevation slightly greater than the Great Pyramid and most other kings' pyramids, and has the remains of part of the casing surviving near the summit. The pyramid may have been intended to be built somewhat north of its final location. This is because it has essentially two substructures, the northern one with an entrance outside the north face, and a burial chamber 30 m north of the centre of the pyramid. With the pyramid further north (and of somewhat larger dimensions than finally employed), both elements would have been in a conventional position. The second set of galleries placed the final burial chamber roughly at ground level, marking the abandonment of deeply buried sepulchral chambers in pyramids. The new complex was linked to the old by a ramp, and protected by a portcullis slab. The sarcophagus was sunk in the floor of the burial chamber, with a sunken cavity for the canopic equipment to the southeast (pl. XXa), the first surviving example of canopic provision within a pyramid.

The subsidiary pyramid (GIIb, now almost completely destroyed) stood on the south side of the main pyramid. The mortuary temple, causeway and valley building marked a major step towards the standard pyramid complex. All were built from particularly massive limestone masonry, facings of ashlars of granite surviving at the valley building (pl. XXb). Its T-shaped hall contained a large number of fine statues, a number of which were preserved through their placement in a pit in later times; it seems that the complex marked a further upswing in the employment of three-dimensional sculpture following on from that already seen under Djedefre.[34] The complex also incorporated the Great Sphinx and an associated temple; although usually regarded as having been sculpted in the time of Khaefre, it may have been originally carved during the Early Dynastic Period.[35] It is also possible that its head was completely re-carved later, perhaps during the Twelfth Dynasty reign of Amenemhat II, a sphinx of whom may provide the best equivalent of the present form of the face and headdress.[36]

The successor of Khaefre, Menkaure, built a much smaller pyramid than the other kings who had built at Giza (L.IX: fig. 6d; pl. XXIa);[37] indeed, his 'Third Pyramid' seems originally to have been intended to be even smaller. It has lost all its limestone casing, but a large amount of a lower, granite, casing is still in place. The substructure is generally viewed to have undergone at least two changes of plan. The initial small pyramid had a simple descending passage and burial chamber but, with the enlargement of the superstructure, a new entrance corridor was provided, including a small panelled chamber and three portcullises, while a new granite burial chamber – uniquely oriented north-south – and a niched storeroom were added at a lower level.[38] A panelled sarcophagus of basalt was installed in the final burial chamber, placed most unusually along the axis of the burial chamber, reflecting the latter's anomalous alignment.[39]

The pyramid's temples show a further development over those of Khaefre, moving towards what was later to become the standard basic layout. The subsidiary pyramid (GIIIc – pl. XXIa, left)[40] is in the unusual position of being near the southwest corner of the main monument, a position previously used by Djedefre, and later only by Userkaf. Two queens' pyramids (GIIIa–b) were built directly east of it.[41]

Curiously, the last king of the Fourth Dynasty, Shepseskaf, did not build a pyramid. Rather, he constructed a huge mastaba at the then-virgin site of Saqqara-South; now known as the *Mastabat Faraun*, its roof had raised end-pieces reminiscent of those found on the lids of many sarcophagi (L.XLIII: fig. 6e; pl. XXIb).[42] This would seem to be a manifestation of the '*pr-nw*' shrine, a shape that was symbolic of Lower Egypt. The meaning of this change is unclear, although the abandonment of the solar symbol that was the pyramid may be connected in some way with the fact that the king's own name did not, unlike those of his immediate predecessors, contain the name of the sun-god, Re.

The design of the substructure was very similar to that of Menkaure's pyramid, but arranged more regularly, with the burial chamber west of an antechamber, and a room with store-niches to the south-east. The sarcophagus was smashed in antiquity. A conventional mortuary temple and causeway were built on the east side, but the valley building has never been explored. Likewise, nothing is known of any subsidiary tomb.

Royal family tombs of the Fourth Dynasty
From the Fourth Dynasty, royal family burials become far easier to trace. A number of the sons of Seneferu were buried with their wives in large tombs at Meidum (map 8B),[43] while other members of his family were subsequently provided with sepulchres at Dahshur.[44]

The tombs of Princes Rahotep, Ranefer and Nefermaat, and their spouses, at Meidum were huge brick mastabas (numbers 6, 9 and 16), with a pair of small chapels in their eastern faces. That of Rahotep contained remarkable statues of the prince and his wife, while both tombs' chapels were extensively decorated in the latest styles. The burial chambers lay at the bottom of deep shafts, beginning in the roof of the mastaba. Another large mastaba (17) lay close alongside the Meidum pyramid. This had been finished only after the body had been placed in the burial chamber, so that the entrance passage left the latter, only to stop after a short while in the subsequently-laid bricks of the substructure. The body, of an adult, will almost certainly have been that of a royal prince, but no traces of his name have ever been found. Only three probable tombs of children of Seneferu have thus far been identified at Dahshur, those of Princes Netjeraperef (number II/1), Iynefer and Kanefer (28).[45] They each lie in different parts of the area and comprise stone mastabas, marking an advance from the brick structures at Meidum.

Curiously, no queens' tombs have been identified at Meidum or Dahshur.[46] This lack is remedied at Giza, where pyramids, apparently previously the sole possession of kings, were granted to womenfolk of Khufu, three being built on the east side of the Great Pyramid, adjacent to the king's subsidiary example (map 2B; pl. XVIb).[47] The exact identity of their owners is uncertain, but GIc (L.VII) is stated in a much later text to have belonged to Princess Henutsen. Another (GIa/L.VI) may have been intended for Khufu's mother, Hetepheres I, whose funerary equipment was ultimately (re?)buried in a deep shaft tomb (G7000X)[48] just north of the pyramid. The remaining small pyramid is likely to have belonged to another wife of the king. Each pyramid had a chapel on the east side, that of GIc being much later enlarged to become the temple of Isis-Mistress-of-the-Pyramids. On the north face of each pyramid, a passage led into the centre of the monument, ending in a burial chamber.

For other members of his family, Khufu laid out a large complex of stone mastabas on the east of his own tomb, adjoining the queens' pyramids (cemetery G7000)[49] where a series of a dozen cores was constructed as part of Khufu's overall necropolis-project. However, four adjacent pairs were subsequently joined together to form huge double-mastabas, the remaining four single cores then being extended to a similar size. Other tombs were then built around this nucleus cemetery.

At the pyramid-complex of Djedefre at Abu Rowash, two small pyramids existed, one to the south of the mortuary temple and one in the southwest corner of the outer enclosure (fig. 5a).[50] The former appears to have been intended as a subsidiary pyramid, but had been adapted into a tomb, with a limestone sarcophagus and a canopic jar having been found in it. The other structure was presumably a replacement subsidiary. Other members of the king's family were interred in cemetery F, 1.5 km northeast of the king's pyramid.[51] However, Khaefre abandoned pyramids for his wives.[52] Some of them, as daughters of Khufu, retained tombs in Giza cemetery G7000, but at least two began rock-cut tombs south of Khaefre's pyramid causeway. This was a considerable innovation, marking a step away from the 'built' forms of tomb superstructure that had long been standard. One lay in a former quarry south of the king's mortuary temple, and belonged to Persenet (LG88).[53] The other, the 'Galarza Tomb', lay close to the bottom of the causeway, and was apparently begun for Khamerernebty I, but substantially modified by her daughter, Khamerernebty II and perhaps a later prince as well.[54]

Rock-cut tombs were employed for a number of other members of Khaefre's family, clustered around Persenet's tomb in what had once been a quarry, although Prince Babaef had a stone mastaba in the same general area.[55] A similar quarry-cemetery was founded by Menkaure, southeast of his pyramid, including the tomb of his son, Khuenre (MQ1).[56] However, pyramids were revived for two of his wives, with the construction of GIIIa and GIIIb on the south side of the king's monument, directly east of his subsidiary pyramid (pl. XXIa).[57] These small pyramids had mud-brick chapels attached to their east sides, although stone construction may originally have been intended. The chapel of GIIIa contained fragments of a lady's calcite statue but no names were forthcoming from any of the small pyramids.

A monument whose owner's status is somewhat unclear (LG100 – pl. XXIIa) is one sometimes dubbed the 'Fourth Pyramid'.[58] It lies just north of the valley building of Menkaure and comprises a square structure atop a rock-cut podium, in which was excavated a chapel and, below it, a burial chamber. Comprising a square stone-built structure atop a rock-cut podium, its chapel was excavated within the podium, from which access to the burial chamber was to be had. These arrangements were elaborations of the corresponding rock-cut features of late Fourth Dynasty royal family members' tombs. It is possible that the tomb's owner, the King's Mother Khentkawes I, may have been mother of Shepeskaf and Userlaf and may have acted as regent for one of them.[59]

The Fifth Dynasty
As is indicated by the uncertainty of the role of Khentkawes I, little is known of the transition between the Fourth and Fifth Dynasties. During the new dynasty, the principal royal necropolis came to be Abusir, some 11 km south of Giza, although a number of kings were interred at Saqqara, including the first and last three rulers. The size and constructional quality of these

pyramids falls well short of Fourth Dynasty norms, but in contrast, their temples are consistently larger and preserve very fine examples of relief decoration.

The dynastic founder, Userkaf, placed his pyramid (L.XXXI: fig. 7a; pl. XXIIb)[60] at the north end of the east enclosure wall of the Step Pyramid, within the 'dry moat' and thus on the terrace in front of the Third Dynasty complex. Since the 'moat' lay only a short distance from the eastern side of the pyramid, and the builders were apparently unwilling to fill-in the gap, only a small chapel was built on the east, the main elements of the mortuary temple being constructed on the south side of the pyramid; the subsidiary pyramid was placed in the south-west corner of the complex, as had been the case under Djedefre and Menkaure. The entrance to the complex lay at the southern end of the eastern wall, approached by a causeway, only the lower part of which can be traced; it is unclear how it bridged the 'moat' before entering the mortuary temple.[61] The temple had been extensively decorated and included a colossal statue of the king, but had been badly damaged by the building of tombs within it during the Twenty-sixth/seventh Dynasty, obscuring many details. The substructure of the king's pyramid generally followed Shepseskaf's pattern, except that the storeroom was placed half way along the entrance corridor and lacks niches.[62] A broken sarcophagus was found in the burial chamber.

Possibly owing to the problems with finding further suitable pyramid sites at Saqqara (cf. below, pp. 28-9, 32 regarding the pyramids of Menkauhor, Unas and Teti), Userkaf's immediate successors moved their necropolis north to Abusir (map 3B; pl. XXIIIa), close to the already-noted ancient access to the Saqqara cemetery.[63] The first pyramid built there was that of Sahure (L.XVIII: fig. 7b; pl. XXIIIb),[64] a monument whose layout crystallised what was to be the standard royal tomb for the remainder of the Old Kingdom.[65] The mortuary temple covered a considerable area against the east face and was elaborately decorated in painted relief. In plan, the causeway opened into a vestibule and then a peristyle court, beyond which lay a hall with statue-niches and then a winding access corridor to the sanctuary, the whole flanked with storerooms. The subsidiary pyramid lay directly south of the temple, which would be its standard location for the remainder of the Old Kingdom.

The interior of the pyramid was wrecked in mediaeval times by stone robbers, leaving a partly collapsed, irregular set of cavities, with but a single fragment of basalt representing the sarcophagus. The burial chamber lay in the centre of the pyramid; on the basis of later monuments, it is likely that an antechamber lay directly east of it, from which a horizontal passage led north towards the centre of the north face. The actual entrance comprised a short sloping passage, close to ground-level – a final abandonment of the 'high' entrance typical of the Fourth Dynasty – with a vestibule and portcullis at its inner end.

The following pyramid of Neferirkare (L.XXI: fig. 7c; pl. XXIVa),[66] was somewhat larger than that of Sahure, and had a core of stepped form: it is possible that it was left thus, and never cased as a true pyramid. Only the inner part of the mortuary temple was completed in stone, the remainder having been completed in brick and wood after the king's death, with its final plan uncertain.[67] Its causeway was later diverted to serve the pyramid of Niuserre, the valley building thus also being taken over by that king. The interior of the pyramid was another victim of stone robbers, and little more than the general layout can be discerned. This was very similar to that found in the pyramid of Sahure, but included a deviation of the entrance corridor to the east for a considerable distance beyond the entrance vestibule, after which it moved to an approximately north-south line (but apparently deviating slightly to the west) that gave access to the antechamber. The burial chamber lay to the west. The eastern deviation of the main corridor would be a distinctive feature of most of the remaining kings' pyramids of the dynasty.

Neferirkare's successor, Neferefre, was also unable to finish his tomb (L.XXVI: fig. 7d; pl. XXIVa)[68] as originally planned. However, in this case the pyramid had risen only a few courses when the king died and was accordingly finished off by filling much of the incomplete interior with gravel (including the cutting within which the substructure was constructed), thus turning it into a mastaba of uniquely square plan. Since the causeway and valley building were barely begun, the mortuary temple, largely built in brick, was enlarged to incorporate elements usually found in the valley building. The structure is well preserved, and revealed many items, including a wooden boat, statuary and administrative papyri.

The substructure followed the now-established pattern but with the oblique inner corridor continuing to the door of the antechamber. It suffered particularly severely from stone robbery owing to its coverage by little more than rubble. Along with fragments of the sarcophagus were found a number of parts of the royal mummy, including a hand, part of the skull and other fragments. These proved to be those of a young man. Neferefre seems to have been succeeded by an even more ephemeral king, Shepseskare. His may have been the barely-begun pyramid, the outline of which lies under the sand to the north of the other Abusir pyramids.[69] The T-shaped outline of the cut for the substructure is visible, but little else, amounting to perhaps one or two months' work.

Niuserre, however, had a more substantial reign, and succeeded in completing a pyramid whose basic form followed that of Sahure (L.XX: fig. 7e; pl. XXVa).[70] However, the arrangement of the elements of the mortuary temple was adjusted to allow the king to take over most of the unfinished causeway and valley building of Neferirkare, the outer parts being placed further south than usual to facilitate the construction of the new upper, joining, section of the causeway. The substructure of the pyramid was once again badly ruined by the activities of stone robbers.

The pyramid of Niuserre was the last king's tomb to be built at Abusir, the remaining kings of the Fifth Dynasty moving back to Saqqara. That of Menkauhor is known from inscriptions of his mortuary priests, but his ownership of a largely-destroyed pyramid a little to the south of the Early Dynastic private necropolis, close to the edge of the escarpment (L.XXIX: fig. 7f), can be demonstrated only on architectural and topographical grounds.[71] First, the layout of the interior, with an oblique second passageway, is found only in the pyramids at Abusir, and had been abandoned by the time of Menkauhor's successor, Isesi: indeed, the plan of the substructure is essential identical to that of Niuserre. Second, the pyramid complex of Teti displays a number of anomalies in layout and orientation that can only be explained as the result of the previous construction of this pyramid on the site to its east (q.v.).

The location, on the edge of the escarpment, and in a position that required a steep and/or long causeway (now destroyed) probably reflected the lack of a suitable site further to the west, Userkaf having employed the last virgin site capable of accommodating a pyramid-complex in the vicinity of the Step Pyramid. It may also have reflected a desire for a prominent position on the skyline visible from Memphis and beyond (cf. the pyramid of Djedefre at Abu Rowash). The whole of Menkauhor's complex was later swallowed up by the Late/Graeco-Roman Period Anubiaeon temple-complex. The principal remains are of the lower courses of the masonry of the inner parts of the substructure, showing that the design followed the approach seen at Abusir of placing the outer vestibule, portcullises and, as already noted, inner passage at an oblique angle the north-south axis. The latter gave access to an antechamber, with a burial chamber to the east and a storeroom to the west – the latter a pattern seen in all later Old Kingdom kings' pyramids.

The shortage of suitable sites in the main Saqqara cemetery was probably the reason that the next king, Isesi, chose to build his pyramid (L.XXXVII: fig. 7g; pl. XXVb)[72] in a hitherto-virgin location well to the south of the earlier monuments, an area that also lacked the steep escarpment that had complicated the construction of causeways there. The valley building is lost, but the mortuary temple was somewhat larger than those at Abusir, and replicated the arrangement seen at the pyramid of Niuserre of having store rooms flanking the entrance hall. A new feature was a square massif at the southern end of the temple's façade (the situation is less clear to the north), which is unique to Isesi's pyramid.

However, in most of its other aspects, the pyramid of Isesi contained elements that would become standard in all future Old Kingdom pyramids. The pyramid itself was of the usual constructional style, and of the same size as the pyramid of Niuserre, but its substructure differed from that of any preceding monument. First, the entrance (to what is the last example of an oblique entrance passage) lay just outside the limit of the north face, and opened from the floor of a chapel that abutted the pyramid casing, any attempt at concealing the location of the entrance to the substructure having now been abandoned.[73] Second, the inner access corridors no longer ran obliquely, but once again proceeded in a straight line towards the centre of the pyramid. Third, a triple set of portcullises was set a little way along the horizontal corridor beyond the initial vestibule. Finally, the annexe that had been introduced east of the antechamber by Menkauhor was divided into three by stub walls.[74] In the burial chamber, the canopic chest was sunk in the floor, southeast of the foot of the sarcophagus (the situation of the chest in preceding Fifth Dynasty pyramids is unknown). Fragments of the king's mummy were found amid the broken sarcophagus. The substructure-arrangement found in Isesi's pyramid henceforth became standard in all king's pyramids down to the end of the Old Kingdom. In addition, the pyramid's base-dimensions – 150 cubits square[75] – also became standard for the rest of the Old Kingdom, only the immediately succeeding pyramid of Unas deviating from this.

The reason for this – the pyramid was only 110 cubits square – almost certainly lies in the site the king chose for his pyramid (L.XXXV: fig. 7h; pl. XXVIa).[76] Like Userkaf before him, Unas clearly desired to be buried close to the Step Pyramid, the only practicable spot being at west end of the south side of of that monument, in the 'precinct' constructed for the tombs of Hotepsekhemwy and Ninetjer back in the Second Dynasty. Presumably not wishing to undertake the extensive quarrying needed to extend the precinct sufficiently to allow a 'full-size' pyramid, Unas's monument was thus constrained in size by its site.

To allow to be built at all, however, whatever still remained of the superstructure of the tomb of Hetepsekhemwy was demolished in its entirety, the eastern side of the pyramid and inner part of the mortuary temple of Unas being built over it. Further east, the superstructure of Ninetjer was also taken down to clear the route of the upper part of the causeway, which then ran along part of the southeastern arm of the Djoser dry moat, before following the natural slope down through a number of bends to the site of the valley building, three-quarters of a kilometre away. The Unas causeway is around twice the length of the second longest causeway, that of the Sixth Dynasty Pepy II, considerably increasing the amount of engineering work required compared with most complexes for this aspect, emphasising, together with the acceptance of reduced pyramid-dimensions, the importance to Unas of the placement of his pyramid.

The mortuary temple of Unas was very similar to that of Isesi, but without the strange pylons, and remarkably assymetrical in layout, a further impact of the restrictions imposed by the site. Apart from this aspect, the temple's design formed the basis for the 'standard' plan that was carried through the next dynasty. The valley building (pl. XXVIb) continued the basic pattern of design seen in those of Sahure and Niuserre, and which is seen later at the pyramid of Pepy II; unfortunately, the valley buildings of many pyramids remain unexcavated and the detail of architectural evolution thus obscure.

Internally, Unas's monument was essentially identical in design with that of Isesi but with the important difference that it was the first royal substructure to be decorated since the time of Djoser (pl. XXVIIa). A delicate panelled design was incised into walls directly adjacent to the sarcophagus, while the ceiling was adorned with five-pointed stars. Most importantly, however, the rest of the burial chamber, the antechamber and part of the approach corridor were covered with columns of hieroglyphs. These comprised a compilation of religious spells that now became the standard decorative scheme for kingly pyramids until the end of the Old Kingdom. Interestingly, decoration (of a completely different kind) also appears at this very time in some private burial chambers – hitherto likewise devoid of adornment.[77] At least some of the blocks used in the substructure had been reused, at least one preserving traces of a relief of Khufu.[78]

The royal burial-chamber texts, now known as the 'Pyramid Texts',[79] deal with the posthumous destiny of the king, which differed greatly from that of the mass of humanity: as a divine being he would dwell with his fellow gods in the entourage of the sun-god, Re. These texts are a miscellaneous compilation of spells of various kinds and lengths, with no two pyramids having precisely the same sets of spells: indeed, some are unique to a given tomb. They include instructions for ceremonies, hymns and spells to aid the progress and transformation of the spirit, possibly arranged in sets radiating out from the kernel of the pyramid, the sarcophagus.

Royal family tombs of the Fifth Dynasty

The regular appointment of princes to high governmental office was ended early in the Fifth Dynasty, with important implications for royal family tombs, the only easily identifiable examples of which are hitherto queens' pyramids or mastabas adjacent to their husbands' tombs. The relatively few royal offspring with known sepulchres have tombs indistinguishable from those of contemporary commoners.

A pyramid directly south of that of Userkaf at Saqqara belonged to Neferhetepes A (fig. 6a);[80] it appears that some work may have been carried out on the pyramid under Userkaf's successor, Sahure. At Abusir, however, there appears to be no obvious pyramid for a wife of Sahure himself,[81] although a small pyramid that lay south of Neferirkare's monument belonged to Khentkawes II, probably his wife.[82] A further small pyramid (L.XXIV) lay to the southeast of that of Khentkawes II,[83] perhaps associated with the tomb of Neferefre, which lay directly to the west, or perhaps dating to the time of Niuserre, the area around whose pyramid seems to be too congested to have accommodated a queen's pyramid. Close by were built an adjacent pair of unusual mastabas (L.XXV/1 and L.XXV/2), apparently to be dated to the reign of Niuserre, each containing the burial of related females, one perhaps a Princess Hanebu.[84] No names have been recovered from any of these sepulchres. A further mastaba, close to the tomb of Neferefre, contained a quarry mark naming a King's Wife and King's Mother Khentkawes,[85] but this may represent the use of a block originally intended for the nearby tomb of Khentkawes II, as the form and contents of the tomb are not consistent with contemporary queenly practice.

Regarding royal sons, the tomb of Nakhtsare was one of a group of four mastabas south of the mortuary temple of Neferefre.[86] Although Abusir ceased to be the kingly cemetery after the time of Niuserre, a number of Isesi's family were buried in brick mastabas southeast of Niuserre's mortuary temple, including Princess Khekeretnebty, whose body was found partly intact.[87] Isesi's principal wife, however, was presumably the owner of a large pyramid northeast of her husband's at South Saqqara, with one of the most elaborate mortuary chapels known from a queenly monument (fig. 7g; pl. XXVb).[88]

A series of royal spouses and children was buried close to the north wall of the Step Pyramid complex, together with a number of other highly placed individuals,[89] with some a little further west.[90] They have been generally regarded as belonging to the family of Isesi, but some at least may actually be affiliated to Menkauhor, whose pyramid lies due east of them, with Meresankh IV, owner of mastaba 82[91] potentially his queen.

Unas certainly abandoned the use of pyramids for his queens: rather, his principal spouses instead shared a double mastaba positioned, as with Isesi's queen, directly north of the outer part of the king's mortuary temple (L.XXXVIII: fig. 7h; pl. XXVIIb).[92] The eastern half belonged to Queen Nebet, the western to Khenut. Each lady had a separate set of rooms, of apparently identical plan, with its own entrance; the chambers were extensively decorated. Further tombs, belonging to other members of Unas's family lay directly north of the queens' mastaba, including that of Prince Unasankh,[93] and that of the Princess Idut;[94] finally, the Princess Hemetre had a tomb west of the Step Pyramid (D65).[95]

A number of royal daughters married commoners, and so were buried in their husbands' tombs. Examples include Niuserre's daughter, Khamerernebty A, wife of Ptahshepses B, interred in a large tomb in central Abusir,[96] and Sheretnebty, buried with her now-nameless husband at Abusir-South in tomb AS68.[97]

The Sixth Dynasty

The founder of the Sixth Dynasty, Teti, placed his monument (L.XXX: fig. 8a; pl. XXVIIIa)[98] almost directly west of the sepulchre of Menkauhor, a strange location explicable only by the shortage of suitable pyramid sites in the area and/or a decision to emulate Niuserre vis à vis Neferirkare in appropriating the lower portion of the earlier king's causeway. Certainly, the causeway departed the far left-hand end of the façade of the mortuary temple at an angle that took it parallel to the south face of the pyramid of Menkauhor.[99]

Save for the rearrangement of the very outermost part of the temple to allow for this, the plan of the mortuary temple essentially followed that of Unas, with the exception that it was more symmetrical, reflecting the lack of space constraints to the south; the pyramid was also able to revert to the size seen in the pyramid of Isesi. Internally, the monument followed the plan seen the tombs of Isesi and Unas, with the Pyramid Texts repeated, albeit with a slightly different selection of spells.[100] In addition, the royal sarcophagus was decorated with texts for the first time, bands of hieroglyphs being inscribed on the upper surface of the lid and the interior sides and floor of the coffer.

Tradition had it that Teti was murdered,[101] and it appears that he was directly followed by a usurping king, Userkare. No clear evidence exists of any potential tomb, although subsurface geophyisical traces at Tabbet el-Guesh, at Saqqara about a kilometre south of the Step Pyramid and a kilometre north of the pyramid of Isesi, have been suggested as a potential site.[102]

Teti had in any case exhausted the last potential pyramid site at northern Saqqara: no later such monuments of any size would be erected there. For the rest of the Old Kingdom, pyramids were built in areas to the south first colonised by Isesi and Shepeseskaf. Pepy I built his monument a little northwest of that of Isesi,[103] in size and layout (apart from a conventional axial causeway) a near-replica of the pyramid-complex of Teti (L.XXXVI: fig. 8b; pl. XXVIIIb). Its decorative scheme did, however, differ in that the panelling around the sarcophagus was reduced in height to that of the sarcophagus itself, and applied only to the north and south walls, the west side of the sarcophagus being occupied by the dwarf walls on which the sarcophagus lid had been stored until drawn forward into place. Additional Pyramid Texts now occupied the area formerly occupied by the upper section of panelling, while the sarcophagus-inscriptions were moved to the outside of the coffer. A hand from the king's mummy was found in the pyramid.

The pyramid complex of Nemtyemsaf I (L.XXXIX: fig. 8c; pl. XXIXa),[104] built southwest of Isesi's tomb, seems to have been all-but-identical to that of Pepy I, although only the interior of the pyramid has been excavated to date. A mummy found in the sarcophagus is likely to have been intrusive. In the case of both pyramids, the apparent directions taken by their causeways indicate that they lay at the margins of wadis that allowed the cultivation to penetrate deeply into the desert region.

The wadi south of Nemtyemsaf's pyramid separated it from the last pyramids of the Old Kingdom tradition (map 5; pl. XXIXb). The first of these was that of last major king of the dynasty, Pepy II,[105] the final manifestation of the 'standard' pyramid complex, lying close to the Fourth Dynasty giant mastaba of Shepseskaf. Pepy II's pyramid (L.XLI: fig. 8d; pl. XXIXc) is much better preserved than those of his immediate predecessors, and seems to have been built with rather more care. When at least partly built, a 6.5 m thick masonry 'girdle' was added around the lower part of the structure; this may have resulted from a perceived instability of the pyramid, perhaps after an earthquake. The construction of this feature necessitated the dismantling of the north chapel and its reconstruction further out.

Pepy II's complex represented the Old Kingdom royal tomb at its most developed, with all elements preserved to some extent. After his reign there seems to have been a rapid decline in Egypt's fortunes, heralding a period of disunity known as the First Intermediate Period, from which only a handful of royal tombs survives.

Royal family tombs of the Sixth Dynasty

A necropolis grew up on the north side of the pyramid of Teti, including the tombs of major figures in his administration.[106] Pyramids were built for his womenfolk in the northeastern part of this cemetery, one probably for Teti's mother Sesheshet,[107] and one each for his wives Iput I and Khuit II (fig. 8a).[108] The pyramids were small, but had substantial chapels, that of Iput I being the first queen's example to include deities in its decoration. Both of the latter two sepulchres seem to have been first built as mastabas, and then converted to pyramids. In Iput's case, at least, this occurred after the lady's death. Her skeleton and some of her jewellery survived in her sarcophagus, at the bottom of a vertical shaft under the centre of the pyramid, which was sealed by its construction.

As in the Fifth Dynasty, a number of princesses married commoners. One of the most notable was Sesheshet-Watetkhethor, who had a distinct suite of rooms in the very large mastaba of her spouse, the Vizier Mereruka.[109]

A very large queenly cemetery was provided on the south side of Pepy I's pyramid (fig. 8b; pl. XXXa).[110] These pyramids included the tombs of Ankhenespepy II, Nebwenet, Inenek-Inti, Meryetyotes IV, Mehaa, Ankhenespepy III, Behenu and another (perhaps the earliest of them all). All but that of Mehaa (where the tomb of her son Netjerykhethor lay directly east of her pyramid) had substantial chapels, that of Inti having its doorway flanked with small obelisks. The pyramid of Ankhenespepy II was the largest queen's pyramid yet built, including features hitherto specific to a king's sepulchre, including having its burial chamber adorned with the Pyramid Texts.[111] Most of the ladies buried in the cemetery were wives of Pepy I, but Ankhenespepy II subsequently also married her stepson/nephew Nemtyemsaf I, while Ankhesenpepy III was a spouse of Pepy II, as was probably Behenu – most unusually for the period thus interred 1.5 km from their husband. Behenu's pyramid also had Pyramid Texts, of similar type to those found in the pyramids of two queens of Pepy II, contributing to her proposed dating to his reign.

The complex of Nemtyemsaf I has never been excavated, and very little is known of its associated necropoleis. However, a map drawn in the 1840s shows three approximately square mounds around the king's pyramid. Two of these, to the north, are of the right size for queens' pyramids (map 5) and moreover lie in a similar position relative to the king's monument as the tombs of Teti's queens to his.

The pyramid complex of Pepy II is accompanied by the last three queens' pyramids of the Old Kingdom, two at the king's tomb's northwest angle (of Neith and Iput II – pl. XXXb), and the other (of Wedjebten) at the opposite corner.[112] Each monument had a substructure decorated with Pyramid Texts and large decorated chapels, incorporating a subsidiary pyramid (fig. 8d). Iput's chapel was itself used a little later as the tomb of a queen, one of the store-rooms having had had a funerary stela carved into one of its walls, and a sarcophagus placed in the chamber, used for the burial of Queen Ankhenespepy IV. The sarcophagus had been carved from an older block, with a lid made from what had once been a section of the Sixth Dynasty royal annals[113], the contrast between such improvised arrangements and the burial places of the other wives of Pepy II is most striking, reflecting the decline of the royal house following the old king's demise.

This kind of use of an older temple in lieu of a proper tomb is seen in the case of another member of the royal family of the period following Pepy II's death. Prince Ptahshepses was laid to rest in a corridor in the southeast part of the valley building of the funerary complex of Unas, enclosed in a late-Fourth Dynasty sarcophagus.[114] It is likely that other senior members of the court at the end of the Old Kingdom were similarly interred. However, there is a severe lack of material from this period, with only one king's tomb known between the death of Pepy II and the end of the First Intermediate Period, that of Ibi. Furthermore, only one tomb belonging to a member of the royal family has been identified, that of Princess Nebet II, at Koptos, the hometown of her husband. Little is known of its layout, the tomb having been over-built by a modern house, and only the granite false door and three blocks examined in situ.[115]

Chapter 3

The First Intermediate Period

Following the very long reign of Pepy II, there seems to have a rapid decline in central power, manifested in a succession of brief reigns known as the Seventh/Eighth Dynasty. Ultimately, the country split, with a civil war presaging forcible reunification under the southern Eleventh Dynasty, which defeated the last representative of the northern Ninth/Tenth Dynasty.

Very few tombs attributable to kings of the First Intermediate Period have been identified. In the Memphite necropolis, only one of the kings of the rump of the Old Kingdom royal line has a known tomb. However, its miniscule size and poor preservation hint at a likely reason for our lack of knowledge of other such monuments – still hidden in the little-explored sandy wastes of Saqqara-South. The known monument was that of Ibi, no larger than a queen's example of the preceding era (L.XL: fig. 8e; pl. XXXc).[1] Only a few parts of the superstructure survive, along with traces of a small mud brick mortuary temple. The substructure was reduced to two rooms, albeit still decorated with the Pyramid Texts.

A feature of the period is the fragmentation of the state, the detail of which still remains obscure. The existence of a polity centring on Dara (Arab el-Amaiem, Beni Qurra) in Middle Egypt is evidenced principally by a huge funerary monument there (Monument M), dated by pottery to the First Intermediate Period and presumably that of a local ruler – perhaps named Khui on the basis of a name found in nearby tomb (fig. 8f).[2] Built of brick, the monument covers an area approaching twice that of the pyramids of the Fifth and Sixth Dynasties, and significantly more than that of Menkaure's pyramid at Giza. It remains unclear, however, whether the structure was actually a pyramid, or a mastaba with an unusually square plan.

The substructure is unique, apparently entered via a horizontal vaulted passage in the middle of the north side. Beyond this, a vestibule had a stairway running upwards to the left, and a passage to the right; their destination was destroyed along with most of the interior of the superstructure. A passage descended from the end of the vestibule, its roof supported by a series of brick arches until it ended abruptly in a small stone-lined burial chamber.

The end of the First Intermediate Period was marked by a conflict between the Ninth/Tenth Dynasty regime, who were by then ruling in the north, from the city of Herakleopolis (Ihnasiya el-Medina) at the mouth of the Fayyum, and the Eleventh Dynasty one ruling the south from Thebes. No sign of a royal cemetery of the period has been found at Herakleopolis, but at least one of its rulers, its probably-penultimate king, Merykare, seems to have been buried in a pyramid at Saqqara.

Our knowledge of this monument derives solely from the texts on the stelae of a number of its mortuary priests (pl. XXXIa),[3] a number of whom shared its priesthood with that of the pyramid of Teti, with the possible implication that the pyramids of Teti and Merykare lay near one another. On the other hand, there are examples from Egyptian history where mortuary priests were buried away from the tomb to which they were affiliated, while the area of the pyramid of Teti was a perennial favourite for tombs for many centuries, possibly attracted by the easy access provided by Teti's causeway. As a result, the ruined pyramid to the east of Teti's pyramid was argued by a number of scholars to be Merykare's;[4] however it is now clear that this monument is of Fifth Dynasty date (p. 28). Accordingly, the precise location of Merykare's tomb remains obscure: one possibility may be that, like the Queen Anknesenpepy IV and Prince Ptahshepses noted above (pp. 34-5), he had a tomb constructed somewhere within the temple-structures of Teti or Menkauhor – now largely destroyed – or perhaps a simple shaft-tomb of the kind found for at least one king of the Thirteenth Dynasty (pp. 54-5), with an offering-place within the mortuary temple of Teti, which may explain why they shared some mortuary priests.

The Herakelopolitans' Theban opponents' tombs are better known. Located at Thebes-West, the earliest of them lay at El-Tarif, at the northern end of what would grow into a national necropolis during the New Kingdom (maps 11–12; fig. 9; pl. XXXIb). Typical private tombs of this period in the area were cut into the desert gravel and bedrock, with their offering places fronted by a wide but shallow fore-hall, the front of which consisted of a series of pillars, giving such sepulchres their Arabic name, 'saff', which implies 'a line', or 'many doorways'. Those of the local kings were simply greatly enlarged versions of these, the earliest example, attributed to Inyotef I, and known as the *Saff el-Dawaba*,[5] having a sunken courtyard measuring 65 x 300 m, a double colonnade across the rear providing the façade for the royal offering place. A series of doorways at the sides gave access to tombs of members of the court.

Inyotef II's tomb, the *Saff el-Qisasiya*,[6] was very similar, but slightly wider, with many more chambers at the rear of the court. It is likely that the king's burial lay at the end of a sloping passage at the rear of the central chapel, but this remains unverified. The tomb was described anciently in Papyrus Abbott, a record of an inspection of Theban royal tombs during the reign of Rameses IX, as having 'the pyramid fallen down upon it, before which its stela stands; the figure of the king stands upon this stela, his dog between his feet'.[7] The stela in question (pl. XXXIIa) was found in a brick chapel, apparently being of pyramidal form, at the eastern end of the court – 250 m from the main façade.

The *Saff el-Baqar*, attributed to Inyotef III,[8] was essentially identical with the previous two monuments, but with a more elaborate stone-lined offering place. Sarcophagus fragments recovered from the site also suggest more elaborate burial arrangements than in the earlier two *saff*s. The whole courtyard of the tomb is today filled with modern houses, as is that of Inyotef II and nearly all of that of Inyotef I.

Inyotef III was the last ruler of the line to control the south only, his successor Montjuhotep II reuniting the country and founding the Middle Kingdom mid-way through his reign of half a century. He also abandoned El-Tarif in favour of a new location not far from the Old Kingdom governors' tombs at the head of a valley now known as Deir el-Bahari, but still oriented towards Karnak. Although in a very different environment from the flat plain of El-Tarif, the concept of the approach to the royal tomb being flanked by the sepulchres of his court was continued. The rock-cut tomb-chapels of the nobility were cut high in the walls of the valley, overlooking the causeway that led from the edge of the cultivation (and perhaps a valley building) to the site of the royal tomb, which will be discussed in the next chapter.

Chapter 4

The Middle Kingdom

The later Eleventh Dynasty

The funerary monument of Montjuhotep II[1] took a completely novel form: a temple-tomb on two levels, each fronted by colonnades, which went through four phases of evolution before reaching its ultimate form (figs. 10a, 19; pl. XXXIIb). The upper terrace's central focus was a large square massif, variously reconstructed as a tumulus, a mastaba or a pyramid,[2] although the latter option is clearly suggested by the designation of the monument as a pyramid in Papyrus Abbott. This was surrounded by a pillared hall, behind which was a colonnaded court and then a hypostyle hall, at the back of which lay the main offering place, together with the entrance to the king's rock-cut tomb. Montjuhotep's temple was adorned with a wide range of motifs, including military activities, hunting in the desert, agricultural narratives, the king in the presence of the gods and episodes from the *ḥb-sd* festival. The temple also included the small tomb-chapels of six female members of the royal household,

The burial place of the king himself (DBXI.14) lay at the end of a 150 m-long passageway, partly lined with sandstone, which descended from the rear part of the temple (pl. XXXIIIa). This gave access to a chamber with a pointed roof, within which was constructed an alabaster shrine which served in lieu of a conventional sarcophagus (fig. 10b). This contained a wooden coffin and wooden-lidded canopic jars, together with sceptres, walking sticks and bows and arrows, while models typical of the Middle Kingdom were found, not only in the burial chamber, but also in niches in the walls of the descending corridor. The temple-complex also incorporated a heb-sed jubilee-cenotaph in the form of a passageway – known as the *Bab el-Hosan* – that descended from the temple forecourt to a chamber under the pyramid and may have been intended to be the actual royal burial chamber during the earliest phase of the temple's evolution. This room contained offerings, an empty wooden coffin and a sandstone statue of the king in jubilee dress, wrapped in linen. Some wooden model boats has also been placed in a chamber at the bottom of a shaft below the chamber.

Later graffiti refer to priests of the mortuary cult of the next king,

Montjuhotep III,[3] but the identification of the structure within which they officiated has been a matter for debate. It has often been equated with an unfinished structure behind the Sheikh Abd el-Qurna hill (TT281),[4] which comprises grading in preparation for the construction of a temple and causeway of the kind built for Montjuhotep II, together with a corridor-tomb and a number of subsidiary shaft-tombs (pl. XXXIIIb). However, this had never been a functional temple of the kind implied by the aforementioned graffiti, and has also been proposed as being an initial monument for Amenemhat I, the founder of the next, Twelfth, dynasty before his intended burial place was shifted to the north (see p. 41).[5] Another possible owner is the last king of the Eleventh Dynasty, Montjuhotep IV: a text in the Wadi Hammamat records an expedition to obtain the lid for the king's sarcophagus-lid,[6] but nothing related to a verified actual burial place has been identified.

Montjuhotep III did, however, build a temple on a high peak known today as Thoth Hill to the north-west of the Theban necropolis (fig. 10c; pl. XXXIVa–b), oriented in exactly the same way as his predecessor's Deir el-Bahari monument.[7] The structure was erected on a platform, supported by rough stone retaining walls on two sides, and comprised a brick pylon and enclosure, with a chapel housing three parallel inner rooms, a common arrangement in Middle Kingdom sanctuaries.[8] The chapel itself was plastered in white, and equipped with a limestone doorway inscribed for Montjuhotep III, with an inner wooden shrine. A fragment of statuette has been reconstructed as a figure in jubilee dress and a piece of naos-roof interpreted as a sarcophagus-lid, the structure being thus long regarded as a jubilee-cenotaph, but it is now clear that the formal dedication was to Horus. The whole chapel had been erected on the site of a much earlier structure of rough stonework, which has been dated to the Early Dynastic Period.

It is possible, however, that the temple also formed the mortuary chapel of Montjuhotep III, given that it is the only known West-Theban monument definitely attributable to him. It may thus be that a subterranean complex, cut into the side of the hill and ultimately transformed into a decorated Coptic hermitage, was actually Montjuhotep's burial place.[9] Lying at the bottom of a water-worn 'chimney' in the rock half-way up the cliff in the wadi on the north side of the hill, and accessed via a ledge running along the flank of the hill (pl. XXXVa), the innermost room contains what appears to be a sarcophagus carved as one with the rock (pl. XXXVb). The 'lid' – with raised end-pieces – is integral with the walls, but the southern end of the whole monument was apparently composed of a separate slab of stone. All material found in the hermitage was Coptic in date, and if indeed originally the king's tomb, the cutting of all but the sarcophagus chamber was almost certainly secondary, the inner room having originally been accessed by a simple tunnel.

A factor in favour of the attribution of the sarcophagus to Montjuhotep III is that its unusual form would fit well as the successor to the unique shrine employed by Montjuhotep II in lieu of a sarcophagus.

Royal Family Tombs of the later Eleventh Dynasty

The idea of the approach to the king's tomb being flanked by the graves of his followers was perpetuated by Montjuhotep II at Deir el-Bahari, the cliffs along the causeway to his mortuary temple containing many rock tombs of his court. Those close to the temple included that of Queen Neferu II (TT319), a small finely decorated chapel, from which a corridor led to the burial chamber, which was lined with sandstone and decorated with offering-texts.[10]

Within the temple itself, close to the king's own tomb, was that of another wife, Tem, a corridor descending to a transverse chamber containing a large alabaster sarcophagus made from separate slabs (DBXI.15).[11] Other members of the royal family were buried within the confines of the mortuary temple itself, in particular in shafts associated with a series of six decorated mortuary shrines (pl. XXXVIa) in front of the ramp of the royal tomb entrance (Kemsit [TT308], Sadhe, Kawit, Henhenet, Ashayet and Mayet [DBXI.7, 9, 11, 17 and 18]).[12] These also employed 'built' sarcophagi, and in one case (TT308) the burial chamber walls were adorned with images of the deceased and offerings.

Nothing is known of the burial arrangements of royal family members of the latter part of the dynasty, not surprisingly given the obscurity of the sepulchres of the kings themselves.

The Twelfth Dynasty

The dynastic founder, Amenemhat I was responsible for moving the Egyptian capital back to the north of Egypt, to a city known as Itjtawi. This seems to have lain near modern Lisht (map 7B), where the king built his tomb. As has been noted above, it is possible that he had begun a temple-tomb at his previous city, but at Lisht a broadly conventional pyramid complex was erected (L.LX: fig. 11a; pl. XXXVIb).[13] It has been suggested that prior to the inception of this monument, Amenemhat may have begun both a temple-tomb at Thebes (p. 40) and perhaps a pyramid at Saqqara, but both these suggestions are without proof;[14] the only tomb unequivocally associated with the king is the Lisht pyramid, and only one pyramid-name preserved in texts. The Lisht pyramid was of stone, albeit of poor quality, and incorporated numerous blocks from Old Kingdom pyramid complexes. These may simply be a reflection of a desire for economy, but it is also possible that they were used to link Amenemhat physically with the great kings of the past. Certainly, his propaganda presented him as the founder of a new era, which would restore Egypt to her past glories.

Nothing is known of the valley building and causeway, while the mortuary temple has been so destroyed that virtually nothing is known of its plan. However, surviving terracing shows that it had two levels, suggesting some affinity with Montjuhotep II's sepulchre at Deir el-Bahari. There are indications that the design of the temple was altered while under construction. No trace of a subsidiary pyramid was found.

The substructure was entered from ground level on the north side, a granite-lined corridor leading to a square chamber under the centre of the pyramid. From the centre of this room, a vertical shaft led down over 11m. Unfortunately, rising ground water has inundated whatever lies below, and all attempts at pumping have come to naught. Likewise, no items of the king's funerary equipment have come to light.

On the other hand, some such pieces (in particular the canopic jars) are known from the pyramid of his successor, Senwosret I (L.LXI: fig. 11b; pl. XXXVIIa),[15] displaced by robbers from his likewise-submerged burial chamber, which lay some 24 m below the pyramid base at the end of the steeply-sloped entrance corridor: the shaft found in Amenemhat's pyramid was omitted. The substructure was entirely constructed in a deep cutting in the desert surface.

Senwosret's pyramid lay some 1,750 m south of that of his father, with an innovative structure. This comprised a series of solidly-built limestone retaining walls, with the intervening spaces filled with smaller blocks and rubble, embedded in mortar. The complex, of which the valley building remains unknown, closely follows late Old Kingdom norms in its design, including a chapel erected over the pyramid entrance and the last known example of a subsidiary pyramid. An unusual feature was that at least part of the causeway was lined with statues of the king. The outer part of the enclosure wall of the complex had finely-carved bastions bearing the Horus-name of Senwosret I.

The next king abandoned Lisht, and moved north to the ancient necropolis of Dahshur (map 6B). In contrast with Seneferu, who had built his pyramids there some 2,000 m out into the desert, Amenemhat II built his monument (L.LI: fig. 11c; pl. XXXVIIb)[16] on a high ridge lying only a short distance from the edge of the cultivation. It lay directly south of an Old Kingdom cemetery, of which at least four tombs were annexed into the northwest corner of the king's new enclosure. The pyramid itself is so destroyed – the remaining stone chippings giving it its modern name, the White Pyramid – that even the dimensions of its base have yet to be determined. However, it seems to have used the same structural scheme as that of Senwosret I.

The rest of the complex is also in a bad state, but it can be seen to diverge once more from the Old Kingdom prototype. First, the enclosure is extended both to the east and to the west. The latter area holds a number of tombs, while the former accommodated the vanished mortuary temple, as well as two masonry massifs that may, like similar elements at the pyramid of Isesi, represent some kind of pylon gateway.

The substructure was at first sight simple, but nevertheless has a number of interesting features. A corridor from the north, blocked by two portcullises, led to a flat-ceilinged burial chamber; above this was a set of gabled relieving beams. Inside the chamber, the sarcophagus was made up from a series of quartzite slabs and concealed under the floor. In some previous tombs, for example that of Khaefre, sarcophagus lids had been arranged to lie flush with the floor, but in Amenemhat II's pyramid, filling and paving slabs had been laid over the sarcophagus cover. Hitherto, canopic chests had always lain south or southeast of the body. Now, this one lay in the floor of a short passage that led back under the pyramid entrance passage, ending up northeast of the body. These departures were clearly intended to enhance the protection given to the corpse; the next reign saw yet further divergence from time-hallowed tradition.

The pyramid of Senwosret II at Lahun (L.LXVI: map 8C; fig. 11d; pl. XXXVIIIa)[17] marked a significant departure. First, he constructed his tomb in the Fayyum region (map 8A), an area remote from the usual royal necropoleis in the Memphite area. This would seem to have been a reflection of the interest in the Fayyum shown by kings of his dynasty, a number of whom appear to have undertaken irrigation and land reclamation work there.

Second, while the basic concept of the pyramid, mortuary temple, causeway and valley building remained intact, the execution of the first element incorporated fundamental re-thinks. The pyramid itself was built of mud brick for the first time since the end of the Third Dynasty. Like the Brick Pyramid at Abu Rowash, a considerable portion of the core was composed of a native rock knoll. The brick was keyed into the rock by a set of radial stone walls built atop it, very similar to the system employed at the pyramid of Senwosret I, except that the filling was now of brick. The usual Tura limestone was employed for the outermost casing.

The entrance to the substructure was switched from the time-hallowed north face to the south side, with the burial chamber shifted away from the centre of the monument. At the same time, the entrance became a shaft and the corridors and chambers a tunnelled system. The latter shift seems to have been the result of the use of the rock knoll for the pyramid core, which prevented the usual 'cut and cover' approach. The inability to introduce heavy blocks from above resulted in the main entrance shaft being supplemented with a larger 'construction' shaft further south. This was concealed after use under the floor of a dummy tomb, reflecting the underlying motivation for the entrance position changes: security. This is also seen elsewhere in the complex. On the north side were eight mastabas and the queen's pyramid, like the main pyramid with their cores cut from the living rock.

The layout of Senwosret II's substructure was fairly simple, but has some curious features, including a deep shaft near the entrance, leading down to the water table, and a corridor that runs around three sides of the burial chamber to enter it through the north wall. It is possible that this feature was intended to make up for the southern approach of the actual entrance passage, much as the 'air shafts' of the Great Pyramid may have compensated for its anomalous ascending access corridors. The gable-roofed granite burial chamber held a sarcophagus with an irregular undersurface and a thick lip around the rim, perhaps reflecting an early plan for it to be partly sunk in the burial chamber floor (pl. XXXVIIIb). The room contained an alabaster offering table, while a gold cobra from the king's crown and a pair of leg bones represented the last traces of the burial of the pharaoh himself.

The rest of the complex has been badly destroyed, and comprised a small temple against the east face of the pyramid, and a valley building 1.2 km away, near the edge of the cultivation – although apparently lacking a built causeway. The settlement that adjoined the valley building ('Kahun') has preserved much information on daily life in the Middle Kingdom.

The next monarch, Senwosret III, built two funerary complexes, one at Dahshur and one at Abydos. The former was a pyramid, placed 1500 m north of that of Amenemhat II (L.XLVII: fig. 12a; pl. XXXIXa).[18] It continued the use of brick for the actual pyramid, but without the use of an underlying rock knoll, while the complex itself was very different from what had come to be the standard. It underwent at least two phases of building, the first being to a design not dissimilar to that found at Lahun, with royal family tombs placed within the enclosure, north and south of the king's pyramid. However, the final version produced a rectangular enclosure strikingly similar in appearance to that of Djoser of the Third Dynasty. Both this outer enclosure wall and the one marking out the original extent of the enclosure were panelled in imitation of the wall of the Step Pyramid exclosure, with the entrance in the southeast corner, an arrangement not seen since Third Dynasty times.

The causeway that led from this was extensively decorated. An explicit link with Djoser many be found at the northern end of the complex where, in an area enclosed by the final enlargement, were two shafts each holding a Third Dynasty alabaster sarcophagus, apparently not used for burials. They are identical with examples found under the Step Pyramid, and it seems likely that they were actually removed from there.

On the other hand, Djoser's model was not followed slavishly, there being no major temple on the north side of the pyramid, or the dummy-building complexes seen there. Instead, in addition to the original eastern mortuary temple, there was a large temple in the (later) southern portion of the enclosure, while small pyramids were also placed within the complex, one of which (Pyramid VII) may have represented the temporary revival of the subsidiary pyramid, as all that lay below it was a shrine, with no sign of a burial-installation.

The main pyramid was unusual in that the lowest few courses of its outer casing took the form of vertical panelling, on the same model as that of the enclosure walls. As in the case of the pyramid of Senwosret II, a chapel was placed in the middle of the north face, although once again the actual entrance to the substructure lay elsewhere, in this case being approached via a shaft on the west side. The interior layout was of a fairly simple form, recalling that of Fifth/Sixth-Dynasty royal sepulchres with, interestingly, the granite walls of the burial chamber whitewashed, contradicting the usual Egyptian practice of flaunting the use of expensive hard stones. The king's sarcophagus had a panelled motif applied to its lower part, apparently intended to replicate the actual pattern of bastions seen on Djoser's enclosure wall.

It remains uncertain whether Senwosret III was ever buried in his pyramid: no traces of an interment were found, while the king, most unusually, had the aforementioned second tomb at Abydos (map 10; fig. 13; pl. XXXIXb).[19] This comprised a temple at the edge of the desert and, 700m to the west, at the base of a high eminence, known in ancient times as the 'Mountain of Anubis', a complex comprising an enclosure (but no significant cult-place) and a subterranean tomb of an unprecedented kind, and with no monumental element: perhaps the *gebel* rising behind was regarded as the equivalent.[20] Indeed, it appears that the modest walling and associated structures adjacent to the tomb entrance were intentionally dismantled after its closure.

The tomb's corridors descended to a point some 40 m below the level of the entrance, the distance from this to the end of the final corridor being around 170 m. The plan was most unusual, with many of its elements explicable as security features. From the entrance, a corridor led first to a limestone-lined chamber with a roof carved in the form of a series of wooden poles. The tomb continued above the ceiling at the far end, the next passage leading to a pair of limestone-lined chambers-cum-shafts, joined at the top and bottom; ascending the second of them to a doorway, a descending corridor was then entirely filled with granite plug-blocks and terminated in a small quartzite-lined chamber, behind the right-hand wall of which was concealed the sarcophagus. Beyond this, a curving passageway descended to two quartzite-lined chambers, the second of which marked the end of the tomb. In spite of its protective features, the sepulchre was robbed in antiquity, a robbers' passageway, cut from the second shaft-chamber alongside the plug-blocks, having broken through into the hidden cavity holding the sarcophagus.

There is no evidence that Senwosret's successor, Amenemhat III, had an Abydene sepulchre. However, he did construct two funerary monuments, albeit in his case apparently as a result of misfortune. The first was erected at a site due east of the Fourth Dynasty Bent Pyramid at Dahshur (L.LVIII: map 6B; fig. 12b; pl. XLa).[21] A brick pyramid, known today as the Black Pyramid, its stone pyramidion was the first extant example known to have been be decorated. The surrounding complex reverted to a more standard form as compared with the neo-Third Dynasty pattern adopted by Senwosret III, although lacking any potential subsidiary pyramid. On the other hand, the pyramid's substructure introduced a greater degree of elaboration than seen before, with the tombs of two of the king's wives also wholly within the pyramid's structure, approached from a separate entrance, although connected with the king's tomb chambers underground (p. 51).

For the first time in a pyramid since the time of Djoser, the entrance passages had stairs, while the corridors had an average height of some 2 m, contrasting in particular with the very low ceilings of Old Kingdom pyramids. The king's burial complex comprised a burial chamber near the centre of the pyramid, approached by a corridor flanked with storerooms. Curiously, the canopic chest was intended to lie some 40 m from the burial chamber. Apparently as a substitute for a subsidiary pyramid, a shallow shaft under the main entrance passage led to a series of corridors under the south face of the pyramid, equipped with chapels and three dummy canopic chests (presumably respectively for the king and the two queens buried under the pyramid). These were unique features, not revived in any later pyramid.

The monument was not, however, used for the king's burial, the Black Pyramid's substructure displaying numerous indications of structural failure – perhaps indicating a common geological problem across this part of the Dahshur necropolis. However, the queens' interments seem to have gone ahead, with further burial places improvised in the corridors and vestibules of the king's chambers. The latter may date to the Thirteenth Dynasty, when two shaft tombs on the north side were converted into royal tombs (see p. 54).

To replace the Dahshur monument, Amenemhat III turned to the site of Hawara in the Fayyum, where he erected a pyramid complex with a number of unique or innovative features (L.LXVII: map 8A; fig. 12c; pl. XLb).[22] Its temple lay predominantly on the south side of the pyramid itself, and covered an area of over 60,000 m².[23] Later destruction has made its plan difficult to recover, but its north part included a number of quartzite shrines, each with two royal figures inside them. The entrance seems to have been in the southeast corner, and thus the whole structure may, like that of Senwosret III, be paying tribute to the pyramid complex of Djoser. The complexity of the cult buildings at Hawara is described by a number of Classical visitors, including Herodotus and Diodorus Siculus, who dubbed it the 'Labyrinth'. It is unclear whether there was any causeway or valley building, since there is no obvious location for the latter owing to the topography of the area.

The entrance to the pyramid substructure was on the south side, and had even more elaborate protective devices than the Black Pyramid. Each change of direction was via a sliding quartzite portcullis slab in the ceiling, while the burial chamber was a single block of the same stone, beyond and below the antechamber. Access was via a trench in the antechamber floor leading to a gap between the burial chamber's end wall and one of the roofing slabs, kept raised until the funeral. The slab was supported on props, bedded in a series of sand-filled 'chimneys'. The latter had plugs at the bottom: when these were removed the sand would flow out, the props would sink down, and the quartzite roof-beam would bed on the top of the chamber, sealing it completely. Security was further enhanced by filling an apparently blind corridor near the pyramid entrance with stone blocks – through which the inevitable robbers had dutifully mined.

The burial chamber had nevertheless been robbed, and the king's body burned. His granite sarcophagus, with the panelled lower part as introduced in the previous reign, lay in the centre of the room, a canopic chest beyond its foot. An additional sarcophagus had been created by placing granite slabs between the east side of the king's sarcophagus and the wall, and adding a lid; an offering table in the room showed this extra sarcophagus to have been made for Princess Neferuptah. Her body was, however, removed prior to her father's death, and placed in a new pyramid, built 2 km to the south (p. 52).

The tombs of the last two rulers of the Twelfth Dynasty, Amenemhat IV and Queen Sobekneferu are unknown, although the former's tomb may have been a pyramid at Dahshur noted below (p. 53).

Royal family tombs of the Twelfth Dynasty
Amenemhat I's pyramid-complex at Lisht contains a number of tombs that may have been built for members of his family, but their attribution remains uncertain (fig. 11a).[24] In particular, on its lower terrace, north of the mortuary temple we find two mastabas (954 and 956[25]) in a location employed for royal

family tombs in many of the complexes of the late Old Kingdom,[26] and also in the slightly later pyramid complex of Senwosret I. The western structure (954) has been completely destroyed, but had beneath it two burial complexes, both beginning with shafts themselves cut in the bottom of a very large, 3 m deep shaft, one of which is only partially explored owing to water infiltration that prevented the burial chamber(s) from being reached. The other, however, led at one level to six intact burial chambers, distributed in a star formation about the shaft. They proved to be fairly poor, with only one name, of a Lady Sitsobek, being recovered. Another six similar chambers lay further down the shaft, and yet another six at the bottom, these last half-dozen having been unused.

A double row of shaft tombs west of the king's pyramid may have included royal family sepulchres, given that an inscribed fragment bearing the name of a princess was found in the filling above them, in particular the four which had been made for single, rather than multiple, burials.[27] Presumably buried in this area was the king's mother, Neferet I, since her offering table was found reused nearby.

The pyramid-complex of Senwosret I provides rather more data on its arrangements available for members of the royal family (fig. 11b).[28] It had an unusual, and exceptionally large, outer temenos, within which were built a series of nine small pyramids, only two of whose owners are known. One (1) belonged to Queen Neferu IV, and another (2) to the Princess Itakayet A.

In their design, these small pyramids differed considerably from their Old Kingdom precursors, with that of Neferu IV being rather different from the rest. It was entered via a deep shaft in the middle of the north face, directly in front of an extension of the pyramid casing, against which formerly abutted a chapel. A passage led from the bottom the shaft to an antechamber, in the floor of which was sunk the entrance to the burial chamber, a niche at its end.

The position of Neferu's tomb conformed to earlier Old Kingdom practice, in particular that of the time of Khufu. If one were to use other Old Kingdom practice as a guide, the two pyramids directly north of the mortuary temple (8 and 9) would appear to be candidates for containing further queenly burials, their dual nature, with a common enclosure wall, being suggestively reminiscent of the tombs of Nebet and Khenut, in Unas's complex, not to mention tombs 954 and 956 in that of Amenemhat I. Pyramid 8's chapels have disappeared, but the substructure was entered via a shaft on the centre of the north side, from the bottom of which a passageway led to a chamber under the centre of the pyramid, with a coffin-cut in the middle of the floor, and another room beyond. The adjacent pyramid 9 had a core of brick, an unusual feature which, together with the evidence of the pottery found in its foundation deposits, suggests that it may have been built during the reigns of Amenemhat II or Senwosret II, presumably for a wife or daughter of Senwosret I who had lived into one of these reigns. The location of the substructure is uncertain, as none of the shafts in the vicinity led to rooms that obviously related to the pyramid.

The aforementioned pyramid 2 (Itakayet) had a decorated chapel and a substructure of elaborate form, also found in the adjacent pyramid 3. This involved employing both an entrance shaft and a 'construction' one, covered over by the erection of the chapel against the north face of the pyramid: the actual burial was made via the entrance shaft. From this, a corridor ran towards the burial chamber; in pyramid 2, this was little more than an extension of the corridor, with a canopic niche in the left-hand wall, but in 3, two sets of sliding stone doors were incorporated to block access, and a quartzite sarcophagus and canopic chest placed in the chamber. Fragments of bone were found in the chamber, and a piece of a female statue was found in the chapel, but nothing is known of the name or title of the owner of the pyramid.

Four more small pyramids stood on the west and north sides of the king's pyramid, both 4 and 5 presenting problems as to the location and original forms of their substructures: in marked contrast with the Old Kingdom, Middle Kingdom tombs show very little standardisation in the forms of their substructures. The two final pyramids, 6 and 7, seem to have been built as a co-ordinated pair, begun around Year 13 of Senwosret I; the substructure of the former has not been identified, while that of the latter was found choked with mud and never fully excavated.

Amenemhat II's enclosure at Dahshur had in its western section three tombs of an apparently new type (fig. 11c; pl. XLIa).[29] Each was a built structure of masonry sunk in a pit, covered by a brick relieving arch; a passage ran the entire length of the tomb, off which opened two niches, each containing a sarcophagus. From the west side of each sarcophagus-cut, three low openings gave access to an offering/canopic chamber, below the paving of the passage above. At the time of the burial, the niche was filled with stone slabs, locked in place by a vertical keystone. With their passages filled with plug blocks, the tombs became effectively solid masses of stone (pl. XLIb); doubtless this explains the fact that two of the tombs remained intact, yielding the funerary equipment of Princesses Ita and Khnemet (Northern Tomb), Sithat(hormeryet) and Itaweret (South West Tomb). The southern sarcophagus of the third tomb was that of Queen Keminub but, curiously, the northern sarcophagus was not that of a royal lady, but apparently belonged to a high official named Amenhotep. Found reused in the area, and presumably originally from a tomb there, are the re-used remains of the false-door of Prince Amenemhat-ankh.

With the plethora of tomb types and locations seen under the first three kings of the Twelfth Dynasty, one might have expected some move towards stability under the fourth, Senwosret II. However, his complex at Lahun exhibits yet more innovations (fig. 11d).[30] The superstructures of eight mastabas and a pyramid lie along the north side of the main temenos, all, like the king's pyramid, partially cut from the bedrock. Inscribed fragments allow the attribution of the small pyramid to a queen, but the only names recovered from the mastabas were the king's.

Just as the king's pyramid has concealed its entrance by shifting its entrance away from the give-away location of the middle of the north face, the substructure of the queen's pyramid (belonging to Weret I, mother of Senwosret III?) was placed just north of the enclosure wall (621). Its plan was reminiscent of a king's substructure of the late Old Kingdom, and had little in common with the tomb of Keminub at Dahshur (pl. XLIc).

The substructures of the royal family mastabas were placed on the south side of the king's pyramid (tombs 7–16). They all followed the same basic design: an entrance shaft leading to an antechamber, its floor sunk to a lower level, at the end of which was the burial chamber. Virtually all of the area of this was occupied by the sarcophagus, a niche in the right-hand wall containing the canopic equipment, a further opening at the far end of the wall giving access to the offering chamber.

As at Lahun, a row of royal family tombs lay along the north side of the enclosure of Senwosret III at Dahshur.[31] In this case, however, their substructures actually lay below their four (pyramidal) superstructures and comprised four individual sepulchres joined by a single east-west gallery, the entrance to which lay in the north-east corner of the king's enclosure. Two revealed the names of their owners, tomb II belonging to Queen Neferethenut and tomb III to a Princess Itakayet (C); tomb IV was that of a now-anonymous queen, while tomb I had been usurped by a later official. While each tomb on the gallery differed in detail, all resembled the queen's in basic form: a chamber led off the main east-west corridor, a stairway and passage sunk in the floor leading to a burial chamber with two subsidiaries. A canopic niche lay at the end of a short passage west of the stairway.

Further down the shaft giving access to the four tombs lay a further royal tomb of a wholly different design, apparently added later in the reign. It comprised two conjoined vestibules with niches, each containing a sarcophagus. Two of the eight sets of sarcophagi and canopics named king's daughters, while two jewellery caches, one in each vestibule, yielded the names of two further princesses.

Three further pyramids lay to the south of the king's pyramid, the westernmost (tomb IX) belonging to Queen Weret II.[32] Its entrance lay some distance to the northeast of the superstructure, the shaft joining a north-south passage half way along its 60 m length. To the north, this gave access to an antechamber, a canopic room and a burial chamber, the latter with a fine granite sarcophagus with a panelled lower part. This all lay under the body of the king's pyramid, some 50m away from the queen's own monument. Under the latter, the southern part of the passage led to a small subterranean shrine.

Of the other two pyramids, pyramid VIII belonged to Senwosret III's mother, Weret I. However, its substructure comprised merely a shaft, dug under the centre of the pyramid and inaccessible after its construction, with a granite canopic chest, plus jars, in a small room at the bottom. This may have represented a cenotaph for the queen, who may have been actually buried at Lahun (see above).

Amenemhat III's pyramid at Dahshur further develops the arrangements of the substructure of pyramid IX by providing for two of his wives to rest wholly under the his own pyramid, without any separate superstructures for the ladies.[33] The queens' chambers were primarily approached via a stairway and passage from the west side of the pyramid, leading first to a chamber, with a canopic in its eastern side, and then a stairway leading northwards to two chambers forming the tomb of Queen Aat. Apparently to be regarded as part of the same complex was a chamber lying south of the main approach passage, perhaps the equivalent of a king's subsidiary pyramid. An almost identical complex lay immediately to the east of Aat's, connected to it by a passage that ultimately led with the king's chambers, under the eastern part of the pyramid. A number of other subsidiary burials appear to have been added following Amenemhat III's death, comprising sarcophagi and canopics athwart both pyramid entrances (that in the queens' passage belonging to a Princess Sithathor) and in the two vestibules directly south of the king's burial chamber.

Amenemhat III's second pyramid at Hawara has thus far failed to yield any dependent royal family tombs, although a small pyramidion found on the site might have come from a queen's pyramid. The king's pyramid substructure has a corridor almost exactly corresponding to that which connected the king's chambers at Dahshur with those of his wives, but is normally regarded as a blind intended to fool thieves, with no indication that it ever led to further chambers.

In addition, the king's daughter Neferuptah B was temporarily buried in the king's burial chamber of the pyramid. Dying prematurely with an enhanced status that demanded a monumental tomb,[34] an interim installation was provided within the king's Hawara pyramid while building work could get under way elsewhere. A sarcophagus was created by fitting slabs between the king's coffer and the wall of the chamber, a stone canopic chest also being provided. She was later re-buried under a pyramid at Hawara-South (map 8A; pl. XLIIa),[35] designed with a burial chamber that would be roofed over and embedded in the mass of brickwork and the pyramid built over it, without any entrance passageway. This preserved the tomb intact until 1955, but the body had been destroyed by infiltrating water. The burial chamber was divided in two by a partition wall, a huge sarcophagus lying in the southern section. The northern part held an offering table, a silver vase and a series of pots. The first two items were inscribed, as were further silver vessels from the compartment that held the sarcophagus. Another offering table and the canopics had been left behind in the main Hawara pyramid.

Chapter 5

The Second Intermediate Period

The Thirteenth Dynasty

Subsequent to the death of Amenemhat III, the sequence of known royal tombs fails. As already noted, the tombs of the last two kings of the Twelfth Dynasty remain unidentified, and of the large number of kings who ruled during the following Thirteenth Dynasty, only a handful can be associated with a particular funerary monument. Indeed, such monuments are rare, and it is clear that very many of the dynasty's kings lacked monumental tombs – or at least not in the Memphite necropolis: two known tombs of the period were at Abydos.

In the Memphite area, known Thirteenth Dynasty royal tombs are to be found in an area spanning some 9 km between southern Saqqara-South and Mazghuna, to the south of Dahshur. Perhaps the earliest monument is a never-investigated structure at Dahshur (L.LIV; map 6B),[1] comprising an area of limestone rubble, some 40m square, with the line of a causeway leading from it. A fragment bearing the name 'Amenemhat' was found in the area, suggesting that the owner of this monument may have been Amenemhat IV, V or VI – although the fragment might have been 'stray' from the nearby pyramid of Amenemhat II.

At least one Thirteenth Dynasty pyramid lies at Dahshur-South (map 7A).[2] This contained the canopic jars of a king named Ameny-Qemau (fig. 14a),[3] a monarch is not otherwise known. However, a king of the first part of the dynasty, Hornedjhiryotef, appears to have been surnamed 'son of Qemau', and it is not improbable that his predecessor, apparently with the prenomen Smenkare but no known nomen, was Ameny-Qemau. On a prominent hill overlooking the cultivation, the pyramid is located in an area previously used only for Old Kingdom private tombs. Probably never finished, only some parts of the brickwork survive, while there may be indications of a north chapel, but no certain remains of other elements of the complex. Only the inner part of the substructure survives, from the point where a large vertically sliding block prevented access through the ceiling of the vestibule at the bottom of the entrance passage into the rest of the tomb. From here a series of vestibules, closed off by a lateral portcullis, led to the burial chamber. It embodied what seems to be typologically the earliest of a new kind of combined sarcophagus/canopic chest, with cavities for both the body and its internal organs within the same block. This formed the floor of the room, and was sealed by a lid that was slid on top from the antechamber-area, which lay directly north of the sarcophagus. The lid was locked into place by a sideways-sliding portcullis-slab (fig. 14g); owing to its being in contact with the chamber walls on three sides, and the portcullis on the other, the inevitable tomb robbers had to resort to smashing the north end of the lid to gain access to the coffin, and then push the remains northwards, to rifle the canopic cavity. This is one of two basic burial chamber designs found during the Thirteenth Dynasty, to be termed here type 13/1.

A very similar, but slightly more evolved, substructure is to be found at the North Pyramid at Mazghuna (fig. 14b),[4] at the southernmost extension of the Memphite pyramid-field (map 7A). Nothing of the core is now traceable, and in view of the lack of any brick debris, it may have been of stone, unlike preceding pyramids. The only part of the complex that has been traced in detail is a 116 m section of the foundations of the exceptionally wide causeway.

The actual entrance to the pyramid is destroyed, the first preserved part being steps descending from the north. However, since the size of the pyramid is very uncertain, it is not clear whether this was the actual entrance or whether further now-lost galleries existed under what would have been an exceptionally large pyramid for the period. In contrast with the state of the superstructure, the roofing of the rest of the substructure is intact, the plan being reminiscent of that of Qemau, albeit with additions; the arrangement of the combined sarcophagus/canopic chest, portcullis and antechamber is exactly the same. It seems likely that the pyramid had never been used for a burial, as the sarcophagus lid was found still stored in the antechamber.

As already noted, far fewer pyramid remains exist than kings of the Thirteenth Dynasty, and it is thus likely that many were buried in much less impressive sepulchres. One example of such a tomb has been identified, belonging to a king named Hor (fig. 14c).[5] It was enlarged out of a simple shaft tomb on the north side of Amenemhat III's Black Pyramid, with a new stone burial chamber added. Except for the omission of a portcullis and the use of a separate sarcophagus and canopic chest, the arrangement of Hor's chambers mirrors the type 13/1 integral burial chamber found in contemporary pyramids. The tomb suffered relatively lightly at the hands of the tomb-robbers, thus providing us with our only sizable body of information as to what accompanied a Middle Kingdom monarch to the grave. The antechamber contained, principally, a naos containing a statue of the king's *ka*, two alabaster stelae, a case for staves and a number of pottery and (dummy) wooden vessels. Inside his sarcophagus, the king's body lay within a decorated rectangular coffin, wearing a gilded wooden mask. A wooden inner canopic chest contained four human-headed canopic jars.

A more elaborate form of integrated burial chamber, incorporating the roof-lowering mechanism first seen in the Hawara pyramid of Amenemhat III was employed in the South Pyramid at Mazghuna (L.LIX: fig. 14d).[6] It differed, however, from the Twelfth Dynasty monument in that the chamber, sarcophagus and canopic chest were made from a single block of quartzite (type 13/2 – fig. 14h). Compared with earlier integral sarcophagi/canopic chests, the block was considerably deepened, leaving a appreciable void above the coffin- and canopic-cavities; the use of a single lid was abandoned in favour of two much more massive blocks. One was intended as a fixture, cut away below to give additional headroom for the burial party, but the other was supported by a pair of props, lowered by the use of 'sandraulics'. The outer part of the descending corridor is lost, but it gave access to the interior via two granite portcullises – of a design and workmanship identical with that seen in the North Pyramid.

The South Pyramid itself has been entirely destroyed, along with much of the roofing of the substructure, although the remains of a brick enclosure wall of a wavy form are preserved, along with a simple mortuary temple of the same material on the east side, and another structure in the south-east corner of the enclosure. Quarry marks indicate that work was being carried on in the third year of an un-named king. The pyramid was 100 cubits square, a size that it seems was employed for a number of pyramids of the period, and was half the size of the majority of Twelfth Dynasty pyramids.

A very similar monument was built for Khendjer at southern Saqqara-South, (L.XLIV: map 6A; fig. 14e; pl. XLIIb),[7] albeit with a slightly larger and more developed burial chamber, suggesting a somewhat later date. In any case, Khendjer appears securely placed as the sixteenth king of the dynasty, two places after Hor. The pyramid's enclosure apparently had originally had a 'wavy' mud-brick wall, but ultimately this had been replaced by a niched one of stone. Remains of an eastern mortuary temple and a north chapel have both been located, together with fragments of the decorated pyramidion. The pyramid's structure represented a further development of the arrangements found at the South Mazghuna pyramid.

Perhaps the latest known Thirteenth Dynasty pyramid in the Memphite necropolis was built near that of Khendjer (L.XLVI: fig. 14f),[8] although until the traces of another monument that can be detected under the sand just to the southeast are investigated,[9] this cannot be certain. Other traces northwest of the pyramid of Khendjer may also represent at least one other pyramid.[10]

Three-quarters larger than most pyramids of the dynasty, the substructure of Khendjer's neighbour was one of the most elaborate of any Egyptian sepulchral monument, with a series of vestibules, changes of level and portcullises. One of its most remarkable features was its possession of two burial chambers. The principal one was carved out of a block of quartzite, with a conventional-looking sarcophagus and canopic chest within, but carved as one with the chamber. Closure of the chamber was to be by the now-usual 'sandraulic' means, but the tomb was never used. The other burial chamber lay to the west and had an arrangement of sarcophagus/lid/portcullis similar to Qemau's, but reversed, with a separate canopic chest. The chamber has been described as a queen's, but no equivalent installation is known elsewhere. Given the elaboration of the substructure, clearly inspired by the desire for security, its being a decoy to draw plunderers away from the real burial, being perhaps the most attractive explanation.

The pyramidion of the pyramid of Aya (pl. XLIIIa) came to light at Kataana in the Delta, but it is likely that it was taken there as booty by the later invading Hyksos kings, and the king's tomb may actually have been in the Memphite necropolis or elsewhere in the Nile valley. In contrast to the elaborate pyramidia of Amenemhat III and Khendjer, it bears merely an image of the king offering to Ptah.

At Abydos, two royal tombs of the period have been located just northeast of the Abydene tomb of Senwosret III (fig. 13).[11] While their substructures were of designs closely resembling those of pyramids of the period, it remains unclear whether or not their superstructures were mastabas or pyramids. One, S9, employs the twisting, quartzite portcullis-blocked plan seen in all the pyramids of the dynasty, together with the combined burial chamber/sarcophagus/canopic chest typified by the pyramid of Khendjer, including the 'sandraulic' mechanism for lowering the access block of the burial chamber. Only some elements of the mud-brick complex survive, including what may be parts of the chapel and inner enclosure, together with part of a 'wavy' enclosure wall. Apart from the relative orientation of the substructure, the S9 complex is very similar to that of the Mazghuna-South pyramid, suggesting a similar date.

The other tomb, S10, is less regular than S9, and more badly damaged, although a typical late Middle Kingdom stairway flanked with benches survived in the main corridor. However, fragments of the funerary stela were found in the enclosure that was attached to the eastern side and appears to have housed the mortuary temple. One fragment named a king Sobek[hotep], and as the coffin apparently deriving from the tomb (see just below) bore

Coffin Texts not attested before the middle of the Thirteenth Dynasty, it seems probable that the tomb was that of one of Sobekhotep III, IV or VI, the longer reigned kings of the period. It has been suggested that Sobekhotep IV may be the most likely of them, on the basis of his reign-length, and in particular that he certainly undertook other work at Abydos. On this basis, S9 is likely to have belonged to another king of this group, which also included Neferhotep I – who is also known to have undertaken work at Abydos and, with his long reign, is thus perhaps the leading candidate for S9's owner. It is possible that a naos containing the seated figure of a king, found in a secondary context elsewhere at Abydos, and with (incomplete) texts similar in style to those of the Sobekhotep stela, may have come from the chapel of S9 or S10. As to why these two kings had been buried away from the Memphite necropolis, it may be noted that Sobekhotep III was of (Theban) non-royal birth and was thus beginning a new royal line, which may therefore have wished to cement its new status by burial in the hallowed cemetery of Osiris, the kings of the First Dynasty – and the soon-to-be-deified Senwosret III.

The poor state of S10 was due partly to Roman/Coptic quarrying (which also badly damaged S9 and the monument of Senwosret III), but also to the fact its quartzite combined sarcophagus/canopic chest had been extracted from the tomb for reuse in a cemetery that was established directly northeast (pl. XLIIIb – its lid has not yet been located). Here, the sarcophagus/chest formed part of a tomb (CS6), approached by a shallow mud-brick-lined shaft, of a type that also comprised tombs CS12–14. The remaining tombs in the cemetery comprised a series of axial galleries gently descending into the desert gravel (CS4, 5, 7, 8 and 9), walled with brick and roofed either by a brick vault or with logs, culminating in a stone-lined burial chamber.[12]

All these tombs are now anonymous, apart from CS9, which belonged to a king Useribre Senebkay (pl. XLIVa). Its limestone burial chamber, 3.48 m long x 1.48 m wide and made entirely of re-used blocks, was decorated in paint, with a winged sun-disk on its end wall, below which was a panel bearing a pair of *wadjet*-eyes, flanked by female figures presumably representing Isis and Nephthys. A winged sun-disk, with one of the king's cartouches below it, and a female figure also appeared on the two side-walls of the chamber, between a pair of vertical yellow bands. The remains of the king's plundered wooden coffin, canopic equipment and mummy (of a man who had died in battle) were found in the tomb, the gilded canopic chest having been manufactured from wood salvaged from the coffin of a king Sobekhotep, all-but-certainly the owner of tomb S10.

It is thus clear that Sobekhotep's S10 was stripped for materials by the owners of at least two tomb-builders in the adjacent cemetery, which may have belonged to either the Theban Sixteenth Dynasty, or perhaps a local

'Abydos Dynasty' of the same general period;[13] in either case, the plundering and dismantlement of S10 will have occurred within a few decades of the original burial. Reuse of material is also found in other tombs in the cemetery, including a limestone sarcophagus incorportated into tomb CS10, suggesting a centrally-sanctioned stripping of tombs of material for recycling following a change in regime in the area. Certainly, there is no way that the operations at S10 could have been in any way clandestine.

Royal Family Tombs of the Thirteenth Dynasty

Only a few royal family tombs from the Thirteenth Dynasty have been identified to date. At the complex of Khendjer, dependant tombs were restricted to the south side of the outer enclosure, with three shaft tombs; the western two are collapsed, but the other tomb was found jam-packed with three quartzite sarcophagi and canopic chests, all without indication of ownership.[14] To the east lay a small pyramid containing two burial chambers, reached via two quartzite portcullises as found in the king's pyramid (L.XLV; fig. 14e).[15] Neither chamber, each with a close-fitting sarcophagus and canopic chest, was ever used. Here we see yet another example of a dependant royal tomb equipped for multiple burials in a single substructure, something not found in Old Kingdom.

The only other royal family tomb recorded from the Thirteenth Dynasty is that of Nubheteptikhered,[16] presumably the daughter of Hor, who was buried in the adjacent shaft on the north side of the Black Pyramid at Dahshur. Like that king's tomb, a stone-lined extension had been built into the simple original Twelfth Dynasty structure, with a stone sarcophagus containing her intact coffin.

The Sixteenth and Seventeenth Dynasties

Somewhere around 1650 BC, Egypt split between a group of rulers of Palestinian origin, ruling from the northeast Delta (the Fifteenth Dynasty, often dubbed the Hyksos), and Egyptian line(s) ruling from Thebes in the south (the Sixteenth and Seventeenth Dynasties, probably separated by a Hyksos incursion into the far south).[17] Nothing is known of any royal cemetery at the Hyksos royal city of Avaris (Tell el-Daba), but we have already noted the possibly-Sixteenth Dynasty royal cemetery at Abydos-south, while a Theban royal cemetery of (at least) the Seventeenth Dynasty lay on the west bank at Dra Abu'l-Naga (maps 11 and 12; pl. XLIVb).[18] Only one of the tombs of this latter group is currently positively identified, but others were seen and/or plundered in the nineteenth century, and yet more were listed in Papyrus Abbott. Having recorded the inspection of the tombs of Amenhotep I (p. 62, below) and Inyotef II (p. 38, above), the papyrus then notes in turn the condition of the sepulchres of Inyotef VI, Inyotef V, Sebekemsaf I, Taa,[19] Kamose and (Prince) Ahmose-Sapairi, before concluding with the tomb of Montjuhotep II at Deir el-Bahari (p. 39, above).

The remains of the pyramid of Inyotef VI[20] have been found roughly a quarter of the way along the Dra Abu'l-Naga hill (pl. XLVa), and given that the Papyrus Abbott sequence terminates at Deir el-Bahari, one would assume that it represented the northernmost of a series of Seventeenth Dynasty royal tombs running southward from that point. This is supported by the presence of a number of high-status tombs of the period a little to the south.[21] The papyrus notes that plunderers had attempted to tunnel under the pyramid from the adjacent tomb of Shuroy (TT13), a Ramesside tomb-chapel that lies directly to the right of the pyramid.

The pyramid itself, with a steep slope, was built on top of an earlier shaft tomb (K02.2), on the slope of the hill, and comprised an outer skin of bricks, now reduced to a few courses, with a rubble fill, with an inscribed cap-stone, surrounded on three sides by an enclosure wall. The eastern side may have been terraced, and was in any case was adorned by a pair of small obelisks, bearing the king's names and titles. No substructure has been located in the immediate vicinity of the pyramid, which would thus seem to have been some distance from the monument itself. The only information available is that the king's intact gilded coffin[22] was found in 1827 in 'a small and separate tomb, containing only one chamber, in the centre of which was placed a sarcophagus, hewn out of the same rock, and formed evidently at the same time as the chamber itself; its base not having been detached'.[23]

A similar separate substructure seems to have held the burial of Inyotef V (to which the coffin of Inyotef VII was later added) high on the Dra Abu'l-Naga hill, in a chamber at the end of a corridor accessed by a brick-lined shaft some 7 m deep.[24] Inyotef V's gilded coffin had been made for him by his brother Inyotef VI,[25] while that of Inyotef VII was a 'stock' piece, presumably reflecting his premature death.[26] The burial chamber presumably also held Inyotef V's canopic chest.[27] As for the actual pyramid of Inyotef V, mentioned in Papyrus Abbott as 'in the course of being tunneled into by the thieves at the place where the stela of its pyramid was set up', fragments of its cap-stone have been found just southeast of the pyramid of Inyotef VI (pl. XLVb).[28] This suggests that the pyramid of Inyotef V itself lay close by, reflecting the aforementioned expectations on the basis of the Papyrus Abbott itinerary.

In contrast to these actual remains, neither the tomb of Sobekemsaf I nor anything deriving from it has yet to be positively identified – although the latter is not surprising, given that Papyrus Abbott describes the tomb as having been robbed-out shortly before the inspection in Year 16 of Rameses IX. However, the account in the papyrus (supplemented by the transcript of the trial of those responsible in Papyrus Leopold II-Amherst) does indicate that the tomb included provision for the king's wife.

Likewise, no candidates for the tomb of Taa have yet been localised, although his mummy and coffin survive, having been removed from his tomb no later than the early Third Intermediate Period, ultimately being placed with other royal mummies in tomb TT320 (see p. 79, below). On the other hand, a monument in the Birabi (the southern end of Dra Abu'l-Naga/western edge of the Asasif – fig. 16) has been posited as a possible option for one of the last two tombs of the Papyrus Abbott Seventeenth Dynasty sequence, of Kamose and Ahmose-Sipairi.[29] This comprises a pyramid within a large enclosure, with a built chapel, but with its innermost part set into the pyramid – much like the contemporary pyramid of Tetisherit at Abydos noted below – together with a rock-cut substructure.

On the other hand, it is possible that rather than being strung out along the flank of the hill, the Seventeenth Dynasty royal necropolis was concentrated in the immediate area of the known sites of the pyramids of Inyotef V and VI. In that case, a large rock-cut tomb-chapel of late Seventeenth/ early Eighteenth Dynasty date (K94.1) that lies high above the Iyoef tombs on the Dra Abu'l-Naga hill could become a possibility for the sepulchre of Kamose.[30] In any case, his coffin[31] was found secondarily buried at the foot of the hill, perhaps near TT155, at the mouth of the Khawi el-Amwat, some 200m north of the Inyotef VI pyramid. It had presumably been moved at some point after Year 16 of Rameses IX, when Kamose's tomb was found to be intact.

Royal family tombs of the Sixteenth and Seventeenth Dynasties

It would appear that, like the tombs of the kings, the principal burial place of members of the royal family was Dra Abu'l-Naga, where various fragments have been found.[32] That at least some royal wives were interred in the same structure as their husband is indicated by Papyrus Abbott's report on the robbery of the tomb of Sobekemsaf I, which implies that Queen Nubkhaes B lay in a separate chamber close to that of her husband.[33]

That the late Second Intermediate necropolis extended somewhat further north is indicated by the interment in rubble near the road to the Valley of the Kings, at el-Khor (see map 12; pl. XXXIb, top), of a woman who appears to have been a king's wife (pl. XLVIa).[34] Such burials simply in rubble may have been common at the period, it having been suggested that the presence of the coffins of King Kamose and Queen Ahhotep I in such contexts may reflect their original interment, rather than later reburial, as has generally been assumed.

Chapter 6

The New Kingdom

The Eighteenth Dynasty

The matter of the burial place of the founder of the New Kingdom, Ahmose I, has long been the subject of debate.[1] Given the interment of his immediate predecessors and successors at Thebes and the discovery of his mummy in a cache there, the general assumption has been that his own original burial had been in the Theban necropolis, perhaps in the ancestral cemetery of Dra Abu'l-Naga. However, no unequivocal original tomb of his has been identified at Thebes, while at Abydos the king constructed an extensive funerary complex, spread out along a 1.4 km axis across the desert (map 10, bottom).

First, a rubble-cored, but limestone-sheathed, pyramid stands near the cultivation (map 10; pl. XLVIb); its angle seems to have been 63°. A temple adjoined its east side, and was once decorated with extensive, but now-fragmentary, battle scenes, perhaps recording the king's defeat of the Hyksos; a smaller chapel lay just to the north, apparently dedicated to the king's wife, Ahmes-Nefertiry. At the opposite end of its axis was another temple, rising in terraces against the cliff face.

In the expanse of desert between the pyramid and temple, Ahmose constructed two monuments. The first was a pyramidal brick chapel dedicated to the king's grandmother, Tetisherit. The second was a subterranean tomb of unusual form (fig. 15a): mostly cut only a few metres below the surface, a pit entrance gave access to a twisting passageway that eventually opened into a great hall, its roof formerly supported by eighteen columns. Below the hall, a further passage, seemingly unfinished, led deeper into the matrix. Little was found in the tomb, only a few bricks, stamped with Ahmose's prenomen, and a number of fragments of gold leaf, all in the debris of the pillared hall. Interestingly, some of the rubble from the construction of the tomb was used in the core of the king's pyramid. The whole complex was long dismissed as a cenotaph, but in view of the lack of any known funerary monuments at Thebes, it is possible that Ahmose had been initially interred at Abydos but been re-buried at Thebes a few years later – perhaps in the tomb of his successor, Amenhotep I. Ultimately, Ahmose I's mummy and coffin were cached in TT320.

The identity of the burial place of Amenhotep I also presents problems, in spite of being mentioned in Papyrus Abbott.[2] It appears at the head of the list, but it is unclear what – if anything – this implies about its position. It is unlikely to have lain north of the tomb of Inyotef II, while the relative prominence of the king *vis à vis* the other tomb-owners involved (Montjuhotep II excepted) may have led to Amenhotep's tomb being given special attention and visited out of strict topographical order.

Papyrus Abbott states that the tomb lay 120 cubits below some elevated element (the exact translation of which remains moot) and north of the 'House of Amenhotep of the Garden'. Unfortunately there is no clarity on the location of the latter, and it has been variously identified with a number of buildings. Candidate tombs to the north of one or more of these loci have included: KV39, above the southern end of the Valley of the Kings;[3] a putative yet-undiscovered tomb in the cliff above the temples at Deir el-Bahari;[4] a tomb in the wadis behind Dra Abu'l-Naga (AN B);[5] and a rock-cut tomb-chapel high up at Dra Abu'l-Naga (K93.11 – map 12).[6] Both the latter candidates lie close to the north-south axis of a temple constructed in the names of Amenhotep I and his mother Ahmes-Nefertiry in front of the hill.[7]

However, while probably originally constructed early in the Eighteeth Dynasty, both K93.11 and the adjoining K93.12 were extensively modified by the high priests of Amun Ramesesnakht and Amenhotep G during the later Twentieth Dynasty.[8] This is precisely the period during which the tomb of Amenhotep I was reported by Papyrus Abbott as being 'intact' in Year 16 of Rameses IX, making it seemingly impossible to identify K93.11 with a tomb in the process of being transformed into a private sepulchre.

AN B (fig. 15b) contained many items bearing the names of Amenhotep I, Ahmes-Nefertiry and also Ahmose I. Although originally argued to be that of Amenhotep I, it was subsequently generally regarded as actually that of Ahmes-Nefertiry, but since it seems likely that the latter's tomb was elsewhere (see p. 79), its ownership by Amenhotep I seems most likely. It comprises a vertical shaft leading to a corridor (with two annexes), then a deep pit, followed by a further corridor leading to a burial chamber. The latter seems to have been cut in two phases, perhaps to allow a second burial to be included – possibly that of the mummy of Ahmose I, 'repatriated' from Abydos.[9] The pit is a feature found in many later New Kingdom royal tombs (including that of Amenhotep I's wife, Meryetamun B, see pp. 79-80), and was known, at least in later times, as the 'hall of hindering'. It thus seems most likely to have had a protective purpose, to frustrate robbers and to prevent any water that penetrated the entrance from entering the innermost chambers. Wherever his tomb actually lay, Amenhotep I's mummy had been removed by late Rameside times and was eventually reburied in TT320.

As has already been noted, it appears that the substructures of the Seventeenth Dynasty royal pyramids were some distance from their public monument. Similarly, the substructure of Ahmose I's Abydos monument was not actually below any part of the complex, although aligned with it. If correctly identified, the tomb of Amenhotep I was a considerable distance from both of the west bank temples associated with him – a kilometre from one in front of Dra Abu'l-Naga (map 12) and a little more from one at Deir el-Bahari (fig. 16).

The latter structure was extant for only a few decades, until it was demolished during the extension of Hatshepsut's memorial temple (p. 67). A rectangular building, built of bricks stamped with the cartouches of Amenhotep I and queen-mother, Ahmes-Nefertiry (pl. XLVIIa),[10] its decoration included a series of osirid statues of the king (pl. XLVIIb).[11] It would appear that Hatshepsut's temple was originally designed to leave the brick structure in place, Amenhotep's temple being removed only when a final extension was decided upon.

The other Amenhotep I temple (fig. 17a),[12] has an unusual strict north-south axis and was apparently originally built for the king's ḥb-sd. Its ultimate dedication was, however, jointly to Amenhotep and Ahmes-Nefertiry, probably following some rebuilding. One wonders whether the latter may represent a repurposing of an original ḥb-sd chapel as a memorial temple following the decommissioning of Amenhotep I's Deir el-Bahari sanctuary. Unfortunately, the destroyed state of the Dra Abul-Naga building makes definitive conclusions problematic.

The separation of superstructure from substructure was institutionalised from the reign of Thutmose I onwards, when the substructures of kings' tombs began to be placed in a complex of wadis directly behind the curtain of cliffs separating the low desert from the high desert at Thebes-West. Now known as the Valley of the Kings, this housed all but a handful of the burial chambers of New Kingdom monarchs, as well as those of some members of the royal family and senior officials (map 13; pl. XLVIIc).

While it is generally agreed that the first king interred there was Thutmose I, debate continues as to the identity of that tomb.[13] The main candidates have been KV38,[14] in which a sarcophagus and canopic chest manufactured for him by his grandson Thutmose III, were found,[15] and KV20,[16] in whose burial chamber a sarcophagus modified for him by his daughter Hatshepsut[17] was discovered. This sepulchre, featuring a sinuous descending corridor, over 200m in length, and reaching over 90m vertically below its entrance, leading to two chambers, the innermost columned and lined with limestone blocks, also contained a sarcophagus and canopic chest naming Hatshepsut (fig. 15c). In contrast, KV38 was much smaller, comprising a short descending passage, an antechamber and an oval burial chamber (imitating the form of a cartouche – fig. 15d; pl. XLVIIIa).

Accordingly, for many years KV20 was regarded as purely Hatshepsut's, with Thutmose I added secondarily, the female king having removed him thither from KV38. However, it has also been argued that only the innermost chamber was the work of Hatshepsut, the remaining parts of the tomb having already been constructed for Thutmose I[18] or for Thutmose II.[19] If the former, KV38 would have been the work of Thutmose III, who was certainly the author of the sarcophagus found within. The body of Thutmose I would have been first interred in the outer chamber of KV20, presumably in a wooden sarcophagus, given the lack of any traces of a stone example. Then, the tomb will have been taken over by Hatshepsut (adding foundation deposits outside) and extended, the new burial chamber housing both monarchs. Subsequently, Thutmose III will have removed Thutmose I to a new tomb, equipped with a stone sarcophagus and canopic chest.[20] On the alternative scenario that KV38 was cut from the outset for Thutmose I,[21] he will have been originally interred there, removed by Hatshepsut, and returned by Thutmose III, at which point he provided the new items of stone furniture. Either way, the king's mummy appears to have been destroyed by the early Twenty-first Dynasty, when his outermost coffin was usurped by Panedjem I.[22]

The question of the tomb of Thutmose II has long been problematic since, unlike the case of his father, no known tomb contains material bearing his name.[23] The most oft-cited candidate has been KV42 in the Valley of the Kings,[24] essentially a larger, more regular, version of KV38, with a sharp right-angled turn towards the burial chamber (fig. 15e). The walls of KV42's burial chamber had been plastered and given a dado of *kheker*-motifs, clearly with the intention of adding a hand-drawn copy of the Book of *Amduat* (pl. XLVIIIb), found in a number of later royal tombs (see pp. 65-6); remains of such a dado survived in KV38 (cf. pl. XLVIIIa). The tomb also contained an unfinished quartzite sarcophagus of a size and design consistent with it being the earliest of the sequence of such containers known from kings' tombs of the Eighteenth Dynasty. However, the tomb showed no signs of a primary burial, while outside were found foundation deposits, naming Meryetre, a wife of Thutmose III. KV42 has thus been proposed as having been founded for her – although it is perfectly possible that they may represent a secondary appropriation of an unused tomb for the queen, but once again apparently not used for her burial, as the sarcophagus shows no signs of having been closed.[25]

As noted above, another option could be that KV20 was founded for

Thutmose II, which might be further supported by the fact that the final burial chamber has three annexes – potentially one for each king buried there.[26] However, one might in this case have expected a stone sarcophagus to have been provided by either Hatshepsut or Thutmose III, unless this is still concealed in an as-yet-undiscovered 'final' tomb of Thutmose II (which must, however, have been plundered, given the presence of his mummy in TT320). The question of where Thutmose II was interred remains for the time being a mystery.

On the other hand, a mortuary chapel of the king lies in the southern part of the Theban necropolis, west of Deir el-Medina (fig. 17b).[27] The location of that of Thutmose I is uncertain, perhaps near that of Amenhotep I at Deir el-Bahari and later over-built. A (replacement?) chapel may have been built for him by Thutmose III, which was named 'Akheperkare-United-with-Life', but its location is unknown.[28] Thutmose II's sanctuary was a building of fairly simple design, which appears to have undergone reconstruction under Thutmose III, who was responsible for most of the fragmentary carved scenes that survive from the building. Fragments of a colossus of Thutmose II also survived, together with a number of stelae, attesting to his posthumous cult.

Thutmose II left behind a young son, Thutmose III, for whom the dowager Hatshepsut acted as regent for some seven years. She was, however, later crowned as Thutmose III's co-regent, and prepared a funerary complex suited to a fully-fledged king. As a female king, Hatshepsut certainly intended to be buried in KV20, whether by usurpation or original commission. It seems in any case that the inner burial chamber was her work, equipped with storerooms and three columns. In view of the extremely poor rock from which the tomb was cut – a key reason for its irregular form – any attempt to simply plaster the walls to receive decoration was impossible. Therefore, the aforementioned limestone lining blocks were installed, upon which were delineated in black and red a cursive version of the Book of *Amduat* ('What is in the Underworld': pl. XLIXa), the earliest of a series of texts that describe and illustrate the sun-god's passage through the twelve hours of the night, from 'death' and sunset to rebirth at dawn.[29] It would be supplemented, and sometimes replaced, by a series of further 'books' from the end of the Eighteenth Dynasty onwards, which followed it in dealing with aspects of the sun-god's nocturnal journey though the underworld (for a summary of the evolution of the books and their location in the tomb, see Table 2). Throughout the New Kingdom these books were used only in royal tombs – with the anomalous exception of one of the very early examples, in the burial chamber of tomb of the vizier User, a contemporary of Thutmose III (TT61), where one also finds parts of the Litany of Re, a regular feature of royal tombs, starting with that of Thutmose III.[30] The version of the *Amduat* found in KV20 is fragmentary but the intact decoration of the tomb of Thutmose III shows that its execution will have resembled a great papyrus, unrolled against the walls of the burial chamber.

At her accession, Hatshepsut had replaced the sarcophagus that had been made for her as regent and already placed in her tomb in the Wadi Siqqat Taqa el-Zeide (see p. 80, below), with a larger, more elaborately decorated, one. This was subsequently re-worked for Thutmose I, and replaced by an even larger piece, this time with the plan of a cartouche, i.e. exhibiting a square-cut foot, but rounded head. This form was to be almost universal for kingly sarcophagi for the rest of the New Kingdom. When placed in the burial chamber, the sarcophagus head, most unusually, faced south, the reverse of normal practice. However, the canopic chest lay in the traditional orientation of east of the south end of the coffer, even though this meant that it lay opposite the head of the mummy, rather than its feet, as was usual practice.

The associated offering place of Hatshepsut was in the form of a terraced temple in the great bay of Deir el-Bahari, directly north of the Eleventh Dynasty temple of Montjuhotep II (figs. 16, 17c; pl. XLIXb). Its construction (possibly actually begun under Thutmose II[31] – or perhaps even by Thutmose I, given the lack of any known memorial temple for him) led to the destruction of the brick chapel of Amenhotep I (see above, p. 63). KV20 lay just on the other side of the cliff from Deir el-Bahari, which may have been intentional. As the first full-scale New Kingdom royal funerary temple, it is of the greatest interest and provides a prototype for all succeeding examples, although the resemblance is superficially obscured by its construction in deep terraces. In this, Hatshepsut's temple followed its Eleventh Dynasty neighbour, and that of Ahmose I at Abydos. For its elegance and unity with its surroundings, the building has long been recognized as a gem of Egyptian architecture. It appears also to have incorporated many knowing references to earlier periods' mortuary monuments, reflecting a reverence for the past to be seen in many aspects of the culture of the middle of the Eighteenth Dynasty.[32]

It is now clear that the meaning of the temple-element of a New Kingdom royal funerary complex was rather different from that of the mortuary temples attached to Old and Middle Kingdom pyramids.[33] Most fundamentally, rather than being dedicated solely to the personal cult of the dead king, the primary dedicatee was a local version of the god Amun, whose sanctuary lay at the end of the main axis (fig. 17c/A). An open altar to Re lay at the northern extremity of the rear of the temple (B), the chapel of the king (C) – accompanied by a smaller sanctuary of their father (D) – being relegated to the southern extremity. Accordingly, such New Kingdom temples have come to be referred to as 'memorial temples' to distinguish them from the earlier 'mortuary temples' (their ancient Egyptian name was 'Mansions of Millions of Years').

Hatshepsut's complex[34] began in the plain,[35] near the edge of the cultivation, with an unfinished valley building on two levels, a lower court, and an upper terrace fronted by a colonnade of square pillars (pl. La). A causeway, lined with sphinxes, led for over a kilometre westwards to a gate in the main temple's temenos wall. Beyond this, a path flanked with seven pairs of sphinxes led up to a ramp, flanked by colonnades. It seems that these were constructed after other parts of the temple, and it seems that it may originally have been intended to leave the chapel of Amenhotep I intact. However, this decision was presumably later rescinded and the chapel demolished to make way for the northern colonnade. The decoration of the colonnade showed Hatshepsut fowling, fishing and offering to the gods, but only fragments survive. The southern colonnade was adorned with reliefs depicting the transport of a pair of obelisks from the granite quarries at Aswan to the great temple of Karnak.

The second court was also backed with a ramp flanked by colonnades. The southern one contained representations of a trading expedition sent to the land of Punt, probably located on the Red Sea coast of modern Sudan or Somalia. Its northern counterpart contained a sequence showing the myth of Hatshepsut's paternity by the god Amun, who had taken the form of (or become incarnate in) Thutmose I in order to impregnate her mother, Ahmes B. A similar sequence appeared in the memorial temple of Rameses II, as well as in the temple of Amenhotep III at Luxor, and it is likely that it was a standard feature of such 'personal' temples (it is also found in the temple of Khonsupakhered at Karnak, of uncertain date); however, the destroyed state of the decoration of the majority of such sanctuaries makes it impossible to be definitive on the matter.[36]

At either extremity of the second court was a chapel. That at the southern end was dedicated to the goddess Hathor (fig. 17c/E); the northern belonged to Anubis (F), adjacent to which was a further colonnade, running along the north side of the court, equipped with four niches. This structure was never finished, and was built directly over the old tomb of Queen Meryetamun (p. 79).

The upper terrace of the temple, fronted once more by a pair of colonnades and with a decorated trilithon gate, was occupied by a peristyle court. At the back of the court, on the main axis of the temple, was the principal sanctuary, of Amun of *Djeser-djeseru* (the ancient name of the temple: 'Holy-of-Holies'. This originally comprised two rooms, but a third was added in Ptolemaic times, under Ptolemy VIII Euergetes II, dedicated to two deified mortals, Imhotep, architect of the Step Pyramid of Saqqara, and Amenhotep-son-of-Hapu, a celebrated official of Amenhotep III. To the north of the peristyle, a columned vestibule gave access to a court with an open-air altar dedicated to the sun-god in his manifestation of Horemakhet. Leading off this court was a small room, dedicated to Anubis, but heavily featuring Hatshepsut's parents.

A doorway in the south wall of the peristyle led into a vestibule giving access to two chapels, the smaller having been dedicated to Thutmose I, the larger to Hatshepsut herself (pl. Lb), each housing a false-door stela. This linking of the owner of the temple with their father is found in a number of other such structures (e.g. of Sethy I), but it is unclear whether it was an invariable feature of a memorial temple, since the memorial temples of the remaining kings of the Eighteenth Dynasty are all in very poor condition, making assessment problematic.

Unlike Hatshepsut's monument, the earlier of these temples employed considerable quantities of mud-brick in their structures, supplementing the limestone and sandstone that were used primarily for decorated elements. That of Thutmose III (fig. 17d; pl. LIa)[37] was constructed opposite the Sheikh Abd el-Qurna hill where many of the officials of the time were buried, and originally comprised a structure on two levels, the upper terrace being partly rock cut, partly the result of filling and grading, supported by a brick retaining wall. This contained the main body of the temple, fronted by a portico of osiride figures, behind which lay a peristyle court. This in turn gave access to a hypostyle hall, and finally the sanctuaries, arranged as at Deir el-Bahari (pl. LIb). A lower terrace was later added, fronted by a large brick pylon, while a Hathor-sanctuary was subsequently inserted to the south of the main temple-axis, equipped with its own ramp and portico leading up from what was now the middle terrace.

Thutmose III's tomb (KV34)[38] was cut high above the floor of the Valley of the Kings in a 'chimney' in the rock. This kind of location was employed for a number of tombs of the general period, apparently to encourage the obliteration of their precise position by the deposition of debris by floodwater running off the high desert and emptying into wadis such as the Valley via such water-worn routes. KV34 had the same 'bent' plan seen in a number of other contemporary royal tombs (fig. 15f), starting with two sets of steps and two corridors, all somewhat roughly cut, leading to a chamber whose floor was cut away after the funeral to form a shaft some 19 m deep. The walls of the room were whitewashed and topped with a *kheker*-frieze. The preparation of the wall below this suggests that further decoration was contemplated, but never carried out; the ceiling was adorned with five-pointed yellow stars, on a deep blue background. A once-sealed doorway, painted over to match the rest of the wall, led into the antechamber, its roof supported by a pair of pillars. The shape of the room was rather odd, each wall being of a different length; it was adorned with long lists of the denizens of the Underworld, many of whom were not found outside the restricted world of the royal tombs. In keeping with the fashion of the period, they were drawn in pen on a golden-yellow background, in the imitation of a papyrus roll.

A sunken stairway in the floor of the chamber led down into the burial chamber, of the oval form already noted in KV38 and KV42 (pl. LIIa). Its walls bear the earliest intact version of the 'papyrus-written' *Amduat*, seen in fragmentary form in Hatshepsut's sepulchral chamber. On five faces of the two pillars were placed an abbreviated version of another of the funerary 'books', the Litany of Re. The sixth pillar-face, however, was given a unique scene, of the king with three wives and a daughter, and suckled by his mother, Iset, in the guise of a tree, the first and last time that members of the royal family would be included in the decoration of an orthodox royal tomb (cf. p. 73). The stick figures and cursive hieroglyphs, together with those in the antechamber, appear to have been applied during the funerary ceremonies, perhaps as part of the 'activation' of the magical mechanism that was the tomb. Four small annexes, all roughly cut and undecorated, opened out of the burial chamber, and were intended to hold funerary equipment, some fragments of which survived when the tomb was excavated in modern times. These annexes had been closed by wooden doors, but all other openings in the tomb, where closed, had been blocked with masonry.[39]

Thutmose III's sarcophagus was a further development of those of Hatshepsut, but no canopic chest survives. It may have been removed in the Late Period, when the tomb was entered to allow the copying of the sarcophagus's decoration for use on that of a noble named Hapymen.[40] The king's mummy was found in TT 320, within what had once been his outer wooden coffin, although now in very poor condition, almost the entire gilded surface having been hacked away.

The next king, Amenhotep II, placed his tomb (KV35)[41] at the base of the western cliffs of the Kings' Valley, once again below an occasional waterfall. Its plan followed the general arrangement of KV34 (fig. 15g), but was more regular and, most importantly, abandoned the cartouche-form burial hall in favour of one of rectangular plan, approached via an additional corridor, at the end of which a single-leafed wooden door closed the way into the burial chamber (as would be the case in all tombs down to Rameses II). The burial chamber (pl. LIIb) was the only room of the tomb to be decorated, its walls carrying the *Amduat* in the same cursive style as found previously. The pillars, however, were now six in number and showed the king receiving life from various deities. The floor of the chamber was apparently originally intended to be on one level, as in earlier tombs, but at a relatively late stage in construction its south end was lowered by around 1.5m, thus forming a kind of crypt. In this was placed the king's sarcophagus, similar to that of his predecessor, but somewhat larger and less elegant. The construction of the crypt may be explained by an emerging desire to surround the sarcophagus with one or more wooden shrines. Four or more were employed during the late Eighteenth and Twentieth Dynasties, and the sunken floor was probably the easiest way of gaining the requisite vertical clearance.

Although comprehensively robbed in antiquity, large quantities of funerary equipment was found surviving when the tomb was opened. These included fragments of Amenhotep II's canopic chest, which differed completely from those of Hatshepsut and Thutmose I, which had been made from the same material as their sarcophagi. In Amenhotep's case it had been carved from a block of translucent calcite (Egyptian alabaster), and at each corner bore the raised figure of one of the protective goddesses, Isis, Nephthys, Nut and Selqet. Inside, canopic jars were carved as one with the box, each stoppered with a small head of the king. This basic design was retained for royal canopics down to the middle of the Nineteenth Dynasty. As a further innovation, the king was equipped with multiple shabti figures, replacing the single shabti that had been used in burials prior to Amenhotep II's reign. The king's mummy remained in the tomb until modern times, KV35 having been used as a cache for royal mummies removed from their own tombs during the Twentieth/Twenty-first Dynasty.

Amenhotep II's memorial temple[42] was constructed some way south of that of his father, but was almost entirely destroyed in antiquity, part having been used for a Twenty-second Dynasty cemetery (pl. LIIIa). Only the portico and peristyle court of the main temple survive, which seems to have undergone some rebuilding under Thutmose IV and Amenhotep III; on the basis of sculptured fragments it is possible that the latter appropriated at least part of the building for his eldest daughter, Sitamun. Comparing the visible portion of Amenhotep II's temple with the corresponding part of Thutmose III's, an additional row of columns was added around the inside of the peristyle, as well as to the rear of the fronting colonnade.

The memorial temple of Amenhotep's successor, Thutmose IV,[43] continued this trend, the sides and rear of the peristyle now having three rows of columns (fig. 17e). The main body of the temple otherwise followed the plan of Thutmose III's quite closely, although without the latter's Hathor complex. Part of Thutmose IV's first pylon, built of sun-dried brick, still remains standing to some height; behind it, the temple rose on two terraces, but little more than a grey granite doorsill and some paving otherwise remains in situ (pl. LIIIb).

Thutmose IV constructed his tomb (KV43)[44] in the Valley of the Kings on the opposite side of the wadi from that of his father. It is instructive to note that Amenhotep II had also selected a site a considerable distance from the tomb of his predecessor. This practice continued down to the end of the dynasty, but not beyond. The design of the tomb represented a further development of that of Amenhotep II, most notably adding a third flight of stairs and an antechamber before the burial chamber, which is turned through a further ninety degrees (fig. 15h). The antechamber and well-room received decoration (showing the king before various deities, all for the first time in the Valley in polychrome), this was never completed (pl. XLIVa), and the remainder of the tomb was never even plastered in preparation for decoration.

However, the sarcophagus that lay in the burial chamber's sunken crypt was completely carved and painted: twice the height and width of that of Thutmose III it reflects the increasing size of royal sarcophagi from reign to reign. The tomb was robbed on more than one occasion, the first time within a century of the burial, the restoration of the tomb being recorded in a hieratic graffito on the south wall of the antechamber, dating to Year 8 of Horemheb. Later plundering resulted in the destruction of much of the tomb's funerary equipment and the removal of the king's mummy, which eventually found rest in the cache in KV35.

Besides KV43, in which he was actually buried, Thutmose IV was responsible for the foundation of a second tomb in the Valley of the Kings. Foundation deposits naming him have been found outside a tomb, WV22, in a hitherto-virgin branch known as the West Valley.[45] The reason for this is unclear; in any case the tomb was actually completed for his successor, Amenhotep III. In basic plan, the tomb followed that of its immediate precursors, with the principal exception that, uniquely for a kingly tomb, the entrance to the burial hall was not on the main axis, but at one end of a sidewall (fig. 15i). In addition, it had two pillared chambers opening off the crypt, each with its own annex. That at the end of the chamber seems to have been part of the original plan of the tomb, and seems likely to have been intended for the burial of Queen Tiye. The second complex, on the other hand, preserves traces that show that it was enlarged out of what had been one of the standard four store-rooms found in earlier kingly tombs. As a late addition to the tomb plan, it would seem reasonable to attribute it to Sitamun, Amenhotep III's eldest daughter, who obtained the dignity of Queen in the last decade of the king's reign (see further below, p. 81).

The burial chamber was decorated with the 'hand-written' version of the *Amduat* seen in earlier sepulchres, although its style differed somewhat from that found in the tombs of Thutmose III and Amenhotep II, since the upper parts of the figures were properly drawn, and only the legs left as 'sticks' (pl. LIVb). The remaining chambers followed Thutmose IV's lead in being decorated with fully coloured paintings, depicting the king in the company of deities (pl. LVa);[46] the outer pillared hall was not decorated. Only the lid of the sarcophagus survives in the crypt of the burial chamber. Made of granite, it is the first use of the material for a king since the time of Amenemhat III, back at the end of the Twelfth Dynasty; it was once gorgeously decorated in gold foil. Of its coffer, however, no trace has ever come to light. It is most likely that it was removed for reuse during the Third Intermediate Period, when many tombs were stripped of such salvageable material (cf. pp. 64, 106, below).

For his memorial temple,[47] Amenhotep III selected a site south of that of his father for a structure that was in its final configuration without precedent in both size and form (fig. 18, inset; pl. LVb, LVIa). It was but one element of a much larger West-Theban scheme that included his palace-complex at Malqata, two kilometers further south. The temple was rather different in conception from the memorial temples of Amenhotep III's predecessors, both in layout and in size – it ultimately had a peristyle court as large as the whole of the Deir el-Bahari temple of Hatshepsut, with a series of pylon-fronted courts and an enclosure that covered some three square kilometers. This area also embraced a number of subsidiary sanctuaries, including a separate temple of Ptah-Sokar-Osiris, approached from a northern gateway (guarded by colossal standing figures) and processional way.

The memorial temple itself had the unique feature for a West-Theban temple of having the outer courtyards built largely on the floodplain, in contrast to the wholly-desert locations of other temples, and must thus have been intended to flood annually.[48] The main (eastern) entrance to the temple was marked by a brick pylon and a pair of quartzite colossi (now known as the Colossi of Memnon), followed by two further brick pylons, fronted respectively by quartzite and alabaster colossi. An area apparently devoid of structures preceded a peristyle court, with two stelae flanking the entrance, and with standing colossi between the pillars of the front row, those on the north side being of quartzite and those on the south of granite, reflecting the respective geographical origins of the two stones. Little of the plan of the inner temple can, however, be traced, the whole temple having been severely damaged by an earthquake, probably early in the reign of Merenptah, who subsequently used it as a quarry for his own memorial temple (p. 86). This included not only blocks, but also stelae and even sculpture, sliced up to produce building material. Many other items of sculpture were re-worked from at least the reign of Rameses II and became widely distributed around Thebes, and perhaps even further afield.

As well as its funerary role, the temple fulfilled a role during the king's lifetime, as a major venue for his his First Jubilee celebrations.[49] This may explain the range of unusual sculptures included in the temple's furnishings, adding up to an unprecedented collection of images, including many statues of the goddess Sekhmet and divine images that are in some cases without direct parallel elsewhere. Given the building of the outer courtyards on the floodplain, it may have been intended that these deities were to have been perceived during the Inundation as being in the process of emerging from the primaeval ocean of Nun.[50]

Amenhotep III's successor, Amenhotep IV, temporarily changed the pattern of Egyptian royal burial when he transformed the cult of the solar disk Aten into that of a sole god, changed his own name to Akhenaten and moved the capital and royal cemetery to the virgin site of Tell el-Amarna (Akhet-Aten), in Middle Egypt (map 9). Prior to this move, in his fifth regnal year, it is likely that a burial will have been contemplated in the Valley of the Kings, and there is indeed an unfinished tomb in the West Valley (WV25) that may well have been intended as his.[51] It comprises a staircase and descending corridor, beyond which work had been abandoned. The form and dimensions of the corridor are consistent with a late Eighteenth Dynasty date, while there is no evidence for the use of this branch of the valley before Amenhotep III or later than Ay.[52] The tomb was found containing eight intrusive burials of the Third Intermediate Period.

Following the move to Amarna, a wadi to the east of the city was taken over as the new royal place of burial, the establishment of which was included in the decree creating the new city.[53] Now dubbed the Royal Wadi, the first tomb to be founded there was for the king and his family (TA26),[54] 5km up the wadi, and ten from the heart of the city (map 9; fig. 19a). It differed from earlier royal tombs, with corridors of much greater width and height than previously, and also making significant provision for the burial of members of the royal family in chambers and galleries opening off the main corridor.

The main axis. parts of which had stairs, is of interest as being the earliest in a royal tomb to have a ramp down the centre, to aid the introduction of the funerary equipment, and led down to a shallow well-room. A doorway at the back of the well-room gave access to what was used as the burial chamber for not only the king, but his mother Tiye as well: fragmentary sarcophagi of both were found.[55] In its final form, it had only two pillars, but seems to have been designed for four: two were cut away when a sarcophagus-plinth was cut from the floor. It is likely that the original plan was for a further passage to lead beyond it to a definitive burial chamber.

The main corridor of the tomb was undecorated, but the well-room (E) had depictions (now badly damaged, like all the reliefs in the tomb) of the worship of the Aten. For the first time in a New Kingdom royal tomb, relief was employed for its scenes; previously, paint alone had been used. The burial chamber was also decorated with scenes of sun-worship and two scenes of mourning. Provision was made for other royal family burials in suites opening off the main corridor (see p. 82). The burial equipment in the tomb was all reduced to fragments in antiquity, but it is clear that while the same basic elements were carried over from orthodoxy, decoration differed greatly. Thus the sarcophagus of the king depicted the Aten and was protected, not by the four traditional tutelary goddesses, but by his wife, Nefertiti (pl. LVIb), while his canopic chest had the early avian form of the Aten around its corners. Shabti figures were provided, but with inscriptions that gave no more than names and titles.

Two other apparently-kingly tombs (TA27 and TA29) were begun in the Royal Wadi, with the barely-started TA30 possibly another.[56] One, TA27, comprises most of the first corridor, penetrating 13 m into the rock, but no more. In contrast, TA29 was no less than 45m long when work was terminated part way down what would have been a stairway, following on from three full corridors (fig. 19b; pl. LVIIa). The candidates for the owners of these tombs would appear to be Akhenaten's two co-rulers, Smenkhkare and Neferneferuaten, and his successor, Tutankhaten (later -amun), all of whom were resident at Amarna at some point. However, in the absence of texts, allocation is problematic. In any case, Neferneferuaten never received a pharaonic burial, much of her equipment being eventually reused in the burial of Tutankhamun.[57]

This latter interment ultimately took place in a small tomb in the Valley of the Kings, KV62,[58] which was certainly originally intended as a non-kingly sepulchre, but was moderately enlarged to hold a king's burial. Scans of the walls of the burial chamber have revealed traces reminiscent of doorways under the plaster covering the north and west walls of the burial chamber but, at the time of writing, it is unclear whether these are in actuality anything more significant than suggestive relics of the cutting of the chamber.[59]

The identity of Tutankhamun's originally-intended tomb is uncertain, but consensus tends towards WV23, a tomb in the West Valley in which Tutankhamun's successor, Ay, was interred, close to WV25. Although it has been speculated that Tutankhamun had originally been placed in WV23, and moved secondarily to KV62,[60] it seems more likely that it was decided at the time of Tutankhamun's death that the smaller KV62 (perhaps Ay's intended private sepulchre) should be adapted for him during the time occupied by the embalming process.

The original tomb appears to have been restricted to a descending passage and a rectangular chamber – very similar to the plan of the tomb of Amenhotep III's parents-in-law, Yuya and Tjuiu (KV46).[61] When converted (fig. 19c), a sunken crypt was added to the north end of its chamber, together with two small store-rooms. Into the new burial chamber was inserted the king's fine quartzite sarcophagus; its form resembled that of Akhenaten's, but with its protective female figures on its corners representing Isis, Nephthys, Neith and Selqet, rather than the queen. The decoration of the sarcophagus had been largely recut at some stage, probably at the time of the amendment of the king's nomen from Tutankhaten to Tutankhamun, although it has also been suggested that the sarcophagus was among the items from the burial ensemble of Neferneferuaten appropriated for use in KV62, in which case it would have been her texts that needed replacement. The quartzite sarcophagus coffer was closed by a granite lid, broken while being lowered into place; the occasion for this accident may have been the discovery that the toes of the outermost coffin of the king were higher than the rim of the sarcophagus-coffer, and needed adzing down.

The sarcophagus was surrounded by a series of four gilded wooden shrines, which provide the earliest examples of a number of funerary 'books' that came to supplement the *Amduat* during the period following the death of Akhenaten and would later appear on the walls of later royal tombs. The decoration of KV62 itself was restricted to the burial chamber and was entirely polychrome, the 'drawn' schemes of earlier times having been definitively abandoned (pl. LVIIb). It was applied after the interment, since the paintings cover the partition-wall between the chamber and the antechamber that can only have been erected after all items had been placed within.

In contrast with the complete versions of the *Amduat* found hitherto, only part of the first section of the work was provided, opposite the head of the sarcophagus. It would appear that, owing to the lack of space, this was intended to stand for the whole of the work, the remainder being provided magically. The opposite wall showed the royal catafalque being dragged by nobles to the tomb, a scene not normally otherwise found in a royal burial chamber (and in any case normally found in a funerary chapel, not a burial chamber). The long walls of the chamber showed the king before various deities, together with a unique scene of Tutankhamun's successor, Ay, performing the Opening of the Mouth ceremony, a tableau that seems to be an extension of the catafalque-dragging scene on the adjacent wall. While generic Opening of the Mouth sequences were placed in later royal tombs, this is the only case of the celebrant being named; this seems likely to be a result of the issues surrounding the succession after Tutankhamun's death, which may have resulted in Ay's making his claim clear (as Horus burying Osiris) in the ritual context of the tomb.[62]

KV62 was found almost intact, and thus provides an example of the sheer variety of material placed in the tomb of a king of the New Kingdom. Indeed, while many of the objects found had parallels in the debris of other tombs, the richness of some of them was significantly greater, gilding having been applied to pieces whose parallels had been merely of black-varnished wood. The ensemble had very clearly been intended for a much larger tomb, the lack of space in the tomb may have led to the construction of an annex, a shaft-tomb now numbered KV63, to hold the debris from the king's embalming that would under normal circumstances have been, presumably, housed somewhere in the main tomb.[63] Like that of KV62, the entrance to KV63 became sealed by flood-debris within a year of the burial (during which interval robbers briefly penetrated KV62),[64] ensuring that they remained undisturbed until the twentieth century AD.

The flood, which engulfed the lowest part of the Valley in which KV62 and KV63 were cut, also sealed at least one other known tomb there, KV55.[65] This contained a range of material, including a mutilated funerary shrine of Queen Tiye, a set of canopic jars that had originally been made for Kiya, a wife of Akhenaten, a coffin almost certainly made for Kiya that had been reworked for a king (whose names had subsequently been cut out from its inscriptions), and a mummy within the coffin. The interpretation of the material found in KV55 has been the subject of endless Egyptological discussion, but the tomb seems to have been intended to hold a number of burials removed from the Royal Wadi at Amarna when the city ceased to be a royal residence around Years 3/4 of Tutankhamun. Soon after Tutankhamun's death, it seems to have been re-entered, some burials removed and the remaining one mutilated, before being resealed and the site covered by flood debris until modern times. The identity of this remaining burial has been variously argued as being either Akhenaten or Smenkhkare, with the latter apparently the more likely.[66]

Nothing is known of any memorial temple of Akhenaten – given the fundamental change in beliefs that accompanied his reign, it is unclear whether he would have had such a building: perhaps any posthumous cult will have been wrapped-up in that of the Aten itself. Of his successors, an apparent memorial temple of Smenkhkare is mentioned in a graffito of the time of Neferneferuaten,[67] but nothing at all is known of that of Tutankhamun, unless it was one of the two(?) structures of his from which blocks have been found re-used at Karnak.[68] These have been usually been regarded as having originally lain at Karnak, but as it is known that blocks were moved from one side of the Nile to the other for the purpose of reuse, it is not impossible that they came from a west bank memorial temple.

As for a site for a Tutankhamun memorial temple (regardless of the status of the Karnak blocks), a potential clue is that both Amenhotep III and

Tutankhamun's own successor founded their memorial temples just north of what is now Medinet Habu. Indeed, the remains of two anonymous temples exist between these two sanctuaries, close to the place where Thutmose II's temple had also been built.[69] That the temples should date to the later Eighteenth Dynasty is suggested by their plans, while the fact that Rameses IV laid out a temple over part of the site of the North Temple (see p. 97, below) shows that the latter had been demolished by the early Twentieth Dynasty, if not many years earlier.

The West-Theban memorial temple of Tutankhamun's successor, Ay, lay a little way to the south of these potential temple-sites (fig. 18). Equipped with original foundation deposits in Ay's name (showing that he had not usurped a building of Tutankhamun), it was to be usurped and completed by the next king, Horemheb.[70] As laid out by Ay, the structure comprised a tripartite inner temple, with the Amun and royal sections equipped with a pair of hypostyle halls, all fronted by a colonnade. In front of this, a terrace at a lower level was closed by a pylon, with a further pylon representing the façade of the temple a little further to the east. Between the two pylons was erected a palace for occupation during festivals, a feature that would become standard for royal memorial temples.

The other part of Ay's burial installation was his tomb in the West Valley of the Kings, WV23 (fig. 19d).[71] As noted above, the tomb might have been begun for Tutankhamun, although no definitive evidence – e.g. foundation deposits – has been found. The tomb's plan is clearly truncated as compared with its original design, which was presumably akin to that later executed for Horemheb (pp. 78-9, below). Whether this was a result of emergency action on Ay's premature demise or a planned down-sizing is of course a moot point. On the other hand, Ay's likely advanced age at accession (he had been in a senior role since at least the early years of Akhenaten) may have led him to take a conservative approach to providing himself with a royal tomb. Indeed, this may have been the reason for his putative taking over of the tomb from Tutankhamun – to provide himself with a ready-to-use sepulchre.

Only the burial chamber of WV23 was decorated and, like the tomb of Tutankhamun, its decoration was both abbreviated and innovative (pl. LVIIIa). Once again the *Amduat* was cut down to elements of the First Hour, with images of the king and gods distributed along one long wall. Alongside some other mythological elements, however, is a double-scene of the king spearing a hippopotamus and fowling in a canoe, with Queen Tey looking on (pl. LVIIIb). This is unusual in two particular aspects: first, it is the only time that a queen has substantive representation in a king's tomb; second, while the hunting/fowling motif goes back to the Old Kingdom, its use in a burial chamber is not otherwise attested, although a standard feature of pre-Amarna Theban private tomb-chapels and also known in royal memorial temples (pp. 39, 67 above and 94, below). Its frequent modern characterisation as a 'non-royal' feature, perhaps reflecting some ambiguity as to Ay's status, thus misses the point – it is simply in the wrong part of the tomb, paralleling the intrusive mummy-dragging scene in Tutankhamun's burial chamber. As the style of the two tombs' decoration is so similar, a common draughtsman is likely (who may have also worked on the tombs of Horemheb and Rameses I)[72] – and possibly one who was keen to test the boundaries of what was possible in the post-Amarna climate, which generated many significant changes in mortuary decoration.[73]

WV23 was equipped with a sarcophagus of the same basic design as that of Tutankhamun; as in Tutankhamun's tomb, the head of the sarcophagus was oriented towards the wall bearing the abbreviated *Amduat*.[74] However, no sign of any canopic material, or shabti figures has ever came to light, the sum of recovered items having been put forward as evidence for a hurried and incomplete burial. This may tie in with the later destruction of the names and faces of the king and queen in the tomb:[75] there is evidence for difficulties between Ay and his successor, Horemheb,[76] and the latter may have carried out the bare minimum burial ritual necessary to legitimise his succession to Ay.

While commander of the army under his predecessors, Horemheb had built a tomb at Saqqara[77] but, although a uraeus was added to the brow of the now-king's figures where they appeared on the walls of his chapel, a new sepulchre was constructed to hold the now-divine body of Horemheb. This tomb, KV57 (fig. 19e),[78] was cut in the old, eastern, branch of the Valley of the Kings, thus marking an end to the experiment of the West Valley. The tomb is interesting in being the first structurally-complete royal tomb known since the time of Amenhotep III. In many ways its plan closely follows that of WV22, but with the crucial difference that it is laid out along a straight axis. This is usually explained as being a reflection of Atenist practice, since Akhenaten's tomb certainly lacks a turn. On the other hand, the latter's plan is clearly abbreviated, and it is possible that a turn was intended.

The outer galleries of KV57 were undecorated, with the exception of the well-chamber, the walls of which showed the king before the usual Theban mortuary deities. The fundamental difference between these scenes and the corresponding ones in earlier tombs is that, as well as being painted, they were carved in low relief. Thus, unlike earlier tombs where decoration could be applied after the burial had taken place, the adornment of KV57 had to be carried out at the same time as its cutting. Scheduling and resourcing implications following on from this innovation may explain why the decoration of the tomb was still incomplete at the king's death.

The antechamber (I – pl. LIXa) was the next room to possess decoration, with the well-room motifs repeated. In addition to the wooden door leading from it into the burial chamber, a door lay at the antechamber's own entrance for the first time, an feature that continued in later tombs. The reliefs in the burial chamber, comprising parts of the new Book of the Gates, replacing the *Amduat* of earlier tombs, were never finished. Their unfinished state is interesting in that they show every stage of their preparation, from initial red sketch, through black outlining (pl. LIXb), to exquisite carving (pl. LXa). Other indications of the incomplete state of the tomb were the quantities of masons' debris that littered the rooms.

Many fragments of the royal funerary equipment remained in the tomb when discovered, including a granite sarcophagus, the last of the 'corner goddess' type known, fragments of the canopic chest and guardian and divine figures of the kind found complete in the tomb of Tutankhamun. A quantity of skeletal material has been found in the tomb, possibly suggesting use of the tomb as a cache during the Third Intermediate Period: certainly, graffiti in the sepulchre show that there was official activity there around the beginning of that period.

As noted above, Horemheb took over the unfinished memorial temple of Ay, enlarging it by the addition of a peristyle court and an extra pylon, extending the axis to nearly 300m long, and usurping its sculptural programme (fig. 18; pl. LXb).[79] Original relief-work appears to have been in a poorer style than that carried out by Ay. The temple was later demolished, a number of blocks ending up reused on the east bank in the temple of Khonsu at Karnak during the Twentieth Dynasty.

Eighteenth Dynasty Royal Family Tombs
During the New Kingdom, many of the known tombs of the royal family were placed in the southern part of the Theban necropolis, including the area that came to be known as the Valley of the Queens (map 14; pl. LXIa). It was here that at least one daughter of Taa, Ahmes A, had a tomb (QV47),[80] while a large number of other shaft tombs datable to the Eighteenth Dynasty lies in and around the outer part of the valley.[81]

However, the earliest known potential queens' tombs are around Deir el-Bahari, where a long corridor-tomb (TT320 – fig. 20a), later used as the tomb of the Twenty-first Dynasty high priest of Amun, Panedjem II, and still later, as has already been noted more than once, as a cache for royal mummies, has been argued to have originally been that of Ahmes-Nefertiry, wife of Ahmose I.[82] Also, a rather smaller tomb, TT358 (fig. 16, 20b), was found to contain the restored burial of Meryetamun, wife of Amenhotep I, and seems certain to have been her original sepulchre, its location likely to be linked with the presence of that king's later-demolished chapel nearby.[83] A little further south, the unfinished Middle Kingdom mortuary temple behind Sheikh Abd el-Qurna (pp. 39-40; pl. XXXIIIb) hosted a shaft tomb (MMA1019) belonging to Princess Ahmes-Tumerisy, datable to the earlier part of the dynasty.[84]

A series of particularly remote southern wadis[85] were employed for a number of tombs during the reign of Thutmose III, including that of Hatshepsut as regent in the Wadi Siqqat Taqa el-Zeide. It lies in a fairly dramatic location, the entrance being at the base of a cleft in the rock, some 70 m above the bed of the wadi (pl. LXIb). Of a fairly simple right-angled plan (fig. 20c), it contained a small quartzite sarcophagus, lacking only its final polish.[86] A potential tomb of her daughter Neferure (fig. 20d)[87] and a collective burial of three spouses of Thutmose III (fig. 20e)[88] lay in the adjacent Wadi el-Qurud. On the other hand, as noted above, p. 64, KV42 in the Valley of the Kings was constructed (or appropriated) for the king's last Great Wife, Meryetre.

Burials of royal family members during the reign of Amenhotep II are obscure, as it is possible that the tomb prepared for his wife Tiaa, in the Valley of the Kings (KV32 – fig. 20g),[89] was actually constructed, like all her other known monuments, during the reign of her son, Thutmose IV. The tomb conforms to the simple form of a chamber accessed by stairs, as also found in KV21, probably belonging to Eighteenth Dynasty royal family members, but anonymous.[90] On the other hand, it seems likely that KV39, high above the southern end of the Valley of the Kings (fig. 20f),[91] is to be dated (in its final form at least) to Amenhotep II's reign by foundation deposits.[92] It is clear that the final form of KV39 was the result of a number of phases of construction, starting as a simple corridor-tomb, but later extended in three directions. At least nine bodies and many fragments from coffins were found distributed between each of the three main chambers, the coffins to be dated typologically to the middle of the Eighteenth Dynasty. Given the location of the tomb on the margin of the Valley of the King, a view that the tomb was a sepulchre for members of the family of Amenhotep II seems a likely one.

If this interpretation is correct, then KV39 will be the first certain example of a New Kingdom tomb (re)designed for the communal burial of members of the royal family, echoing some of Senwosret III's earlier arrangements at Dahshur. Such apparent originality fits in well with what we know of other aspects of Amenhotep II's funerary activities, which incorporated a number of major innovations in the construction and furnishing of KV35 (pp. 69-70, above). The latter is also the first king's tomb definitely to have held a family member, canopic jars and shabtis belonging to Prince Webensennu having been found there.[93]

In addition, the presence of a tomb for the Great Wife of each of the immediately preceding kings would suggest that one or more of the holders of that title under Thutmose IV (Nefertiry C, Iaret and Mutemwia) will have had a tomb in the Valley of the Kings, with KV21, very similar in plan to Tiaa's KV32, being a potential tomb of one or more of them. Nevertheless, the practice of deceased family being buried in the king's tomb continued, with canopic jars of Prince Amenemhat C and Princess Tintamun being found in Thutmose IV's KV43, together with a complete mummy, probably that of the prince, and other debris that may represent the remains of the princess. As already noted, in Amenhotep III's WV22, two suites of rooms (fig. 15i[Jb and Jc]), created by extending store-rooms were clearly intended for burials, the female gender of at least one intended occupant being indicated by two sets of shabti-fragments; it seems probable that these rooms were intended for Tiye and Sitamun, thus shifting from the previous practice of a separate Valley of the King's tomb for Great Wives.

For lesser members of the royal family during the reigns of Thutmose IV and Amenhotep III, as well as individual shafts,[94] a number of multiple-occupant shaft tombs were provided. At least one such tomb lay in the Valley of the Kings, the four chambers of KV40[95] holding at least thirty-three original burials (plus a similar number of Third Intermediate Period intrusives), the latest of which seemingly dated to the reign of Amenhotep III. Over half the original burials belonged to royal children, the remainder to their retainers.[96] A similar multi-roomed pit-tomb, KV30, probably also represents such a sepulchre of the same period.

A group of such tombs of the same date lie on a raised site (WB1) overlooking the Wadi Bariya at the southwestern extremity of the Theban Necropolis.[97] Two unfinished shafts accompany four multi-chambered shaft tombs, some at more than one level (WB1/2 with nine chambers at three levels), from which derive large quantities of debris from funerary equipment datable by pottery to the period from Thutmose III to Amenhotep III, with coffin-debris of the latter reign. In addition a large quantity of canopic jar fragments preserve the names or titles of a number of members of the royal family (a queen, two princesses and a prince).[98] A number of princesses of the same period (possibly including Tia, originally buried in the single-chambered WB1/3) were later reburied, at an uncertain date, in an abandoned private tomb-chapel at Sheikh Abd el-Qurna.[99]

The picture that thus emerges of royal family burial arrangement during the Eighteenth Dynasty at Thebes appears rather less consistent than during earlier periods, with the innovations of communal burial and the placement of bodies within the area of the king's burial chamber itself. From the time of Amenhotep I there seems to have been a general preference for the southern end of the Theban necropolis, centring on the Valley of the Queens. At least two queens had individual tombs assigned in the Valley of the Kings, suggesting that this may have been the case of others as well, culminating in the provision of apparent dedicated chambers in the tomb of Amenhotep III.

Against this background, we find in the Royal Wadi at Amarna an 'integrated' royal tomb, with specific architectural provision for the entire royal family (fig. 19a). Akhenaten shared his own burial chamber with his mother, while a long corridor-annexe (1–6) may have been intended for his wife Nefertiti and a suite of rooms for prematurely-deceased royal daughters (α–γ). Elsewere in the Royal Wadi, the design of TA28, with two principal chambers (fig. 20h),[100] is highly suggestive of having been intended for multiple burials, and may well have been intended for some of the royal princesses.

The final years of the Eighteenth Dynasty provide little clear data on royal family burial provisions. Two foetus burials found in Tutankhamun's KV62[101] and multiple dismembered human remains from Horemheb's KV57[102] suggest that kings continued to share their tombs with prematurely-deceased relatives. On the other hand, at least some of the remains in KV57 may represent a plundered later cache. Female remains found in Horemheb's old private Saqqara tomb have been argued to represent his wife, Mutnedjmet, perhaps supported by the alleged Memphite provenance of her extant canopic jar.[103]

The Nineteenth Dynasty
Horemheb appears to have died without a direct heir, his successor being his former vizier, Paramesse, an army officer and scion of a military family from the eastern Delta; probably of advanced years, he reigned as Rameses I for less than two years. By the time of his death, only the first two flights of steps and the corridor joining them appear to have been cut for his tomb, KV16 (pl. LXIIa; fig. 19f),[104] founded in the centre of the Valley of the Kings in a more prominent location than had hitherto been employed. Beyond these entrance elements, a small square burial chamber was hurriedly cut, its rough walls covered with thick plaster and painted. The decoration was very similar in style to that of the reliefs in Horemheb's sepulchre, featuring the Book of Gates and the king before the gods.

The burial chamber held the king's unfinished granite sarcophagus, which discarded the elaborate corner-goddess design in favour of the cartouche form of Amenhotep III and his predecessors. The chamber had three small annexes, in which were found various damaged items of wooden funerary equipment, in particular guardian and deity figures. The royal mummy is recorded as having been transported to TT320, via a sojourn in the tomb of Sethy I, but the final fate Rameses I's mummy remains uncertain.[105] No trace survives of any memorial temple founded by Rameses I, although it is possible he began the temple that bears the name of his son Sethy I (pl. LXIIIa; fig. 21a).[106] This incorporated a triple-chapelled suite to Rameses I in his role as the king's father (D) – but with a degree of elaboration that seems to have reflected its being Rameses's principal mortuary sanctuary. It is likely that Sethy's own sanctuary is represented by the scanty remains of what seems to have been an identical triple suite (C) directly west of that of Rameses I.[107]

As in earlier temples, the suite on the main axis (A) was dedicated to Amun, but with the addition of flanking shrines of Mut (E) and Khonsu (F), with the solar court to the north (B). The main part of the temple was fronted by a colonnade, with its outer portion comprising two open courtyards and two mudbrick pylons, the first of which had a palace on its south side, as had also appeared in the temple of Ay and Horemheb. In contrast with the earlier Eighteenth Dynasty temples, the degree of terracing from east to west was modest, the whole aspect of the temple being more that of a normal cult temple than had been the case with previous memorial temples. Decoration was still incomplete at Sethy I's death, with large areas of relief carved subsequently by Rameses II. Some took place directly after his father's death, more after a break of some two decades. The temple was built significantly further north than other memorial temples, apparently with the intention of aligning it with the processional route from Karnak across to the west bank

Sethy I cut his tomb (KV17 – pl. LXIIb, LXIVa; fig. 20g)[108] directly next to that of his father (pl. LXXIVb). In its plan, it represented a logical development of Horemheb's KV57, but now introduced the major innovation of being decorated throughout, including corridors, rather than having paintings and reliefs restricted to a few chambers. This began at the very entrance, with a decorated lintel and welcoming figures of Re-Horakhty. A twin-leaved wooden doorway was secondarily added to the first doorway, a feature also found in later royal sepulchres. The first corridor (B) contained the full text of the Litany of Re, followed, from the second stairway of the tomb, by parts of the *Amduat* (C and D). The well-room (E) was adorned, as was by now traditional, with scenes of the king before the gods, but the following pillared hall (F) received parts of the Book of Gates, first encountered in Horemheb's burial chamber. A subsidiary chamber beyond (Fa) had its decoration, comprising more of the *Amduat* on the walls, and the king and deities on the pillars, left in line-work only, the only part of the tomb never finished.

A stairway and corridor (G and H) descended from the hall F, on whose walls appeared the rituals of the Opening of the Mouth and accompanying texts, ultimately leading into the antechamber (I), with reliefs of the king in the company of the gods, before giving access to the burial chamber (J). Of the same basic form as all such completed chambers since the time of Amenhotep II, this was innovative in that its crypt was given a vaulted ceiling, covered with a huge depiction of constellations of the night sky, bracketed by the body of the sky-goddess Nut. The decoration of the pillared section was taken from the Book of Gates, but that of the crypt came from the *Amduat*, supplemented by other stand-alone motifs.

Five annexes opened from the burial chamber. One (Ja) contained part of the Book of Gates, another the Book of the Divine Cow (Je), a composition found hitherto only on the outer shrine of Tutankhamun; a two-pillared chamber (Jb) contained yet more extracts from the *Amduat*, with rock-cut benches presumably intended to support funerary equipment; the other annexes were devoid of decoration. Their contents included wooden divine figures, shabtis in wood and faience and a sacrificed bull.

From the floor of the crypt, a tunnel, once concealed by over-paving, dived steeply into the rock for over one hundred and seventy metres. Although the upper part is now very rough owing to the nature of the rock at this point, the deepest part has regular stairs and smoothly carved walls, divided into sections by jambs and lintels. It is without known parallel and its purpose has never been properly explained, but may have been intended to reach the water table, which is certainly not far below the point where cutting was stopped.

No trace of a stone sarcophagus has been found in KV17; however, in the crypt lay a calcite outer anthropoid coffin, decorated with the Book of Gates. A fragment of a canopic chest in the same material also came to light. The coffin is of a kind not before found in a royal burial, but which would subsequently become a standard feature of royal burials until the early Twentieth Dynasty. The lack of sarcophagus-remains would suggest that the introduction of such coffins accompanied by a temporary abandonment of the stone sarcophagus, probably in favour of a wooden one of a type found in private tombs since at least the middle of the Eighteenth Dynasty;[109] this idea is supported by a similar situation in the tomb of Rameses II, with a calcite coffin but no sarcophagus-traces.

In addition to his actual tomb, Sethy I also built a cenotaph (the Osireion) behind his temple at Abydos (pl. LXIVc). Although of a totally different form, and incorporating an island on which a dummy sarcophagus and canopic chest were once placed, its decoration comprised compositions otherwise found in kings' tombs and seems to have been intended, like private cenotaphs at the site, to allow the king to be posthumously associated with the festivals of Osiris.[110]

Rameses II's KV7 (fig. 20h)[111] was cut some 80 m from the tombs of his father and grandfather. Unlike them, it has suffered badly from flooding, leaving its finely carved decoration in a very poor state (pl. LXIVb). Its plan was unique for a Ramesside royal tomb in that the tomb turned to the right at the antechamber, directly before the sepulchral hall. This was at least partly owing to problematic geology further along the main axis, but possibly also because of a need to maintain the correct orientation of the burial. This took place in a hall that marked a change from the type that had been standard since the time of Amenhotep II. The long axis was shifted to lie across the room, with eight (rather than six) columns placed in front and behind the sunken crypt-area.

Elsewhere in the tomb, there were more subtle changes from the previous standards, with a decrease in the angle of descent, and an extension of the decoration to the outer part of the entrance (suggesting that the tomb's entrance was never intended to be wholly concealed). A wooden door was fitted at the entrance and exit of the well-room (in lieu of the masonry blocking found in earlier tombs), placing the upper pillared hall straddling the axis (rather than marking its lateral shift). Stairways were also added to either side of a central ramp, an arrangement only previously seen in the tomb of Akhenaten. As far as can be determined, given the flood-damaged state of the walls of the tomb, decoratively, the sepulchre largely continued the pattern established by KV17. Thus the Litany of Re occupied most of corridors B and C, with the *Amduat* in D and well-room E, the following upper pillared hall (F) being adorned with parts of the Book of Gates. The Opening of the Mouth ritual occupied corridors G and H, while extracts from the Book of the Dead were placed in the antechamber (I) and in one of the annexes (Jddd) to the burial hall (J); the *Amduat* was to be found in four of the other annexes (Jb, Je, Jd and Jdd) and part of the Gates also in two of them (Ja and Jd), and the Book of the Divine Cow in yet another (Jf). In the burial hall itself, parts of the *Amduat* were mixed with elements of the Book of Gates. A tunnel of the kind found in KV17 may be suggested by the pattern of collapse of one of the walls of the hall.[112] The mummy of Rameses II joined that of Rameses I in the tomb of Sethy I early in the Twenty-first Dynasty, all three burials being ultimately moved to TT320.

The memorial temple of Rameses II, known today as the Ramesseum (pl. LXVa; fig. 21b),[113] lay between the Eighteenth Dynasty temples of Amenhotep II and Thutmose IV, its great enclosure containing, besides the temple itself, a chapel possibly dedicated to his mother Tuy and wife Nefertiry D, plus perhaps some royal children;[114] assessment is, however, hampered by its state of destruction. The temenos also held a large number of brick vaulted store-houses, some of which were used for burials in the Third Intermediate Period.

The temple's plan was considerably more elaborate than earlier examples of the genre – although retaining the same fundamental layout and function – additionally being built of stone throughout as against the extensive use of brick for the outer elements of most temples down to that of Sethy I. Beyond the pylon, a First Court was flanked by colonnades, that on the right supported by Osiride columns, that on the left fronting the now-standard palace. A ramp led from the First Court to the Second, flanked on the right by what was one of the largest of all Egyptian colossi, the seated figure towering 17.5m above the courtyard and weighing over a thousand tonnes.

The Second Court was surrounded on three sides by colonnades, with osiride pillars on the east and west sides and contained a number of granite colossi. Like the temple's pylon, the wall separating the two courts was decorated with scenes from the Battle of Qadesh, a feature of a number of Rameses II's temples. The west colonnade of the Second Court included another of Rameses's favourite motifs, a procession of his sons. In the following Great Hypostyle Hall, the east wall displayed scenes of war in Syria, the west, processions of princes, and the gods. The usual three complexes led from the hall, but the sanctuary areas are almost entirely destroyed.

The Ramesseum provided the blueprint for subsequent memorial temples, the next of which was that of Merenptah (fig. 21c).[115] Constructed on a smaller scale, much of its masonry was provided by the nearby temple of Amenhotep III, as were stelae and statuary (see p. 72, above). The construction of the temple had been carried out in at least two phases, one presumably beginning at the opening of the reign, and one perhaps commencing around Year 5 – perhaps after the ruin of the temple of Amenhotep III in an earthquake made its materials available for reuse. This latter phase included the replacement of the original mudbrick First Pylon with one of stone and an enlargement of certain elements of the temple structure.

Merenptah's tomb (KV8 – fig. 19i),[116] was constructed close to that of his father. It broadly conformed to the revised royal tomb layout established by the latter, but further enhanced its symmetry around the axis. Decoratively it followed what was now becoming the convention, employing the Litany of Re in the outer parts, with the remainder of the decoration centring on the *Amduat* and Book of Gates (pl. LXVb). However, it introduced a new composition into the decoration of the royal tomb, in the form of the Book of *Aker*, or the Earth, a new composition that also appeared in the Osirion at Abydos, much of the decoration of which had been carried out by Merenptah.[117]

One of the most notable features of KV8 was the number of sarcophagi employed in the royal interment, reversing the lack of such pieces during the previous two reigns. No fewer than three granite outer cases were employed, along with an alabaster outer coffin. The rectangular innermost sarcophagus coffer had actually been made for Merenptah while he had been crown prince, and had been equipped with a new lid with a recumbent figure on its upper surface when later adopted for his kingly burial. This was enclosed in a cartouche-form sarcophagus with another recumbent figure, all enclosed in a gigantic outermost rectangular sarcophagus; it seems that a casing of such huge dimensions had not initially been planned, since various decorated door-jambs had had to be cut away to allow its passage down the tomb, which were subsequently repaired with pieces of sandstone.

The outer two coffers were reduced to fragments and their floors removed entirely in antiquity. The inner sarcophagus was, however, appropriated intact and reused at Tanis for the burial of the Twenty-first Dynasty king Pasebkhanut I (see p. 108, below). The king's mummy ended up cached in KV35, resting in the trough of the coffin of Sethnakhte.

The decade following Merenptah's death saw conflict within the royal family, including a usurpation of power in Nubia and Upper Egypt by one Amenmeses from the legitimate ruler, Sethy II.[118] The latter's tomb, built close to the site of Thutmose I's KV38, was intended to have been of the same basic design as Merenptah's (fig. 22a), albeit with a yet more reduced angle of descent. This was associated with the introduction of wooden doors at the beginning of *each* passage and room of the tomb: in Merenptah's sepulchre doors were provided only at the main entrance and those of the antechamber and burial chamber.

The state of Sethy's tomb (KV15)[119] has been an important piece of evidence in a long-running debate over the exact chronology of the events of the period.[120] It had never been finished and, most importantly, its construction had been interrupted and resumed at least once before work had stopped with the king's death. Crucially, after the outermost walls of the first two corridors of the tomb had been laid out, and carved as far as part of the way through the Litany of Re in the second corridor, work stopped. This left the remainder of that composition, and the 3rd, 4th and 5th Hours of the *Amduat*, merely sketched out in red ink. At this point, the cartouches so far carved in the scenes at the entrance to the tomb (but not those in the Litany) were erased, strongly implying the overthrow of Sethy II at this point.

Decoration was later resumed, but further work was done neither on the Litany, nor on carving the other decoration that had been sketched out prior to the interruption of work. Rather, the erased cartouches were reinstated and work re-started by adorning the pillared hall with some low-quality relief-work that contrasts very strongly with the fine style seen in the outer parts of the tomb; this was not, however, ever finished. This second cessation of work will undoubtedly have coincided with the king's death and the urgent need to prepare the tomb to receive a burial. Thus, the corridor leading from the pillared hall was converted into a burial chamber through the addition of some crude paintings and the introduction of what would have been the innermost of a nest of sarcophagi (pl. LXVIa).

Presumably at the same time, the planned well-room was painted with two-dimensional representations of the three-dimensional statuettes of the king and deities that are typically included amongst the furnishings of New Kingdom royal burials. Such paintings are unique to KV15, and one wonders whether their depiction implies that actual statuettes were unavailable at the time of the burial. A mummy anciently labelled as that of Sethy II was found in the KV35 cache.[121]

The usurping Amenmeses did not take over Sethy's tomb, but began a new tomb of very similar design (fig. 22b) in the central area of the Valley (KV10).[122] When abandoned on Amenmeses's defeat, it had reached beyond the four-pillared hall, with the decoration carved at least as far as that hall. The subsequent treatment of the tomb was most singular. In most cases where a monarch had become a *persona non grata*, their names and figures were excised from their monuments, but other decorative elements left intact. In KV10, however, the entire decoration was sliced from the walls, often leaving ghostly outlines on the surface, especially in those places where raised relief had been employed (pl. LXVIb). The effect of this technique was that in many cases the king's cartouches remained readable on the tomb's walls and pillars – yet were no longer physically there. The best explanation would seem to be that the physical removal of the sacred images and symbols was intended to 'turn off' the magic of the tomb, just as the earlier approach of adding such images and symbols after the burial had taken place seems to have been intended to 'turn on' the magical machine represented by a Egyptian sepulchre.

The inner parts of the tomb were later replastered and redecorated for two royal ladies, Takhat and Baketwernel, a sarcophagus lid usurped for a Queen Takhat also being present in the tomb. Their relationships and precise dating remain unclear:[123] though Amenmeses's mother was named Takhat, it is quite possible that she and the KV10 Takhat(s) were simply homonyms (Takhat was a common name) and there is no reason why the KV10 women could not actually date to the Twentieth Dynasty.

No mortuary temple of Amenmeses has thus far been noted, or anything attributable to his rival, Sethy II, although various foundation deposit plaques of the latter are known from Western Thebes, apparently from secondary contexts or without any context. Since the original ownership of the temples of their immediate successors is guaranteed by foundation deposits found in situ, the foundations of the temple(s) presumably remain hidden under the sand of Western Thebes.

Sethy II was succeeded by Siptah, for whom was founded tomb KV47 (fig. 22c),[124] a little downhill from KV15. Once again, the tomb's plan essentially follows Merenptah's prototype, and came far closer to structural completion than any of the intervening royal sepulchres, with decoration in place at least as far as the entrance to the burial chamber; however, it is unclear whether the latter was ever adorned, as the tomb has suffered severely from flooding, almost the entire stone surface of the floor, walls and ceiling beyond the four-pillared hall having been destroyed. The outer galleries are, however, in almost perfect condition, displaying the now-usual basic decorative scheme, with most of the first two galleries taken up by the Litany of Re, with a number of divine vignettes at the end of the second passage. The ceiling of the first part of the tomb is also in a good state, but from the third corridor onwards all is ruin (pl. LXIIa). Some fragments of the *Amduat* survive, but little more: most of the remainder of the tomb has the aspect of a natural cave.

The burial hall was initially started directly beyond antechamber I, but work was stopped when the quarrymen broke through into tomb KV32 (Queen Tiaa – pp. 80-1, above) on the other side of the bluff into which the tomb was cut. The cavity produced so far became an additional vestibule (J1), beyond which a fresh start was made. The definitive burial hall (J2) omitted the usual rear range of pillars, but the crypt contained the usual granite cartouche-form sarcophagus with a recumbent figure on its lid, plus many calcite fragments, including the king's outer coffin and canopic chest. However, confusion was subsequently sown by floodwaters washing calcite and other debris into KV47 from KV32, making the attribution of some material problematic.

Throughout the tomb, the king's cartouches were erased and later reinstated (pl. LXVIIb). The erasures were probably carried out around the time of Siptah's death, at which point Queen Tawosret, the widow of Sethy II and hitherto the young Siptah's regent, took full pharaonic titles and continued the regnal years of Siptah. She was soon faced by the rebellion of the founder-to-be of the Twentieth Dynasty, Sethnakhte, who overthrew her some two years later, and following his victory was probably responsible for the reinstatement of Siptah's names.[125] The mummy of Siptah was later moved to KV35.

The memorial temple of Siptah lay between the Eighteenth Dynasty monuments of Thutmose III and Amenhotep II, north of the Ramesseum (fig. 21d). Nothing now survives apart from the foundation trenches of its rear part. Jar sealings from the site indicate that work was going on during the king's third and fourth regnal years. The portion of the plan that survives shows that two hypostyle halls were intended to precede the usual threefold sanctuaries, but little else can be said, given the loss of the outer parts. Foundation deposits named not only the king, but the Chancellor Bay, who had played a key role in the king's accession and was a power behind the throne until his execution in Year 5.

The prominence of a noble such as Bay in these deposits is unusual, and still more so was his possession of a tomb of royal proportions and design in the Valley of the Kings (KV13),[126] close to the tombs of Sethy II, Tawosret and Siptah. The overall decorative scheme seems to have closely resembled that of the tomb of Tawosret as queen and regent (see pp. 92-3, below). The original constructional work in KV13 stopped at the end of the corridor after its pillared hall, but during the Twentieth Dynasty it was continued for the burial of two princes (see. p. 104).

As king, Tawosret extended a tomb (KV14)[127] that had been begun for her early in her husband's reign and continued and extended during the regency (fig. 22d). In the outer parts of the tomb, Tawosret's images were modified into those of a king (pl. LXVIIIa), while those of Siptah were renamed as representing Sethy II; no other substantive changes were made. However, at the rear of the tomb, beyond the original burial chamber, a long corridor was driven further into the hillside leading to a new, even larger, burial chamber. Decoratively, the new corridor was adorned with the Book of *Amduat*, the ultimate burial chamber with the Book of Gates although, in contrast to the superlative quality of the relief in the outer parts of the tomb, the extension's poor and hurried style shows clear evidence of haste. Tawosret's queenly sarcophagus was replaced by a more massive item in typical kingly style,[128] the original piece ultimately being reused for burying a Twentieth Dynasty prince in KV13. Tawosret's tomb was reused within a few years for the burial of her conqueror, Sethnakhte and, given the circumstances of her vacating the throne, it seems unlikely that she was ever actually buried there.

To go with her enlarged tomb, Tawosret founded a memorial temple (fig. 21f)[129] just south of the ancient sanctuary of Thutmose IV. Although almost nothing survives of the building apart from the foundation trenches, foundation deposit plaques make it clear that the structure was founded only after Tawosret had become king. Although it may not have been completed, the temple seems to have been considerably advanced prior to its eventual dismantlement to reuse the stone. The recoverable plan shows the temple to have been fronted by a pylon, with a first court probably colonnaded on the right and left, with the usual complex of halls and sanctuaries beyond.

Since the foundation blocks are dated to Tawosret's 8th (and probably final) year and that no temple of her successor Sethnakhte is known, it is possible that much of the construction might actually have been carried out during Sethnakhte's reign. While no definite trace of his name survives, that of Tawosret is known only from the foundations, and any trace of this putative Sethnakhte-phase will have been lost in the utter destruction of the walls and ceilings of the temple.

Royal Family Tombs of the Nineteenth Dynasty

The Nineteenth Dynasty saw a major change in provision for members of the royal family, with decorated rock-cut tombs starting to be provided for the most senior scions, which were in some cases miniature versions of the sepulchres of the kings of the period. With a few exceptions (e.g. the Pyramid Texts in queens' pyramids of the late Old Kingdom), the substructures of earlier royal family tombs were almost universally unadorned; now extensive decoration is often seen. Their locations are also more focused than had been the situation in the Eighteenth Dynasty, with the Valleys of the Kings and the Queens sheltering most of the known royal family tombs of the Ramesside Period.

In the Valley of the Queens (map 14; pl. LXIa) the earliest of this new generation of tombs to be identified is that of Sitre (QV38), mother of Sethy I,[130] indicating a move from the mid-Eighteenth Dynasty practice of burying Great Wives in the Valley of the Kings. QV38 was simple in form and unfinished, but far more elaborate was QV80, that of Tuy, mother of Rameses II.[131] This had a four-pillared hall, with an antechamber and connecting stairway, as did the tomb of Nefertiry D (QV66),[132] which also preserves a rich decoration in painted relief (pl. LXVIIIb). This largely centred on the queen in the company of the gods, together with the Book of Gates. The burial chamber had contained a granite sarcophagus of which only the lid survived, the first example of such a stone monument provided for a queen-consort since the Middle Kingdom (it was only as queen-regent Hatshepsut had a stone sarcophagus).

The daughter-wives of Rameses II, together with Henutmire (probably his sister-wife), all had tombs in the Valley, although nothing is known of the sepulchre of Nefertiry's counterpart as Great Wife, Isetneferet A, who may perhaps have been buried at Saqqara, where her best-known son, Khaemwaset C, had his monuments (see below). Those of Bintanat (QV71),[133] Henutmire (QV75)[134] and Meryetamun E (QV68)[135] were similar in design to QV66, but with much more modest unpillared burial chambers. There is also another tomb in the Valley, QV40,[136] which belonged to the daughter-wife of a king; its cartouches were, however, apparently never filled in, and the identity and precise date of the lady remain uncertain, although the style of the decoration suggests the time of Rameses II.

Of the sons of Rameses II, a number had places allocated in a vast sepulchre in the Valley of the Kings (KV5 – fig. 23a).[137] It seems to have been an extension of a much smaller tomb of the Eighteenth Dynasty, the rear part of which was enlarged into a sixteen-pillared hall, work perhaps begun in Year 19 of Rameses II, on the basis of a graffito on the roof. A large room on the left-hand side of the hall seems to have been a pillared burial chamber, the storeroom of which contained the remains of dozens of storage jars and the bones of food offerings. Another pillared room on the right may also have been intended for a burial, but a T-shaped set of corridors at the back of the main pillared hall gave access to no fewer than fifty-six small rooms of unknown purpose.

On the opposite wall, two further corridors plunged into the bedrock, lined with yet more small chambers, leading to further pillared rooms and descending passages: the total number of passages exceeded 130. Much of the tomb was once decorated, with the outer rooms showing Rameses II and some of his sons in acts of worship or before tables of offerings. The T-shaped corridor was also decorated, tableaux of the gods and offerings to them lying between the chamber-doorways. Depictions or funerary equipment of only five royal sons have yet been found, together with a limited quantity of human remains, making it unclear exactly how many burials were made in this huge tomb.

Of other sons, it is likely that Khaemwaset C was buried at Saqqara, where so many of his monuments lay (he was High Priest of Ptah at Memphis), including what seems to have been a memorial chapel at the western extremity of Abusir-South (map 4).[138] Other offspring of Rameses II were also probably buried in northern Egypt, perhaps at Per-Rameses, the new east Delta residence city established by the king, or at the harem-town of Gurob, where Prince Rameses-meryamun-Nebweben was interred in a coffin originally made for Rameses I before his accession.[139] This is likely to have applied to most of the known royal family members of the remainder of the Nineteenth Dynasty, who have no known tombs at Thebes.[140]

The principal exception to this is Tawosret, for whom a tomb (KV14)[141] was begun alongside that of her husband Sethy II in the latter's Year 2. However, work was soon stopped (presumably owing to Amenmeses's interregnum) and was not apparently resumed until the beginning of Tawosret's regency for Siptah. As begun, and resumed, the tomb was intended as a reduced version of a 'standard' royal tomb, but close to the end of Siptah's reign, a new, larger, burial chamber (Ka/b) was begun just beyond the eight-pillared hall (pl. LXIXa; fig. 22d[J]) that had been initially intended to hold the queen's sarcophagus.

In the tomb's decoration, Tawosret was everywhere prominent (e.g. pl.

LXVIIIa), occupying pillars and the usual positions in offering scenes; however, figures of a king were also initially incorporated into the scheme, originally Siptah, but later altered to Sethy II. The overall decorative scheme of the tomb comprised, apart from such vignettes, extracts from the Book of the Dead in the outer corridors, and the Book of Gates in the queenly burial chamber. As noted above, on Tawosret's becoming king, the tomb was significantly enlarged and new wholly-kingly inner corridors and a burial chamber added.

The Twentieth Dynasty

The founder of the Twentieth Dynasty, Sethnakhte, began his intended tomb, KV11 (fig. 22e),[142] in the central area of the Valley of the Kings, some way from the tombs of his immediate predecessors, but directly adjacent to Amenmeses's KV10. Its outer corridors adopted the same minimal angles of descent introduced by Sety II and followed by Siptah, and which would be a feature of all remaining kings' tombs to be constructed in the Valley of the Kings (pl. LXIXb).

Although a pair of unique cow-headed pilasters flanked the very entrance, decoration otherwise began in a conventional manner, with the customary solar disk and kneeling goddesses on the lintel, and scenes showing the king's greeting to the netherworld by Re-Horakhty at the beginning of corridor B. The rest of this corridor and the following C were adorned with the Litany of Re and the usual subsidiary figures, but the element beyond was carved with figures of the king before deities, rather than the usual *Amduat*. However, this seems not to have been a theological statement, but was a result of a constructional incident that led to a large vestibule (D) being created at this point in the tomb.

This was the outcome of the cutting of the nascent corridor D being interrupted by its collision (at Da) with room Faa of the pre-existing KV10. As a result, the axis of KV11 had to be shifted to the right to allow construction to continue, thus creating the aforementioned rectangular vestibule. Decoration of this room had been completed as far as the doorjambs of the entrance to corridor Db before Sethnakhte's death, as is indicated by the presence of his cartouches there, but stonecutting must have proceeded considerably further by then, perhaps as far as the upper pillared hall (F); the drafting of portions of the decoration may also have extended significantly in that direction. The floor of Db was constructed with an upward slope, presumably to ensure a safe clearance between it and the ceilings of KV10.

However, while the tomb was reasonably advanced, with chamber D large enough to have accommodated, if necessary, a burial at the king's death,

Tawosret's apparently-unused KV14 seems to have represented a more attractive alternative. It was therefore appropriated for Sethnakhte's burial, albeit in some haste, presumably during the period of embalmment. Thus, while the figures of the queen in corridor B were extensively further re-cut to change them to representations of Sethnakhte (pl. LXVIIIa), most of the remaining figures of Tawosret were simply covered with plaster and just Sethnakhte's names and titles drawn in black on the unpainted plaster (pl. LXXa); only occasionally was the king's actual figure sketched in outline. The names on the sarcophagus were erased and re-cut for its new owner. Although the inner coffin of Sethnakhte was found (reused) in KV35, his mummy has never been identified.

As noted above, it is possible that Sethnakhte took over Tawosret's memorial temple, although no proof exists. On the other hand, his son and successor, Rameses III, would soon found the last of the New Kingdom memorial temples to be fully completed, and which remains the best-preserved temple of its kind.

This structure, erected adjacent to the temple of Ay and Horemheb at Medinet Habu (fig. 21g; pl. LXXI),[143] was designed essentially as an enlarged copy of the Ramesseum. It was placed adjacent to an Eighteenth Dynasty temple, which was enclosed within a new mudbrick wall erected as part of Rameses III's project, the wall including the unique eastern High Gate, the principal entrance. This incorporated features of Syrian *migdol*-fortresses, and was externally adorned by images of the king smiting his enemies, while the rooms within its ramparts were decorated with domestic scenes, of the king and his womenfolk engaged in leisure activities.

Rameses III's actual memorial temple was fronted by a First Pylon bearing the usual 'smiting' scenes. Complementing these, the exterior walls of the temple were devoted to the king's physical prowess, either on the hunting field or in battle, and generosity to the gods. Their sequence began on the rear wall of the building, where one finds an account of a Nubian campaign, continuing on the northern walls with depictions of the campaigns in which the king defended Egypt from two aggressions by Libyans and one by the 'Sea Peoples' of the Aegean. The decoration of the southern exterior of the temple started at the First Pylon with a series of scenes of the king hunting antelope, wild donkeys and bulls. Then, covering almost the whole length of the temple was a vast festival calendar, listing the various daily feasts and services celebrated in the temple, together with the offering involved on each occasion.

Inside, a palace abuts the southern exterior wall of the First Court, while the north side of the court had seven piers, each fronted by a colossal statue of the king. The decoration of the court featured the celebratory aftermath of battles depicted on the exterior of the temple, along with those referring to festivals that took place in the temple. The Second Pylon bore 'historical' texts and scenes of captives, the Second Court to which it gave access being colonnaded on all four sides, its walls adorned with scenes of divine festivals.

The portico on the west side of the court was fronted by two rows of pillars, the outermost originally bearing engaged osirid figures of the king. The upper parts of its walls were decorated with scenes taken from the royal coronation ritual, but the lower sections contained almost mirror-image processions of the king's children, on either side of the doorway leading into the First Hypostyle Hall. This latter motif was explicitly copied from the Ramesseum, but the figures were not labelled until after Rameses III's death, and then only some of them. This lack of names is found elsewhere in the temple as well.

Beyond the two open courts, the main (Amun) axis of the temple is in a poor condition, the hypostyle halls having been denuded down to the lowest drums of their supporting columns. The First Hypostyle Hall had a series of small shrines along its northern side and in the south-west corner, while the Second Hypostyle Hall gave access to the three principal cult-complexes of the temple – of Amun, Mut and Khonsu (centre), the dead king (south – without any provision for the king's father) and Re (north). The rear section thus represented the ultimate completed development of the classic New Kingdom mortuary temple, the king's complex including a depiction (in fig. 21g [A]) of the Fields of *Iaru* from the Book of the Dead (pl. LXXb), a feature not known from earlier royal offering places.

Rameses III continued the unfinished tomb KV11 in his own name, the extant cartouches of Sethnakhte being surcharged by those of his son. In addition, a series of side-chambers were added, opening off corridors B and C, resulting in the destruction of some existing elements of the Litany of Re, with substitute texts added to the doorjambs of the new rooms. These were decorated with images of food production, boats, craftsmen and musicians, of kinds that are otherwise unknown in the Valley.

In contrast, corridor Db was conventionally adorned with the *Amduat*, well-room E with images of deities and upper hall F with the Book of Gates and the shrine of Osiris, as had been the case since the time of Sety I. Similarly, the Opening of the Mouth once again featured in corridor G, before giving access to a pair of antechambers (H and I) adorned with images of divinities. Beyond lay the burial chamber, with the central transverse crypt of the type introduced under Rameses II, but with the sarcophagus placed along, rather than across the axis – a feature continued in later Twentieth Dynasty tombs.[144] Although the majority of the decoration was taken from the Book of Gates, the room also contained scenes from the Book of the

Earth, previously found in Merenptah's KV8. Its side-chambers contained a variety of decorative elements, including depictions of the Fields of Iaru (Jd) and the Book of the Divine Cow (Jc). Various further elements were placed on the walls of the small rooms directly beyond the burial chamber.

The sarcophagus in which Rameses III was buried was of the same basic design as that of his immediate predecessors. However, the decoration of its coffer and details of its lid were more reminiscent of the sarcophagi of Merenptah, and it has been suggested that Rameses III's monument may have been begun as the external sarcophagus of Sethy II, not used in his makeshift burial and eventually finished for the later king.[145] The king's mummy was found in TT320.

As completed, KV11 represented a logical enlargement of the tomb-type instigated by Rameses II and Merenptah, with the exception of the aforementioned side-chambers in the outer corridors. However, the tomb of Rameses III was to be the last royal tomb in the Valley of the Kings to be fully completed and decorated in accordance with this design, the sepulchres that followed were all truncated to a greater or lesser degree.

The tomb of Rameses IV (KV2, fig. 22f)[146] was started with the apparent intention of surpassing KV11 in size, the corridors of KV2 being nearly 20% wider than those laid out under Sethnakhte: the corridor-width established for KV2 would then become the standard through to the end of royal tomb building in the Valley of the Kings. However, the burial chamber of KV2 would ultimately occupy the space where one would normally have found the four-pillared upper hall, and be a relatively modest square room (pl. LXXIIa), rather than the monumental pillared rectangular hall of the post-Rameses II 'standard' design (figs. 19, 22). A papyrus plan of the tomb as completed survives, with notations showing the ancient names of various parts of a Rameside royal tomb.[147]

Nevertheless, this seems to have been something more than a simple hurried finishing-off of the tomb following the king's premature death, as was the case with (e.g.) Sethy II's KV15 (cf. p. 89), because the rooms beyond the burial chamber indicate that no substantive progress can have been made towards any descent below the embryonic upper pillared hall when the plan was changed. Accordingly, it would appear that a conscious decision to abbreviate the plan of the tomb was made before any major work had been done beyond well-room E. The burial chamber was given a flat ceiling at the same level as that room, but additional height was provided by the construction of an unbroken slope that ran from the middle of corridor D into the first part of the burial chamber. Corridor D was also unusual in that its central section was vaulted, something not found in any other tomb in the Valley. As for the reasons for this truncation, it may be noted that the initiation of the tomb had been delayed into the king's second regnal year; the relatively advanced age of the king may also have suggested some recasting of the design as time went by, in spite of a bolstering of Deir el-Medina manpower soon after the beginning of work.

The decoration of the tomb began as usual with the king, Re-Horakhty (although for once only on the left wall) and the Litany of Re, but introduced the new Book of Caverns to the repertoire in the third corridor. The *Amduat* and the Opening of the Mouth were, however, omitted, although the loss of the former may have been for reasons of space rather than for any conceptual reasons, as it reappeared in the tombs of Rameses VI and IX. The Book of Gates occupied the burial chamber walls, with the ceiling providing the only Valley of the Kings example of the very rare Book of Nut. Increasing haste by the decorators can be detected in the fact that most of the burial chamber and the rooms beyond were adorned in paint only, rather than painted relief.

The burial chamber of KV2 was dominated by a gigantic granite sarcophagus of the usual recumbent-figure design, placed along the axis of the room, and accompanied by a set of similarly-outsize canopic jars.[148] That the sarcophagus was once surrounded by a series of shrines is indicated by the aforementioned detailed plan of the tomb on papyrus.[149] While an accurate document, it does not appear to have been a working blueprint, and its purpose remains obscure. The king's mummy was eventually moved to KV35.

The situation concerning Rameses IV's mortuary temple is somewhat complex, since three unfinished structures at Thebes-West have revealed the king's names. Two lie in the area of the lower end of the causeways leading up to the temples of Deir el-Bahari (the Asasif). Of one, only two column bases and a single foundation deposit survived. Rameses IV changed his prenomen in his second year, and the use of both forms in the deposit allow it to be dated around the change.[150] The second temple lies some way to the south and was intended to follow the basic plan of Rameses III's Medinet Habu edifice, but one and a half times larger (fig. 16; pl. XLIX).[151] Rameses IV's name appeared in a series of foundation deposits, although the never-finished structure itself yielded only the names of Rameses V and VI, indicating that the unfinished structure was appropriated in turn by these kings as their memorial temple, the latest known structure of its kind at Thebes.

A third west bank foundation was begun just southwest of the by-now demolished mortuary temple of Amenhotep III (fig. 18).[152] Its scanty remains have never been excavated, but its modest dimensions may suggest that it could have been completed, to serve as the cult-centre of Rameses IV that we know to have functioned soon after his death. One might speculate that the decision to abandon the gigantic Asasif temple coincided with one to scale down the royal tomb, to ensure that a complete burial complex was available to the king. On the other hand, a pair of foundation deposits in the name of Rameses IV was found in the northwest corner of the temple-enclosure of Ay and Horemheb, suggesting that something more expansive had been contemplated at one point.

The other side of the papyrus with the plan of the tomb of Rameses IV preserves details of the measurements of the outer corridors of KV9,[153] the next tomb to be begun in the Valley (fig. 22g).[154] Its original intended occupant was Rameses V, and the data in the papyrus extend as far as the well-room (E), which is also the part of the tomb furthest from the entrance in which that king's cartouches can be detected. That work had actually reached just beyond the upper pillared hall (F) before Rameses V's death in his Year 4 is shown by an ostracon dated to that year. It is unclear where Rameses V was actually buried, as KV9 would be continued as the sepulchre of his successor, Rameses VI, with no architectural provision for a second interment. That it took some time to make alternative provisions is indicated by the fact that Rameses V's actual interment did not take place until Year 2 of Rameses VI.[155] This burial presumably occurred somewhere in the Valley of the Kings, given that Rameses V's mummy was later cached in KV35.

Although the outer part of the tomb had been entirely decorated by Rameses V, it appears that his plaster was removed and decoration begun anew in parallel with the resumed cutting of inner part of KV9 by Rameses VI. The plan for this continuation of the tomb was apparently re-cast on a considerably enhanced scale during Rameses VI's Year 2/3, when work was re-started on the tomb, with the final decorative scheme deviating greatly from earlier standards.

Thus, although the decoration of corridor B was as usual begun with the king's reception by Re-Horakhty, the latter was now accompanied by Osiris, and the usual Litany of Re and extracts from the *Amduat* in corridors B through D were replaced by a combination of the Book of Gates and the Book of Caverns. In addition, astronomical ceilings, previously specific to the burial hall, were employed from the very entrance as far as the upper pillared hall F, being supplemented in corridor D and the room E by the Book of the Night. Room E also lost its time-hallowed scenes of the king and divinities in favour of more of the Gates/Caverns mix, which also extended into hall F. In corridors G and H, the Opening of the Mouth tableaux found in this part of a tomb down to the time of Rameses III were replaced by the returning *Amduat*, the ceilings being adorned with the Books of the Day and the Night and a set of cryptographic texts that continue into the antechamber (I). That room's walls were covered with a mixture of the Book of the Dead and images of the king and the gods. Finally, the walls of the burial hall were entirely devoted to the first extant full version of the Book of the Earth, its ceiling to the Books of the Day and Night (pl. LXXIIb). This comprehensive revision of the mythological environment of the tomb has been interpreted as a demotion of Osirian conceptions in favour of those centring on the sun-god and Amun,[156] although it is interesting that many of these changes were reversed under Rameses IX.

During its construction, KV9's axis, at the end of corridor H, intersected that of the anonymous Eighteenth Dynasty KV12. This required a slope to be incorporated into the floor of this corridor, to permit the antechamber and the burial chamber to be cut comfortably below the floor of KV12. The breach having been closed, it received magical protection through a unique vignette that sealed it via the fire of the sun god.

The burial chamber of KV9 is structurally incomplete, the rear row of columns not having been released from the matrix, and the rearmost parts of the chamber never begun, although almost all its surfaces are fully decorated. Thus, like the tomb of Rameses IV, the plan appears to have undergone an intentional truncation, rather than an emergency one occasioned by the premature demise of the king. Substantive quarrying may have been terminated in Year 6, nearly two years before Rameses's death, when most of the copper tools used by the Deir el-Medina workforce were withdrawn. As in the immediately preceding tombs, the sarcophagus lay on the axis of the chamber. Its lid has never been found, while the coffer was broken in antiquity, as was the granite outer coffin that had now replaced the calcite type of earlier reigns.

The tomb seems to have been entered by robbers within two decades of the interment, perhaps via KV12 (see map 13), as some shabtis of Rameses VI were found outside the entrance of that tomb, where they had doubtless been discarded by the robbers. This penetration is probably to be dated to Year 9 of Rameses IX by a graffito on the ceiling of the burial chamber, perhaps written by those responsible for re-sealing the breach from KV12. The royal mummy ended up in KV35.

The locations of KV9 and KV2 were rather different from most earlier tombs, as they were cut into prominent tongues of rock overlooking the main path through the centre of the Valley, in marked contrast to the inconspicuous locations chosen for the earliest tombs there. The development of entrances that were not easily susceptible to obliteration had begun during the Nineteenth Dynasty as a concomitant of the extension of decoration to the very entrance of tombs, and by the latter part of the Twentieth Dynasty it is possible that 'pylons' of rubble were arranged to flank gateway-entrances that lay several metres above the contemporary ground level. A similar location was chosen for Rameses VII's KV1,[157] although to find such a spot the entrance to the tomb would have to lie some way back from the main axis of the Valley and a significant distance north-east of its core area.

Although begun on the same scale as the tombs of Rameses VII's immediate predecessors, the plan of KV1 was even more truncated than KV2, comprising only an entrance corridor, a burial chamber and a small room and niche beyond (fig. 22h; pl. LXXIIIa). Unfortunately, no documentary material survives to account for the degree of curtailment of the plan, given that Rameses VII's reign equalled in length the tenures of Rameses IV and VI, both of whom achieved significantly more in the time available.

On the other hand, the decoration was complete, and showed a number of changes in detail from earlier tombs. In particular, the king became an active player in the scenes at the entrance, making offerings to the greeting deity, who was now seated, rather than standing, as found in preceding sepulchres. In addition, while the left-hand god was, as usual, Re-Horakhty, on the right he was Ptah-Sokar-Osiris, each tableau also now being enclosed in a shrine. Beyond, the left wall had the first part of the Book of Gates, the right the first part of the Book of Caverns, both clearly intended to invoke the remainders of these compositions, excluded for lack of space. In the burial chamber beyond, scenes from the Book of the Earth occupied the lower right wall, but the remainder of the side-walls contained images that were not apparently taken directly from any identifiable 'book'. While the vaulted ceiling of the burial chamber was astronomical, the outer corridor reverted to pre-Rameses VI patterns, in that it was adorned with images of vultures with outstretched wings.

In addition to his representations at the entrance, the king also appeared in the corridor just before the entrance to the burial chamber, on its end-wall, flanking the door into the inner chamber, and on the side-walls of that room. In the first case, he was shown as Osiris, receiving the ministrations of the *Iwn-mwt.f* priest (the latter's first appearance since the Nineteenth Dynasty), in the second in a solar form and in the third offering to Osiris. The sarcophagus in KV1 took a new form, with a rock-cut coffer and very high lid, the whole construct also incorporating locations for the canopic jars.

No tomb is known for Rameses VIII, nor has any of his funerary equipment ever come to light. It has been suggested that KV19 (see p. 105, below), begun for a prince Sethirkopeshef who may have been Rameses VIII before his accession, might have been continued as Rameses VIII's kingly sepulchre, but clearly was not used as such, as it was finally decorated for prince Mentuhirkopeshef C, son of Rameses IX. Given Rameses VIII's very short reign – perhaps a year at most – it is likely that the construction of any new monumental tomb would have progressed minimally, at best. Assuming that he was indeed buried at Thebes, rather than in the north, where the kings were now generally resident, it would seem probable that he was buried in a small tomb that may have been so utterly plundered as to now be unidentifiable – or may, just possibly, remain undiscovered.

Any new beginning made in the name of Rameses VIII would probably have been continued for Rameses IX as his KV6 (fig. 22i).[158] The tomb was once again in the central area, occupying the last prominent tongue of rock in the Valley, although perhaps a problematic site on the grounds of the numerous tombs already in the area, given that Rameses VII had implicitly eschewed it in favour of the remote site actually used for KV1.

Although the king was to rule for some two decades, progress in the construction of this tomb seems to have been slow or intermittent. The design was once again intentionally truncated as compared to the 'standard' plan: although the descent from the upper pillared hall was achieved, a much-reduced burial chamber was constructed directly beyond, without any intervening corridors and chambers.

There was in addition a clear discontinuity in the decorative process in and beyond the second corridor (C – pl. LXXIIIb), with the third corridor, well-room and burial chamber (D, E and J) adorned with work purely in paint or in lower quality relief. This combination of techniques is rather curious, as their use is intermixed on the same wall. It has been argued that this later phase of work is to be dated to the period following the king's death, although it is also possible that it was attributable to a hiatus in the construction process, followed by a need to expedite work, perhaps owing to the king's poor health. It is also clear that work in the Valley was further hampered by ongoing bandit attacks from the western desert, a problem that would endure for some time.

As far as the actual composition of the decoration of KV6 is concerned, the tableaux of the king before the sun-god at the entrance were enshrined in the manner introduced by Rameses VII. However, the gods were once again standing, and while on the left Re-Horakhty (accompanied by Osiris, following the example of KV9) stood with the quadruple-ram-headed Amun-Re-Horakhty, supported by the Goddess of the West.

Beyond, the Litany of Re was reintroduced into the first two corridors and the *Amduat* into the third, supplemented by images of the king and the gods and an 'enigmatic' composition, although the Litany was now accompanied by elements from the Book of Caverns and the Book of the Dead. The burial chamber was given a combination of vignettes from the Books of Caverns, the Earth and the *Amduat* on the walls and the Book of the Night on the ceiling. The mix and choice of elements from the various funerary compositions within the tomb of Rameses IX were unique, and included some texts and scenes that are not found elsewhere.

Architecturally, KV6 reintroduced side-rooms into the first corridor, although these seem never to have been finished or decorated. In its truncated form, the burial chamber was relatively small but seems to have been dominated by a large sarcophagus installation, the exact form of which is uncertain, since nothing remains apart from a two-level cutting in the floor (pl. LXXIVa). The tomb of Rameses IX appears to have been the last royal tomb in the Valley of the Kings to be employed for a primary burial: his is also the latest New Kingdom pharaoh's mummy to have been found in a royal cache, in his case in TT320.

KV18, the tomb of Rameses X,[159] was cut adjacent to the earlier tombs of Rameses I and Sethy I, a site unlike the prominent positions employed by the preceding kings and probably reflecting the increasingly limited number of sites appropriate for the large Ramesside tombs left in the Valley (pl. LXXIVb). Work on the tomb was interrupted frequently, and during the king's third (final) regnal year, only one working day in five actually saw work on it, including interruptions caused by the incursion of foreign bandits, something also attested under Rameses IX.

Such conditions were clearly not conducive to royal tomb construction, and the state of Rameses X's sepulchre when work was discontinued reflects this. Only the entrance to the tomb, the first corridor and a small fragment of the second had been cut (fig. 22j), while decoration was limited to the entrance-lintel and the initial tableaux on each wall of the first corridor. The latter employed the same distribution of deities as the tomb of Rameses IX, but with an additional figure of the king directly inside the entrance to the tomb. There is no indication of the tomb's having been made ready for even an improvised interment, and thus it is unclear where the king was buried, his posthumous fate (and perhaps even demise) probably having been influenced by the tumultuous state into which the country seems to have been falling at the end of Rameses X's reign.[160]

The final royal tomb to be constructed in the Valley was KV4, the intended sepulchre of Rameses XI.[161] Unlike many of the immediately preceding tombs, KV4 seems not to have undergone any significant truncation of its plan (fig. 22k), having a large four-pillared burial chamber at the end of a set of corridors that are the widest and highest found in any royal tomb, continuing a new trend of enlargement also found in KV18 (pl. LXXVa). On the other hand, the inner rooms were by no means complete, with a number of elements only partly released from the rock matrix.

Compared with KV9, the previous tomb to approach structural completion, the upper pillared hall (F) was rectangular rather than square, with the longest dimension along the axis of the tomb, resulting in a deeper stairway leading down towards the burial chamber. The latter diverges even further from previous post-Rameses II practice, abandoning the usual pattern of eight square pillars in favour of four rectangular piers. In addition, a deep rectangular pit in the centre of the hall replaced the sunken crypt, standard since the time of Amenhotep II. Unfortunately, while foundation deposits of Rameses XI were found at the corners of the pit, the exact intended mode of burial is unknown as the tomb was never occupied by the king, the shaft containing debris apparently from the restoration/recycling of earlier funerary equipment during the Twenty-first Dynasty, together with an intrusive burial of the mid-Twenty-second Dynasty.

Although the cutting of the tomb was complete in the outer corridors (contrasting with the unfinished state of the pillared halls), decoration was hardly begun, being restricted to red-ink sketches in the first corridor. These indicate a development of the arrangement of material glimpsed in KV18. On the left wall, the king was shown twice, the second time before a raptor-headed Amun-Re-Horkahty. On the right wall, the king was first shown alone and then within a shrine before quadruple-ram-headed Amun-Re-Horakhty, supported by the Goddess of the West. Beyond her figure was a solar disk, perhaps intended to introduce the Litany of Re, no traces of which, however, survive.

As in the case of Rameses X, there is no indication of where the eleventh Rameses was finally interred. However, it appears that Panedjem I had briefly contemplated taking over KV4 for his own, as on the left-hand wall of KV4, just beyond the point where the last sketch for Rameses XI's decoration had been applied, the raptor-headed figure of Amun-Re-Horakhty was duplicated, together with the accompanying text containing the god's speech, albeit amended by the substitution of Panedjem's names for those of Rameses XI. This can be dated to very soon after Panedjem transitioned from being High Priest of Amun to King, since here he followed the preceding high-priest-cum-king Herihor in using 'High Priest of Amun' as his prenomen, rather than his definitive Khakheperre. However, this new phase of decoration was, like Rameses's original work, left as a simple ink-sketch and the tomb was never occupied by Panedjem, whose original place of interment remains unknown.

Royal family tombs of the Twentieth Dynasty

The Valley of the Queens continued in use during the Twentieth Dynasty, a large number of tombs belonging to members of the family of Rameses III being cut there, largely concentrated in the southern part (map 14; pl. LXXVb). Curiously, the two sepulchres belonging to his wives were decorated under their sons, rather than their husband. QV52, of Tyti, the mother of Rameses IV,[162] the better-preserved of the two, comprised a corridor leading to a burial chamber with three annexes, and was decorated with images of the deceased and deities. QV51, of Rameses VI's mother, Iset

D,[163] was of a similar layout, albeit with only two annexes and some differences in the arrangement of the decoration.

The wife of Rameses IV, Tentopet, was apparently the ultimate owner of QV74, although the plan of the tomb is very similar to those of the womenfolk of Rameses II (and dissimilar to those of other Twentieth Dynasty queens), and thus was probably usurped.[164] QV73, now decorated for a female whose name and titles were never filled in,[165] has a plan that was clearly intended to be the same as Tentopet's, and must therefore be of the same date as to construction – and perhaps ultimate ownership. In connection with the latter, it may be noted that, as remarked above, none of the names of Rameses III's family was filled in during the king's lifetime in his memorial temple. Also probably to be dated to the Twentieth Dynasty is the usurpation of KV10 for a Takhat (or Takhats) and a Baketwerel (see p. ***, above).

A whole series of tombs in the Valley of the Queens seems to have been commissioned simultaneously by Rameses III for his sons: QV42 (Parehirwenemef B);[166] QV43 (Sethhirkopeshef B);[167] QV44 (Khaemwaset E);[168] QV53 (Rameses C);[169] QV55 (Amenhirkopeshef B).[170] Certain dedicatory inscriptions suggest that some tombs were fully decorated, but initially left nameless. A further princely tomb of the same type was constructed in the Valley of the Kings (KV3),[171] although its owner is now unknown, most of its decoration now being lost. Apart from QV42, equipped with a four-pillared burial chamber (and usurped from an unknown queen), and the presence in KV3 of a four-pillared hall at half-length, they all had broadly similar plans, with a straight axis and one or two side chambers. The decoration of all the Valley of the Queens princely tombs centred on the king introducing his sons to the gods (pl. LXXVIa), which would probably also have been the case with KV3.

Under Rameses VI, to judge from a fragmentary text in the tomb naming his wife Queen Nubkhesbed,[172] two princely burials appear to have been made in KV13, the tomb constructed for the Chancellor Bay. The figures of Bay were changed into those of a woman – presumably Nubkhesbed – and a rough extension was added. The latter contained the burial of a Prince Amenhirkopeshef, who was interred in Tawosret's queenly sarcophagus, modified for its new owner – presumably Amenhirkopesef D, a son of Rameses VI.[173] Subsequently, the burial of a Prince Montjuhirkopeshef was inserted into the main corridor of the tomb.[174] While it is possible that he was also an otherwise-unknown son of Rameses VI, he may more likely have been Montjuhirkopeshef B, known from the processions of sons of Rameses III at Medinet Habu, and conceivably the father of Rameses IX.

The last known royal family tomb of the New Kingdom is that of

Montjuhirkopeshef C, a son of Rameses IX. His tomb, KV19 in the Valley of the Kings,[175] had been founded by a Prince Sethhirkopeshef, probably a son of Rameses III (and perhaps the future Rameses VIII), possibly to replace QV43. It was decorated with scenes of Montjuhirkopeshef before the gods, but was incomplete when occupied, a rough rock-cut sarcophagus being provided in front of the unfinished end of the corridor.

Chapter 7

The Third Intermediate Period

The Twenty-first Dynasty

The end of the New Kingdom marked a fundamental change in both the Egyptian state itself and royal burial arrangements. First, the unity of the country fluctuated with time. Upper Egypt (and Thebes) had its own king for a time at the beginning of the new Third Intermediate Period, and eventually became a separate state for over a century. Other parts of the country also became independent polities from time to time.[1] Second, the role of Western Thebes as the default royal cemetery ended. Although the royal residence had been moved definitively to the north under Rameses II, royal corpses were still returned to the ancient burial ground at Thebes for burial (although neither Rameses X nor XI seem ever to have been interred in their Valley of the Kings tombs). Now, each royal residence-city would have its own royal necropolis.

At the beginning of the Twenty-first Dynasty, two former high priests of Amun, Herihor and Panedjem I, successively obtained royal titles in Thebes. Nothing is known of Herihor's posthumous fate, although the body of his wife, Nedjmet A, was eventually reburied in TT320.[2] Similarly, the mummy of Panedjem I, in an extensively reworked coffin of Thutmose I, was also found in that cache, together with those of his own wife, Henttawy A, and offspring Masaharta and Maatkare A (respectively high priest and God's Wife of Amun),[3] but without evidence of their primary sepulchre(s). As noted above, Panedjem seems to have contemplated the appropriation of Rameses XI's unused KV4, but did not go so far as to complete doing so. Since no material referable to Herihor's tomb has ever come to light, it is likely that the tomb remains untouched. Similarly, the burial places and funerary equipment of the Twenty-first Dynasty Theban high priests Menkheperre, Djedkhonsiufankh I, Nesibanebdjedet II and Pasebkhanut III/IV are also unknown, suggesting that a highest status cemetery of the period remains hidden somewhere in the Theban hills – conceivably in the little-explored southern wadis where, however, there is graffiti-evidence of Twenty-first Dynasty interest.

For the Twenty-first Dynasty and the first part of the Twenty-second Dynasty, however, the primary king of Egypt ruled from the city of Tanis (San el-Hagar) in the northeastern Delta. Because the topography of the Delta did not provide for the desert cemeteries found in the Nile valley, and exemplified on a monumental scale by the Memphite and Theban necropoleis, Delta necropoleis had been placed on relatively high ground within settlement zones, in particular within temple precincts, since the earliest times.[4] Thus, at Tanis the substructures of the royal tombs were built from masonry in back-filled cuttings in the ground within the enclosure of the Great Temple of Amun (fig. 24; pl. LXVIb). It seems likely that chapels of mudbrick were erected on the surface above them, but any traces of these were destroyed without record when the tombs were excavated. To judge from later tombs of similar form at Thebes (p. 117, below), such superstructures would have resembled miniature temples; it is conceivable that these might have incorporated small pyramids, often found as part of such 'temple-tombs' during the New Kingdom.[5]

The first king to rule from Tanis was Nesibanebdjedet (Smendes) I, and although the only known traces of Nesibanebdjedet I's burial are a pair of his canopic jars, obtained on the antiquities market,[6] it seems certain that he was the original owner of NRT-I in the Tanite necropolis which was, on the basis of its location, the earliest of the royal tombs built there (part of its north wall had been cut back to make room for the adjacent monument of Nesibanebjedet's successor).[7] However, NRT-I was later usurped and rebuilt by the Twenty-second Dynasty king Osorkon II (see pp. 110-12, below).

There appears to be no doubt as to Pasebkhanut I's original ownership of tomb NRT-III,[8] a structure built of limestone, with the exception of two granite burial chambers, and decorated in relief. Entry was by way of a shaft (fig. 24/III[1]) at the eastern end of the tomb, which led into an antechamber (2). On the north and west walls (pl. LXXVIIa), processions of genii surmounted scenes of the king offering to Osiris and Isis while, on the east, Pasebkhanut offered to Re-Horakhty, above which scene was a series of demons.[9] In the south wall, a doorway surrounded by bands of texts led to a chamber almost completely filled with a sarcophagus intended for the king's son, Ankhefenmut (3); this was evidently never used, the prince's disgrace being suggested by the erasure of his figures, names and titles from the walls of his chamber, where he had been depicted adoring the gods. Directly to the east lay another chamber, completely embedded in masonry and accessible only from above (4). Here was found the untouched burial of the General Wendjebaendjed, lying inside granite, gilded wood and silver coffins, a gold mask on his face.

On the walls of the chamber, the favoured courtier did homage to Osiris, Horakhty and Apis. His coffin had been made for a Nineteenth Dynasty Third Prophet of Amun Amenhotep and, like many such items found at Tanis, had been salvaged from a plundered Theban tomb for re-use in the north.

Two concealed doorways in the west wall of the antechamber, sealed with granite plugs and then covered with limestone reliefs, gave access to a pair of parallel chambers, prepared for Pasebkhanut himself (5) and his wife, Mutnedjmet (6). The king's burial was found intact, with his canopic jars and the debris of their chest at the foot of the sarcophagus, together with shabtis, whose boxes had decayed in the humidity of the tomb, vessels of metal and stone, and the skeleton of an animal, whether a sacrifice or a pet. On the rear wall of the chamber, the dead king was depicted as a mummy before a table of offerings. The sarcophagus, as noted above, had been usurped from Merenptah, while the black granite anthropoid coffin found within proved likewise second-hand. The silver inner coffin was, however, an original, together with the gold mask and mummy-board over the mummy within – reduced by the damp to a skeleton.

Mutnedjmet's chamber, while unrobbed, held not her burial, but that of Pasebkhanut I's successor, Amenemopet. That this was his primary burial is suggested by the fact that the doorway leading to the chamber from the antechamber had been filled with blocks carved with a scene of Amenemopet designed to match the adjacent decoration of Pasebkhanut: a significantly later reburial is unlikely to have taken such care. Amenemopet's name now replaced the queen's on the lid of her sarcophagus and on her chamber's wall, where it now incongruously accompanied Mutnedjmet's carved female figure. It is possible that Mutnedjmet was actually buried in Amenemopet's original tomb, NRT-IV (see just below), as remains of a coffin were found there.[10]

Amenemopet's burial was less rich than that of Pasebkhanut I, the coffin being of gilded wood, rather than silver, with the gold mask that covered the decayed mummy's face far less massive than that of the earlier king. At the foot of the sarcophagus stood the canopic jars and other vessels, while beside it were the remains of a further gilded coffin, bearing Amenemopet's name. Perhaps too large to fit into the borrowed sarcophagus, the coffin may have been simply dumped. Amenemopet had previously constructed NRT-IV, a small tomb of but one chamber just to the west, containing a Middle Kingdom sarcophagus reinscribed for the king.[11]

Nothing is known of the burial of the next king, Osorkon the Elder, but the last two kings of the Twenty-first Dynasty, Siamun and Pasebkhanut II were buried in the antechamber of NRT-III, on a low podium erected directly outside the burial chamber of Pasebkhanut I. Each burial comprised no more than the mummy and a gilded wooden coffin, plus usurped canopic jars, but both bodies and coffins were utterly decayed when found, the attribution of the interments being possible only on the basis of shabtis belonging to the kings that lay nearby.[12]

Royal Family tombs of the Twenty-first Dynasty

As noted above, the tomb of Pasebkhanut I incorporated burial places for a wife and a son, but nothing else is known of royal family burial arrangements in Tanis during the Twenty-first Dynasty. At Thebes, as has also been noted, the original burial places of the two local kings and their wives are unknown, but those of some of the offspring of Panedjem I are known from primary burials.[13]

Like those of lesser families of the period, these did not take place in purpose-built individual tombs, but in collective and/or reused sepulchres. Thus, Djedmutesankh A (possibly the wife of the High Priest of Amun Djedkhonsiufankh, son of Panedjem I) and Henttawy B (daughter of Panedjem I) and Henttawy C (daughter of High Priest Menkheperre, another son of Panedjem I) were buried together in a small tomb at Deir el-Bahari (MMA60).[14] A further likely daughter of Panedjem I, Nauny, was buried in the outer part of TT358,[15] the old Eighteenth Dynasty tomb of Meryetamun B, wife of Amenhotep I (p. 79, above), which lay close to MMA60 and a number of other tombs of similar date

Although not kings, the high priests of Amun during the Twenty-first Dynasty were all descendants of Panedjem I – who was also the father of King Pasebkhanut I at Tanis. Only one original burial place of any high priest is known – Panedjem II, grandson of Panedjem I; in this he was accompanied by his two wives, a daughter and a son-in-law. This tomb, TT320 just south of Deir el-Bahari, appears to have been cut in the early Eighteenth Dynasty as the sepulchre of Queen Ahmes-Nefertiry, (p. 79, above), whose body was allowed to remain in the company of the new occupants.

As already noted, when found in modern times TT320 also contained a large number of New Kingdom kings, members of the royal family and a number of other individuals, together with some of the royal/high priestly family of the first half of the Twenty-first dynasty. The date of introduction of these bodies has been a matter of debate, but it seems most likely that Panedjem II and his family were interred between the reigns of Siamun (when the high priest himself and one wife were definitely buried, as evidenced by dockets) and Shoshenq I (by dated linen on the mummies of Panedjem II's daughter and son-in-law) in the innermost part of the tomb, with the earlier royal mummies added subsequently.[16] However, another suggestion has been that the bulk of the royal mummies were placed in TT320 before the Panedjem II group began to be buried in the tomb, with only a small group of royal mummies added later.[17]

The Twenty-second Dynasty

No trace of actual tombs belonging to the first kings of the next, Twenty-second, Dynasty have been indentified at Tanis. Later tradition linked the new line with the city of Bubastis (Tell Basta), and it is not impossible that a new royal necropolis was founded there.[18] On the other hand, other sites are possible, with suggestions including another area at Tanis itself, Herakleopolis, and the precinct of Ptah at Memphis, both of which latter sites later received high status burials of the period. Indeed, Memphis hosted a 'House of Millions of Years of Shoshenq-meryamun' – by its name apparently a mortuary establishment of the dynastic founder, Shoshenq I.[19] One clue is that a body probably originally buried in this 'new' cemetery was later reburied at Tanis, and showed clear indications that it had lain for a while in standing water (see just below) – for which there is no evidence in the known tombs at Tanis. It also suggests that the 'new' necropolis may have ultimately been abandoned owing to flooding problems.

Nevertheless, the canopic chest of Shoshenq I survives – unfortunately having come from the antiquities market with no evidence for its original provenace.[20] The chest is interesting in that it was clearly inspired by prototypes of the mid-New Kingdom, and has no obvious Third Intermediate Period parallels. Since the reign of Shoshenq I probably saw the final reburials of New Kingdom pharaohs in the TT320 cache (see p. 109, above) one wonders whether his canopic chest was based on a piece seen or retrieved by reburial commissioners at this time.

Datable by the formulation of his names to the first part of the Twenty-second Dynasty is King Shoshenq IIa, although his exact place in the royal succession remains problematic.[21] His coffin and mummy, accompanied by shabtis and canopic equipment,[22] were placed between Siamun and Pasebkhanut II in the antechamber of NRT-III after they had lain for a period in standing water – and the coffin having had its trough broken.[23] It may have been the implied inundation of the 'new' necropolis that led to a resumption of the use of the original Tanis necropolis under Osorkon II.

As already noted, Osorkon II took over what had originally been the tomb of Nesibanebdjedet I (NRT-I).[24] This may have followed the plundering of the tomb during the hiatus in the area's use as the royal cemetery, or perhaps had been undertaken during the building of NRT-III, especially in view of the work required on NRT-I to accommodate NRT-III. The full extent of Osorkon's rebuilding of this sepulchre is unclear, but certainly involved the tomb's complete decoration and the provision of a new entrance from the west (fig. 24/I[a]), replacing an original shaft on the east.

The new doorway contained an unusual tableau in which the general Pashereneset son of Hori is shown mourning and reciting an elegy for the late king Osorkon:[25] that a king should be mourned like a mortal is a new departure.[26] Beyond this entrance lay what was initially a single antechamber (1, 1a), decorated with extracts from various mortuary books, including the Books of the Earth, the Day, the Night and the Dead. The latter included the weighing of the heart (pl. LXVIIb) and the Negative Confession – elements that were quite new to a kingly tomb: no longer is the king a god on earth gone to join his brothers in heaven, but one who must now submit to judgment like a mere mortal. The first king known to have been so depicted is Panedjem I,[27] on his Book of Dead papyrus, the change seemingly the final manifestation of the development first seen in the chapel of Rameses III at Medinet Habu, where that king was depicted in the Fields of Iaru (pl. LXXb). A very similar vignette is also found in chamber 2, along with other material taken from the Book of the Dead and from the Books of *Amduat* and the Earth. More of the Book of the Dead adorned the adjacent square room, which had probably been the Twenty-first Dynasty entrance shaft, along with elements from the Book of *Amduat*.

Side-room 2, although primarily decorated for Osorkon II himself, was employed as a burial chamber for his father Takelot I – whose intended tomb was presumably either too liable to flooding or otherwise untenable. The room was equipped with an appropriated Twelfth Dynasty sarcophagus of one Ameny (pl. LXXVIIIa).

The granite-lined main burial chamber (pl. LXXVIIIb) had minimal decoration, comprising two vignettes from the Book of the Earth. The eastern end was later rebuilt to take the sarcophagus of the king's son Hornakhte C, while most of the remainder was occupied by a large granite sarcophagus – by its form apparently an original Twenty-second Dynasty piece of work (albeit reusing a Ramesside slab for the lid), rather than a usurped Middle or New Kingdom piece as had been the case in the interments of many earlier kings of the Third Intermediate Period. Unfortunately, NRT-I had been robbed in antiquity, and thus only fragments of the funerary equipments of the occupants survived. Of the burial of Osorkon II himself, only the eyes from his cartonnage and the remains of a gilded coffin survived, together with canopic jars, shabtis and various other debris.

Like Pasebkhanut I, Osorkon and his family did not retain sole occupancy of their tomb for long. A large sarcophagus was introduced into the northern half of the antechamber (1a), and the 'new' room sealed off by a wall bearing figures of Osorkon II and Shoshenq III offering to divine figures. It is unclear who was the intended occupant of the sarcophagus, as while fragments of shabtis of a King Shoshenq were found, Shoshenq III had his own tomb some distance away (see below). These might represent a later intrusive interment of Shoshenq V, replacing a member of Shoshenq III's family, perhaps after a

111

robbery. Alternatively, the shabtis may relate to NRT-VII, an annexe of uncertain date built in front of Osorkon II's entrance to NRT-I.[28]

The successor of Osorkon II, Shoshenq III, built his own tomb (NRT-V)[29] to the northwest of the earlier sepulchres, at a significantly higher level – perhaps a reaction to the putative flooding of the 'new' necropolis. Compared with the tombs of Pasebkhanut I and Osorkon II, it was of a much simpler design, comprising a single compartment, divided into an antechamber and a burial chamber (pl. LXXIXa). The entire structure was of reused blocks, its decoration largely derived from the *Amduat*, supplemented by various less-usual scenes. The south wall of the burial chamber was adorned with scenes of the king's reawakening, including his welcome into the boats of the Sun God (pl. LXXIXb). The cornices of the vaulted chamber bore vignettes from the Book of the Dead. Two sarcophagi were found within the chamber, one belonging to Shoshenq III himself, and bearing a very shallow recumbent figure on the lid. The other was associated with fragments of canopic jars, which belonged to Shoshenq III's successor, Shoshenq IV.[30]

An undecorated tomb (NRT-II)[31] of very similar plan was built against and shared a wall with NRT-I (pl. LXXXa). It contained a limestone sarcophagus and the debris of three coffins, one of silver and two of wood, plus canopic fragments, one bearing the prenomen Usermaetre-setpenamun. This identifies the owner as Pamiu, successor of Shoshenq IV, as all other users of this prenomen of the period have otherwise-known tombs and canopics.

During the reign of Osorkon II, Thebes once again acquired a king of its own. The first of these was Horsieset I, apparently a grandson of Osorkon I and son of a recent high-priest, Nesibanebdjedet III.[32] He built his tomb (MH1 – fig. 26a; pl. LXXXb)[33] within the enclosure of the memorial temple of Rameses III at Medinet Habu, just south of Eighteenth Dynasty temple there (see pl. LXXI). The sepulchre was once surmounted by a chapel, the substructure comprising a sandstone construction sunk in the floor of the courtyard and made up of a single undecorated chamber approached by a stepped ramp, and equipped with niches for the canopic jars, now placed flanking the body, rather than at its feet as had formerly been the custom. The tomb contained, apart from the remains of a skeleton, a set of canopic jars, a set of shabtis and a stone anthropoid coffin, the trough removed from the tomb of Henutmire, sister wife of Rameses II (QV75). The lid was a Twenty-second Dynasty original, showing the king with the head of a raptor. This avian visage is also found on the coffin and cartonnage of Shoshenq IIa, and seems to be distinctive of the Twenty-second Dynasty.

After a short hiatus, the independence of Thebes was reasserted by Takelot II, but the region soon fell into civil war, the ultimate winner of which was his son, Osorkon III. No tomb of any of these kings of Thebes (sometimes referred to as the 'Theban Twenty-third Dynasty') has yet been identified, but Theban documents of the Twenty-sixth-and-seventh Dynasties mention a *ḥwt* (temple/tomb) of a king *Wsrtn* that seems likely to have been that of Osorkon III.[3] Given that Horsieset I had his tomb at Medinet Habu, and that the God's Wives of Amun, the effective rulers of the Thebaid during the Twenty-fifth/sixth Dynasties has their tombs there (see p. 117, below), it seems likely that this lost tomb was also located there.

Royal family tombs of the Twenty-second Dynasty

It is difficult to discern any clear pattern for burials of the royal family during the Twenty-second Dynasty.[35] A son of Osorkon II was buried with him in NRT-I, but this seems very much to have been a makeshift arrangement; a nameless sarcophagus in the same tomb's antechamber may have been inserted for a member of the family of Shoshenq III, but this is uncertain.

Away from Tanis, a Queen Kama was buried in a stone-built tomb of the Tanite type at Tell Moqdam (Leontopolis);[36] it had two chambers, one containing a broken limestone sarcophagus, and another holding the queen's intact granite example. Kama's room had been decorated in relief, unfortunately in poor condition, while her water-rotted mummy had been equipped with an extensive set of jewelry. It is uncertain who was the other occupant of the tomb, as no name was preserved there; it might have been Kama's husband, or another relation, but this remains problematic while her own antecedents remain uncertain.[37]

Under Osorkon II, the high priesthood of Ptah at Memphis passed to one of his sons, his descendants holding the post for a number of generations. Their necropolis lay just outside the southwest corner of the precinct of the temple of their god at Kom Rabia.[38] Comprising the sepulchres of Shoshenq D (eldest son of Osorkon II), Takelot B, Pedieset A and Horsieset H (Shoshenq's direct descendants), they broadly resembled the royal tombs of Tanis in form (pl. LXXXc). That of Pedieset A was a two-floored structure, with both levels (each comprising two chambers) having pointed ceilings. The upper level, embedded in brickwork, housed the two reused sarcophagi of Amenhotep-Huy, city steward under Amenhotep III, with the silver coffin of Pedieset himself. That of Shoshenq D was similar (pl. LXXXIa), the lower level being elaborately decorated with scenes from the Book of the Dead, but ground water had badly damaged its contents.

At least two princely tombs were built at Abydos during the late Twenty-first/early Twenty-second Dynasties. One belonged to Pasebkhanut A, a son of the Theban high priest Menkheperre, and was a brick mastaba (D22 – map 10, in area D of the North Cemetery), containing a chapel and burial shaft, and from which came a fine stela.[39] The other belonged to the High Priest of Amun Iuput A, son of Shoshenq I and interestingly enough points directly towards the Early Dynastic royal necropolis at Umm el-Qaab. It was a fairly remarkable structure built in a long, narrow pit, with a chamber of granite, decorated with scenes from the *Amduat*.[40]

At Thebes, following the re-establishment of a local monarchy under Takelot II, the area around the old mortuary temple of Rameses II, which had in any case become an important cemetery during the Twenty-second Dynasty, became a place of burial for members of the royal family.[41] Among royal children and relations buried there were Osorkon G (son of Takelot III, in B27), Ankhpakhered ii (great-grandson of Takelot II – B29) and Tabeketenasket B (granddaughter of Takelot II – B28), as were probably Shepensopdet A (granddaughter of Osorkon II) and God's Wife of Amun Karomama G. The tombs were simple shaft graves, some of which may have had some form of offering place attached to them. Medinet Habu also hosted similar tombs, some under the floors of the Rameses III temple, including that of Nesterwy, a daughter of King Rudamun.[42]

The Twenty-fifth Dynasty

At the end of the New Kingdom, Egyptian control over Nubia (Kush) was ended and a new native, but Egyptianised, polity grew up, centred on the former Egyptian colonial capital of Napata, close to the holy mountain of Gebel Barkal, sacred to Amun. By the mid eighth century, southern Upper Egypt had come under the control of the kings of Kush; finally by the end of the century, the Kushite king had seized control of the whole of Egypt, establishing a formal dual monarchy with Kush.[43]

By now, the Kushite royal cemetery had been established for some time at El-Kurru, a few kilometres from the Kushite religious capital of Gebel Barkal (fig. 25; pl. LXXXIb), but there remains a debate as to how far back an unbroken series of tombs can be traced.[44] The earliest tombs on the site were tumuli, which were then succeeded by a series of mastabas that continues through to the Kushite expansion into Egypt under Kashta, who may have been the owner of the largest of the mastabas, Ku8 (pl. LXXXIIa).[45]

These mastabas were followed by a sequence of pyramids, the first being built by Piye, who was the first Kushite king to penetrate into the Delta and receive the allegiance of the majority of the Egyptian local rulers. Now numbered Ku17,[46] the pyramid was only 8 m square and is now wholly vanished; to judge from later Kushite pyramids, it is likely that it had a high angle of elevation, appearing tall and slender. The substructure was approached by a stairway, once covered by the now-destroyed chapel, the burial chamber being a corbel-roofed room (fig. 26b; pl. LXXXIIb). Sets of canopic jars and shabtis were provided, but instead of a sarcophagus a rock-cut bench lay in the middle of the burial chamber. It had a cut-out in each corner, to receive the legs of a bed: interment on a bier has been characterized as a typical feature of Nubian burials since at least Kerman (Second Intermediate Period) times. Such small pyramids, with chapels on their east sides built above the stairway entrance to the substructrure, became the standard form of tomb for Kushite kings, soon extended to queens and later to other royal family members as well.

Piye has long been assumed to have been succeeded by Shabaka, but a good historical case can be made for Piye being directly followed by Shabataka, and only then by Shabaka.[47] Certainly, the tomb of Shabataka (Ku18)[48] shows much greater structural similarities to that of Piye, having an open-cut burial chamber (fig. 26c; pl. LXXXIIb) that contrasts with the fully-tunnelled substructures of the tombs of Shabaka and unequivocally later kings. It was placed some way from the tomb of Piye, amongst some of the more ancient tombs in the cemetery, and it was its somewhat awkward position that led to its descending stair incorporating an unusual right-angled turn in its descending stairway.

The vaulted rock-cut burial chamber of Shabaka's pyramid (Ku15 – fig. 26d; pl. LXXXIIIa-b)[49] was plastered and painted, apparently with scenes from the New Kingdom books of the underworld, as were employed in later Kushite royal tombs, of which only traces survive. The simple substructure design seen in this and the earlier Twenty-fifth Dynasty royal tombs was replaced in the pyramid of the next king, Taharqa, by something vastly more elaborate. In the case of his sepulchre, built at the hitherto-virgin site of Nuri (Nu1),[50] the usual stairway in front of the east face and small antechamber were followed by a six-pillared burial hall, the aisles of which were vaulted (fig. 26e). A curious corridor completely surrounded the subterranean rooms, at a slightly higher level, accessible via a flight of steps at the far end of the sepulchral chamber, and also a pair of stairways just outside the doorway of the antechamber. The usual bench lay in the centre of the burial chamber, upon which had lain a nest of coffins, some pieces of whose gold foil and stone inlay remained, together with a fragment of skull. The canopic jars were of very fine quality, and introduced new textual formulations, which become standard in subsequent Egyptian burials. A vast number of shabtis were recovered, in a variety of hard and soft stones, and many in remarkably large sizes – some up to 60 cm in height.

Not only was the substructure greatly enlarged, but the pyramid that surmounted it (pl. LXXXIVa) was substantially larger than any built in Kush before (or anywhere else for many centuries), this desire for size probably determining the shift to a new site, since limited space remained at El-Kurru.

The first phase of construction of Nu1 produced a pyramid with a 29.5 m base – nearly three times that the pyramid of Shabaka – a second phase, with a slightly higher elevation, enlarging this to something nearly seven times the size of the monument of Piye. Curiously, this second phase was not aligned with the first, leaving the substructure off-centre.

Interestingly, the next king, Tanutamun – the last Kushite king to rule any of Egypt-proper – returned to El-Kurru for his burial, inserting his pyramid (Ku16)[51] alongside that of Shabaka (fig. 26f; pl. LXXXIIIb), whose design it closely followed, although curiously omitting the previously-obligatory coffin-bench. In Tanutamun's case, the decoration of the substructure has been substantially preserved, with images of the king and the gods in the antechamber and scenes deriving from the books of the underworld (pl. LXXXIVb).

Although no Kushite king would rule in Egypt after Tanutamun's overlordship of the Thebaid ended in 654BC, the line continued to rule Upper (and sometimes parts of Lower) Nubia until the fourth century AD. During this period pyramids of the type established during the Twenty-fifth Dynasty continued to be employed, although their contents and ornamentation showed a steady shift towards a distinctly Kushite interpretation of the ancient motifs. Canopic jars initially remained in use, supplemented for a short period by, for the first time in Kush, stone sarcophagi, but both types of container had disappeared soon after the reign of Melanaqeñ, sixth successor of Tanutamun. At first, the royal tombs were primarily built at Nuri (plus one at El-Kurru), but they later shifted further south to Meroë, although a few were constructed back at Gebel Barkal (pl. LXXXIVa, LXXXVa–b, LXXXVIa).[52]

Royal family tombs of the Twenty-fifth Dynasty

Royal wives were buried in even smaller versions of the pyramids adopted by the Kushite kings. At El-Kurru,[53] Piye's wives, Kheñsa and Tabiry were buried in Ku4 and Ku53 respectively, the latter being much the smaller of the two; adjacent were four other similar tombs, one belonging to Neferukakashta (Ku52), who was possibly another of his spouses. Three other definite royal ladies' tombs have also been identified at El-Kurru, those of Qalhata (Ku5 – wife of Shabaka and mother of Tanutamun), Arty (Ku6 – wife of Shabataka) and Ñaparaye (Ku3). The latter is interesting in that her husband, Taharqa, was buried not at El-Kurru, but at Nuri. On the other hand, another wife of that king, Atakhebasken, was interred in Nuri Nu36,[54] where many subsequent queens' pyramids were erected. The substructure of Ku5 contains well-preserved decoration (focussing on the Book of the Dead) suggesting that, like those of the kings, queen's burial chambers were generally decorated as well (pl. LXXXVIb).

While the vast majority of the Kushite royal family seem to have been buried in their home cemeteries, a number of female members were buried in the ancient necropolis of Abydos.[55] The Kushites employed the same cemetery, D, as their Twenty-first/second dynasty predecessors, those buried there including a wife of Piye, Peksater (un-numbered), Shabaka's daughter, Isetemkheb H (D3), together with Paabtameri, apparently the wife of a king of the dynasty (D9). The Lady Taniy, a senior member of the household of a Kushite queen, was also interred in the area. Also probably buried there was Princess Meryetamun G, of unknown parentage, whose stela almost certainly came from Abydos.

Unfortunately, little is known of the structures of the tombs, which may have been reuses of New Kingdom structures. On the other hand, a substantial stone doorway survives from the sepulchre of Peksater, implying a monument of some solidity. It is interesting to see royal wives apparently being buried at Abydos, far away from their husbands in Nubia, as there is no evidence to suggest that they were in any way just cenotaphs.

The other significant group of royal family tombs of the dynasty are those of the God's Wives of Amun at Medinet Habu (fig. 26g; pl. LXXXVIIa).[56] Under Osorkon III, the office of God's Wife was significantly advanced in dignity, ultimately coming to replace that of high priest of Amun during the Twenty-sixth Dynasty. In keeping with this, the bearers possessed substantial tomb-chapels at Medinet Habu, opposite that of King Horsieset I (p. 112). The earliest (MH17), apparently belonging to Shepenwepet I (daughter of Osorkon III), was a brick structure, now almost entirely destroyed, with a simple burial chamber sunk into the ground beneath. In contrast, the directly adjacent chapel of Amenirdis I (sister of Piye), apparently originally built in brick, was reconstructed as a stone-built structure fronted by a pylon, leading to a four-pillared hall (pl. LXXXVIIb) and then to a sanctuary, surrounded by a corridor, under Shepenwepet II (daughter of Piye), leaving only the original burial chamber unchanged.

Shepenwepet II occupied a rather simpler monument directly adjoining that of Amenirdis, begun as a near duplicate of her predecessor's tomb. However, it was subsequently modified, the structure ultimately being shared with the subsequent God's Wife Neitiqerti (Nitokris) I, daughter of Psametik I, and her mother, Mehytenweskhet C. Thus, a court with two pillars now gives access to three parallel offering places, Shepenwepet's in the centre.

The chambers that held the ladies' sarcophagi lay directly under the floor of their sanctuaries, in all cases but that of Amenirdis equipped with a vaulted roof. Shepenwepet I's tomb may have had an entrance passage from the north (destroyed by a later tomb) but the others seem to have been accessed directly from above. The chambers were only large enough to hold a sarcophagus – in all cases subsequently removed: two were subsequently re-used in Ptolemaic tombs at Deir el-Medina.[57]

Chapter 8

The Saite and Later Periods

The Twenty-sixth Dynasty

During the Twenty-sixth Dynasty, the royal residence lay at Sais (Sa el-Hagar). An account of the royal cemetery there survives in the work of Herodotus, who visited the city around 450 BC. He records that Wahibre (Apries), fourth king of the dynasty, was buried 'in the family tomb in the temple of Athena [Neith], nearest to the shrine, on the left-hand as one goes in.' He then continues:

> The people of Sais buried all the kings who came from the province inside this area. The tomb of Amasis (Ahmose II) is also in the temple court, although further from the shrine than that of Apries and his ancestors. It is a great cloistered building of stone, decorated with pillars carved in the imitation of palm trees and other costly adornments. Within the cloister is a chamber with double doors, and behind the doors stands the sepulchre.

This may imply that the earliest Saite kings were buried in a single tomb – or perhaps that each had a separate tomb below a single superstructure. The description of Ahmose II's monument seems to conjure up a standard Egyptian peripteral shrine, with a central cella surrounded by a colonnade. The cella would have contained the cult-image of the dead king; presumably, the burial chamber was sunk in the ground beneath, following the patterns seen at Tanis and Medinet Habu during the Third Intermediate Period.

However, the area of the temples at Sais is now completely destroyed, and largely occupied by a lake (pl. LXXXVIIIa). There is thus little or no chance of recovering any in-situ trace of the royal cemetery.[1] From here presumably came a fragment of granite that would appear to derive from the sarcophagus of Psametik II (pl. LXXXVIIIb).[2] The heart-scarab of Nekau II,[3] some twenty-five shabtis,[4] and two canopic jars belonging to Wahibre[5] are also known.

118

Royal family tombs of the Twenty-sixth Dynasty

Funerary remains belonging to four queens of the Twenty-sixth Dynasty survive. Mehytenweskhet C, a wife of Psametik I, was buried alongside her daughter, the God's Wife of Amun, Neitiqerti I, in the tomb of Shepenwepet II at Medinet Habu (p. 117, above), additional shrines being installed either side of Shepenwepet's.[6] The sarcophagus of Nekau II's wife, Khedebneith-hirbinet I,[7] was allegedly found at Sebannytos, but little is known of the circumstances of its discovery or the form of her tomb.[8] On the other hand, the intact tomb of Psametik II's wife, Takhuit, was found at Athribis (Tell Atrib), near the apex of the Nile Delta.[9] It comprised a brick structure, sunk into the ground surface, in which lay the quartzite sarcophagus. Inside lay the rotted remains of the queen's wooden coffin and mummy. Various gold items were found on the body, while a small gold mask had been sewn on to the shroud. Doubtless other such tombs are lost under the mud of the Delta.

The remaining tomb, Giza LG83,[10] was shared between Nakhtsebastetru, wife of Ahmose II, her son, Ahmose C, and a certain Lady Tashentihet. It lay in a row of tombs of the period along the northern edge of the causeway of Khaefre, but little is known of its form.

The Twenty-seventh and Thirty-first Dynasties

In 525 BC, Egypt became part of the Persian Empire and the kings of Persia accordingly became the kings of Egypt. The first two adopted full Egyptian royal titularies, but the Persian rulers' self-identifiction as pharaohs declined after Darius I.[11] Burial places can be attributed to almost all these monarchs, but only one unequivocally on the basis of inscriptions, the other monuments being assigned on more subjective grounds.

The sepulchre of the first Persian 'pharaoh', Kambyses II, is problematic. It is known from the writings of Aristobulus of Cassandreia, who witnessed its examination under Alexander the Great, as well as those of Strabo, that the tomb of Kyrus II, the founder of Persian imperial power, lay at Pasagardae in central Iran, and is generally identified with an extant monument at the site, the *Qabr-e Madar-e Sulaiman*, a vaulted burial chamber raised on a stepped podium (pl. LXXXIXa). However, no tradition exists as to the location of Kambyses' tomb, potential candidates being the lower part of a podium similar to that of the *Qabr* at Takht-e Rustam, 45km southwest of Pasagardae,[12] and two towers, one at Pasagardae (the *Zendan-e Soleiman* – pl. LXXXIXb)[13] and one at Nashq-e Rustam (the *Kabah-e Zardusht* – fig. 27a; pl. LXXXIXc, XCb),[14] just north of Takht-e Rustam and the royal cemetery from the time of Darius I.

The towers are roughly the same size, although the *Kabah* is built upon a stepped base, with an exterior displaying dummy windows, and a single chamber at the top, approached by a stairway at the front. They have been interpreted variously as fire-temples and tombs, with the latter perhaps the more likely.[15] It has also been noted on architectural grounds that the *Kabah* may have been built later than the *Zendan*.[16] On this basis it is possible that the *Zendan* may have been built as the original tomb of Kambyses II while the royal centre was at Pasagardae, and replaced by the *Kabah* when the centre shifted to the south, near where the vast ceremonial terrace of Persepolis[17] was erected by Kambyses' successors, and where later kings were interred.

Nothing can be said of any tomb for 'Bardiya', the usurper whose brief reign separated the death of Kambyses II from the seizure of power by Darius I;[18] however, Darius inaugurated a series of distinctive rock-cut sepulchres that were constructed at or near Persepolis until the collapse of the Persian empire. His own tomb (I)[19] was hewn into the centre of the vertical cliff-face at Nashq-e Rustam (fig. 27b; pl. XCIa), just to the east of the *Kabah-e Zardusht*, and comprised a cruciform cutting whose horizontal bar housed an engaged colonnade and entrance to the burial chambers. The upper vertical bar was adorned with a tableau of the king before a fire altar, supported by representative figures of thirty subject-nations; figures of solidiers adorned the side-walls of this part of the façade. The latter were identified by inscriptions, while texts also occupied the area behind the king in the upper register (comprising his political philosophy) and all but the lefthandmost of the panels formed by the pillars of the main façade (comprising his personal philosophy). These texts were written in the three principal cuneiform-written languages of the empire, Old Persian, Elamite and Akkadian (in that order from the left on the main façade).

The entrance to the interior of the tomb was framed by an Egyptianising doorway, and opened onto a transverse vestibule, only the lefthand part of which had been completed, giving access to three burial chambers, one on the axis of the entrance and two more to the left. It seems likely that (as in some later tombs) it had originally been intended that there should be a central chamber flanked by two others, but poor rock to the right frustrated this plan, an additional chamber being cut to the left. Each chamber had three gabled-lidded burial-cuts, but while the king presumably occupied one of those in the axial chamber (perhaps the innermost), there is no evidence as to who was buried in the sepulchre, although it probably included some of Darius' five known wives, some offspring and perhaps his parents. Curiously, the extensive inscriptions found on the tomb of Darius I are absent from the rest of the series of sepulchres inspired by it, and thus the allocation of the remainder of the series to specific kings has been based on the architectural and locational detail.

The sepulchre of Xerxes I has usually been identified with tomb II,[20] cut in a rock-face east of, and at 90 degrees to, that of Darius I (pl. XCb). The attribution has been made principally on the basis of its being a location requiring less stone-removal than other tomb-sites and the regularity of the design of the inner chambers (fig. 27c).[21] However, against this is the fact that the layout of these chambers differs from any other Persian royal tomb except for tomb VI, and that tomb II is the only one of the monuments at Nashq-e Rustam not easily visible from Persepolis (cf. pl. XCa). It might thus rather be interpreted as the last of the tombs cut in the Nashq-e Rustam cliff prior to the move of the royal necropolis to Persepolis itself, and to be placed directly before tomb VI in the chronological sequence.

Topographically, the more likely candidate for Xerxes' burial place is tomb IV (conventionally assigned to Darius II),[22] which is in the second most prominent location at Nashq-e Rustam – one also aligned directly with the *Kabah-e Zardusht* – and has a triple-chambered interior of the type apparently intended for tomb I (fig. 27c). The fact that these chambers are not placed fully perpendicular to the façade has been used to argue that the tomb represents a decline from the standards seen in the tomb of Darius I. This feature may actually, however, represent an attempt to maintain the interior orientation seen in the latter tomb, in spite of local topography requiring the façade to be aligned further towards the southwest than that of tomb I. The three chambers open from a vestibule, its shape defined by the need to orient the chambers, and in this case have a single burial-cut each. The façade of tomb IV represents in all key features a duplicate of that of Darius I (as is the case with all the Persian royal tombs), except for the absence of any texts.

On the basis of the criterion of location, the sepulchre of the next king, Artaxerxes I, would seem most likely to have been tomb III, which is actually that conventionally associated with him.[23] In all features it follows tomb IV, with the attempt at maintaining burial chamber orientation resulting in the southwest corner of the transverse vestibule breaking through the façade (fig. 27d). Each chamber once again held a single burial-cut. After Artaxerxes I's death, the throne was held successively by the short-lived (murdered) Xerxes II and Sogdianus; it is possible that a smoothing of the rock east of the tomb of Darius I was the beginning of a burial place for one of them.

As already noted, the position of tomb II strongly suggests that it was the last sepulchre completed at Nashq-e Rustam, and was thus probably the tomb of Darius II (rather than the generally-assumed Xerxes I). While the façade once again closely follows the design initiated by Darius, the interior is very different from the tombs discussed thus far (fig. 27e). Rather than a transverse hall giving access to multiple chambers, tomb II had a single, rather larger, chamber, preceded by a slightly wider vestibule. This contained three burial-cuts, thus equipping the tomb for the same number of interments as tombs III and IV. This interior arrangement supports the placement of tomb II at the end of the Nashq-e Rustam sequence, as the same interior-form is also found in one of the tombs at Persepolis (pl. XCIb), which are certainly later than those at Nashq-e Rustam – and also share the orientation of tomb II.

The single-chambered Persepolis tomb is number VI (fig. 27f; pl. XCIIa),[24] usually attributed to Artaxerxes III, but in view of the link with tomb II, and the fact that it occupies a site that dominates the Persepolis terrace, it seems far more likely that it was built by Artaxeres II – who lost the rule of Egypt early in his reign, the country managing to shake off Persian domination during Artaxerxes' struggle for power with his brother Kyrus (B) that followed Darius II's death and subsequent conflicts in the Aegean. The Persepolis tombs differed from the Nashq-e Rustam ones in that they were cut in the side of a sloping hill, rather than into a near-vertical rock-face, abandoning the cruciform approach for one that included a terrace in front of the entrance to the interior, which was thus far more accessible than in the Nashq-e Rustam tombs. On the other hand, the remainder of the façade continued the pattern inaugurated by Darius I.

Persia, in the person of Artaxerxes III, regained control over Egypt in 342, to whom the second completed tomb (V)[25] at Persepolis should probably be attributed (fig. 27g; pl. XCIIb), since it lies in a less favourable location further from the terrace, and also reverts to the usual tripartite burial chamber arrangement, albeit with chambers more widely spaced than in earlier tombs; it also has trilingual label-texts on the figures of the thirty supporting figures in the façade, for the first and only time since Darius I. The final tomb constructed at Persepolis (VII)[26] was never finished, only part of the façade having been smoothed and adorned with the upper part of the main tableau. Given its position, it was clearly the last sepulchre begun at the site and may represent a monument begun by Arses, continued by Darius III and abandoned on the latter's defeat by Alexander III and his subsequent murder.

The Twenty-ninth Dynasty

In 404BC, the latest of a series of rebellions against Persian rule had begun, when one Amenirdis (Amyrtaeus) of Sais proclaimed himself king. His authority had expanded as far as Aswan by 400, establishing an independence that would last for six decades before Egypt was once again conquered by the Persians. Nothing is known of any tomb built for this first king of the newly-independent country – presumably at Sais – which he may have occupied prematurely following the seizure of the throne by Naefarud (Nepherites) I, the founder of Twenty-ninth Dynasty, from Mendes (Tell el-Rub'a).

Naefarud I is the last ancient king of Egypt itself to have a tomb whose actual remains have been identified (pl. XCIIIa). This had been constructed in the southeast corner of the enclosure of the main temple at the site, close to its wall, and partly cutting an early iteration of the wall. It had comprised a brick-lined cutting, the lining perhaps forming the foundation for some kind of superstructure – possibly a mastaba and/or chapel. The bottom of the cutting had been given a 30cm deep layer of sand, probably to form a foundation for the limestone burial chamber that was built within the cutting. Entirely destroyed, with only fragments remaining, it seems to have resembled the burial chambers employed at Tanis, and been similarly decorated with extracts from the books of the underworld, although only the *Amduat* is now recognisable; also present was at least one depiction of the king before the Ram-god of Mendes. The entrance appears to have been from the north, the chamber containing an outer sarcophagus of limestone (perhaps originally sunk into the floor of the room) and an inner one of basalt. Nothing has been found of the tombs of the three other kings who comprised the dynasty, apart from a few shabti figures of the Hagar.

The Thirtieth Dynasty
The last king of the Twenty-ninth Dynasty, Naefarud II, was deposed by Nakhtnebef (Nektanebo) I of Sebennytos (Sammandud/Behbeit el-Hagar), who thus became the first king of the Thirtieth Dynasty. No trace of his tomb has yet been identified, but fragments of his sarcophagus were found in reused contexts in Cairo,[27] while a few shabtis are also known. The sarcophagus coffer of the last king of the dynasty – and last native king of Egypt – Nakhthorheb (Nektanebo II) has also been recovered from a reused context, this time in Alexandria.[28] As this king is known to have fled to Nubia in the face of a Persian reoccupation, it is clear than it was never used for his burial. Suggestions have been made, however, that it might have been employed for the interment of Alexander the Great (see below).

Royal Family Tombs of the Thirtieth Dynasty
The sarcophagus of Udjashu, the mother of Nakhthorheb, was found at the apparently Coptic site of Kom Yetwal wa Yeksar, near Masara in the northern Delta;[29] like granite columns from the same place, it had clearly been brought here for building stone. As for its original location, the texts on the sarcophagus mention the site of Behbet el-Hagar, some 30 km to the south, and only a few kilometers from Sebannytos, the home of the dynasty, suggesting that it originally came from there.

The burial place of Khedebneithirbinet II, wife of Nakhthorheb was, in contrast, many kilometers to the south, at Saqqara. There, her burial was made in the tomb of two men named Psametik at Saqqara, the inner chamber of which was taken over for her, and from which were recovered her canopic jars. The tomb is interesting in that the approach corridor was lines with niches holding very fine deity statues associated with the Psametik burials.[30]

Khedebneithirbinet's burial seems to have been a secondary one, inserted into a private tomb of some years earlier. This unusual arrangement may have been the result of her husband Nakhthorheb's flight from Egypt, with the former queen buried during the early Ptolemaic Period in an imposing, but improvised, tomb.

The Argaeid and Ptolemaic Dynasties

Egypt was annexed to the Persian Empire for a decade, before the onslaught of the young Macedonian king, Alexander III, brought that entity to a sudden end. Alexander ('the Great'), was recognised by the oracle of Amun at Siwa Oasis as legitimate Pharaoh. Amongst his acts in Egypt was the foundation of the city of Alexandria in the northwest Delta, which is where he was ultimately buried following his premature death.[31]

The Satrap (governor) of Egypt, Ptolemy, son of Lagos, managed to obtain the royal body during its journey through Syria from Babylon, where Alexander had died, and transport it to Egypt as part of the process that led to his becoming king after the murder of Alexander's son, Alexander IV. At first the body was interred at 'Memphis' in 321/20: it has been suggested that this burial might have taken place at the Serapeum at Saqqara, the cemetery of the sacred bulls whose popularity had made major advances during the Thirtieth Dynasty. This might account for the presence in the complex of a group of 3rd century statues of Greek philosophers,[32] a feature that is otherwise difficult to explain. A linked suggestion has also been made that the body was placed in the unused sarcophagus of Nakhthorheb, which tradition long held to have been Alexander's sepulchre. However, Alexander's definitive burial was at Alexandria, sometime in the reign of Ptolemy II, perhaps around 290, in a location that is wholly obsure. However, a massive calcite structure that had once formed the antechamber of a large tumulus-tomb of Macedonian type (pl. XCIVa), in what later became the Terra Sancta cemetery in the eastern part of the city (the 'Alabaster Tomb'),[33] might conceivably have been Alexander's – or perhaps that of one of the first three Ptolemies.

A tomb (II) within the Great Tumulus at the site of Vergina, back in Macedonia,[34] seems to have been the burial place of one of the kings of the Argaeid line, although debate continues over whether the king interred was Alexander III's assassinated father, Philip II, or his half-brother and successor, Philip III Arrhidaeus; the argument seems to favour the former.[35]

In any case, tomb II comprised two vaulted chambers, fronted by a two-columned portico, the first containing the cremated remains of a woman, the inner those of a man with rich burial goods. The similar tomb III nearby held the cremated remains of a youth, who has been identified as Alexander IV.

Regardless of whether the Alabaster Tomb belonged to Alexander III or an early Ptolemy – or someone else entirely – Ptolemy IV established a new funerary enclosure, the 'Sema', in which were concentrated not only the body of Alexander, but also those of earlier members of the Ptolemaic Dynasty, and which would thence be the royal mausoleum.[36] As with most Alexandrine topographical matters, the precise location of this enclosure, the 'Soma', is unclear, but seems to have lain in the 'Palaces' district, south or southwest of the Lochias (now Silsila) peninsula, possibly close to the main crossroads of the ancient city (fig. 28; pl. XCIVa). The forms of the tombs within this are also obscure, but at least some seem to have had pyramidal roofs, perhaps inspired both by Egyptian monuments and the mausoleum of Mausolus at Halicarnassus. The golden coffin of Alexander was pillaged by Ptolemy X in 88 BC and replaced by one of 'crystal', 'glass' or perhaps alabaster, and his tomb is mentioned on various occasions until at least to the visit of the Emperor Caracella in AD 215. The Soma may have survived until at least the second half of the 3rd century, albeit perhaps damaged in one of the political/military upheavals of that period, but was probably destroyed during the late 4th century, perhaps in the earthquake of 365, although there is a reference to Alexander's corpse being on display around 390.

Tantalising references to a 'tomb' of Alexander are found from the ninth and tenth centuries and on into the sixteenth century AD, the latter associating it with a site by then occupied by the Attarin Mosque – in a domed pavilion within which the sarcophagus of Nakhthorheb lay for many years (which had became generally described as that of Alexander by the 18th century).[37] However, it is difficult to determine whether these structures had any direct link with the actual burial places of Alexander (or the other royal tombs in the Sema).

While it would seem from the available data that most of the Ptolemies were interred in the Sema, Kleopatra VII is reported to have had a separate tomb, 'adjacent to the Temple of Isis'.[38] Unfortunately, our source for this, Plutarch, does not define which of the many Isis-shrines was involved, while the tomb's design remains obscure.

The Roman Emperors
With the fall of Kleoptra VII, Egypt became part of the Roman Empire, the emperors accordingly becoming nominal kings of Egypt, and thus their imperial burial places the now the royal tombs of Egypt. Augustus

constructed a mausoleum close to the banks of the Tiber in Rome (pl. XCIVb),[39] circular in plan, consisting of several concentric rings of earth and brick, covered with a tumulus, planted with trees and topped with an 8+m gilded bronze statue of himself; the entrance was flanked with a pair of uninscribed Egyptian obelisks, now in the Piazza dell'Esquilino and Piazza del Quirinale in Rome. A corridor ran from the entrance to a chamber with three niches to hold the urns containing the ashes of the wider Augustan imperial family, down to Claudius. Nero's remains were placed in the Mausoleum of the Domitii Ahenobarbi on the Pincian Hill, while Galba was buried near the Aurelian Road, Otho at Brixellum, with the ultimate fate of Vitellius' body uncertain. Vespasian and Titus(?) had their ashes initially interred in the Augustan mausoleum,[40] but these were moved to the Temple of the Flavian Gens, built by Domitian, whose remains were also placed there. Nerva became the last emperor to be buried in the Augustan Mausoleum, although Julia Domna, wife of Septimius Severus had her ashes temporarily placed there, before transfer to the Mausoleum of Hadrian (below).

Trajan's ashes were placed in a chamber at the base of his triumphal column, which commemorated his wars with the Dacians (101–102 and 105–106) in the emperor's Forum (pl. XCVa),[41] while a new monumental imperial mausoleum was built by Hadrian.[42] On a larger scale than that of Augustus, it retained a circular plan for its main section, but on a square base (divided into sixty-seven brick-lined compartments; it is unclear whether these were subsidiary burial chambers or had a structural purpose). The interior was also more elaborate, the entrance leading to a gallery that ascended in an anticlockwise manner just inside the perimeter of the cylindrical section to a vestibule above the entrance. From here, a passage led to the burial chamber under the centre of the monument, 12 m above ground level. It was equipped with niches for urns in three of its walls, which were used for burials down to the time of Caracella; the chamber was desecrated and the urns and ashes scattered during the sacking of Rome in 410. The form of much of the building was hidden by its reconstruction into the Castel Sant'Angelo from the fourteenth century onwards (pl. XCVb), but literary evidence suggests it was originally topped by a monumental sculpture, perhaps an enormous quadriga (four-horse chariot).

Most of the emperors who were murdered or otherwise died violently over subsequent decades are without known or surviving tombs, until Diocletian built a monumental mausoleum at Split in Croatia – which now forms the core of the Cathedral of St Domnius.[43] It comprised a domed subterranean chamber, surmounted by an also-domed public area (pl. XCVIa).

126

Diocletian and his immediate successors are the last Roman emperors for whom hieroglyphic names and titles are known, the conversion of Constantine I to Christianity early in the 4th century fatally undermining the conception under which the emperors had simultaneously been divine kings of Egypt. It appears that the emperor was initially buried in a porphyry sarcophagus in his Church of the Holy Apostles at Constantinople, the new capital, surrounded by twelve empty sarcophagi representing the twelve apostles (Constantine holding himself to be the thirteenth). He was, however, transferred to a new circular, domed, mausoleum nearby in 356/7.

The original Church of the Holy Apostles was demolished by the Emperor Justinian in the early 530s and a new building dedicated in 540, the new mausoleum following the same form as the original, now placed east of the church. An additional mausoleum was constructed for Justinian himself at the end of the northern arm of the church, the complex remaining the imperial burial place until the death of Constantine VIII in 1028 (pl. XCVIb).[44] The last of the emperors buried there to rule Egypt was Constans II, interred in 668 in Justinian's annexe, apparently in the same sarcophagus as his ephemeral father Constantine II.[45] The very last Byzantine ruler to have effective rule of Egypt was Hercalius, under whom the Arab conquest of Egypt began at the start of 640, and who died in February 641, by which time much of the country was in Arab hands and Alexandria was under siege; the city fell in September, the remaining Byzantine forces withdrawing in 642.

Notes

INTRODUCTION
[1] With one exception: see p. 65.
[2] Hays 2011.

CHAPTER 1
[1] Case and Payne 1962; Payne 1973.
[2] Friedman 2011; Friedman, Van Neer and Linselle 2011.
[3] Dreyer 1998.
[4] Petrie 1901: 7; Kaiser and Dreyer 1982: 222–25; Dreyer et al. 1996: 49.
[5] Petrie 1901: 7; Kaiser and Dreyer 1982: 221–22; Dreyer et al. 1996: 86.
[6] See Dreyer 1991.
[7] Porter and Moss 1937: 88; Kaiser and Grossmann 1979: 157–58; Kaiser and Dreyer 1982: 220–21; Dreyer et al. 2003: 85–86
[8] Porter and Moss 1937: 88; Kaiser and Grossmann 1979: 159–61; Kaiser and Dreyer 1982: 213–20; Dreyer 1990: 62–64; Dreyer et al. 1996: 48–57; Dreyer et al. 1998: 138–41; Dreyer et al. 2000: 90–97.
[9] Bestock 2009; 2012: 38–39.
[10] Bestock 2012: 39–44.
[11] Porter and Moss 1937: 54–55; Kemp 1966; Kaiser and Dreyer 1982: 253–60; O'Connor 1989; for examples at Saqqara, see p. 8, below.
[12] Porter and Moss 1937: 78–81; Dreyer 1991: 96; 2009: 165–66; 2010: 143–44; Dreyer et al. 2011: 55–62.
[13] Dodson 1997–98, with full references.
[14] Cf. Zink and Nerlich 2003.
[15] Porter and Moss 1937: 82–83; Dreyer 1993: 57.
[16] Dreyer 1991.
[17] Porter and Moss 1937: 82.
[18] Porter and Moss 1937, 83–85; Dreyer 1990: 72–79; 1993: 57–61; Dreyer et al. 1998: 141–64; 2000: 97–118; 2003:88–107.
[19] E.g. Saqqara S3035, S3036, S3506 (Porter and Moss 1974–81: 440–42, 446
[20] Saqqara S2185 (Porter and Moss 1974–81: 437).
[21] O'Connor 1995.
[22] E.g. Saqqara S3357, dating to the reign of Hor-Aha (Porter and Moss 1974–81: 444).
[23] Porter and Moss 1937: 82.
[24] Reginald Clark suggests to me (personal communication 22 August 2015) that this may be secondary, having been added during the Middle or New Kingdoms; on security features in Early Dynastic and early Old Kingdom tombs, see Clark 2016.
[25] Porter and Moss 1937: 85–86; Dreyer et al. 2000: 119–21; 2006: 93–98; 2011: 72–83.
[26] Porter and Moss 1937: 86–87; Dreyer et al. 1996: 57–66.
[27] Callender 2011: 7–47; cf. Stadelmann 2011b.
[28] Porter and Moss 1937: 118–19.
[29] Porter and Moss 1974–81: 436–48.
[30] Cf. Morris 2007.
[31] Regulski 2009.

[32] On approach routes to Saqqara, see Dodson 2016c.

[33] Porter and Moss 1974–81: 613; Lacher 2008.

[34] Reisner 1936: 138–43; Lacher 2008: 433–39.

[35] Lacher 2008: 440–47.

[36] But cf. Lacher 2008: 431–33.

[37] See further Dodson 2016c: 6–10.

[38] Porter and Moss 1974–81: 613; Munro 1983: 278–82; Lacher-Raschdorff 2014.

[39] See Dodson 2016c: 6–9.

[40] Mathieson and Tavares 1993: 27–28; cf. Spencer 1974: 3.

[41] There are some indications on the ground that could suggest that it was actually square, but if these potential features are actually unrelated to the enclosure, one would assume a rectangular form, with roughly the proportions of the Abydos enclosures, or the *Gisr el-Mudir*, discussed just below.

[42] Mathieson and Tavares 1993: 28–31; Mathieson et al. 1997.

[43] Showing that old suggestions that the *Gisr el-Mudir* might be the unfinished remains of a Third Dynasty pyramid complex are extremely unlikely; in addition, the walls show no signs of the facings akin to those of the Step Pyramid enclosure wall, alleged by some writers (cf. Mathieson and Tavares 1993: 28 n.29).

[44] It should be noted, however, that it has also been suggested that the *Gisr el-Mudir* was unrelated to the tombs, and should be attributed to the time of Khasekhemwy, with its purpose, however, left moot (for references, see Regulski 2009: 226–27; cf., however, the discussion in Dodson 2016c: 8–9).

[45] MMA 60.144 (Porter and Moss 1974: 870).

[46] Sakkara tomb B 3 (Porter and Moss 1974–81: 490); its precise location is now unknown, but certainly lay in the area to the north of the Step Pyramid complex.

[47] A stamped brick, found near the tomb of Ninetjer, bears the cartouche Nefer*senedj*re (Leclant and Clerc 1988: 330), which has been suggested as being a variant of the simple name 'Sened/Senedj', but if so it will be the earliest known cartouche by nearly a century, and of a format not attested until well into the Fourth Dynasty.

[48] Stadelmann 1985; 1991: 37, 39.

[49] On the other hand, these could possibly represent Djoser's queens' tombs: see p. 17, below.

[50] Porter and Moss 1937: 81; Kaiser and Grossmann 1979: 161–62; Dreyer et al. 2006: 98–110; 2011: 83–90.

[51] Porter and Moss 1937: 54.

[52] Fairman and Blackman 1935, 1944.

[53] Newberry 1922; Dodson 1996a.

[54] Porter and Moss 1937: 196; Kemp 1963; Alexanian 1998; Friedman and Raue 2007.

[55] O'Connor 1989: 83-84.

[56] Porter and Moss 1937: 87; Dreyer et al. 1998: 164–66; 2000: 122–28; 2003: 108–24; 2006: 110–27.

[57] See p. 5 above for Saqqara S2185; they were also employed at Helwan.

[58] Porter and Moss 1937: 52–53; M.D. Adams and O'Connor 2010.

[59] Porter and Moss 1974–81: 444.

[60] Porter and Moss 1974–81: 436.

[61] Saad 1957: 5, 41, 8.

[62] Porter and Moss 1937: 37.

CHAPTER 2

[1] Until the late 1990s, it was thought that Sanakhte reigned between these two kings. However, excavations in the tomb of Khasekhemwy then revealed numerous sealings of Djoser (Dreyer 1998), with the implication that the latter provisioned his putative father's burial, and thus was his direct successor. The two kings' sealings have also been found together in a series of galleries below the northernmost edge of the Step Pyramid complex.

[2] Porter and Moss 1974–81: 399–415.

[3] Kaiser 1969.

[4] Suggestions that they might have held (e.g.) the king's internal organs are nullified by the presence of canopic chests in many pyramids possessing subsidiaries.

[5] It is possible that this installation was the result of a rebuilding during the construction of the pyramid: for the debate, see Lauer 1962: 75–76; Stadelmann 1996; Kaiser 1992 and 1997.

[6] Strouhal et al. 1998.

[7] Vyse 1840–42: III, 9; Palanque 1902; Macramallah 1932; Swelim 1987: 91–95.

[8] Porter and Moss 1937: 37; Incordino 2008: 82–83.

[9] Porter and Moss 1974–81: 415–17.

[10] For this, and all other Old Kingdom sarcophagi, see Donadoni Roveri 1969.

[11] On the evolution of sarcophagi, see Dodson 2016a.

[12] Porter and Moss 1974–81: 313; Lehner 1996; Dodson 2000.

[13] Swelim 1987.

[14] Both monuments are close to the edge of the cultivation, perhaps to aid in the brickmaking process.

[15] Porter and Moss 1974–81: 401–5.

[16] Dodson 1988c.

[17] Porter and Moss 1974–81: 417.

[18] Porter and Moss 1935: 89–90; Maragioglio and Rinaldi 1964–77: III, 6–53; El-Khouli 1991; Reader 2015.

[19] On the evolution of causeways, see Awady 2009: 86–120.

[20] Porter and Moss 1974–81: 877–82; Stadelmann 2011a.

[21] Porter and Moss 1974–81: 877–80; Alexanian, Bebermeier and Blaschta 2012.

[22] Porter and Moss 1974–81: 876; Stadelmann and Sourouzian 1982; Stadelmann 1983; Stadelmann et al. 1993.

[23] Kaiser and Dreyer 1980.

[24] Edwards 1997.

[25] At Zawiyet Sultan (Zawiyet el-Maiyitin, Zawiyet el-Amwat), Nubt (El-Zawayda, Naqada), Sinki (Nag Ahmed Khalifa, Abydos-South) El-Kula (Nag el-Miamariya, Edfu-North), El-Ghenimiya (Edfu-South) – see Kaiser and Dreyer 1980; Dreyer and Swelim 1982.

[26] Porter and Moss 1974–81: 11–16; Romer 2007.

[27] For these and other decorative elements from the complex, see Flentye 2011: 77–84.

[28] Hawass 1997.

[29] Porter and Moss 1974–81: 14–16; Yoshimura and Kurokochi 2013.

[30] Edwards 1994.

[31] Porter and Moss 1974–81: 1–3; Valloggia 2011.

[32] Porter and Moss 1974–81: 312–13; Edwards 1994.

[33] Porter and Moss 1974–81: 19–26.

[34] Cf. Flentye 2011: 85–91.

[35] Reader 2005; 2006.

[36] Louvre A23 (Fay 1996).

[37] Porter and Moss 1974–81: 26–34.

[38] Others have argued for a single unified plan, or even that the final phase dated to the reign of Shepseskaf: for references, see Verner 2014: 16.

[39] This was lost at sea en route to England in 1838. The king's burial was renewed during the Twenty-fifth/sixth Dynasty, when a new coffin was provided for his despoiled mummy. This is now in the British Museum, together with human remains that might be part of Menkaure's body, although Carbon-14 dates suggest a much later date.

[40] Cf. Jánosi 1996: 22–26.

[41] Ricke (1950: 120) proposed that GIIIa was used for the temporary burial of the king while the main pyramid was finished-off by Shepseskaf (cf. n.102, above).

[42] Porter and Moss 1974–81: 433–34.

[43] Porter and Moss 1934: 90–94; Harpur 2001.

[44] Alexanian 1999.

[45] Porter and Moss 1974–81: 893–94; Alexanian 1999.

[46] Jánosi 1996: 5–9.

[47] Porter and Moss 1974–81: 16–18; Jánosi 1996: 9–19, 77–82, 105–14, 123–28; Callender 2011: 81–83, 105–6, 119–21.

[48] Porter and Moss 1974–81: 179–82; Lehner 1985; Callender 2011: 60–63.

[49] Porter and Moss 1974–81: 187–94; Callender 2011: 93–99.

[50] Callender 2011: 87–88.

[51] Porter and Moss 1974–81: 4–5 (dated to Fifth Dynasty); for re-dating, see Gourdon 2006.

[52] Jánosi 1996: 20–21.

[53] Porter and Moss 1974–81: 233; Callender 2011: 103.

[54] Porter and Moss 1974–81: 273–74; Callender 2011: 110–16, 129.

[55] Porter and Moss 1974–81: 230–34, 239.

[56] Porter and Moss 1974–81: 293.

[57] Porter and Moss 1974–81: 34–35; Jánosi 1996: 21-28, 82–86, 105–14, 128–37.

[58] Porter and Moss 1974–81: 288–89; Maragioglio and Rinaldi 1964–77: VI, 168—95; Callender 2011: 136–47; Lehner, Jones, Yeomans, Mahmoud and Olchowska 2011.

[59] On the various theories, see Verner 2001: 165–78; 2014: 20–24; see also now Awady 2006.

[60] Porter and Moss 1974–81: 397–98; Labrousse and Lauer 2000.

[61] Cf. Dodson 2016c: 12.

[62] Jánosi 2013.

[63] On the potential reasons for the choice of this site, see Verner and Brůna 2011; Verner 2014: 158–60.

[64] Porter and Moss 1974–81: 326–35.

[65] Cf. Verner 2014: 160–62; on the principal motifs to be found in the various parts of the pyramid complex during the Fifth Dynasty, see Verner 2014: 186–98.

[66] Porter and Moss 1974–81: 339–40.

[67] See Verner 2014: 166–68.

[68] Porter and Moss 1974–81: 340; Verner (ed.) 2006.

[69] Verner 1982; 2014: 169–70.

[70] Porter and Moss 1974–81: 335–39; Maragioglio and Rinaldi 1964–77: VIII, 8–53; Krejči 2011.

[71] Berlandini 1979; Maragioglio and Rinaldi 1964–77: VIII, 59–63; Hawass 2010; Dodson 2016c: 13–15. The monument has also been proposed as belonging to a Tenth Dynasty king, Merykare (see p. 37); Silverman (2009: 74–75) has suggested that the pyramid might have been usurped by Amenemhat I.

[72] Porter and Moss 1974–81: 424. Maragioglio and Rinaldi 1964–77: VIII, 64–97.

[73] It is possible that this feature had been introduced by Menkauhor, but as neither anying of the perimeter of the pyramid, nor of the outer entrance corridor, survives, Isesi's is the earliest pyramid with any actual evidence.

[74] It is also possible that these divisions were present in Menkauhor's devastated annex.

[75] Also found at the earlier pyramids of Sahure and Niuserre.

[76] Porter and Moss 1974–81: 417–22; Labrousse, Lauer and Leclant 1977; Labrousse and Moussa 1996; Labrousse 1996–2000: I, 15–41; Labrousse and Moussa 2002.

[77] E.g. in the tomb of Mereruka (Porter and Moss 1974–81: 534); for a full list, see Dodson and Ikram 2008: 183–85.

[78] Youssef 2011.

[79] Faulkner 1969; Allen and Manuelian 2005.

[80] Labrousse and Lauer 2000: 141–62; Jánosi 1996: 87–89; Callender 2011: 158–61.

[81] Cf. Callender 2011: 166.

[82] Verner 2001.

[83] Krejčí, Callender and Verner 2009: 69–150; Callender 2011: 171–75.

[84] Krejčí, Callender and Verner 2009: 151–233.

[85] Krejči. 2011.

[86] Krejčí, Callender and Verner 2009: 37–68.

[87] Verner and Callender 2002.

[88] Porter and Moss 1974–81: 424; Maragioglio and Rinaldi 1964—77: VIII, 98–107; Megahed 2011; Callender 2011: 187–90.

[89] Porter and Moss 1974–81: 485–89, 496–98; Baud 1997.

[90] Porter and Moss 1974–81: 482; Callender 2011: 194.

[91] Callender 2011: 192.

[92] Porter and Moss 1974–81: 623–25; P. Munro 1993b; Callender 2011: 195–99, 204-5.

[93] Now reconstructed in the Field Museum of Natural History, Chicago.

[94] Porter and Moss 1974–81: 617–19.

[95] Hassan 1975: 1–10.

[96] Porter and Moss 1974–81: 340–42.

[97] Bárta et al. 2014: 20–33.

[98] Porter and Moss 1974–81: 393–96; Lauer and Leclant 1972; Labrousse 1996–2000: I, 43–72.

[99] Cf. Dodson 2016c: 14.

[100] Hays 2012.

[101] Kanawati 2002.

[102] Dobrev 2006a: 127–29; 2006b: 234–35; 2010.

[103] Porter and Moss 1974–81: 422–24; Labrousse 1996–2000: II, 1–45.

[104] Porter and Moss 1974–81: 425; Labrousse 1996–2000: II, 47–76.

[105] Porter and Moss 1974–81: 425–31; Labrousse 1996–2000: II, 77–99.

[106] Porter and Moss 1974–81: 508–37.

[107] Hawass 2011; Callender 2011: 206–9, 228–29; Wahba 2015.

[108] Porter and Moss 1974–81: 396–97; Labrousse, 1994; Jánosi 1996: 39–45, 90–93, 170–75; Hawass 2000: 414–19, 422–44; Callender 2011: 217–19, 221–23.

[109] Porter and Moss 1974–81: 534–35.

[110] Labrousse 1999; Callender 2011: 235–37, 238–39, 242–43, 244–45, 258–62, 288–90, 293–95; Labrousse 2012.
[111] Dobrev, Labrousse and Mathieu 2000.
[112] Porter and Moss 1974–81: 431–33; Jánosi 1996: 46–50, 138–44; Callender 2011: 271–75, 280–81, 283–86.
[113] Baud and Dobrev 1995; 1997; Dobrev 2000; Callender 2011: 299–303.
[114] Dodson 1992a; Labrousse and Moussa 1996: 8–9 n.11.
[115] Habachi 1983: 205—13.

CHAPTER 3

[1] Porter and Moss 1974–81: 425.
[2] Porter and Moss 1934: 258; Weill et al. 1958.
[3] Porter and Moss 1974–81: 538, 562, 563, 902.
[4] E.g. Malek 1994.
[5] Porter and Moss 1960–64: 594; Di. Arnold 1976: 19–22.
[6] Porter and Moss 1960–64: 595; Di. Arnold 1976: 25–32.
[7] pBritish Museum EA 10221, 2:1–3:14 (Kitchen 1983: 469–72).
[8] Porter and Moss 1960–64: 595; Di. Arnold 1976: 33–38.

CHAPTER 4

[1] Porter and Moss 1972: 381–400; Thomas 1966: 11–22; Di. Arnold 1974–81; 1979a.
[2] Cf. Polz 2007, 200–11.
[3] Winlock 1947: pl. 42–43.
[4] Porter and Moss 1972: 400; Thomas 1966: 26–28.
[5] Do. Arnold 1991.
[6] Porter and Moss 1952: 331; Thomas 1966: 28–30.
[7] Porter and Moss 1972: 340; Vörös 1998; 2003; 2007, 82–95; Vörös and Pudleiner 1997; 1998.
[8] E.g. Medinet Madi and Qasr el-Sagha.
[9] Weeks 1983: 53–54; Vörös 1998: 65–67; I am most grateful to Professor Weeks for the provision of unpublished material from his work.
[10] Porter and Moss 1960–64: 391–93.
[11] Porter and Moss 1960–64: 657; Thomas 1966: 22.
[12] Porter and Moss 1960–64: 385–86, 656–57; 1972: 386–90; Thomas 1966: 22–26.
[13] Porter and Moss 1934: 77–78; Di. Arnold 1988: 70–71.
[14] Silverman's proposal to place a pyramid at Saqqara (2009: 72–78) is based primarily on the burial there of officials associated with a pyramid of the king (cf. n. 135, above, for his proposal that he might have usurped the Fifth Dynasty pyramid attributed to Menkauhor).
[15] Porter and Moss 1934, 81–83; Di. Arnold 1988; 1992.
[16] Porter and Moss 1974–81: 885–86.
[17] Porter and Moss 1934: 107–9.
[18] Porter and Moss 1974–81: 882–85; Di. Arnold 2002; Oppenheim 2011.
[19] Porter and Moss 1937: 92; Wegner 1995; 2006a; 2006b; 2007a; 2007b; 2009; 2013; Wegner and Abu El-Yazid 2006.
[20] Cf. the later possible role of El-Qurn as the 'pyramid' of the tombs in the Valley of the Kings.
[21] Porter and Moss 1974–81: 887–88; Di. Arnold 1987.
[22] Porter and Moss 1934, 100–1; Di. Arnold 1979b; Uphill 2000.

[23] For a catalogue of the material from the site – but with a fundamentally flawed attempt at a reconstruction – see Uphill 2000.

[24] Cf. Jánosi 1996: 52–54.

[25] Di. Arnold 2008: 82–83.

[26] For example, Isesi, Unas, Teti, Nemtyemsaf I and Pepy II.

[27] Mace 1922: 12.

[28] Di. Arnold 1992; Jánosi 1996: 54–59, 116–20.

[29] Porter and Moss 1974–81: 886; Jánosi 1996: 59–60. There has been controversy over the date of these ladies and the others buried in the western area of the enclosure, attempts having been made to push them into the Thirteenth Dynasty (Williams 1975–76). However, the position and design of their tombs make it difficult to doubt that the tombs (two of which were found intact) were designed integrally with the pyramid-complex. Their principal occupants were thus all-but-certainly related to Amenemhat II, and buried within fifty years of his death – i.e no later than the reign of Senwosret III or the earlier part of that of Amenemhat III (cf. Fay 1996: 43–44, although she fails to fully appreciate the architectural context of the tombs).

[30] Porter and Moss 1934: 109–10; Jánosi 1996: 60–62.

[31] Porter and Moss 1974–81: 883–84; Di. Arnold 2002: 58–74; Stünkel 2006.

[32] Arnold 2002: 75–87.

[33] Di. Arnold 1987: 37–53; Jánosi 1996: 65–67.

[34] It seems probable that Amenemhat III had only daughters, and that Neferuptah may have been regarded as the king's heir; later, after the reign of Amenemhat IV, a further daughter, Sobekneferu, came to the throne as the first certain female pharaoh.

[35] Farag and Iskander 1971; Jánosi 1996: 67–70.

CHAPTER 5

[1] Porter and Moss 1974–81: 887; Swelim 1994, 343 n.16.

[2] One or two may lie uninvestigated under the sand (see Arnold and Stadelmann 1975: 174; cf. Alexanian 1999: fig. 1).

[3] Porter and Moss 1974–81: 890; Swelim and Dodson 1998.

[4] Porter and Moss 1934, 76.

[5] Porter and Moss 1974–81: 888–89.

[6] Porter and Moss 1934: 76.

[7] Porter and Moss 1974–81: 434–35.

[8] Porter and Moss 1974–81: 435.

[9] Schiestl 2008: 249–51.

[10] Schiestl 2008: 241–43.

[11] McCormack 2006; 2010: 75–77; Wegner and Cahail 2015; I am most grateful to Dr McCormack for the latest results of her excavation of S9.

[12] Wegner 2014; Wegner and Cahail 2015: 128–32, 149–53; Wegner 2016.

[13] For a discussion, see Ilin-Tomich 2014.

[14] Jéquier 1938: 38–39.

[15] Porter and Moss 1974–81: 435; Jánosi 1996: 70–71, 120–22.

[16] Porter and Moss 1974–81: 889.

[17] On the classification of the royal lines of the time, see Dodson 1991; Ryholt 1997: 151–83; Polz 2007: 20–56.

[18] Winlock 1924; Thomas 1966: 34–45; Miniaci 2011; Polz and Seiler 2003.

[19] Duplicated in the papyrus, apparently in error: cf. Biston-Moulin 2012.

[20] Porter and Moss 1960–64: 603; Polz and Seiler 2003; Polz 2007: 31–33, 133–38.

[21] Under excavation by a Spanish team.
[22] British Museum EA6652 (Porter and Moss 1960–64: 602–3).
[23] Athanasi 1836, xi.
[24] Miniaci 2011: 70–72.
[25] Louvre E.3019 (Porter and Moss 1960–64: 603).
[26] Louvre E.3020 (Porter and Moss 1960–64: 603).
[27] Louvre N.491=E.2538 (Porter and Moss 1960–64: 603; Dodson 1994: 37–47, 117–18[25], 150–51[25]).
[28] Porter and Moss 1960–64: 603; Polz 2007: 31–33, 133–38.
[29] Porter and Moss 1960–64: 600; Polz 2007: 138–60.
[30] Polz 2007: 162–72.
[31] Cairo TR 14/12/27/12 (Porter and Moss 1960–64: 600).
[32] E.g. Parkinson and Quirke 1992; Geisen 2004.
[33] Winlock 1924: 237–40.
[34] The contents of the burial are now in Edinburgh (Porter and Moss 1960–64: 606; Eremin et al 2000; Manley and Dodson 2010: 22–27).

CHAPTER 6

[1] Harvey 1994; 2001; 2004; 2008; Dodson 2010a; 2013: 24.
[2] Polz 1995; Dodson 2013: 23–24.
[3] Which now seems to be a royal family tomb of the middle of the Eighteenth Dynasty (Dodson 2003: 188–89; Aston 2013: 16–17; 2015).
[4] Niwiński 2009.
[5] Porter and Moss 1960–64: 599–60.
[6] Polz 2007: 172–97.
[7] Porter and Moss 1972: 422–23; Van Siclen 1980.
[8] Respectively as a cenotaph and an actual tomb (Polz 1998; Rummel 2009; 2010; 2013; 2014; Polz, Rummel, Eichner and Beckh 2012: 123–27).
[9] Dodson 2013.
[10] Porter and Moss 1972: 343; Di. Arnold 1979a: 67, pl. 42, 44.
[11] Moved to the temple of Montjuhotep II after the demolition (Porter and Moss 1972: 343).
[12] Porter and Moss 1972: 422–23; Van Siclen 1980.
[13] Polz 2007: 211–29.
[14] Porter and Moss 1960–64: 557–59; Thomas 1966: 71–83; Reeves 1990: 17–18; Weeks (ed.) 2000: 24; Piacentini and Orsenigo 2004: 195–96, 285–86.
[15] On the royal sarcophagi and canopics of the New Kingdom, see Dodson 2016a and b.
[16] Porter and Moss 1960–64: 546–47; Thomas 1966: 75–77; Reeves 1990: 13–17; Weeks (ed.) 2000: 21–22.
[17] Manuelian and Loeben 1993a; 1993b.
[18] Romer 1974.
[19] Roehrig 2007: 122.
[20] On the royal sarcophagi and canopic equipment of the New Kingdom, see Dodson 2016a and b; for funerary equipment in general, see Price 2016.
[21] Cf. Roehrig 2016: 184–88.
[22] Cf. Dodson 2012: 50–52; an anonymous mummy found in the coffin when found in TT320 (Cairo CG61065 – Smith 1912: 25–28) has often been called that of Thutmose I, but on arm position alone, as well as likely age at death, this cannot be so. Starting with Amenhotep I, kings were buried with their arms crossed at the breast: 'Thutmose I' has his extended.

²³ Roehrig 2006: 247, 248–50. Reeves 1990: 18–19 has the unusual tentative suggestion that TT358, found containing the restored burial of Meryetamun, wife of Amenhotep I (see pp. 79), might have been originally that of Thutmose II, reused for Meryetamun reburial during the Twenty-first Dynasty; however, there is no evidence in the tomb to suggest that it was anything other than the queen's original sepulchre.

²⁴ Porter and Moss 1960–64: 559; Thomas 1966: 78–80; Hornung 1975; Reeves 1990: 24–25; L. Gabolde 1991; El-Bialy 1999; Eaton-Krauss 1999; 2012; Weeks (ed.) 2000: 25; Preys 2011: 333–37.

²⁵ There is some evidence that might suggest that Meryetre was disgraced during the reign of her grandson, Thutmose IV (Bryan 1991: 98–99).

²⁶ Cf. Roehrig 2007.

²⁷ Porter and Moss 1972: 456–57; L. Gabolde 1989: 128–39.

²⁸ Known from a door (Porter and Moss 1972: 535); it has been suggested that the king's original chapel lay on the site of what became the sanctuary of his son, Wadjmose (Porter and Moss 1972: 444–46; see Quirke 1990: 174).

²⁹ Usefully summarized and described by Hornung 1999, with references.

³⁰ Porter and Moss 1960–64: 125; Dziobek 1994: 42–47.

³¹ Wysocki 1986.

³² See Ćwiek 2014.

³³ Haeny 1998; Ullmann 2016.

³⁴ Porter and Moss 1972: 340–77, 423–24; Weeks (ed.) 2001: 66-75.

³⁵ On the complex's relationship with Old and Middle Kingdom royal funerary monuments, see Ćwiek 2014.

³⁶ The Hatshepsut sequence has often been cited as being included specifically owing to her unusual status, but as there is no substantive reason to doubt the legitimacy of Amenhotep III and Rameses II, it seems far more likely that such sequences were a standard feature.

³⁷ Porter and Moss 1972: 426–29; Seco Álvarez and Radwan 2010; Seco Álvarez and Radwan and others 2010; Seco Álvarez 2012; http://thutmosisiiitempleproject.org.

³⁸ Porter and Moss 1960–64: 551–54; Thomas 1966: 77; Romer 1975; Reeves 1990: 19–24; Weeks (ed.) 2000: 23–24; Weeks (ed.) 2001: 136–39; Piacentini and Orsenigo 2004: 3–52.

³⁹ On the closing of doors in Valley of Kings tombs, see Roehrig 1995.

⁴⁰ Now BM EA23 (Porter and Moss 1934: 72; Hayes 1935: 153–54 n.42).

⁴¹ Porter and Moss 1960–64: 554–56; Thomas 1966: 77–78; Reeves 1990: 192–99; Weeks (ed.) 2000: 24; Weeks (ed.) 2001: 140–45; Piacentini and Orsenigo 2004: 52–190.

⁴² Porter and Moss 1972: 429-31; Sesana 2002–9; 2013, 2015.

⁴³ Porter and Moss 1972: 446–47.

⁴⁴ Porter and Moss 1960–64: 559–62; Thomas 1966: 80–81; Reeves 1990: 34–38; Weeks (ed.) 2000: 25.

⁴⁵ Porter and Moss 1960–64: 547–50; Thomas 1966: 183–87; Reeves 1990: 38–40; Kondo 1992; 1995; Reeves 1990: 38–40; Yoshimura and Kondo 1995; Weeks (ed.) 2000: 22; Yoshimura 2004; Yoshimura (ed.) 2008; Kawai 2013; Nishisaka, Takahashi and Yoshimura 2015; Kikuchi 2015.

⁴⁶ It has been suggested that the ordering of deities in this tomb was intended to reflect the sequence in which the king encountered them en route to the Duat, represented by the burial chamber and its decoration, and that this concept was also incorporated into the decoration of royal tombs down to Rameses I (Robinson 2010).

[47] Porter and Moss 1972: 449–54; Haeny (ed.) 1981; Weeks (ed.) 2001: 62–65; Sourouzian and Stadelmann 2005a; 2005b; Sourouzian 2010; 2011; Sourouzian et al. 2004; 2006a–c; 2007.

[48] Also a feature of a temple built by the king at Memphis (Porter and Moss 1974–81: 840, 843, 844, 863; Morkot 1990; Garnett 2011).

[49] Cf. Johnson 1998: 83.

[50] Cf. Bryan 1997, 2005 on the potential conceptual basis underlying Amenhotep III's sculpture program.

[51] Thomas 1966: 81–82; Reeves 1990: 40–42; Schaden 1979.

[52] A group of nameless foundation deposits to the east of WV25 can be dated to the late Eighteenth Dynasty (Afifi and Dash 2015).

[53] Murnane and Van Siclen 1993: 41.

[54] Porter and Moss 1934: 235–37; G.T. Martin 1974; 1989.

[55] Raven 1994; Brock 1996.

[56] El-Khouly and Martin 1987.

[57] For Neferuneferuaten and her fate, see Dodson 2009: 27–52.

[58] Porter and Moss 1960–64: 569–86; Thomas 1966: 142–47; Beinlich and Saleh 1989; Reeves 1990: 61–69; Eaton-Krauss 1993; Weeks (ed.) 2000: 28–30; Weeks (ed.) 2001: 146–71; Robins 2007.

[59] Reeves 2015, who goes on to conjecture that the northern 'door' might lead to the (intact) burial chamber of Nefertiti, Tutankhamun's sepulchre having been fashioned out of the outer rooms of her tomb. Although some remote-sensing work had been done by the time this book went to press, no conclusive results had yet been forthcoming.

[60] Drenkhahn 1983.

[61] Porter and Moss 1960–64: 562–64; Reeves 1990: 148–53; Weeks (ed.) 2000: 26.

[62] Cf. Dodson 2009: 89–94.

[63] Dziobek, Höveler-Müller and Loeben (eds) 2009; R.S. Wilson 2010; Schaden 2011; another option could be that the material derives from the Royal Tomb at Amarna, moved to KV63 when a number of mummies were removed to KV55 (see just below).

[64] Cross 2008; 2009; 2014: 141–43, 146–48.

[65] For bibliography see Grimm and Schoske (eds.) 2001, with summaries of the various published theories on pp. 121–136; to this add in particular M. Gabolde 2009. The contents are usefully summarised in Bell 1990.

[66] Cf. Dodson 2014: 165–66.

[67] Porter and Moss 1960–64: 253; Dodson 2009:

[68] Sa'ad 1975; Eaton-Krauss 1988: 2–3; Johnson 2009; Dodson 2009: 66–69.

[69] Robichon and Varille 1936: I, 29, 41–42, pl. iv[3], xii, xiii, xix, xxxvi–xxxviii[1] (North Temple); 47, pl. iv[4], xvi–xix, xli, xlii[1] (South Temple).

[70] Porter and Moss 1972: 457–59.

[71] Porter and Moss 1960–64: 550–551; Thomas 1966: 90–92; Schaden 1984; 2000; Reeves 1990: 70–72; Weeks (ed.) 2000: 22–23; Weeks (ed.) 2001: 172–75.

[72] Robins 1994: 157–59.

[73] Cf. Dodson and Ikram 2008: 252–55.

[74] Schaden 1984: 49–51 argued erroneously that box of the sarcophagus was reversed: see Reeves 1990a: 71, pl. v for the proof that this was not the case.

[75] Wilkinson 2011.

[76] Dodson 2009: 107–8.

[77] G.T. Martin 1989; H.D. Schneider 1996.

[78] Porter and Moss 1960–64: 567–69; Thomas 1966: 92–96; Hornung 1971; Reeves 1990: 75–79; Weeks (ed.) 2000: 28; Weeks (ed.) 2001: 176–89; van Dijk 2008.

[79] Porter and Moss 1972: 457–50.

[80] Porter and Moss 1960–64: 755–76.

[81] Thomas 1966: 184–87; Leblanc 1989a: 53; 1989b: 230–37.

[82] Porter and Moss 1960–64: 383, 658–67; Graefe and Belova (eds) 2010; on original ownership, see Aston 2013, the riposte in Graefe and Bickerstaffe 2013 and Aston's reply (2015).

[83] Porter and Moss 1960–64: 421 (incorrectly dated to Amenhotep II, corrected in Wyzocki 1984).

[84] Porter and Moss 1960–64: 668.

[85] For a recent re-survey of the area, with references, see Litherland 2014.

[86] Porter and Moss 1960–64: 591.

[87] Porter and Moss 1960–64: 592.

[88] Porter and Moss 1960–64: 591–92; Lilyquist 2003; Litherland 2014: 44–45.

[89] Weeks (ed.) 2000: 23; Jenni 2009: 17; Jenni (ed.) in preparation; Preys 2011: 332–33.

[90] Ryan 1991; 1992a; 1992b; 2007a; 2007b; 2010; 2010–11; Weeks (ed.) 2000: 22; Preys 2011.

[91] Weeks (ed.) 2000: 24–25; Rose 2000; Buckley 2005; Buckley, Buckley and Cooke 2005.

[92] Dodson 2003: 188–89; it now seems clear that the tomb cannot have been that of Amenhotep I, as proposed in the past by various writers, including the present author.

[93] The identification of his remains is hampered by the use of the tomb as a cache in the Third Intermediate Period, the mummy of a young male having been found alongside two female bodies that have been argued to be the reburied remains of Queens Tiye and Nefertiti (see Dodson 2014: 165–67 and Dodson and Cross 2016d for discussions).

[94] Probably including KV64, which contained a fragment naming Princess Sitiah (Bickel and Paulin-Grothe 2012) – although this may have been a stray from KV40 (see just below).

[95] Bickel 2014; Bickel and Paulin-Grothe 2014.

[96] A Prince Merymontju was interred in Year 25 (of Amenhotep III, on the basis of seal-impressions).

[97] Litherland 2014: 73–82; 2015.

[98] Litherland 2016; a number of fragments from these jars have been in museums since the early part of the twentieth century (Porter and Moss 1960–64: 769–70).

[99] Dodson and Janssen 1989; contrary to the conclusions reached there, it seems likely that the texts found with these burials date to their original Eighteenth Dynasty depositions (see Bouvier 2009), rather than their reburials (reburial indicated by their presence in the substructure of a tomb-chapel in the main nobles' cemetery, instead of in an a shaft-tomb in the Valley of the Kings or Southern Wadis like all other known royal family burials).

[100] El-Khouli and Martin 1987: 3–6.

[101] Leek 1972: 21–23

[102] Davis 1912: 2.

[103] BM EA36635 (G.T. Martin 1982: 277; Schneider 1996: 44; Thomas 1967 once suggested that she might be the owner of tomb QV33 in the Valley of the Queens; see, however Leblanc and Hassanein 1985: 27–28).

[104] Porter and Moss 1960–64: 534–35; Thomas 1966: 103–4; Robins 1983; Reeves 1990: 91–92; Weeks (ed.) 2000: 20; Weeks (ed.) 2001: 190–93.

[105] Bickerstaffe 2006; 2014: 103–21.

[106] Porter and Moss 1972: 407–21; Osing 1977; Brand 2000: 228–49; Weeks (ed.) 2001: 76–85; cf. Martinez 2007; 2008 on possible traces suggesting a usurpation of at least part of the building from an earlier ruler.

[107] Cf. Bell 1969, pointing out the problems with Hölscher's proposal (1941: 29–30) that post-Eighteenth Dynasty memorial temples lacked royal chapels.

[108] Porter and Moss 1960–64: 535–45; Thomas 1966: 104–7; Reeves 1990: 92–94; Donadoni 1966; Hornung 1991; Weeks (ed.) 2000: 21; Weeks (ed.) 2001: 194–211.

[109] Dodson 2016a: 250–51.

[110] Porter and Moss 1939: 29–31.

[111] Porter and Moss 1960–64: 505–7; Thomas 1966: 107–8; Reeves 1990: 94–95; Weeks (ed.) 2000: 18; Weeks (ed.) 2001: 212–17; Leblanc 2010.

[112] Romer 1981: 75.

[113] Porter and Moss 1972: 431–43; Centre of Documentation 1980; Weeks (ed.) 2001: 86–88; Cain and Martiex 2010.

[114] Uphill 1992.

[115] Porter and Moss 1972: 447–49; Sourouzian 1989: 162–74; Jaritz 1992, 2001; Jaritz, Dominicus and Sourouzian 1995; Jaritz et al. 1996, 1999 and 2001; Bickel 1997; Dominicus 2004.

[116] Porter and Moss 1960–64: 507–09; Thomas 1966: 108–10; Kitchen 1968–90: 68–72; Reeves 1990: 95–98; Brock 1992; Weeks (ed.) 2000: 18–19; Weeks (ed.) 2001: 218–21; Barbotin and Guichard 2004; 2006.

[117] For the Book of the Earth, its origins and later application, see Roberson 2012.

[118] For this period, see Dodson 2010b.

[119] Porter and Moss 1960–64: 532–33; Thomas 1966: 111–14; Reeves 1990: 103–4; Weeks (ed.) 2000: 20.

[120] See Dodson 1999.

[121] On its identity, see Dodson 2010b: 80–82.

[122] Porter and Moss 1960: 517–8; Thomas 1966: 110-11; Kitchen 1968–90: IV, 199-202; Ertman 1993; Schaden 1993; 1994; 2004; 2011; Weeks (ed.) 2000: 19; Schaden and Ertman 1998.

[123] Dodson 2010b: 48–51.

[124] Porter and Moss 1960–64: 564–66; Weeks (ed.) 2000: 26; Jenni 2009: 14–15; Jenni (ed.) forthcoming.

[125] For a discussion of these events, see Dodson 2010b: 111–22.

[126] Porter and Moss 1960–64: 527; Thomas 1966: 115–16; Kitchen 1968–90: IV, 355–56; Altenmüller 1989; 1992a; 1994; Weeks (ed.) 2000: 20.

[127] Porter and Moss 1960–64: 527–32; Thomas 1966: 114–15, 125; Altenmüller 1983; 1992b; 2012; Weeks (ed.) 2001: 222–31.

[128] Altenmüller 1983: 140–43 preferred to see it as a sarcophagus to be used for a putative interment of Sethy II in the tomb (on this theory, see Dodson 2010b: 160 n.4; Altenmüller 2016: 211 now suggests that the sarcophagus had been moved from KV11 by Rameses III).

[129] Porter and Moss 1972: 447; Wilkinson (ed.) 2011; Wilkinson 2012; Creasman, Johnson, McClain and Wilkinson 2014.

[130] Porter and Moss 1960–64: 751; Thomas 1966: 211, 213, 224–25; Leblanc 1989a: 54; 1989b: 240.

[131] Porter and Moss 1960–64: 769; Thomas 1966: 214, 217–18, 225; Leblanc 1989a: 55; 1989b: 241–43.

132 Porter and Moss 1960–64: 762–65; Thomas 1966: 213–14, 217, 219, 224–25; Habachi 1974; Leblanc 1989b: 241–43; McDondald 1996; Weeks (ed.) 2001: 294–311.

133 Porter and Moss 1960–64: 766–67; Thomas 1966: 211, 214, 217–18, 224–25; Leblanc 1989a: 54; 1989b: 241–43.

134 Porter and Moss 1960–64: 769; Thomas 1966: 214, 218, 224–25; Leblanc 1988; 1989a: 55; 1989b: 241–43.

135 Porter and Moss 1960–64: 765–66; Thomas 1966: 211, 214, 217–18, 224–25; Habachi 1974; Leblanc 1989a: 54; 1989b: 241–43.

136 Porter and Moss 1960–64: 751–52; Thomas 1966: 211, 213–14, 218–19, 222, 224–25; Leblanc 1988; 1989a: 54; 1989b: 240.

137 Porter and Moss 1960–64: 501; Thomas 1966: 149–51; Weeks 1998; 2000; Weeks (ed.) 2000: 17.

138 Waseda University, Institute of Egyptology 2001, 2005.

139 Porter and Moss 1934: 114; Polz 1986.

140 But cf. p. 88 for the issues around the royal ladies who were secondary owners of KV10.

141 For refs, see n. 383, above.

142 Porter and Moss 1960–64: 518-26; Thomas 1966: 125-27; Reeves 1990: 115; Marciniak 1982; 1983; Weeks (ed.) 2000: 19; Weeks (ed.) 2001: 232–39.

143 Porter and Moss 1972: 481–527; Murnane 1980; Weeks (ed.) 2001: 96–109.

144 Cf. Wilkinson 1995: 79-81.

145 Dodson 1986.

146 Porter and Moss 1960–64: 497-500; Thomas 1966: 127-29; Reeves 1990: 115–17; Hornung 1990; Peden 1994: 44-46; Weeks (ed.) 2000: 16–17; Weeks (ed.) 2001: 240–43.

147 pTurin 1885 (Carter and Gardiner 1917).

148 Dodson 1996b.

149 Carter and Gardiner 1917.

150 Porter and Moss 1972: 424.

151 Porter and Moss 1972: 424–26.

152 Porter and Moss 1972: 454, 459.

153 Hornung 1988a: 138-42.

154 Porter and Moss 1960–64: 511-18; Thomas 1966: 129-30; Amer 1985: 69-70; Ventura 1988; Abitz 1989; Reeves 1990: 117–19; Weeks (ed.) 2000: 19; Weeks (ed.) 2001: 244–65; Darnell 2004: 163–275; Barwick 2011: 24-30; Brock 2012.

155 Peden 2001: 83–88.

156 Cf. Bács 1992.

157 Porter and Moss 1960–64: 495-97; Hornung 1990; 1999: 109; Thomas 1966: 130-31; Reeves 1990: 119; Weeks (ed.) 2000: 16; Brock 1995.

158 Porter and Moss 1960–64: 501-505; Thomas 1966: 131-32; Reeves 1990: 119–20; Abitz 1990; Weeks (ed.) 2000: 18; Rossi 2001; Weeks (ed.) 2001: 266–69; Darnell 2004, 276-373.

159 Porter and Moss 1960–64: 545; Thomas 1966: 132; Reeves 1990: 120; Jenni (ed.) 2000; Weeks (ed.) 2000: 21.

160 Cf. Dodson 2012: 8-9, 14.

161 Porter and Moss 1964: 501; Thomas 1966: 132-33; Brooklyn Museum Theban Expedition [1979]; Ciccarello [1979]; Ciccarello and Romer [1979]; Reeves 1990: 121–23; Weeks (ed.) 2000: 17;
Jansen-Winkeln 2007: 21[28]; Dodson 2012: 49-50, fig, 35.

[162] Porter and Moss 1960–64: 756–58; Thomas 1966: 214, 219, 223–25; Grist 1985; Leblanc 1989b: 243–45; Collier, Dodson and Hamernik 2010.

[163] Porter and Moss 1960–64: 756; Thomas 1966: 211, 219–20, 223–25; Leblanc 1989a: 54; 1989b: 243–45.

[164] Porter and Moss 1960–64: 767–68; Thomas 1966: 214, 218–19, 224–25; Leblanc 1989a: 55; 1989b: 241–43.

[165] Porter and Moss 1960–64: 767; Thomas 1966: 214, 217–18, 224–25; Leblanc 1989a: 55; 1989b: 240.

[166] Porter and Moss 1960–64: 752–53; Thomas 1966: 219–21, 223–25; Leblanc 1989b: 243–45.

[167] Porter and Moss 1960–64: 753–54; Thomas 1966: 219–25; Leblanc ; 1989b: 243–45; he may have also founded tomb KV19 in the Valley of the Kings: see p. 100, above.

[168] Porter and Moss 1960–64: 754–55; Thomas 1966: 219–25; Leblanc ; 1989b: 243–45; Hassanein and Nelson 1997.

[169] Porter and Moss 1960–64: 759; Thomas 1966: 212, 219–21, 223–25; Leblanc 1989a: 54; 1989b: 243–45.

[170] Porter and Moss 1960–64: 752–53; Thomas 1966: 210, 219–25; Hassanein and Nelson 1976; Leblanc 1989b: 243–45.

[171] Porter and Moss 1960–64: 500; Thomas 1966: 150–51; Weeks (ed.) 2000: 17.

[172] Altenmüller 1994c: 5–6.

[173] Altenmüller 1994a: 4–5.

[174] Altenmüller 1994c.

[175] Porter and Moss 1960–64: 546; Thomas 1966: 151–52; Reeves 1990: 134–35; Weeks (ed.) 2000: 21; Brock 2013: 101–8.

CHAPTER 7

[1] For the Third Intermediate Period and its complexities, see Dodson 2012.

[2] Porter and Moss 1960–64: 662.

[3] Porter and Moss 1960–64: 662–63.

[4] Stadelmann 1971.

[5] Lull 2002: 51–59.

[6] MMA 47.60 and Aubert Collection (Dodson 1994: 79, 128, 172–73).

[7] Montet 1947: 46–47; 1951: 27–30.

[8] Montet 1951; Brissaud 1987: 23–25; Lull 2002: 27-33, 117-35; Aston 2009: 41–54; Le Guilloux 2010.

[9] On the decoration of the Tanite royal tombs, see Roulin 1998.

[10] Cf. Aston 2009: 44, 54.

[11] Montet 1951: 173–75; Jansen-Winkeln 2007–9: I, 95[7.3]; Aston 2009: 54.

[12] Association Française d'Action Artistique 1987: 136-7[19]; Aston 2009: 51. A scarab of Siamun was also found in the chamber (Aston 2009: 51).

[13] For an overview, see Aston 2014: 39–47.

[14] Porter and Moss 1960–64: 629; Aston 2009: 199–202.

[15] Porter and Moss 1960–64: 629–30; Aston 2009: 202.

[16] Reeves 1990: 244–77.

[17] Sheikholeslami 2008; Aston 2014: 44–45.

[18] But cf. Sagrillo 2009: 341–42, 349–50.

[19] Sagrillo 2009: 357–58.

[20] Dodson 1994: 83–84, 131, 178–79; Brandl 2012.

[21] See Dodson 2012: 101.

[22] Montet 1951: 37–50; Aston 2009: 51–54.

[23] Brunton 1939: 546–47.

[24] Montet 1947; Brissaud 1987: 17–18, 23–25; von Känel 1987: 57; Lull 2002: 74-117; Aston 2009: 54–58.

[25] Jansen-Winkeln 2007–9: II, 110[18.5]; Ritner 2009: 347–48[81].

[26] The text ends with the laconic note 'Kapus made it for him'. This has generally been interpreted as an indication that Osorkon II's mother Kapes (the names are slightly different, but within the potential boundaries of orthographic variation) outlived him and acted as intermediary in allowing Pashereneset to add his elegy – or even provided the king with his tomb. However, the lady in question is given no title, while Osorkon II's mother would in any case have been unlikely to be still alive at the end of her son's reign, which seems on broader chronological grounds to have lasted some four decades. Accordingly, 'Kapus' seems more likely to have been a quasi-homonym of the queen – perhaps a daughter of the king, if a member of the royal family at all.

[27] Cairo SR11488 (Saleh and Sourouzian 1987: [235]).

[28] Cf. Aston 2009: 58–59.

[29] Montet 1960; Brissaud 1987: 16–17; Lull 2002: 135–62; Aston 2009: 59–60.

[30] Dodson 1993.

[31] Montet 1947: 87–89; Aston 2009: 60.

[32] Not himself a former high priest, as was long thought: see Dodson 2012: 105–8.

[33] Porter and Moss 1960–64: 772; Lull 2002: 163–68; Aston 2009: 261; 2014a: 18–21.

[34] Lull 2002: 168–69; Jansen-Winkeln 2007–9: II, 294; Aston 2014: 21–23.

[35] Cf. Aston 2014: 23–39, 47–48.

[36] Porter and Moss 1934: 39; Lull 2002: 172–73; Aston 2009: 64–65.

[37] She may have been the wife of the King Iuput II, who was ruling at the site around 735BC, although it has been suggested that she is identical with Karomama B, wife of Osorkon II.

[38] Porter and Moss 1974–81: 846–47; Jeffreys 1985: 70–71; Aston 2009: 78–82.

[39] Porter and Moss 1937: 68.

[40] Porter and Moss 1937: 75; some of these granite blocks were found in the 1970s built into the White Monastery at Sohag, to which area they may have been removed for initial reuse under Ahmose II (Vernus 1976).

[41] Porter and Moss 1960–64: 678–84.

[42] Aston 2009: 265.

[43] See Dodson 2012: 139–68.

[44] Dodson 2014b: 3–6.

[45] Porter and Moss 1952: 196; Dunham 1950: 46–47; Lull 2002: 180–82.

[46] Porter and Moss 1952: 197; Dunham 1950: 64–66; Lull 2002: 182–83.

[47] Broekman 2015.

[48] Porter and Moss 1952: 197; Dunham 1950: 67–71; Lull 2002: 183–85.

[49] Porter and Moss 1952: 196; Dunham 1950: 55–59; Lull 2002: 183.

[50] Porter and Moss 1952: 223; Dunham 1955: 7–16; Lull 2002: 185–93. There were once suggestions that Taharqa had possessed a second pyramid (W T 1) at Sedeinga, nearly 350km away to the north, in which he had actually been buried. However, it has now become clear that the inscribed blocks upon which this attribution was based had been reused: see Leclant 1984; Lull 2002: 193–96.

[51] Porter and Moss 1952: 196; Dunham 1950: 60–63; Gasm el Seed 1985; Lull 2002: 196–97.

[52] Porter and Moss 1952: 195, 203–7, 225–33, 241–61; Dunham 1958; 1963; Dunham and Chapman 1952.

[53] Porter and Moss 1952: 195–97; Dunham 1950: 27–43, 81–90.

[54] Porter and Moss 1952: 231; Dunham 1955: 19–24.

[55] Leahy 1994.

[56] Porter and Moss 1960–64: 772–73; 1972: 476–80; Aston 2009: 263–64.

[57] Porter and Moss 1960–62: 685–86.

CHAPTER 8

[1] Cf. Lull 2002: 173–78; P. Wilson 2006: 19-150, 259-66; Leclère 2008: 159–96.

[2] Louvre E.32580, from a private collection (Barbotin 2000); another potential royal sarcophagus/coffin fragment was found at Ganag, 5km north of Sais (P. Wilson 2016).

[3] Formerly in the collection of the Comte de Caylus in 1767 (Barbotin 2000: 38 n.26).

[4] Barbotin 2000: 37; P. Wilson 2016.

[5] Dodson 1994: 104–5, found respectively reused as the container for a mummified raptor and in an Etruscan tomb in far-away Italy. This dispersion of Wahibre's equipment may derive from his killing in the aftermath of his overthrow by Ahmose II. Although Herodotus records above that he was granted burial in his own tomb, it is possible that the interment was somewhat makeshift, and omitted certain items, which were later reused in various contethusxts.

[6] Cf. Aston 2014: 51.

[7] KHM ÄOS3 (Vittman 1974).

[8] Vittmann 1974.

[9] Adam 1958: 303–4.

[10] Porter and Moss 1974–81: 289.

[11] Cf. Lloyd 2014.

[12] Herzfeld 1935: 36; 1941: 214; Schmidt 1953: 56–57.

[13] Stronach 1965: 11–14; Stronach 1978: 117–37; Dieulafoy 1884: 22 suggested that it was the tomb of Kambyses I, predecessor of Kyrus II.

[14] Schmidt 1970: 18–49.

[15] Although Schmidt 1970: 49 comes out in favour of the former.

[16] Stronach 1965: 17.

[17] Schmidt 1953.

[18] A tomb at Eshaqvan has been suggested as his (Herzfeld 1941: 205–6).

[19] Schmidt 1970: 80–90.

[20] Schmidt 1970: 90–93.

[21] Schmidt 1970: 93, on a highly subjective basis.

[22] Schmidt 1970: 96–99.

[23] Schmidt 1970: 93–96.

[24] Schmidt 1970: 102–7 (called Artaxerxes III).

[25] Schmidt 1970: 99–102 (called Artaxerxes II).

[26] Schmidt 1970: 107; Kleiss and Calmeyer 1975.

[27] Porter and Moss 1934: 72.

[28] Porter and Moss 1934: 3–4; Fraser 1972: II, 39–40.

[29] Porter and Moss 1934: 45.

[30] Porter and Moss 1974–81: 670–71.

[31] For discussions of the history of Alexander III's burial(s), cf. Fraser 1972: I, 15–17, II, 36–42; Chugg 2002; 2004/5; Saunders 2007; there is no evidence whatever for suggestions that he might have been buried at Siwa Oasis, or anywhere other than

'Memphis' and Alexandria.
[32] Lauer and Picard 1955.
[33] Adriani 1939.
[34] Andronicos 1984; Hammond 1991.
[35] Borza and Palagia 2007; Musgrave et al. 2010.
[36] Fraser 1972: I, 15–16, 225; II, 33–36.
[37] A 'tradition' that links it with the Nabi Daniel Mosque, 500m away, appears to date only to AD 1850.
[38] Fraser 1972: II, 33–34.
[39] Hesberg 1994.
[40] Dąbrowa 1996.
[41] Lepper and Frere 1988.
[42] Pierce 1925; Boatwright 1987: 161–81; Mercalli 1998.
[43] Hébrard and Zeiller 1912: 69–100.
[44] Downey 1959. The tombs in the church were desecrated by crusaders in 1204 and the building badly damaged; it was demolished in 1461, its site being used to build the Fatih Mosque. Six sarcophagi survive, displayed in Hagia Eirene and the Archaeological Museum, Istanbul.
[45] See Downey 1959: 36 n.25, 39–40 nn.24, 26.

Chronology of Ancient Egypt

including principal kings

LE = Lower Egypt only; UE = Upper Egypt only.
All dates more or less conjectural prior to 690 BC, with scholarly estimates varying by decades.

PREDYNASTIC PERIOD

Badarian Culture	5000-4000 BC
Naqada I (Amratian) Culture	4000-3500
Naqada II (Gerzean) Culture	3500-3150
Naqada III Culture	3150-3000

		Tomb
EARLY DYNASTIC PERIOD		
Dynasty 1	3050–2810	
Narmer		Umm el-Qaab B17/18
Hor-Aha		Umm el-Qaab B10/15/19
Djer		Umm el-Qaab O
Djet		Umm el-Qaab Z
Den		Umm el-Qaab T
Anedjib		Umm el-Qaab X
Semerkhet		Umm el-Qaab U
Qaa		Umm el-Qaab Q
Dynasty 2	2810–2660	
Hotepsekhemwy		Saqqara
Reneb		
Ninetjer		Saqqara
Sened		
Sekhemib/Peribsen		Umm el-Qaab P
Khasekhem/Khasekhemwy		Umm el-Qaab V
OLD KINGDOM		
Dynasty 3	2660–2600	
Djoser		Saqqara
Sanakht		Abu Rowash 'El-Deir'?
Sekhemkhet		Saqqara
Khaba		Zawiyet el-Aryan
Huni		Abu Roash (?)
Dynasty 4	2600–2470	
Seneferu		Dahshur & Meidum
Khufu		Giza

Djedefre		Abu Rowash
Seth?ka		Zawiyet el-Aryan
Khaefre		Giza
Menkaure		Giza
Shepseskaf		Saqqara-south
Dynasty 5	2470–2360	
Userkaf		Saqqara
Sahure		Abusir
Neferirkare		Abusir
Shepseskare		Abusir?
Neferefre		Abusir
Niuserre		Abusir
Menkauhor		Saqqara
Isesi		Saqqara-south
Unas		Saqqara
Dynasty 6	2360–2195	
Teti		Saqqara
Userkare		
Pepy I		Saqqara-south
Nemtyemsaf I (Merenre)		Saqqara-south
Pepy II		Saqqara-south
Nemtyemsaf II		

FIRST INTERMEDIATE PERIOD

Dynasties 7/8	2195–2160	
Ibi		Saqqara-south
Dynasties 9/10 (LE)	2160–2040	
Dynasty 11a (UE)	2160–2065	
Inyotef I		El-Tarif
Inyotef II		El-Tarif
Inyotef III		El-Tarif

MIDDLE KINGDOM

Dynasty 11b	2065–1995	
Montjuhotep II		Deir el-Bahari
Montjuhotep III		Thoth Hill(?)
Montjuhotep IV		
Dynasty 12	1995–1780	
Amenemhat I		Lisht
Senwosret I		Lisht
Amenemhat II		Dahshur
Senwosret II		Lahun
Senwosret III		Dahshur & Abydos-south
Amenemhat III		Dahshur & Hawara
Amenemhat IV		Dahshur L.LIV?
Sobekneferu		

SECOND INTERMEDIATE PERIOD

Dynasty 13	1780–1650	
Sobekhotep I		
Sonbef		
Nerikare		
Amenemhat V		Dahshur L.LIV?
Ameny-Qemau		Dahshur-south
Amenemhat VI		Dahshur L.LIV?
Nebnuni		
Hornedjhiryotef		
Swadjkare		
Nedjemibre		
Sobekhotep II		
Rensonbe		
Hor		
Amenemhat VII		
Wegaf		
Khendjer		Saqqara-south
Imyromesha		
Inyotef IV		
Seth(y)		Saqqara-south
Sobekhotep III		
Neferhotep I		Abydos-south S9?
Sihathor		
Sobekhotep IV		Abydos-south S10?
Sobekhotep V		
Sobekhotep VI		
Iaib		
Aya		
Ini I		
Sewadjtu		
Ined		
Hori		
Sobekhotep VII		
Ini II		
Neferhotep II		
Dynasty 14 (LE)	1700–1650	
Dynasty 15 (LE)	1650–1535	
Dynasty 16 (UE)	1650–1590	
Senebkay		Abydos-south CS9
Dynasty 17 (UE)	1585–1540	
Sobekemsaf I		
Inyotef V		Dra Abu'l-Naga
Inyotef VI		Dra Abu'l-Naga
Inyotef VII		Dra Abu'l-Naga
Sobekemsaf II		
Ahmose the Elder		

Taa		Dra Abu'l-Naga
Kamose		Dra Abu'l-Naga/Birabi?

Dynasty 18

Ahmose I	1540–1516	Abydos-south/AN B (?)
Amenhotep I	1516–1496	Dra Abu'l-Naga AN B(?)
Thutmose I	1496–1481	KV20?/KV38
Thutmose II	1481–1468	KV20? KV42?
Thutmose III	1468–1414	KV34
(Hatshepsut	1462–1447)	KV20
Amenhotep II	1415–1386	KV35
Thutmose IV	1386–1377	KV43
Amenhotep III	1377–1337	WV22
Akhenaten	1337–1321	TA26
(Smenkhkare	1325–1326)	
(Neferneferuaten	1326–1319)	TA29?
Tutankhamun	1321–1312	TA27?/WV23?/KV62
Ay	1311–1308	WV23
Horemheb	1308–1278	KV57

Dynasty 19

Rameses I	1278–1276	KV16
Sethy I	1276–1265	KV17
Rameses II	1265–1200	KV7
Merenptah	1200–1190	KV8
Sethy II	1190–1185	KV15
(Amenmeses	1189–1186)	KV10
Siptah	1186–1178	KV47
Tawosret	1178–1176	KV14

Dynasty 20

Sethnakhte	1176–1173	KV11/KV14
Rameses III	1173–1142	KV11
Rameses IV	1142–1136	KV2
Rameses V	1136–1132	KV9/?
Rameses VI	1132–1125	KV9
Rameses VII	1125–1118	KV1
Rameses VIII	1118–1116	
Rameses IX	1116–1098	KV6
Rameses X	1098–1095	KV18/?
Rameses XI	1110–1095(LE)	
	+1095–1078	KV4/?

Third Intermediate Period

Dynasty 21

Herihor	1078–1065(UE)	
Nesibanebdjedet I	1078–1053(LE)	NRT-I
Amenemnesut	1065–1049(UE?)	
Panedjem I	1063–1041(UE)	

Pasebkhanut I	1049–999	NRT-III
Amenemopet	1001–992	NRT-IV/NRT-III
Osorkon the Elder	992–985	
Siamun	985–967	NRT-III
Pasebkhanut II	967–941	NRT-III
Dynasty 22		
Shoshenq I	943–922	
Osorkon I	922–888	
Takelot I	888–872	?/NRT-I
Osorkon II	872–831	NRT-I
Shoshenq III	831–791	NRT-V
Shoshenq IV	791–779	NRT-V
Pamiu	779–773	NRT-II
Shoshenq V	773–736	
Dynasty 23	736–666	
Thebes		
Horsieset I	?–840?	MH1
Takelot II	834–810	
Padubast I	824–800	
Shoshenq VI	800–794	
Osorkon III	791–762	Medinet Habu?
Takelot III	768–748	
Rudamun	748–745	
Dynasty 24 (LE)	734–721	
Dynasty 25		
Kashta	?–745	Ku8?
Piye	745–713	Ku17
Shabataka	713–705	Ku18
Shabaka	705–690	Ku15
Taharqa	690–664	Nu1
Tanutamun	664–656+	Ku16

Saite Period

Dynasty 26		
Psametik I	664–610	Sais
Nekau II	610–595	Sais
Psametik II	595–589	Sais
Wahibre (Apries)	589–570	Sais
Ahmose II (Amasis)	570–526	Sais
Psametik III	526–525	Sais

Late Period

Dynasty 27 (Persians)		
Kambyses II	525–522	Pasagardae/Nashq-e Rustam?
Darius I	521–486	Nashq-e Rustam I
Xerxes I	486–465	Nashq-e Rustam IV(?)

Artaxerxes I	465–424	Nashq-e Rustam III(?)
Xerxes II	424	
Darius II	423–405	Nashq-e Rustam II(?)
Dynasty 28		
Amyrtaios	404–399	
Dynasty 29		
Naefarud I	399–393	Mendes
Pasherenmut	393	
Hagar	393–380	
Naefarud II	380	
Dynasty 30		
Nakhtnebef	380–362	
Djehor	362–360	
Nakhthorheb	360–339	
Dynasty 31 (Persians)		
Artaxerxes III Ochus	339–338	Persepolis V(?)
Artaxerxes IV Arses	338–336	Persepolis VII?
Darius III	335–332	Persepolis VII?

Hellenistic Period

Dynasty of Macedonia	332–310	
Alexander III	332–323	Alexandria
Philip III Arrhidaeus	323–317	Vergina(?)
Alexander IV	317–310	Vergina(?)
Dynasty of Ptolemy	310–30	Alexandria
Roman Period	BC 30–395 AD	Rome &c

References

Abbreviations

AJA	*American Journal of Archaeology* (Boston).
ASAE	*Annales du Service des Antiquités de l'Égypte* (Cairo).
A&L	*Ägypten und Levante* (Vienna).
BIFAO	*Bulletin de l'Institut Français d'Archéologie Orientale du Caire* (Cairo).
BMMA	*Bulletin of the Metropolitan Museum of Art* (New York).
CdE	*Chronique d'Egypte* (Brussels).
DE	*Discussions in Egyptology* (Oxford).
E&T	*Études et Travaux* (Warsaw).
EgArch	*Egyptian Archaeology: Bulletin of the Egypt Exploration Society* (London).
GM	*Göttinger Miszellen* (Göttingen).
JAEI	*Journal of Ancient Egyptian Interconnections* (Tucson).
JARCE	*Journal of the American Research Center in Egypt* (New York, &c).
JEA	*Journal of Egyptian Archaeology* (London).
JEH	*Journal of Egyptian History* (Leiden).
JHS	*Journal of Hellenic Studies* (London).
JMFA	*Journal of the Museum of Fine Arts, Boston* (Boston).
JNES	*Journal of Near Eastern Studies* (Chicago).
JSSEA	*Journal of the Society for the Study of Egyptian Antiquities* (Toronto).
Kmt	*Kmt: a Modern Journal of Ancient Egypt* (San Francisco, &c).
MDAIK	*Mitteilungen des Deutschen Archäologischen Instituts, Kairo* (Mainz).
MMJ	*Metropolitan Museum Journal* (New York).
NARCE	*Newsletter of the American Research Center in Egypt* (New York).
OMRO	*Oudheidkundige Mededelingen uit het Rijksmuseum van Oudheden te Leiden* (Leiden).
RdE	*Revue d'Egyptologie* (Leuven).
SAK	*Studien zur altägyptschen Kultur* (Hamburg).
ZÄS	*Zeitschrift für Ägyptische Sprache und Altertumskunde* (Leipzig, Berlin).

Bibliography

ABITZ, F. 1990. "Der Bauablauf und die Dekorationen des Grabes Ramesses' IX."
SAK 17: 1-40.

– 1989. *Baugeschichte und Dekoration des Grabes Ramses' VI.* Freiburg:
Universitätsverlag/Göttingen: Vandenhoeck und Ruprecht.

ADAM, S. 1958. 'Recent Discoveries in the Eastern Delta (Dec. 1950-May 1955)'.
ASAE 55: 301–24.

ADAMS, M.D. and D.B. O'Connor 2010. 'The Shunet el-Zebib at Abydos:
architectural conservation at one of Egypt's oldest preserved royal monuments'. In
*Offerings to the discerning eye: an Egyptological medley in honor of Jack A.
Josephson*, edited by S.H. D'Auria, 1–8. Leiden: Brill.

ADRIANI, A. 1939 'Tombeau en alabatre du cimetière Latin', *Annuaire du Musée
Gréco-Romain 1935–1939*: 15–23.

AFIFI, R.A. and G. DASH 2015. 'The Discovery of Intact Foundation Deposits in the
Western Valley of the Valley of the Kings'. In *Current Research in Egyptology 2014:
Proceedings of the Fifteenth Annual Symposium*, edited by M.S. Pinarello, J. Woo, J.
Lundock and C. Walsh, 1–12. Oxford: Oxbow.

ALEXANIAN, N. 1998. 'Die Reliefdekoration des Chasechemui aus dem sogenannten
Fort in Hierakonpolis'. *In Les critères de datation stylistiques à l'ancien empire*,
edited by N. Grimal, 1–29. Cairo: Institut français d'archéologie orientale.

– 1999. *Dahschur*, II: *Das Grab des Prinzen Netjer-aperef. Die Mastaba II/1 in
Dahschur.* Mainz: Philipp von Zabern.

ALEXANIAN, N., W. BEBERMEIER and D. BLASCHTA 2012. 'Untersuchungen am
unteren Aufweg der Knickpyramide in Dahschur'. *MDAIK* 68: 1–30.

ALLEN, J.P. and P. DER MANUELIAN 2005. *The Ancient Egyptian Pyramid Texts.*
Atlanta: Society of Biblical Literature.

ALTENMÜLLER, H. 1983.'Das Grab des Königin Tausret im Tal des Könige von
Thebes'. *SAK* 10: 1–24.

– 1989. 'Untersuchungen zum Grab des Bai (KV 13) im Tal der Könige von Theben.'
GM 107: 43–54.

– 1992a. 'Zweiter Vorbericht in die Arbeiten des Archäologischen Instituts der
Universität Hamburg am Grab des Bay (KV 13) im Tal der Könige von Theben.'
SAK 19: 15–36.

– 1992b. 'Bemerkungen zu den neu gefundenen Daten im Grab der Königin Twosre
(KV14) im Tal der Könige von Theben.' In *After Tut'ankhamūn*, edited by C. N.
Reeves, 141–64. London and New York: Kegan Paul International

– 1994. 'Dritter Vorbericht in die Arbeiten des Archäologischen Instituts der Universität
Hamburg am Grab des Bay (KV 13) im Tal der Könige von Theben', SAK 21 (1994),
1-18.

– 2012. 'A Queen in a Valley of Kings: The Tomb of Tausret'. In *Tausret: forgotten
queen and pharaoh of Egypt*, edited by R.H. Wikinson, 67–91. New York: Oxford
University Press.

– 2016. 'Royal Tombs of the Nineteenth Dynasty'. In *The Oxford Handbook to the*

Valley of the Kings, edited by R.H. Wilkinson and K.R. Weeks, 200–17. New York: Oxford University Press.

AMER, A.A.A. 1985. 'Reflections on the Reign of Ramesses VI'. *JEA* 71: 66–70.

ANDRONICOS M. 1984. *Vergina: the royal tombs and the ancient city*. Athens: Ekdotike Athenon.

ANDRZEJEWSKI, T. 1962. 'Le Livre des portes dans la salle du sarcophage du tombeau de Ramsès III'. *ASAE* 57: 1–6.

ARNOLD, Di. 1974–81. *Der Tempel des Königs Mentuhotep von Deir el-Bahari*, 3vv (Mainz: Philipp von Zabern).

– 1976. *Gräber des Alten und Mittleren Reiches in El-Tarif*. Mainz: Philipp von Zabern.

– 1977. 'Fajjum'. In *Lexikon der Ägyptologie*, edited by W. Helck and E. Otto, 87–93. Wiesbaden: Otto Harrassowitz.

– 1979a. *The Temple of Mentuhotep at Deir el-Bahri*. New York: Metropolitan Museum of Art.

– 1979b. 'Das Labyrinth und seine Vorbilder'. *MDAIK* 35: 1–9.

– 1987. *Der Pyramidbezirk des Königs Amenemhet III in Dahschur*, I: *Die Pyramide*. Mainz: Philipp von Zabern.

– 1988. *The Pyramid of Senwosret I*. New York: Metropolitan Museum of Art.

– 1992. *The Pyramid Complex of Senwosret I*. New York: Metropolitan Museum of Art.

– 1998. 'Royal Cult Complexes of the Old and Middle Kingdoms'. In *Temples in Ancient Egypt*, edited by B.E. Schafer, 86–126. London: I.B. Tauris, 1998).

– 2002. *The Pyramid Complex of Senwosret III at Dahshur: architectural studies*. New York: Metropolitan Museum of Art.

– 2006. 'Changing the shape of the pyramid of Senusret III'. In *Abusir and Saqqara in the Year 2005*, edited by M. Bárta, F. Coppens and J. Krejčí, 108–15. Prague: Czech Institute of Egyptology.

– 2008. *Middle Kingdom Tomb Architecture at Lisht*. New York: Metropolitan Museum of Art.

ARNOLD, Di. and R. STADELMANN 1975. 'Dahschur: Erster Grabungsberichte'. *MDAIK* 31: 169–174.

ARNOLD, Do. 1991. 'Amenemhat I and the early Twelfth Dynasty at Thebes'. *MMJ* 26: 5–48.

ASSOCIATION FRANÇAISE D'ACTION ARTISTIQUE 1987. *Tanis: L'or des pharaons*. Paris: Ministère des Affaires Étrangères/Association Française d'Action Artistique.

ASTON, D.A. 2009. *Burial Assemblages of Dynasty 21–25: Chronology – Typology – Developments*. Vienna: Verlag der Österreichen Akademie der Wissenschaften.

– 2013. 'TT 320 and the ḳȝy of Queen Inhapi – A Reconsideration Based on Ceramic Evidence'. *GM* 236: 7–20.

– 2014. 'Royal Burials at Thebes during the First Millennium BC'. In *Thebes in the First Millennium BC*, edited by E. Pischikova, J. Budka and K. Griffin, 15–60. Newcastle upon Tyne: Cambridge Scholars.

– 2015. 'TT 358, TT 320, and KV 39. Three Early Eighteenth Dynasty Queen's Tombs in the Vicinity of Deir el-Bahri'. In *Deir el-Bahari Studies,* edited by Z. Szafranski, 14-42. Warsaw: Polish Centre of Mediterranean Archaeology.

ATHANASI, G. 1836. *A brief account of the researches and discoveries in Upper Egypt made under the direction of Henry Salt*. London: John Hearne.

AWADY, T. el 2006. 'The royal family of Sahura. New evidence'. In *Abusir and*

Saqqara in the Year 2005, edited by M. Bárta, F. Coppens and J. Krejči, 191–218. Prague: Czech Institute of Egyptology.

– 2009. *Sahure – The Pyramid Causeway: history and decoration program in the Old Kingdom*. Prague: Charles University.

AYRTON, E.R., C.T. CURRELLY and A.E.P. WEIGALL 1904. *Abydos*, III. London: Egypt Exploration Fund.

BÁCS, T.A. 1992. 'Amun-Ra-Harakhti in the late Ramesside royal tombs.' In *The intellectual heritage of Egypt: studies presented to László Kákosy by friends and colleagues on the occasion of his 60th birthday*, edited by Ulrich Luft, 43–53. Budapest: Chaire d'Égyptologie.

BARBOTIN, C. 2000. 'Un bas-relief au nom de Psammétique II (595–589 av. J.-C.), une récente acquisition du Louvre.' *La revue du Louvre et des Musées de France* 5: 33–38.

BARBOTIN, C. and S. GUICHARD 2004. 'La tombe de Merenptah: Projets et travaux récents'. *Memnonia* 15: 153–64.

– 2006. 'Fouilles du Louvre dans la tombe de Merenptah, 2005–2006'. *Memnonia* 17: 151–69.

BARSANTI, A. 1912. 'Fouilles de Zaouiét el-Aryân (1911–1912)', *ASAE* 12: 57–63.

BÁRTA, M., H. VYMAZALOVÁ, V. DULÍKOVÁ, K. ARIAS, M. MEGAHED and L. VARADZIN 2014. 'Exploration of the Necropolis at Abusir South in the Season of 2012: Preliminary Report'. *A&L* 24: 15–38.

BARWICK, M. 2011. *The Twilight of Ramesside Egypt: Studies on the History of Egypt at the End of the Ramesside Period*. Warsaw: Agade.

BAUD, M. 1997. 'Aux pieds de Djoser: les mastabas entre fosse et enceinte de la partie nord du complexe funéraire'. In *Études sur l'Ancien Empire et la nécropole de Saqqâra dédiées à Jean-Phillipe Lauer*, edited by C. Berger and B. Mathieu, 69–87. Montpellier: Université Paul Valéry-Montpellier III.

EL-BIALY, M. 1999. 'Récentes recherches effectuées dans la tombe no. 42 de la Vallée des Rois'. *Memnonia* 10: 161–78.

BEINLICH, H. and M. SALEH 1989. *Corpus der Hieroglyphischen Inschriften aus dem Grab des Tutanchamun*. Oxford: Griffith Institute.

BELL, M. 1990. 'An Armchair Excavation of KV 55'. *JARCE* 27: 97–137.

BELZONI, G. 1820. *Narrative of the Operations and Recent Discoveries within the Pyramids, Temples, Tombs and Excavations in Egypt and Nubia*. London: John Murray.

BERLANDINI, J. 1979. 'La pyramide "ruinée" de Sakkara-nord et le roi Ikaouhor-Menkaouhor'. *RdE* 31: 3–28.

BESTOCK, L. 2009. *The development of royal funerary cult at Abydos: two funerary enclosures from the reign of Aha*. Wiesbaden: Otto Harrassowitz.

BICKEL, S. 2014. 'The Tomb of 18th Dynasty Princesses and Princes'. *Kmt* 25/3: 22–32.

BICKEL, S. and E. PAULIN-GROTHE 2012. 'KV 64: Two Burials in one Tomb'. *EgArch* 41: 36–40.

– 2014. 'KV 40: A burial place for the royal entourage'. *EgArch* 45: 21–24.

BICKERSTAFFE, D. 2006. 'Examining the mystery of the Niagara Falls mummy: was he from the royal mummies cache? And is he Rameses I?' *Kmt* 17/4: 26–34.

– 2014. *An Ancient Egyptian Case Book*. N.p.: Canopus Press.

BISTON-MOULIN, S. 2012. 'Le roi Sénakht-en-Rê Ahmès de la XVIIe dynastie'. *Égypte nilotique et méditerranéenne* 5: 61–71

BOATWRIGHT, M.T. 1987. *Hadrian and the City of Rome*. Princeton, NJ: Princeton University Press.

BORZA E.N. and PALAGIA O. 2007. 'The chronology of the Macedonian royal tombs at Vergina'. *Jahrbuch des Deutschen Archäologischen Instituts* 122: 81–125.

BOUVIER, G. 2009. 'Les princesses de Gourna'. In *Texte – Theben – Tonfragmente: Festschrift für Günter Burkard*, edited by D. Kessler, R. Schulz, M. Ullmann, A. Verbovsek and S.J. Wimmer, 59–69. Wiesbaden: Harrassowitz.

BRAND, P.J. 2000. *The Monuments of Seti I: epigraphic, historical and art historical analysis*. Leiden: Brill.

BRANDL, H. 2012. 'Engel mit nur einem flügel? Der Grabstein der Eheleute Loewy und sein altägyptisches Vorbild, der Berliner Eingeweideschrein Scheschonqs I'. *Pharaonen an der Spree: Ägyptisierende Architektur und Skulptur in Berlin*, 1, edited by M. Loth, 143–52. Norderstedt: Books on Demand GmbH.

BRISSAUD, P. 1987. 'Les fouilles dans le secteur de la nécropole royale (1984–1986)'. In *Cahiers de Tanis: Mission français des fouilles de Tanis* I, edited by P. Brissaud, 7–43. Editions Recherche sur les Civilisations.

BROCK, E.C. 1992. 'The Tomb of Merenptah and its Sarcophagi'. In *After Tut'ankhamūn*, edited by C. N. Reeves, 122–40. London and New York: Kegan Paul International.

– 1995. 'The Clearance of the Tomb of Ramesses VII'. In *Valley of the Sun Kings: New Explorations in the Tombs of the Pharaohs*, edited by Richard H. Wilkinson, 47–67. Tucson: The University of Arizona Egyptian Expedition.

– 1996. 'The sarcophagus of Queen Tiy'. *JSSEA* 26: 8–21.

– 2012. 'Chaos reversed: the reconstruction of the inner sarcophagus of Ramses VI'. In *Achievements and problems of modern Egyptology: proceedings of the international conference held in Moscow on September 29–October 2, 2009*, edited by G.A. Belova and S.V. Ivanov, 49–63. Moscow: Russian Academy of Sciences.

– 2013. 'Some Observations on the Valley of the Kings in the Twentieth Dynasty'. In *Archaeological Research in the Valley of the Kings & Ancient Thebes: Papers Presented in Honor of Richard H. Wilkinson*, edited by P.P. Creasman, 101–22. N.p.: University of Arizona Egyptian Expedition.

BROEKMAN G.P.F. 2015. 'The order of succession between Shabaka and Shabataka; A different view on the chronology of the Twenty-fifth Dynasty'. *GM* 245: 17–31.

BROOKLYN MUSEUM THEBAN EXPEDITION. [1979]. *Theban Royal Tomb Project: A Report of the First Two Seasons*. San Francisco: Privately Printed.

BRUNTON, G. 1939. 'Some Notes on the Burial of Shashanq Heqa-kheper-Re', *ASAE* 39: 541–47.

BRYAN, B.M. 1991. *The reign of Thutmose IV*. Baltimore: Johns Hopkins University Press.

– 1997. 'The statue program for the mortuary temple of Amenhotep III'. In *The temple in ancient Egypt: new discoveries and recent research*, edited by S. Quirke, 57–81. London: British Museum Press.

– 2005. 'Аменхотеп III и мемфисская теология / Amenhotep III and the Memphite Theology: Royal and Divine Statuary'. In *Петербургские сфинксы: солнце Египта на берегах Невы*, edited by V.V. Solkin, 153–90, 270–90. St Petersburg: Zurnal-Neva.

BUCKLEY, I.M. 2005. 'Excavations at Theban Tomb KV 39'. In *Current Research in Egyptology II*, edited by A. Cooke and F. Simpson, 21–28. Oxford: Archaeopress.

BUCKLEY, I.M., P. BUCKLEY and A. COOKE 2005. 'Fieldwork in Theban Tomb KV 39: The 2002 Season'. *JEA* 91: 71–82.

CAIN, K. and P. MARTINEZ 2010. 'Face to face with the past: a decade of insight at the Ramesseum'. In *Les temples de millions d'années et le pouvoir royal à Thèbes au Nouvel Empire: sciences et nouvelles technologies appliquées à l'archéologie*, edited by C. Leblanc and G. Zaki, 231–42. Cairo: Dar el-Kutub.

CALLENDER, V.G. 2004. 'Queen Tausret and the End of Dynasty 19'. *SAK* 32: 81–104.

– 2011. *In Hathor's image*, I: *The wives and mothers of Egyptian kings from Dynasties I–VI*. Prague: Charles University in Prague.

CALLENDER, V.G. and P. JÁNOSI 1997. 'The Tomb of Queen Khamerernebty II at Giza. A Reassessment'. *MDAIK* 53: 1–22.

CALMEYER, P. 1975. 'Das Unvollendete Achaemenidische Felsgrab bei Persepolis'. *Archaeologische Mitteilungen aus Iran* 8: 81–113.

CARTER, H. and A.H. GARDINER 1917. 'The Tomb of Ramesses IV and the Turin Plan of a Royal Tomb'. *JEA* 4: 130–58.

CASE, H. and J.C. PAYNE 1962. 'Tomb 100: the decorated tomb at Hierakonpolis'. *JEA* 48: 5–18.

CENTRE OF DOCUMENTATION 1980. *Le Ramesseum*, 11 vv. Cairo: Centre of Documentation.

CHUGG, A.M. 2002. 'The Sarcophagus of Alexander the Great?' *Greece & Rome* 49: 8–26.

– 2004/5. *The Lost Tomb of Alexander the Great*. London: Richmond Editions.

CICCARELLO, M. [1979]. T*he Graffito of Pinutem I in the Tomb of Ramesses XI* San Francisco: Privately Printed.

CICCARELLO, M. and J. ROMER. [1979]. *A Preliminary Report of the Recent Work in the Tombs of Ramesses X and XI in the Valley of the Kings*. San Francisco: Privately Printed.

CLARK, R.J. 2016. *Tomb Security in Ancient Egypt from the Predynastic to the Pyramid Age*. Oxford: Archaeopress.

COLLIER, M., A. DODSON and G. HAMERNIK 2010. 'P. BM EA 10052, Anthony Harris, and Queen Tyti'. *JEA* 96: 242–47.

CORDINGLEY R.A. and I.A. RICHMOND 1927. 'The Mausoleum of Augustus'. *Papers of the British School at Rome* 10: 23–35.

CREASMAN, P.P., W.R. JOHNSON, J.B. MCCLAIN and R.H. WILKINSON 2014. 'Foundation or completion? The status of Pharaoh-Queen Tausret's temple of millions of years'. *JNES* 77: 274–83.

CROSS, S.W. 2008. 'The Hydrology of the Valley of the Kings'. *JEA* 94: 303–12.

– 2009. 'The Re-Sealing of KV62'. *AncEg* 10/2: 16–22.

– 2014. 'The Workmen's Huts and Stratigraphy in the Valley of the Kings'. *JEA* 100: 133–50.

ĆWIEK, A. 2014. 'Old and Middle Kingdom Tradition in the Temple of Hatshepsut at Deir el-Bahari'. *E&T* 27: 61–93.

DĄBROWA, E. 1996. 'The Origin of the "Templum Gentis Flaviae": A Hypothesis'. *Memoirs of the American Academy in Rome* 41: 153–61.

DARNELL, J.C. 2004. *The enigmatic Netherworld Books of the Solar-Osirian unity: cryptographic compositions in the tombs of Tutankhamun, Ramesses VI and Ramesses IX*. Fribourg; Academic Press/Göttingen: Vandenhoeck & Ruprecht.

DAVIS, T.M. 1912. *The Tombs of Harmhabi and Touatânkhamanou*. London: Constable.

DE MORGAN, J. 1895. *Fouilles à Dahchour*, I. Vienna: Adolphe Holzhausen.

DIEULAFOY, M.A. 1884. *L'art antique de la Perse: Achéménides, Parthes, Sassanides*, I. Paris: Librairie centrale d'architecture.

DOBREV, V. 2000. 'The South Saqqara Stone and the sarcophagus of Queen Mother Ankhesenpepy (JE 65 908)'. In *Abusir and Saqqara in the year 2000*, edited M. Bárta and J. Krejčí, 381–96. Prague: Academy of Sciences of the Czech Republic, Oriental Institute.

– 2006a. 'A new necropolis from the Old Kingdom at south Saqqara'. In *The Old Kingdom art and archaeology: proceedings of the conference held in Prague, May 31 – June 4, 2004*, edited by M. Bárta, 127–31. Prague: Czech Institute of Egyptology, Faculty of Arts, Charles University in Prague.

– 2006b. 'Old Kingdom tombs at Tabbet al-Guesh (south Saqqara)'. In *Abusir and Saqqara in the year 2005: proceedings of the conference held in Prague (June 27 July 5, 2005)*, edited by M. Bárta, F. Coppens and J. Krejčí, 229–35. Prague: Czech Institute of Egyptology, Faculty of Arts, Charles University in Prague.

– 2010. 'Quest for the lost kings of Dynasty 6'. In *Recent discoveries and latest researches in Egyptology: proceedings of the First Neapolitan Congress of Egyptology, June 18th–20th 2008*, edited by F. Raffaele, M. Nuzzolo and I. Incordino, 51–65. Wiesbaden: Harrassowitz.

DOBREV, V. and M. BAUD 1995. 1995. 'De nouvelles annales de l'Ancien Empire égyptien: une "Pierre de Palerme" pour la VIe dynastie'. *BIFAO* 95: 23–92.

– 1997. 'Le verso des annales de la VIe dynastie: pierre de Saqqara-Sud'. *BIFAO* 97: 35–42.

DOBREV, V., A. LABROUSSE and B. MATHIEU 2000. 'La dixième pyramide à textes de Saqqâra: Ânkhesenpepy II. Rapport préliminaire de la campagne de fouilles 2000'. *BIFAO* 100: 275–96.

DODSON, A. 1986. 'Was the Sarcophagus of Ramesses III begun for Sethos II?'. *JEA* 72: 196–98.

– 1998a. 'The Tombs of the Queens of the Middle Kingdom'. ZÄS 115: 123–36.

– 1998b. 'Egypt's first antiquarians?' *Antiquity* 62/236: 513–17.

– 1991. 'On the Internal Chronology of the Seventeenth Dynasty'. *GM* 120: 33–8.

– 1992a. 'On the Burial of Prince Ptahshepeses'. *GM* 129: 49–51.

– 1992b. 'Death after Death in the Valley of the Kings', In *Death and Taxes in the Ancient Near East*, edited by S. Orel, 53–59. Lewiston: The Edwin Mellen Press.

– 1993. 'A new King Shoshenq confirmed?' *GM* 137: 53–58.

– 1994. *The Canopic Equipment of the Kings of Egypt*. London: Kegan Paul International.

– 1996a. 'The Mysterious Second Dynasty.' *Kmt* 7/2: 19–31.

– 1996b. 'A canopic jar of Ramesses IV and the royal canopic equipment of the Ramesside Period'. *GM* 152: 11–17.

– 1997–98. 'The So-Called Tomb of Osiris at Abydos'. *Kmt* 8/4: 37–47.

– 2000. 'The Layer Pyramid at Zawiyet el-Aryan: Its Layout and Context'. *JARCE* 38: 81–90.

– 2003. 'The burial of members of the royal family during the Eighteenth Dynasty'. In *Egyptology at the dawn of the twenty-first century: proceedings of the Eighth International Congress of Egyptologists, Cairo, 2000,* edited by Z. Hawass and L.P. Brock, II, 187–93. Cairo: American University in Cairo Press.

– 2009. *Amarna Sunset: Nefertiti, Tutankhamun, Ay, Horemheb and the Egyptian Counter-Reformation*. Cairo: American University in Cairo Press.

– 2010a. 'The Burials of Ahmose I'. In *Thebes and Beyond: Studies in Honour of Kent R. Weeks*, edited by Z. Hawass and S. Ikram, 25–33. Cairo: Conseil Supréme des Antiquités.

– 2010b. *Poisoned Legacy: The Fall of the Nineteenth Egyptian Dynasty*. Cairo: American University in Cairo Press.

– 2012. *Afterglow of Empire: Egypt from the fall of the New Kingdom to the Saite Renaissance*. Cairo: American University in Cairo Press.

– 2013. 'On the burials and reburials of Ahmose I and Amenhotep I'. *GM* 238: 19–24.

– 2014a. *Amarna Sunrise: from Golden Age to Age of Heresy*. Cairo: American University in Cairo Press.

– 2014b. 'The Coming of the Kushites and the Identity of Osorkon IV'. In *Thebes in the First Millennium BC*, edited by E. Pischikova, J. Budka and K. Griffin, 3–12. Newcastle-upon-Tyne: Cambridge Scholars.

– 2016a. 'Sarcophagi'. In *The Oxford Handbook to the Valley of the Kings*, edited by R.H. Wilkinson and K.R. Weeks, 245–59. New York: Oxford University Press.

– 2016b. 'Canopics'. In *The Oxford Handbook to the Valley of the Kings*, edited by R.H. Wilkinson and K.R. Weeks, 260–73. New York: Oxford University Press.

– 2016c. 'Go West: on the ancient means of approach to the Saqqara Necropolis'. In *Mummies, Magic and Medicine: Multidisciplinary Essays in Egyptology for Rosalie David*, edited by C. Price, P. Nicholson, R. Morkot, J. Tyldesley, A. Chamberlain and R. Forshaw, 3–18. Manchester: Manchester University Press.

DODSON, A. and S. CROSS 2016. 'The Valley of the Kings in the reign of Tutankhamun'. *EgArch* 48: 3–8.

DODSON, A. and S. IKRAM 2004. *The Tomb in Ancient Egypt*. London: Thames and Hudson.

DODSON, A. and J.J. JANSSEN 1989. 'A Theban Tomb and its Tenants'. *JEA* 75: 125–38.

DONADONI, S. 1966. *La decorazione della tomba di Seti I nella Valle dei Re*. Milan: Fratelli Fabbri.

DONADONI ROVERI, A.M. 1969. *I sarcophagi egizi dalle origini alla fine dell' Antico Regno*. Rome: Università degli Studi di Roma.

DOWNEY, G. 1959. 'The Tombs of the Byzantine Emperors at the Church of the Holy Apostles in Constantinople'. *JHS* 79: 27–51.

DRENKHAHN, R. 1983. 'Ein Umbettung Tutanchamuns?' *MDAIK* 39: 29–37.

DREYER, G. 1990. 'Umm el-Qaab: Nachuntersuchungen im frühzeitlichen Königsfriedhof. 3./4. Vorbericht'. *MDAIK* 46: 53–90.

– 1991. 'Zur Rekonstruktion der Oberbauten der Königsgräber der 1. Dynastie in Abydos'. *MDAIK* 47: 93–104.

– 1993. 'Umm el-Qaab: Nachuntersuchungen im frühzeitlichen Königsfriedhof. 5./6. Vorbericht'. *MDAIK* 49: 23–62.

– 1998a. *Umm el-Qaab*. 1: *das prädynastische Königsgrab U-j und seine frühen Schriftzeugnisse*. Mainz: Philipp von Zabern.

– 1998b. 'Der erste König der 3. Dynastie'. In *Stationen: Beiträge zur Kulturgeschichte Ägyptens, Rainer Stadelmann gewidmet*, edited by H. Guksch and D. Polz, 31–34. Mainz: Philipp von Zabern.

– 2009. 'Report on the 21st campaign of reexamining the royal tombs of Umm el-Qaab at Abydos 2006/2007'. *ASAE* 83: 165–75.

– 2010. 'Report on the 22nd campaign of reexamining the royal tombs of Umm el-Qaab at Abydos 2007/2008'. *ASAE* 84: 143–56.

DREYER, G., A.I. BLÖBAUM, E.-M. ENGEL, H. KÖPP and V. MÜLLER 2011. 'Umm el-Qaab. Nachuntersuchungen im frühzeitlichen Königsfriedhof 19./20./21. Vorbericht'. *MDAIK* 67: 53–92.

DREYER, G., A. EFFLAND, U. EFFLAND, E.-M. ENGEL, R. HARTMANN, U. HARTUNG, C. LACHER, V. MÜLLER and A. POKORNY 2006. 'Umm el-Qaab. Nachuntersuchungen im frühzeitlichen Königsfriedhof 16./17./18. Vorbericht'. *MDAIK* 62: 67–129.

DREYER, G., E.M. ENGEL, U. HARTUNG, T. HIKADE, E. V. KÖHLER and F. PUMPENMEIER 1996. 'Umm el-Qaab. Nachuntersuchungen im frühzeitlichen Königsfriedhof 7/8. Vorbericht'. *MDAIK* 52: 11–81.

DREYER, G., R. HARTMANN, U. HARTUNG, T. HIKADE, H. KÖPP, C. LACHER, V. MÜLLER, A. NERLICH and A. ZINK 2003. 'Umm el-Qaab. Nachuntersuchungen im frühzeitlichen Königsfriedhof, 13./14./15. Vorbericht'. *MDAIK* 59: 67–138.

DREYER, G., U. HARTUNG, T. HIKADE, E.C. KÖHLER, V. MÜLLER and F. PUMPENMEIER 1998. 'Umm el-Qaab. Nachuntersuchungen im frühzeitlichen Königsfriedhof, 9./10. Vorbericht'. *MDAIK* 54: 77–167.

DREYER, G., A. VON DEN DRIESCH, E.-M. ENGEL, R. HARTMANN, U. HARTUNG, T. HIKADE, V. MÜLLER and J. PETERS 2000. 'Umm el-Qaab. Nachuntersuchungen im frühzeitlichen Königsfriedhof, 11./12. Vorbericht'. *MDAIK* 56, 43–129.

DREYER, G. and N. SWELIM 1982. 'Die kleine Stufenpyramide von Abydos-Süd (Sinki)'. *MDAIK* 38: 83–95.

DUNHAM, D. 1950. *El-Kurru*. Boston: Museum of Fine Arts.

– 1955. *Nuri*. Boston: Museum of Fine Arts.

– 1958. *Royal Tombs at Meroe and Barkal*. Boston: Museum of Fine Arts.

– 1963. *The West and South Cemeteries at Meroe*. Boston: Museum of Fine Arts.

DUNHAM, D. and S.E. CHAPMAN 1952. *Decorated Chapels of the Meroitic Pyramids at Meroe and Barkal*. Boston: Museum of Fine Arts.

DZIOBEK, E. 1994. *Die Gräber des Vezirs User-Amun: Theben Nr, 61 und 131*. Mainz: Philipp von Zabern.

DZIOBEK, E., M. HÖVELER-MÜLLER and C.E. LOEBEN (eds) 2009. *Das geheimnisvolle Grab 63 – die neueste Entdeckung im Tal der Könige: Archäologie und Kunst von Susan Osgood*. Rahden: Leidorf.

EATON-KRAUSS, M. 1988. 'Tutankhamun at Karnak'. *MDAIK* 44: 1–11.

– 1993. *The Sarcophagus in the Tomb of Tutankhamun*. Oxford: Griffith Institute.

– 1999. 'The Fate of Sennefer and Senetnay at Karnak Temple and in the Valley of the Kings'. *JEA* 85: 113–29.

– 2012. 'Who commissioned KV 42 and for whom?' *GM* 234: 53–60.

EDWARDS, I.E.S. 1994. 'Do the Pyramid Texts suggest an explanation for the abandonment of the subterranean chamber of the Great Pyramid?'. In *Hommages à Jean Leclant,* edited by C. Berger, G. Clerc and N. Grimal, I, 161–67. Cairo: Institut français d'archéologie orientale.

– 1997. 'The Pyramd of Seila and its Place in the Succession of Snofru's Pyramids'. In

Chief of Seers: Egyptian Studies in Memory of Cyril Aldred, edited by E. Goring, N. Reeves and J. Ruffle, 88–96. London: Kegan Paul International.

EMERY, W.B. 1961. *Archaic Egypt*. Harmondsworth: Penguin.

ENGELBACH, R. 1934, 'A Foundation Scene of the Second Dynasty'. *JEA* 20: 183–84.

EREMIN, K.A., E. GORING, W.P. MANLEY AND C. CARTWRIGHT 2000. 'A Seventeenth Dynasty Egyptian Queen in Edinburgh'. *Kmt* 11/3: 32–40.

ERTMAN, E. 1993. 'A First Report on the Preliminary Survey of Unexcavated KV10'. *Kmt* 4/2: 38–46.

FAIRMAN H.W. and A.M. BLACKMAN 1935, 1944, 'The Myth of Horus at Edfu'. *JEA* 21: 26–36; 30: 5–22.

FARAG, N. and Z. ISKANDER 1971. *The Discovery of Neferwptah*. Cairo: General Organization for Government Printing Offices.

FAY, B. 1996. *The Louvre Sphinx and Royal Sculpture from the Reign of Amenemhat II*. Mainz: Philipp von Zabern.

FAULKNER, R.O. 1969. *The Ancient Egyptian Pyramid Texts*. Oxford: Griffith Institute.

FIRTH, C.M. and J.E. QUIBELL 1935. *The Step Pyramid*. Cairo: Institut français d'archéologie orientale.

FLENTYE, L. 2011. 'The decorative programmes of the pyramid complexes of Khufu and Khafre at Giza'. In *Old Kingdom, new perspectives: Egyptian art and archaeology 2750–2150 BC*, edited by N. Strudwick and H. Strudwick, 77–92. Oxford: Oxbow Books.

FRASER, P.M. 1972. *Ptolemaic Alexandria*, 3vv. Oxford: University Press, 1972.

FRIEDMAN, R.F., 2011. 'The early royal cemetery at Hierakonpolis: An overview'. In *Recent discoveries and latest researches in Egyptology. Proceedings of the first Neapolitan congress of Egyptology, Naples, June 18–20, 2008*, edited by F. Raffaele, M. Nuzzolo and I. Incordino, 67–86. Wiesbaden: Harassowitz.

FRIEDMAN, R.F. and D. RAUE 2007. 'New observations on the Fort at Hierakonpolis'. In *The archaeology and art of ancient Egypt: essays in honor of David B. O'Connor*, edited by Z.A. Hawass and J.E. Richards, I, 309–36. Cairo: Conseil Suprême des Antiquités de l'Egypte.

FRIEDMAN, R.F., W. VAN NEER and V. LINSELLE 2011. 'The Elite Predynastic Cemetery at Hierakonpolis: 2009–2010 update' In *Egypt at its origins 3: proceedings of the Third International Conference "Origin of the state: predynastic and early dynastic Egypt", London, 27th July – 1st August 2008*, edited by R.F. Friedman and P.N. Fiske 157–91. Leuven: Peeters.

GABOLDE, L. 1989. 'Les temples «mémoriaux» de Thoutmosis II et Toutânkhamon (un rituel destiné à des statues sur barques)'. *BIFAO* 89: 127–78.

– 1991. 'La chronologie du règne de Thoutmosis II, ses conséquences sur la datation des momies royales et leurs répercussions sur l'histoire du développement de la Vallée des Rois'. In *Akten des vierten Internationalen Ägyptologen Kongresses München 1985, 4: Geschichte, Verwaltungs- und Wirtschaftsgeschichte, Rechtsgeschichte, Nachbarkulturen*, edited by S. Schoske, 55–61. Hamburg: Buske.

GABOLDE, M. 2009. "Under a Deep Blue Starry Sky." In *Causing his Name to Live: studies in Egyptian epigraphy and history in memory of William J. Murnane*, edited by P.J. Brand and L. Cooper, 109–20. Leiden: Brill.

GARNETT, A. 2011. '"The like of which never existed": the Memphite building programme of Amenhotep III'. In *Current research in Egyptology 2009: proceedings of the tenth annual symposium, University of Liverpool 2009*, edited by J. Corbelli, D. Boatright and C. Malleson, 53–66. Oxford: Oxbow.

GASM EL SEED, A. 1985. 'La Tombe de Tanoutamon à El Kurru (KU. 16).' *RdE* 36: 67–72.

GEISEN, C. 2004. *Die Totentexte des verschollenen Sarges der Königin Mentuhotep aus der 13. Dynastie: ein Textzeuge aus der Übergangszeit von den Sargtexten zum Totenbuch.* Wiesbaden: Harrassowitz.

GONEIM, M.Z. 1957. *Horus Sekhemkhet: The Unfinished Step Pyramid at Saqqara*, I Cairo: Institut français d'archéologie orientale.

GOURDON, Y. 2006. 'The Royal Necropolis of Djedefra at Abu Rowash (seasons 2001–2005)'. In *Abusir and Saqqara in the Year 2005*, edited by M. Bárta, F. Coppens and J. Krejči, 247–56. Prague: Czech Institute of Egyptology.

GRAEFE, E. and G. BELOVA (eds) 2010. *The Royal Cache TT320: A Re-examination.* Cairo: Supreme Council of Antiquities Press.

GRAEFE, E. and D. BICKERSTAFFE 2013. 'Die sogenannte königliche Chachette TT320 was keinesfalls das Grab der Ahmose-Nofretere !' *GM* 239: 115–19.

GRIMM, A. and S. SCHOSKE (eds.) 2001. *Das Geheimnis des goldenen Sarges: Echnaton und das Ende der Amarnazeit.* Munich: Lipp Verlag.

GRIST, J. 1985. 'The Identity of the Ramesside Queen Tyti'. *JEA* 71: 71–81.

HABACHI, L. 1974. 'Lids of the Outer Sarcophagi of Merytamen and Nefertari'. In *Festschrift zum 150jahrigen Bestehen des Berliner Ägyptischen Museuems*, 105–12. Berlin: Akademie-Verlag.

– 1983. 'The Tomb of the princess Nebt of the VIIIth dynasty discovered at Qift'. *SAK* 10: 205–13.

HAENY, G. 1998. 'New Kingdom «Mortuary Temples» and «Mansions of Millions of Years»'. In *Temples in Ancient Egypt*, edited by B.E. Schafer, 86–126. London: I.B. Tauris.

HAENY, G. (ed.) 1981 *Untersuchungen im Totentempel Amenophis' III* (Weisbaden: Otto Harrasowitz, 1981).

HAMMOND, N.G.L. 1991. 'The Royal Tombs at Vergina: Evolution and Identities Author(s)'. *Annual of the British School at Athens* 86: 69–82.

HARPUR, Y. 2001. *The Tombs of Nefermaat and Rahotep at Maidum: Discovery, Destruction and Reconstruction.* Oxford: Oxford Expedition to Egypt.

HARRIS, J.R. 2004. 'En sag om forveksling'. *Papyrus* 24/2: 4–13.

HARVEY, S.P 1994. 'Monuments of Ahmose at Abydos', *EgArch* 4: 3–5.

– 2001. 'Tribute to a Conquering King. Battle scenes at Abydos honor a pharaoh's triumph over Hyksos occupiers and his reunification of Egypt'. *Archaeology* 54/4: 52–55.

– 2004. 'New evidence at Abydos for Ahmose's funerary cult'. *EgArch* 24: 3–6.

– 2008. "Report on Abydos, Ahmose and Tetisheri Project, 2006–2007 season." *ASAE* 82: 143–55.

HASSAN, S. 1975. *Mastabas of Princess Ḥemet-Reʿ and Others.* Cairo: General Organisation for Government Printing Offices.

HASSANEIN, F. and M. NELSON 1976. *La tombe du prince Amon-(her)-khepchef.* Cairo: Centre d'études et documentation sur l'ancienne Égypte.

– 1997. *La tombe du Prince Khaemouaset [VdR nº 44].* Cairo: Conseil Supérieur des Antiquités.

HAWASS, Z. 1997. 'The discovery of the harbors of Khufu and Khafre at Gîza'. In *Études sur l'Ancien Empire et la nécropole de Saqqâra dédiées à Jean-Philippe Lauer*, 1, edited by C. Berger and B.Mathieu, 245–56. Montpellier: Université Paul Valéry-Montpellier III.

– 2000. 'Recent discoveries in the pyramid complex of Teti at Saqqara'. In *Abusir and Saqqara in the year 2000*, edited by M. Bárta and J. Krejčí, 413–44. Prague: Academy of Sciences of the Czech Republic.

– 2010. 'The excavation of the headless pyramid, Lepsius XXIX'. In *Perspectives on Ancient Egypt: studies in honor of Edward Brovarski*, edited by Z.A., Hawass, P. Der Manuelian, and R.B. Hussein, 153–70. Cairo: Conseil Suprême des Antiquités de l'Égypte.

– 2011. 'The discovery of the pyramid of Queen Sesheshet(?) at Saqqara. In *Times, signs and pyramids: studies in honour of Miroslav Verner on the occasion of his seventieth birthday*, edited by V.G. Callender, L. Bareš, M. Bárta, J. Janák and J. Krejčí, 173–89. Prague: Faculty of Arts, Charles University in Prague.

HAWASS, Z., Y.Z. GAD, S. ISMAIL, R. KHAIRAT, D. FATHALLA, N. HASAN, A. AHMED, H. ELLEITHY, M. BALL, F. GABALLAH, S. WASEF, M. FATEEN, H. AMER, P. GOSTNER, A. SELIM, A. ZINK and C.M. PUSCH, 2010. 'Ancestry and Pathology in King Tutankhamun's Family'. *Journal of the American Medical Association* 303/7: 638–47.

HAYES, W.C. 1935. *Royal Sarcophagi of the XVIII Dynasty*. Princeton: University Press.

HAYS, H.M. 2011. 'The death of the democratisation of the afterlife'. In *Old Kingdom, new perspectives: Egyptian art and archaeology 2750–2150 BC*, edited by N. Strudwick and H. Strudwick, 115–30. Oxford: Oxbow Books.

– 2012. *The Organization of the Pyramid Texts: typology and disposition*, 2vv. Leiden: Brill.

HÉBRARD, E. and J. ZEILLER 1912. *Spalato: le Palais de Dioclétien*. Paris: Librairie générale de l'architecture et des arts décoratifs.

HERZFELD, E. 1941. *Iran in the Ancient East: archaeological studies presented in the Lowell lectures at Boston*. Oxford: Oxford University Press.

– 1935. *Archaeological history of Iran*. Oxford: Oxford University Press.

HESBERG, H. von 1994. *Das Mausoleum des Augustus: der Bau und seine Inschriften*. Munich: Verlag der Bayerischen Akademie der Wissenschaften.

HÖLSCHER, U. 1941. *The Excavation of Medinet Habu*, III: *The Mortuary Temple of Ramses III*, Part 1. Chicago: University of Chicago Press.

– 1954. *The Excavation of Medinet Habu*, V: *Post-Ramessid Remains*. Chicago: University of Chicago Press.

HOREAU, H. 1841. *Panorama d'Égypte et de Nubie*. Paris: chez l'auteur.

HORNUNG E. 1971. *Das Grab des Haremhab im Tal der Könige*. Bern: Franke Verlag.

– 1975. 'Das Grab Thutmosis' II.' *RdE* 27: 125–31.

– 1988a. "Zum Turiner Grabplan." In *Pyramid Studies and Other Essays presented to I.E.S. Edwards*, edited by J. Baines, T.G.H. James, A. Leahy, and A.F. Shore, 138–42. London: Egypt Exploration Society.

– 1988b. "Zum Schutzbild im Grabe Ramses' VI." In *Funerary Symbols and Religion. Essays dedicated to Professor M.S.H.G. Heerma van Voss on the occasion of his retirement from the Chair of the History of Ancient Religions at the University of Amsterdam*, edited by J.H. Kamstra, H. Milde and K. Wagtendonk, 45–51. Kampen: J.H. Kok.

– 1990a. *Zwei Ramessidische Königsgräber: Ramses IV. und Ramses VII.* Mainz: Philipp von Zabern.

– 1990b. The Valley of the Kings: Horizon of Eternity (New York: Timken Publishers,

– 1991. *The Tomb of Pharaoh Seti I/Das Grab Sethos' I.* Zurich and Munich: Artemis.

– 1999. *The Ancient Egyptian Books of the Afterlife*, translated by David Lorton. Ithaca: Cornell University Press.

ILIN-TOMICH, A. 2014. 'The Theban Kingdom of Dynasty 16: Its Rise, Administration and Politics'. *JEH* 7: 143–93.

INCORDINO, I. 2008. *Chronological problems of the IIIrd Egyptian Dynasty: a re-examination of the archaeological documents.* Oxford: Archaeopress.

JÁNOSI, P. 1996. *Die Pyramidenanlagen der Königinnen: Untersuchungen zu einem Grabtyp des Alten und Mittleren Reiches.* Vienna: Akademie der Wissenschaften.

– 2013. 'Im Inneren der Userkaf-Pyramide: Beobachtungen und Gedanken zu einem vergessenen Kammernsystem'. *Sokar* 26, 22–33.

JANSEN-WINKELN, K. 2007–9. *Inschriften der Spätzeit*, 3vv. Wiesbaden: Harrassowitz.

JARITZ, H. 1992. 'Der Totentempel des Merenptah in Qurna. 1. Grabungsbericht (1.– 6. Kampagne)'. *MDAIK* 48: 65–91

– 2001. 'The Museum of the Mortuary Temple of Merenptah'. *EgArch* 19: 20–24.

JARITZ, H., M. DOLL, B. DOMINICUS AND W. RUTISHAUSER 2001. 'Der Totentempel des Merenptah in Qurna. 5. Grabungsbericht'. *MDAIK* 57: 141–70

JARITZ, H., B. DOMINICUS and H. SOUROUZIAN 1995. 'Der Totentempel des Merenptah in Qurna. 2. Grabungsbericht (7.und 8. Kampagne)'. *MDAIK* 51: 57–83.

JARITZ, H., B. DOMINICUS, U. MINUTH, W. NIEDERBERGER and A. SEILER 1996. 'Der Totentempel des Merenptah in Qurna. 3. Grabungsbericht (9. und 10. Kampagne)'. *MDAIK* 52: 201–32.

JARITZ, H., B. DOMINICUS, W. NIEDERBERGER, H. SOUROUZIAN and L. STALDER 1999. "Der Totentempel des Merenptah in Qurna. 4. Grabungsbericht." *MDAIK* 55: 13–62.

JEFFREYS, D.G. 1985. *The Survey of Memphis*, I. London: Egypt Exploration Society.

JEFFREYS, D. and A. TAVARES 1994. 'The Historic Landscape of Early Dynastic Memphis'. *MDAIK* 50: 143–73

JÉQUIER, G. 1938. *Deux pyramides du Moyen Empire.* Cairo: Institut français d'archéologie orientale.

JENNI, H. 2009. 'La Vallée des Rois – ses tombeaux et ses ouvriers: travaux concernant les tombes KV 17, 18, 32 et 47 menés par l'Institut d'Égyptologie de l'Université de Bâle'. *Égypte, Afrique & Orient* 54: 11–24.

JENNI, H. (ed.). 2000. *Das Grab Ramses' X (KV18).* Basel: Schwabe & Co.

– in preparation. *Das Grab Siptahs (KV 47) und das Grab der Königin Tiaa (KV 32).*

JOHNSON, W.R. 1998. 'Monuments and Monumental Art under Amenhotep III'. In *Amenhotep III: perspectives on his reign*, edited by D.B. O'Connor and E.H. Cline, 63–94. Ann Arbor: University of Michigan Press.

– 2009. 'Tutankhamen-Period battle narratives at Luxor'. *Kmt* 20/4: 20–33.

KAISER, W. 1969. 'Zu den königlichen Talbezirken der 1. und 2. Dynastie in Abydos und zur Baugeschichte des Djoser-Grabmals'. *MDAIK* 25: 1–21.

– 1992. 'Zur unterirdischen Anlage der Djoserpyramide und ihrer entwicklungsgeschichtlichen Einordnung'. In *Gegengabe: Festschrift für Emma*

Brunner-Traut, edited by I. Gamer-Wallert and W. Helck, 167–90. Tübingen, Attempto.

– 1997. 'Zu den Granitkammern und ihren Vorgängerbauten unter der Stufenpyramide und im Südgrab von Djoser'. *MDAIK* 53: 195–207.

KAISER, W. and G. DREYER 1980. 'Zu den kleinen Stufenpyramiden Ober- und Mittelägyptens'. *MDAIK* 36: 43–59.

– 1982. 'Umm el-Qaab. Nachuntersuchungen im frühzeitlichen Königsfriedhof: 2. Vorbericht'. *MDAIK* 38: 211–69.

KAISER, W. and P. GROSSMANN 1979. 'Umm el-Qaab. Nachuntersuchungen im frühzeitlichen Königsfriedhof 1. Vorbericht'. *MDAIK* 35: 155–63.

KANAWATI, N. 2002. *Conspiracies in the Egyptian Palace: Unis to Pepy I.* London: Routledge.

KAWAI, N. 2013. 'Some Remarks on the Funerary Equipment form the Tomb of Amenhotep III (KV 22)'. In *Archaeological Resaerch in the Valley of the Kings and Ancient Thebes: Papers Presented in Honor of Richard H. Wiliknson*, edited by P.P. Creasman, 149–72. [Tucson]: University of Arizona Egyptian Expedition.

KEMP, B.J. 1963. 'Excavations at Hierakonpolis Fort, 1905: a preliminary note'. *JEA* 49: 24–28.

– 1966. 'Abydos and the Royal Tombs of the First Dynasty'. *JEA* 52: 13–22.

– 1967. 'The Egyptian First Dynasty Royal Cemetery'. *Antiquity* 41: 22–32.

EL-KHOULI, A. 1991. *Meidum.* Sydney: Australian Centre for Egyptology.

EL-KHOULI, A. and G.T. MARTIN 1987. *Excavations in the Royal Necropolis at El-'Amarna 1984.* Cairo: Institut français d'archéologie orientale.

KIKUCHI, T. 2015. 'The Decoration Program in the Burial Chamber of the Royal Tomb of Amenophis III'. In *Proceedings of the Tenth International Congress of Egyptologists, University of the Aegean, Rhodes 22-29 May 2008*, edited by P. Kousoulis and N. Lazaridis, 1709–18. Louvain: Peeters.

KITCHEN, K.A. 1983. *Ramesside Inscriptions: Historical and Biographical*, VI. Oxford: Basil Blackwell.

KLEISS, W. and P. CALMEYER 1975. 'Das Unvollendete achämenidischen Felsgrab bei Persepolis'. *Archaeologische Mitteilungen aus Iran* 8: 81–113.

KONDO, J. 1992. 'A Preliminary Report on the Re-clearance of the Tomb of Amenophis III (WV 22)'. In After *Tut'ankhamūn: Research and Excavation in the Royal Necropolis at Thebes*, edited by C.N. Reeves, 41–54. London: KPI.

– 1995. 'The Re-clearance of Tombs WV 22 and WV A in the Western Valley of the Kings'. In *Valley of the Sun Kings: New Expeditions in the Tombs of the Pharaohs*, edited by R.H. Wilkinson, 25–33. Tucson: University of Arizona Egyptian Expedition.

KREJČÍ, J. 2011. 'Nyuserra Revisited'. In *Abusir and Saqqara in the Year 2010*, edited by M. Bárta, F. Coppens and J. Krejči, 518–29. Prague: Czech Institute of Egyptology.

– 2015. 'Archaeological excavation of the mastaba of Queen Khentkaus III in Abusir (Tomb AC 30)', *Prague Egyptological Studies* XV.

KREJČÍ, J., V.G. CALLENDER, and M. VERNER 2009. *Abusir XII: minor tombs in the Royal Necropolis I (the mastabas of Nebtyemneferes and Nakhtsare, pyramid complex Lepsius no. 24 and tomb complex Lepsius no. 25).* Prague: Czech Institute of Egyptology, Faculty of Arts, Charles University.

LABROUSSE, A. 1994. 'Les reines de Teti, Khouit et Ipout I, recherches architecturales'. In *Hommages à Jean Leclant,* I, edited by C. Berger, G. Clerc and N. Grimal, 231–44.

– 1996–2000. *L'architecture des pyramides à textes*, 2vv. Cairo: Institut français d'archéologie orientale.

– 1999. *Les pyramides des reines. Une nouvelle nécropole à Saqqâra.* Paris: Hazen.

– 2012. 'Recent discoveries at the necropolis of King Pepy I'. In *Ancient Memphis: 'Enduring is the Perfection'. Proceedings of the international conference held at Macquarie University, Sydney on August 14–15, 2008*, edited by L. Evans, 299–308. Leuven: Peeters.

LABROUSSE, A. and A.M. MOUSSA 1996, *Le temple d'accueil du complexe funéraire du roi Ounas.* Cairo: Institut français d'archéologie orientale.

– 2002. *La chaussée du complexe funéraire du roi Ounas.* Cairo: Institut français d'archéologie orientale.

LABROUSSE, A. and J.-Ph. LAUER 2000. *Les complexes funéraires d'Ouserkaf et de Néferhétepes.* Cairo: Institut français d'archéologie orientale.

LABROUSSE, A, J.-P. LAUER and J. LECLANT 1977, *Le Temple haut du complexe funéraire du roi Ounas.* Cairo: Institut français d'archéologie orientale.

LACHER, C.M. 2008. 'Das Grab des Hetepsechemui/Raneb in Saqqara – Ideen zur baugeschichtlichen Entwicklung'. In *Zeichen aus dem Sand: Streiflichter aus Ägyptens Geschichte zu Ehren von Günter Dreyer*, edited by E.M. Engel, V. Müller and U. Hartung, 427–52. Wiesbaden: Harrassowitz.

LACHER-RASCHDORFF, C.M. 2014. *Das Grab des Königs Ninetjer in Saqqara. Architektonische Entwicklung frühzeitlicher Grabanlagen in Ägypten.* Wiesbaden: Harrassowitz.

LAUER, J.-Ph. 1962. *Histoire monumentale des pyramides d'Égypte.* Cairo: 'Institut français d'archéologie orientale.

LAUER, J.-Ph. and J. LECLANT 1972. *Le temple haut du complexe funéraire du roi Téti.* Cairo: 'Institut français d'archéologie orientale.

LAUER, J.-Ph. and C. PICARD 1955. *Les statues ptolémaïques du Sarapieion de Memphis.* Paris: Presses universitaires de France

LEAHY, M.A. 1994. 'Kushite Monuments at Abydos'. In *The Unbroken Reed: Studies in the Culture and Heritage of Ancient Egypt in Honour of A.F. Shore*, edited by C. Eyre, A. Leahy and L.M. Leahy, 171–92. London: Egypt Exploration Society.

LEBLANC, C. 1988. 'L'identification de la tombe de Henout-mi-Re''. *BIFAO* 88: 131–46.

– 1989a. *Ta set neferou; une necropole de Thebes-Ouest et son histoire*, I. Cairo: Nubar.

– 1989b. 'Architecture et evolution chronologique de tombes de la Vallée de Reines', *BIFAO* 89: 227–48.

– 2010. 'The Tomb of Ramesses II (KV 7): From its Archaeological Excavation to the Identification of its Iconographical Program.' *MDAIK* 66: 161–74.

LEBLANC, C. and F. HASSANEIN 1985. 'La Vallée des Reines'. *Archéologia* 205: 24–31.

LECLANT, J. 1984. 'Taharqa à Sedeinga'. In *Studien zu Sprache und Religion Ägyptens. Zu Ehren von Wolfhart Westendorf überreicht von seinem Freunden und Schülern.* Göttingen: F. Junge.

LECLANT, J. and G. CLERC 1988. 'Fouilles et travaux en Égypte et au Soudan, 1986–1987'. *Orientalia* 57: 307–404.

LECLÈRE, F. 2008. *Le villes de basse Égypte au Ier millénaire av. J.-C.* Cairo: Institut français d'archéologie orientale.

LEEK, F.F. 1972. *The Human Remains from the Tomb of Tut'ankhamūn.* Oxford: Griffith Institute.

LE GUILLOUX, P. 2010. *Le mobilier funéraire de Psousennès Ier.* N.p: Actes Sud.

LEHNER, M. 1985. *The Pyramid Tomb of Hetep-heres and the Satellite Pyramid of Khufu.* Mainz: Philipp von Zabern.

– 1996. 'Z500 and the Layer Pyramid of Zawiyet el-Aryan'. In *Studies in Honor of William Kelly Simpson*, edited by P. der Manuelian, II, 507–22. Boston: Museum of Fine Arts.

LEHNER, M., D. JONES, L. YEOMANS, H. MAHMOUD and K. OLCHOWSKA 2011. 'Re-examining the Khentkaues Town'. In *Old Kingdom, new perspectives: Egyptian art and archaeology 2750–2150 BC*, edited by N. Strudwick and H. Strudwick, 143–91. Oxford: Oxbow Books.

LEPPER, F. and S. FRERE 1988. *Trajan's Column. A New Edition of the Cichorius Plates. Introduction, Commentary and Notes.* Gloucester: Alan Sutton Publishing,

LEPSIUS, C.R. 1849–59. *Denkmaeler aus Aegypten und Aethiopien*, 6vv. Berlin/Leipzig: Nicolaische Buchandlung.

LESKO, B. 1969. 'Royal mortuary suites of the Egyptian New Kingdom', *AJA* 73, 453–58.

LILYQUIST, C. 2003. *The Tomb of Three Foreign Wives of Tuthmosis III.* New York: Metropolitan Museum of Art.

LITHERLAND, P. 2014. *The Western Wadis of the Theban Necropolis.* London: New Kingdom Research Foundation.

– 2016. *The Shaft Tombs of Wadi Bairiyah, I.* London: New Kingdom Research Foundation. .

LLOYD, A.B. 2014. 'The Egyptian Attitude to the Persians'. In *A Good Scribe and an Exceedingly Wise Man: Studies in Honour of W.J. Tait*, edited by A.M. Dodson, J.J. Johnston and W. Monkhouse, 185–98. London: Golden House Publications.

LULL, J. 2002. *Las tumbas reales egipcias del Tercer Período Intermedio (dinastías XXI – XXV): Tradición y cambios.* Oxford: Archaeopress.

MACE, A.C. 1921. 'Excavations at Lisht', *BMMA* 16, Part II: 5–19.

– 1922. 'Excavations at Lisht', *BMMA* 17, Part II: 4–18.

MACRAMALLAH, R. 1932. 'Une forteresse du Moyen Empire (?) à Abou-Rawâch'. *ASAE* 32: 161–73.

MALEK, J. 1994. 'King Merykare and his Pyramid'. In *Hommages à Jean Leclant*, edited by C. Berger, G. Clerc and N. Grimal, IV, 203–14. Cairo: Institut français d'archéologie orientale.

MANLEY, W. and A. DODSON 2010. *Life Everlasting: National Museums Scotland Collection of Ancient Egyptian Coffins.* Edinburgh: National Museums Scotland.

MANUELIAN, P. DER and C.E. LOEBEN 1993a. 'From daughter to father: the recarved Egyptian sarcophagus of Queen Hatshepsut and King Thutmose I'. *JMFA* 5: 24–61.

– 1993b. 'New light on the recarved sarcophagus of Hatshepsut and Thutmose I in the Museum of Fine Arts'. *JEA* 79: 121–55.

MARAGIOGLIO, V. and C.A. RINALDI 1964–77. *L'architettura delle Piramidi Menfite*, III–VIII. Rapallo: Officine Grafische Canessa.

MARCINIAK, M. 1982. "Réparations anciennes dans le tombeau de Ramsès III (no. 11) dans la Vallée des Rois." *Africana Bulletin* 31: 37–43.

– 1983. "Deux campagnes épigraphiques au tombeau de Ramsès III dans la Vallée des Rois (no 11)." *Études et Travaux* 12: 295–305.

MARTIN, G.T. 1974–89. *The Royal Tomb at el-'Amarna*, 2vv. London: Egypt Exploration Society.

– 1982. 'Queen Mutnodjmet at Memphis and El-'Amarna' In *L'Égyptologie en 1979: Axes prioritaires de recherches*, II, 275–78. Paris: n.p.

– 1989. *The Memphite Tomb of Ḥoremḥeb, Commander-in-Chief of Tut'ankhamūn*, I. London: Egypt Exploration Society.

MARTINEZ, P. 2007. 'Seti I and the ghosts of what had been: a reappraisal of Qurna temple and its history'. *Kmt* 18/1: 36–46.

– 2008. 'Par des portails anépigraphes: un réexamen des développements architecturaux du début de l'époque ramesside à Thèbes Ouest'. *CdE* 83: 41–74.

MASPERO, G. 1901. *The Dawn of Civilization*, 4th edition. London: Society for Promoting Christian Knowledge.

MATHIESON, I. 2000. 'The National Museums of Scotland Saqqara Survey Project'. In *Abusir and Saqqara in the year 2000*, edited by M. Barta and J. Krejči, 33–42. Prague: Academy of Sciences of the Czech Republic.

MATHIESON, I.J. and A. TAVARES 1993. 'Preliminary Report of the National Museums of Scotland Saqqara Survey Project, 1990–1'. *JEA* 79: 17–31.

MATHIESON, I., E. BETTLES, J. CLARKE, C. DUHIG, S. IKRAM, L. MAGUIRE, S. QUIE and A. TAVARES 1997. 'The National Museums of Scotland Saqqara Survey Project 1993–1995'. *JEA* 83: 17–53.

MCCORMACK, D. 2006. 'Borrowed legacy: royal tombs S9 and S10 at South Abydos'. *Expedition* 48/2: 23–26.

– 2010. 'The significance of royal funerary architecture for the study of Thirteenth Dynasty kingship'. In *The Second Intermediate Period (Thirteenth-Seventeenth Dynasties): current research, future prospects,* edited by Marcel Marée, 69–84. Leuven: Peeters.

MCDONALD, J.K. 1996. *The Tomb of Nefertari: House of Eternity*. Cairo: American University in Cairo Press.

MEGAHED, M. 2011. 'The Pyramid Complex of "Djedkare's Queen" in South Saqqara. Preliminary Report 2010'. In *Abusir and Saqqara in the Year 2010*, edited by M. Bárta, F. Coppens and J. Krejči, 616–34. Prague: Czech Institute of Egyptology.

MERCALLI, M. 1998. *Adriano e il suo mausoleo: studi, indagini e interpretazioni*. Milano: Electa.

MINIACI, G. 2011. *Rishi Coffins and the funerary culture of the Second Intermediate Period*. London: Golden House Publications.

MONTET. P. 1947. *La nécropole royale de Tanis* I: *Les constructions et le tombeau de Osorkon II à Tanis*. Paris: n.p.

– 1951. *La nécropole royale de Tanis* II: *Les constructions et le tombeau de Psousennes à Tanis*. Paris: n.p.

– 1960. *La nécropole royale de Tanis* III: *Les constructions et le tombeau de Chéchanq III à Tanis*. Paris: n.p.

MORKOT, R.G. 1990. '*Nb-m3't-R*'–United-With-Ptah'. *JNES* 49: 323–37.

MORRIS, E.F. 2007. 'On the ownership of the Saqqara mastabas and the allotment of political and ideological power at the dawn of the state'. In *The archaeology and art of ancient Egypt: essays in honor of David B. O'Connor* 2, edited by Z.A. Hawass and J.E. Richards, 171–90. Cairo: Conseil Suprême des Antiquités de l'Egypte.

MUNRO, P. 1983. 'Einige Bemerkungen zum Unas-Friedhof in Saqqara: 3. Vorbericht über die Arbeiten der Gruppe Hannover im Herbst 1978 und im Frühjahr 1980'. *SAK* 10: 277–95.

– 1993a. 'Report on the work of the Joint Archaeological Mission Free University of Berlin/University of Hannover during their 12th Campaign (15th March until 14th May, 1992) at Saqqâra'. *DE* 26: 47–58.

– 1993b. *Der Unas-Friedhof Nord-West*, I. Mainz: Philipp von Zabern.

MURNANE, W.J. 1980. *United with eternity: a concise guide to the monuments of Medinet Habu*. Chicago: The Oriental Institute, University of Chicago/Cairo: American University in Cairo Press.

MURNANE, W.J. and C.C. VAN SICLEN III 1993. *The Boundary Stelae of Akhenaten*. London and New York: Kegan Paul International.

MUSGRAVE, J., A.J.N.W. PRAG, R. NEAVE, R. LANE FOX and H. WHITE 2010. 'The Occupants of Tomb II at Vergina. Why Arrhidaios and Eurydice must be excluded'. *International Journal of Medical Sciences* 7/6: 1–15.

NAVILLE, E. 1895–1909. *The temple of Deir el Bahari*, 6vv. London: Egypt Exploration Fund.

NAVILLE, E. and H.R. HALL 1907–1913. *The XIth Dynasty Temple at Deir el-Bahari*, 3vv. London: Egypt Exploration Fund.

NEWBERRY, P.E. 1922. 'The Set Rebellion of the IInd Dynasty'. *Ancient Egypt* 1922: 40–6.

NISHISAKA, A., K. TAKAHASHI and S. YOSHIMURA 2015. 'Conservation in the Tomb of Amenophis III, 2011–2012'. In *Current Research in Egyptology 2014: Proceedings of the Fifteenth Annual Symposium*, edited by M.S. Pinarello, J. Woo, J. Lundock and C. Walsh, 29–38. Oxford: Oxbow.

NIWIŃSKI, A. 2009. 'The tomb protection in the Theban 21st Dynasty: unknown archaeological facts gathered during the excavation of the Polish-Egyptian "Cliff Mission" at Deir el-Bahari in the seasons 1999–2006'. In *The Libyan period in Egypt: historical and cultural studies into the 21st–24th Dynasties. Proceedings of a conference at Leiden University, 25–27 October 2007*, edited by G.P.F. Broekman, R.J. Demarée, and O.E. Kaper, 277–89. Leiden: Nederlands Instituut voor het Nabije Oosten.

O'CONNOR, D. 1989. 'New Funerary Enclosures (*Talbezirke*) of the Early Dynastic Period at Abydos', *JARCE* 26: 51–86.

– 1995. 'The earliest royal boat graves'. *EgArch* 6: 3–7.

OPPENHEIM, A. 2011. 'The Early Life of Pharaoh: Divine Birth and Adolescence Scenes in the Causeway of Senwosret III at Dahshur'. In *Abusir and Saqqara in the Year 2010*, edited by M. Bárta, F. Coppens and J. Krejči, 171–88. Prague: Czech Institute of Egyptology.

OSING, J. 1977. *Der Tempel Sethos' I. in Gurna*. Mainz: Philipp von Zabern.

PALANQUE, C. 1902. 'Rapport sur les fouilles d'el-Deir (1902)'. *BIFAO* 2: 163–70.

PARKINSON, R. and S. QUIRKE 1992. 'The Coffin of Prince Herunefer and the Early History of the Book of the Dead', In *Studies in Pharaonic Religion and Society in*

168

Honour of J. Gwyn Griffiths, edited by A.B. Lloyd, 37–51. London: Egypt
Exploration Society.

PAYNE, J.C. 1973. 'Tomb 100: the decorated tomb at Hierakonpolis confirmed.' *JEA*
59: 31–35.)

PEDEN, A.J. 1994. *The Reign of Ramesses IV*. Warminster: Aris and Phillips.

– 2001. 'Where did Ramesses VI bury his nephew?' *GM* 181: 83–88.

PETRIE, W.M.F. 1909. *Qurneh*. London: British School of Archaeology in Egypt.

PETRIE, W.M.F, G. BRUNTON and M.A. MURRAY 1923. *Lahun* II: *the pyramid.*
London: British School of Archaeology in Egypt.

PIACENTINI, P. and C. ORSENIGO 2004. *La Valle dei Re Riscoperta: I giornali di
scavo di Victor Loret (1898–1899) e altri inediti*. Milan: Skira/Università degli, Studi
di Milano.

PIERCE, J.R. 1925. 'The Mausoleum of Hadrian and the Pons Aelius'. *Journal of
Roman Studies* 15: 75–103.

POLZ, D. 1986. 'Die Särge des (Pa-)Ramessu'. *MDAIK* 42: 145–66.

– 1995. 'The Location of the Tomb of Amenhotep I: A Reconsideration'. In *Valley of
the Sun Kings: New Explorations in the Tombs of the Pharaohs*, edited by Richard H.
Wilkinson, 8–21. Tucson: The University of Arizona Egyptian Expedition.

– 2007. *Der Beginn des Neuen Reiches: zur Vorgeschichte einer Zeitenwende*. Berlin:
Walter de Gruyter.

POLZ, D., U. RUMMEL, I. EICHNER AND T. BECKH 2012. 'Topgraphical
Archaeology in Dra' Abu'l-Naga: Three Thousand Years of Cultural History.'
MDAIK 68: 116–34.

POLZ, D. and A. SEILER 2003. *Die Pyramidenanlage des Königs Nub-Cheper-Re
Intef in Dra' Abu el-Naga*. Mainz: Philipp von Zabern.

PORTER, B. and R.L.B. MOSS. 1934. *Topographical Bibliography of Ancient
Egyptian Hieroglyphic Texts, Reliefs and Paintings*, IV: *Lower and Middle Egypt.*
Oxford: Clarendon Press.

– 1937. *Topographical Bibliography of Ancient Egyptian Hieroglyphic Texts, Reliefs
and Paintings*, V: *Upper Egypt: Sites*. Oxford: Clarendon Press.

– 1939. *Topographical Bibliography of Ancient Egyptian Hieroglyphic Texts, Reliefs and
Paintings*, VI: *Upper Egypt: Chief Temples (excl. Thebes)*. Oxford: Clarendon Press.

– 1952. *Topographical Bibliography of Ancient Egyptian Hieroglyphic Texts, Reliefs
and Paintings*, VII: *Nubia, Deserts, and Outside Egypt*. Oxford: Clarendon
Press/Griffith Institute.

– 1960–64. *Topographical Bibliography of Ancient Egyptian Hieroglyphic Texts,
Reliefs and Paintings*, I: *The Theban Necropolis*. 2nd edition. Oxford: Clarendon
Press/Griffith Institute.

– 1972. *Topographical Bibliography of Ancient Egyptian Hieroglyphic Texts, Reliefs
and Paintings*, II: *Theban Temples*. 2nd edition. Oxford: Griffith Institute.

– 1974–81. *Topographical Bibliography of Ancient Egyptian Hieroglyphic Texts,
Reliefs and Paintings*, III: *Memphis*. 2nd edition by J. Málek. Oxford: Griffith
Institute.

PREYS, R. 2011. 'Les tombes non-royales de la Vallée des Rois'. *SAK* 40: 315–38.

PRICE, C. 2016. 'Other Tomb Goods'. In *The Oxford Handbook to the Valley of the
Kings*, edited by R.H. Wilkinson and K.R. Weeks, 274–89. New York: Oxford
University Press.

QUIRKE, S. 1990. 'Kerem in the Fitzwilliam Museum'. *JEA* 76: 170–74.

RAVEN, M.J. 1994. 'A sarcophagus for Queen Tiye and other fragments from the Royal Tomb at El-Amarna'. *OMRO* 74: 7–20.

READER, C. 2005. 'The age of the Sphinx and the development of the Giza necropolis'. In *Current research in Egyptology II: January 2001*, edited by A. Cooke and F. Simpson, 47–56. Oxford: Archaeopress.

– 2006. 'Further considerations on development at Giza before the 4th Dynasty.' *PalArch's Journal of Archaeology of Egypt/Egyptology* 3/2: 12–25.

– 2015. 'The Meidum Pyramid'. *JARCE* 51: 203-24.

REDFORD, D.B. (ed.) 2004. *Excavations at Mendes, I: The royal necropolis*. Leiden: Brill.

REEVES, C.N. 1990. *Valley of the Kings: The decline of a royal necropolis*. London: Kegan Paul International.

– 2015. *The Burial of Nefertiti?* Tucson AZ: Amarna Royal Tombs Project/University of Arizona Egyptian Expedition.

REEVES, C.N. and R.H. WILKINSON 1996. *The Complete Valley of the Kings*. London: Thames and Hudson.

REGULSKI, I. 2009 'Investigating a new Dynasty 2 necropolis at South Saqqara'. *British Museum Studies in Ancient Egypt and Sudan* 13, 221–37.

REISNER, G.A. 1936. *The Development of the Egyptian Tomb Down to the Accession of Cheops*. Oxford: University Press/Cambridge, MA: Harvard University Press.

RICKE, H. 1950. *Bemerkungen zur ägyptischen Baukunst des Alten Reichs*, II. Cairo: Schweizeriches Institut für ägyptische Bauforschung und Altertumskunde in Kairo.

RITNER, R.K. 2009. *The Libyan Anarchy: Inscriptions from Egypt's Third Intermediate Period.* Atlanta: Society of Biblical Literature.

ROBERSON, J.A. 2012. *The Ancient Egyptian Books of the Earth*. Atlanta GA: Lockwood Press.

ROBICHON, C. and A. VARILLE 1936. *Le Temple du scribe royal Amenhotep, fils de Hapou.* Cairo: Institut Français d'archéologie Orientale.

– 1938. 'Fouilles des temples funéraires Thébains (1937)'. *RdE* 3: 99–102.

ROBINS, G. 1983. 'The Canon of Proportions in the Tomb of Ramesses I (KV 16)'. *GM* 68: 85–90.

– 2007. 'The Decorative Program in the Tomb of Tutankhamun (KV 62)'. In *The Archaeology and Art of Ancient Egypt: essays in honor of David B. O'Connor*, edited by Z.A. Hawass and J.E. Richards, II, 321–42. Cairo: Conseil Suprême des Antiquités de l'Egypte.

ROBINSON, P. 2010. 'Some Observations on the Route to the Afterlife from Late 18th Dynasty Royal Tombs.' *JSSEA* 37: 59–77.

ROEHRIG, C. 1995. 'Gates to the Underworld: The Appearance of Wooden Doors in the Royal Tombs in the Valley of the Kings.' In *Valley of the Sun Kings: New Explorations in the Tombs of the Pharaohs*, edited by Richard H. Wilkinson, 82–104. Tucson: The University of Arizona Egyptian Expedition.

– 2006. 'The Building Activities of Thutmose III in the Valley of the Kings.' In *Thutmose III: A New Biography*, edited by E.H. Cline and D. O'Connor, 238–59. Ann Arbor: University of Michigan Press.

– 2007. 'Chamber Ja in Royal Tombs in the Valley Of The Kings'. In *Sacred space and sacred function in ancient Thebes. Occasional proceedings of the Theban Workshop,* edited by P.F. Dorman and B.M. Bryan, 117–38. Chicago: Oriental Institute of the University of Chicago.

– 2016. 'Royal Tombs of the Eighteenth Dynasty'. In *The Oxford Handbook to the Valley of the Kings*, edited by R.H. Wilkinson and K.R. Weeks, 183–99. New York: Oxford University Press.

ROMER, J. 1974. 'Tuthmosis I and the Bibân el-Molûk: some some problems of attribution'. *JEA* 60: 119–33.

– 1975. 'The Tomb of Tuthmosis III'. *MDAIK* 31: 315–48.

– 1981. *The Valley of the Kings*. London: Michael Joseph and Rainbird.

– 2007. *The Great Pyramid: ancient Egypt revisited*. Cambridge: Cambridge University Press.

ROSE J. 2000. *Tomb KV39 in the Valley of the Kings: A Double Archaeological Enigma*. Bristol: Western Academic and Specialist Press.

ROSSI, C. 2001. 'The plan of a royal tomb on O. Cairo 25184'. *GM* 184: 45–53.

ROULIN, G. 1998. 'Les tombes royales de Tanis: Analyse du programme decoratif'. In *Tanis: travaux récents sur le Tell Sân el-Hagar*, edited by P. Brissaud and C. Zivie-Coche, 193–275. Paris: Éditions Noêsis.

RUMMEL, U. 2009. 'Grab oder Tempel? Die funeräre Anlage des Hohenpriesters des Amun Amenophis in Dra' Abu el-Naga (Theben–West)'. In *Texte–Theben–Tonfragmente: Festschrift für Günter Burkard*, edited by D. Kessler, 348–60. Wiesbaden: Harrassowitz.

– 2011. 'Two Re-Used Blocks of the God's Wife Isis at Deir el-Bakhit/Dra' Abu el-Naga (Western Thebes)'. In *Ramesside Studies in Honour of K.A. Kitchen*, edited by M. Collier and S. Snape, 423–31. Bolton: Rutherford Press.

– 2013. 'Ramesside tomb-temples at Dra Abu el-Naga'. *EgArch* 42: 14–17.

– 2014. 'War, death and burial of the High Priest Amenhotep: the archaeological record at Dra' Abu el-Naga'. *SAK* 43: 375–97.

RYAN, D.P. 1991. 'Return to Wadi Biban el Moluk: the second (1990) season of the Valley of the Kings Project'. *Kmt* 2/1: 26–31.

– 1992a. 'The valley again'. *Kmt* 3/1, 44–47, 69.

– 1992b. 'Some observations concerning uninscribed tombs in the Valley of the Kings'. In *After Tut'ankhamūn: research and excavation in the Royal Necropolis at Thebes*, edited by C.N. Reeves, 21–27. London: Kegan Paul .

– 2007a. 'Pacific Lutheran University Valley of the Kings Project: work conducted during the 2005 field season'. *ASAE* 81: 345–56.

– 2007b. Pacific Lutheran University Valley of the Kings Project: work conducted during the 2006 field season'. *ASAE* 81: 357–61.

– 2010. 'Pacific Lutheran University Valley of the Kings project: work conducted during the 2007 field season'. *ASAE* 84: 383–88.

– 2010–11. '5 field seasons in the royal necropolis: the second phase of the Pacific Lutheran University Valley of the Kings Project'. *Kmt* 21/4: 30–44.

RYHOLT, K.S.B. 1997. *The Political Situation in Egypt During the Second Intermediate Period, c. 1800–1550 B.C.* Copenhagen: Museum Tusculanum Press.

SA'AD, R. 1975. 'Fragments d'un minument de Toutânkamon retrouvés dans le IXᵉ pylône de Karnak'. In *Cahiers de Karnak V: 1970–1972*, edited by J. Lauffray, S. Sauneron and R. Sa'ad, 93–109. Cairo: Centre Franco-Égyptien d'Étude des Temples de Karnak.

SAAD, Z.Y. 1957. *Ceiling Stelae in the Second Dynasty Tombs from the Excavations at Helwan*. Cairo: Caire: Imprimerie de l'Institut français d'Archéologie orientale.

SAGRILLO, T.L. 2009. 'The Geographic Origins of the "Bubastite" Dynasty'. In *The Libyan Period In Egypt: historical and cultural studies into the 21th – 24th Dynasties. Proceedings of a conference at Leiden University, 25–27 October 2007*, edited by G.P.F. Broekman, R.J. Demarée and O.E. Kaper, 341–59. Leiden: Nederlands Instituut voor het Nabije Oosten/Louvain: Peeters.

SALAH, M. and H. SOUROUZIAN 1987. *The Egyptian Museum Cairo: Official Catalogue*. Mainz: Philipp von Zabern.

SAUNDERS, N.J. 2007. *Alexander's Tomb: The Two-Thousand Year Obsession to Find the Lost Conquerer*. New York: Basic Books.

SCHADEN, O.J. 1979. 'Preliminary Report on the Re-clearance of Tomb 25 in the Western Valley of the Kings (WV-25)'. *ASAE* 63: 161–68.

– 1984. 'Clearance of the tomb of King Ay (WV-23)'. *JARCE* 21: 39–64.

– 1993. 'Amenmesse Project Report'. *NARCE* 163: 1–9.

– 1994. 'Some Observations on the Tomb of Amenmesse (KV-10)'. In *Essays in Egyptology in Honor of Hans Goedicke*, edited by B. Bryan and D. Lorton, 243–54. San Antonio: Van Siclen Books).

– 2004. 'KV-10: Amenmesse 2000'. *ASAE* 78: 129–49.

– 2011. 'KV 63 update: the 2011 season'. *Kmt* 22/2: 33–41.

SCHADEN, O.J. and E. ERTMAN 1998. 'The Tomb of Amenmesse (KV-10): The First Season'. *ASAE* 73: 116–55.

SCHIESTL, R. 2008. 'Dahschur in der 13. Dynastie: Bericht über den im Frühjahr 2006 durchgeführten Survey'. *MDAIK* 64: 239–66.

SCHMIDT, E.F. 1953. *Persepolis, I: Structures – Reliefs – Inscriptions*. Chicago: Oriental Institute.

– 1970. *Persepolis, III: The Royal Tombs And Other Monuments*. Chicago: Oriental Institute.

SCHNEIDER, H.D. 1996. *The Memphite Tomb of Ḥoremḥeb, Commander-in-Chief of Tutʿankhamūn*, II: *Catalogue of the Finds*. Leiden: National Museum of Antiquities/London: Egypt Exploration Society.

SECO ÁLVAREZ, M. 2012. 'Últimos descubrimientos en el proyecto de excavación, restauración y puesta en valor del templo funerario de Tutmosis III en la orilla oeste de Luxor'. In *Novos trabalhos de Egiptologia Ibérica: IV Congresso Ibérico de Egiptologia – IV Congreso Ibérico de Egiptología*, edited by L.M. de Araújo and J. das Candeias Sales (eds), 2, 1065–75. Lisbon: Instituto Oriental e Centro de História da Facultade de Letras da Universidade de Lisboa.

SECO ÀLVAREZ, M. and A. RADWAN 2010. 'Egyptian-Spanish project at the temple of Thutmosis III in Luxor West Bank: results of two seasons'. In *Les temples de millions d'années et le pouvoir royal à Thèbes au Nouvel Empire: sciences et nouvelles technologies appliquées à l'archéologie*, edited by C. Leblanc and G. Zaki, 59–71. Cairo: Dar el-Kutub.

SECO ÁLVAREZ, M. and A. RADWAN and others 2010. 'First season of the Egyptian-Spanish project at the funerary temple of Thutmosis III in Luxor'. *ASAE* 84: 27–61.

SESANA, A. 2002. *4th Preliminary report of the Italian archaeological expedition on the area of the temple of Amenophis II – Western Thebes, 2001/2002*. Como: C.F.B. – Centro Comasco di Egittologia 'Francesco Ballerini'.

– 2003. *5th Preliminary report of the Italian archaeological expedition on the area of the temple of Amenophis II – Western Thebes, 2002/2003.* Como: C.F.B. – Centro Comasco di Egittologia 'Francesco Ballerini'.
– 2004. *6th Preliminary report of the Italian archaeological expedition on the area of the temple of Amenophis II – Western Thebes, 2003/2004.* Como: C.F.B. – Centro Comasco di Egittologia 'Francesco Ballerini'.
– 2007. *7th-8th-9th Preliminary report of the Italian archaeological expedition on the area of the temple of Amenophis II – Western Thebes, 2005/2007.* Como: C.F.B. – Centro Comasco di Egittologia 'Francesco Ballerini'.
– 2008. 'Preliminary Report of the Eighth Italian Archaeological Mission – Temple of Amenophis II at Western Thebes, Egypt – Winter 2005/2006'. *ASAE* 82: 261–87.
– 2009. 'Preliminary report on the ninth Italian archaeological Expedition – temple of Amenhotep II, western Thebes, Egypt – Winter 2006/2007'. *ASAE* 83: 393–416.
– 2013. 'The Temple of Millions of Years of Amenhotep II at Thebes: New Discoveries'. In *Archaeological Resaerch in the Valley of the Kings and Ancient Thebes: Papers Presented in Honor of Richard H. Wiliknson*, edited by P.P. Creasman, 325–31. [Tucson]: University of Arizona Egyptian Expedition.
– 2015. 'Excavation of the Italian mission in the Temple of Millions of Years of Amenhotep II on the West Bank of Luxor / Excavación de la misión italiana en el Templo de Millones de Años de Amenhotep II en la ribera oeste de Luxor'. In *Los templos de millones de años en Tebas / The temples of millions of years in Thebes*, edited by M. Seco Álvarez, and A. Jódar Miñarro, 135–43. Granada: Editorial Universidad de Granada.
SHEIKHOLESLAMI, C.M. 2008. 'A lost papyrus and the royal cache in TT 320 before 1881'. In *The Realm of the Pharaohs: essays in honor of Tohfa Handoussa* I, edited by Z.A. Hawass, K.A. Daoud and S. Abd El-Fattah, 377–400. Cairo: General Organisation for Government Printing Offices.
SILVERMAN, D.P. 2009. 'Non-Royal Burials in the Teti Pyramid Cemetery and theEarly Twelfth Dynasty'. In *Archaism and innovation: studies in the culture of Middle Kingdom Egypt*, edited by D.P. Silverman, W.K. Simpson and J. Wegner, 47–101. New Haven, CT: Department of Near Eastern languages and civilizations, Yale University/Philadelpia, PA: University of Pennsylvana Museum of Archaeology and Anthropology.
STROUHAL, E., G. BONANI, W. WOELFLI, A. NĚMEČKOVÁ and S. SAUNDERS 1998. 'Re-investigation of the remains thought to be of King Djoser and those of an unidentified female from the Step Pyramid at Saqqara'. In *Proceedings of the Seventh International Congress of Egyptologists, Cambridge, 3–9 September 1995*, edited by C.J. Eyre, 1103–7. Leuven: Peeters.
SOUROUZIAN, H. 1989. *Les Monuments du roi Merenptah.* Mainz: Philipp von Zabern.
– 2010. 'The temple of millions of years of Amenhotep III: past, present, and future perspectives'. In *Les temples de millions d'années et le pouvoir royal à Thèbes au Nouvel Empire: sciences et nouvelles technologies appliquées à l'archéologie*, edited by C. Leblanc and G. Zaki, 91–98. Cairo: Dar el-Kutub.
– 2011. 'La statuaire du temple d'Amenhotep III à Thèbes'. In *Statues égyptiennes et kouchites démembrées et reconstituées: hommage à Charles Bonnet*, edited by D. Valbelle and J.-M. Yoyotte, 71-92. Paris: Presses de l'Université Paris-Sorbonne.

SOUROUZIAN, H., H. BECKER, T. HERBICH, D. VLASOV, and A. ZOLOTAREV 2006. 'Three seasons of work at the temple of Amenhotep III at Kom el Hettan. Part IV: magnetometric, geologic and biologic prospections'. *ASAE* 80: 489–520.

SOUROUZIAN, H. and R. STADELMANN 2005a. 'Recent discoveries and new southern place names at the mortuary temple of Amenhotep III, Kom el-Hettan'. *Sudan & Nubia* 9: 76–81.

– 2005b. '«Храм, что принимает Амона и возвышает его красоту»: колоссы Мемнона и заупокойный комплекс Аменхотепа III в Ком-эль-Хеттан (западные Фивы). Археологические исследования и консервация' / 'The Colossi of Memnon and the Mortuary Temple of Amenhotep III in Western Thebes at Kom el Hettan – with his Beautiful Name: "The Temple Who Receives Amun and Raises his Beauty"'. In *Петербургские сфинксы: солнце Египта на берегах Невы*, edited by V.V. Solkin, 107–52, 246–69. St Petersburg: Zurnal-Neva.

SOUROUZIAN, H., R. STADELMANN, M. SECO ALVAREZ, L. BAVAY, H. BECKER, P. BROMBLET, M. EL-AMOURI, S. EMARA, J. LINKE, F. PERNEL, F. SCHUBERT, M. SCHUBERT and F. WENZEL 2004. "The temple of Amenhotep III at Thebes: excavation and conservation at Kom el-Hettân. Third report on the fifth season in 2002/2003." *MDAIK* 60: 171–236.

SOUROUZIAN, H., R. STADELMANN, B. MADDEN and T. GAYER-ANDERSON 2006a. "Three seasons of work at the temple of Amenhotep III at Kom el Hettan. Part I: work at the colossi of Memnon." *ASAE* 80: 323–65.

SOUROUZIAN, H., R. STADELMANN, J. DORNER, N. HAMPIKIAN, M. SECO ALVAREZ, I. NOUREDDINE, M.A. LÓPEZ MARCOS and C. PERZLMEIER 2006b. "Three seasons of work at the temple of Amenhotep III at Kom el Hettan. Part II: investigations at the second pylon and work on the royal colossi." *ASAE* 80: 367–99.

SOUROUZIAN, H., R. STADELMANN, N. HAMPIKIAN, M. SECO ALVAREZ, I. NOUREDDINE, M. ELESAWY, M. ANGEL LÓPEZ MARCOS and C. PERZLMEIER 2006c. 'Three seasons of work at the temple of Amenhotep III at Kom el Hettan. Part III: works in the dewatered area of the peristyle court and the hypostyle hall.' *ASAE* 80: 401–87.

SOUROUZIAN, H., R. STADELMANN, M. SECO ALVAREZ, J. DORNER, N. HAMPIKIAN and I. NOUREDDINE 2007. 'The temple of Amenhotep III at Thebes: excavations and conservation at Kom el-Hettân. Fourth report on the sixth, seventh and eighth season in 2004, 2004–2005 and 2006.' *MDAIK* 63: 247–35.

SPENCER, A.J. 1974. 'Researches on the topography of North Saqqâra'. *Orientalia* 43: 1–11.

STADELMANN, R. 1971. 'Das Grab in Tempelhof. Der Typus des Königsgrabes in der Spätzeit'. *MDAIK* 27: 111–23.

– 1983. 'Die Pyramiden des Snofru in Dahschur: Zweiter Bericht über die Ausgrabungen an den nördlichen Steinpyramide, mit einem Exkurs über Scheintür oder Stelen im Totentempel des AR'. *MDAIK* 39: 225–41.

– 1985. 'Der Oberbauten der Königsgräber der 2. Dynastie in Sakkara'. In *Mélanges Gamal eddin Mokhtar*, II, 295–307. Cairo: Institut français d'archéologie orientale.

– 1991. *Die ägyptischen Pyramiden*. Mainz: Philipp von Zabern.

– 1996. 'Zur Baugeschichte des Djoserbezirks Grabschacht und Grabkammer der Stufenmastaba'. *MDAIK* 52: 295–305.

– 2011a. 'The heb-sed Temple of Seneferu at Dahshur'. In *Abusir and Saqqara in the*

Year 2010, edited by M. Bárta, F. Coppens and J. Krejči, 736–46. Prague: Czech Institute of Egyptology.

– 2011b. 'Where were the queens of the Early Dynastic Period and the queens of Djoser time buried'. In *Times, signs and pyramids: studies in honour of Miroslav Verner on the occasion of his seventieth birthday*, edited by Callender, V.G., L. Bareš, M. Bárta, J. Janák and J. Krejčí, 375–89. Prague: Faculty of Arts, Charles University.

STADELMANN, R., N. ALEXANIAN, H. ERNST, G. HEINDL, and D. RAUE 1993. 'Pyramiden und Nekropole des Snofru in Dahschur. Dritter Vorbericht über die Grabungen des Deutschen Archäologischen Instituts in Dahschur'. *MDAIK* 49: 259–94.

STADELMANN, R. and H. SOUROUZIAN 1982. 'Die Pyramiden des Snofru in Dahschur: Erster Bericht über die Ausgrabungen an der nördlichen Steinpyramide'. *MDAIK* 38: 379–93.

STRONACH, D. 1964. 'Excavations at Pasargadae: second preliminary report'. *Iran* II: 21–39.

– 1965. 'Excavations at Pasargadae: third preliminary report'. *Iran* III: 9–40.

– 1978. *Pasargadae: a report on the excavations conducted by the British Institute of Persian Studies from 1961 to 1963*. Oxford: Clarendon Press

STÜNKEL, I. 'The relief decoration of the cult chapels of royal women in the pyramid complex of Senusret III at Dahshur'. In *Abusir and Saqqara in the Year 2005*, edited by M. Bárta, F. Coppens and J. Krejči, 148–66. Prague: Czech Institute of Egyptology.

SWELIM, N. 1983. *Some Problems on the History of the Third Dynasty.* Alexandria: The Archaeological Society of Alexandria.

– 1987. *The Brick Pyramid at Abu Rowash, Number '1' by Lepsius: a preliminary study*. Alexandria: The Archaeological Society of Alexandria.

– 1988. 'The Dry Moat of the Netjerykhet Complex'. In *Pyramid Studies and Other Essays presented to I.E.S. Edwards*, edited by J. Baines, T.G.H. James, A. Leahy and A.F. Shore, 12–22. London: Egypt Exploration Society.

– 1991. 'Some Remarks on the Great Rectangular Monuments of Middle Saqqara'. *MDAIK* 47: 389–402.

– 1994. 'Pyramid Research from the Archaic to the Second Intermediate Period: Lists, catalogues and Objectives.' In *Hommages à Jean Leclant*, edited by C. Berger, G. Clerc and N. Grimal, I, 337–49 Cairo: Institut français d'archéologie orientale.

SWELIM, N. and A. DODSON 1998. 'On the Pyramid of Ameny-Qemau and its Canopic Equipment'. *MDAIK* 54: 319–34.

TE VELDE, H. 1967. *Seth, God of Confusion*. Leiden: Brill.

THOMAS, E. 1966. *The Royal Necropoleis of Thebes, I: The Major Cemeteries.* Princeton: Privately Printed.

– 1967. 'Was Queen Mutnedjemet the owner of Tomb 33 in the Valley of the Queens?' *JEA* 53: 161–63.

UPHILL, E. 1992. 'Where were the funerary temples of the New Kingdom queens?' In *Sesto Congresso internazionale di egittologia: atti* 1, 613–18. Turin: International Association of Egyptologists.

– 2000. *Pharaoh's Gateway to Eternity. The Hawara Labyrinth of King Amenemhat III.* London: Kegan Paul International.

ULLMANN, M. 2016. 'The Temples of Millions of Years at Western Thebes'. In *The Oxford Handbook to the Valley of the Kings*, edited by R.H. Wilkinson and K.R. Weeks, 417–32. New York: Oxford University Press.

VALLOGGIA, M. 2011. *Abou Rawash, 1: le complexe funéraire royal de Rêdjedef*, 2vv. Cairo: Institut français d'archéologie orientale.

VAN DIJK, J. 2008. 'New evidence on the length of the reign of Horemheb'. *JARCE* 44: 193–200.

– 2009. 'The Death of Meketaten'. In *Causing his Name to Live: studies in Egyptian epigraphy and history in memory of William J. Murnane*, edited by P.J. Brand and L. Cooper, 83–88. Leiden: Brill.

VAN SICLEN, C.C. 1980. 'The Temple of Meniset at Thebes'. *Serapis* 6: 187–207.

VENTURA, R. 1988. 'The Largest Project for a Royal Tomb in the Valley of the Kings'. *JEA* 74: 137–56.

VERNER, M. 1982. 'Eine zweite unvollendete Pyramide in Abusir'. *ZÄS* 109: 75–78.

– 1994b. 'Abusir Pyramids 'Lepseius no. XXIV and no. XXV'. In *Hommages à Jean Leclant*, I, edited by C. Berger, G. Clerc and N. Grimal, 371–8. Cairo: Institut français d'archéologie orientale.

– 1998. 'Pyramid Lepsius no. XXIV: notes on the construction of the pyramid's core'. In *Stationen: Beiträge zur Kulturgeschichte Ägyptens, Rainer Stadelmann gewidmet*, edited by H. Guksch and D. Polz, 145–50. Mainz: Philipp von Zabern.

– 2000. 'Who was Shepseskara, and when did he reign?' In *Abusir and Saqqara in the year 2000*, edited by M. Bárta and J. Krejčí, 581–602. Prague: Academy of Sciences of the Czech Republic, Oriental Institute

– 2001. *Abusir III: the Pyramid Complex of Khentkaus*. Prague: Czech Institute of Egyptology.

– 2002. *The Pyramids: The Mystery, Culture and Science of Egypt's Great Monuments*. London: Atlantic Books.

– 2014. *Sons of the Sun: rise and decline of the Fifth Dynasty*. Prague: Charles University.

VERNER, M. (ed.) 2006. *Abusir IX: the pyramid complex of Raneferef: the archaeology*. Prague: Czech Institute of Egyptology.

VERNER, M. and V. BRŮNA 2011. 'Why was the Fifth Dynasty cemetery founded at Abusir?' In *Old Kingdom, New Perspectives: Egyptian Art and Archaeology 2750–2150 BC*, edited by N. Strudwick and H. Strudwick, 286–94. Oxford: Oxbow Books.

VERNER, M. and V.G. CALLENDER 2002. *Abusir VI: Djedkare's family cemetery. Excavations of the Czech Institute of Egyptology*. Prague: Czech Institute of Egyptology,

VERNUS, P. 'Inscriptions de la troisième période intermédiaire (II): blocs du grand-prêtre d'Amon *iwpwt* remployés dans le Deir-el-Abyad'. *BIFAO* 75: 67–72.

VITTMANN, G. 1974. 'Zwei Königinnen der Spätzeit namens Chedebnitjerbone'. *CdE* 49: 43–51.

VON KÄNEL, F. 1987. 'Notes épigraphiques'. In *Cahiers de Tanis: Mission français des fouilles de Tanis* I, edited by P. Brissaud, 45–60. Editions Recherche sur les Civilisations.

VÖRÖS, G. 1998. *The Temple on the Pyramid of Thebes: Hungarian Excavations on Thoth Hill at the Temple of Pharaoh Montuhotep Sankhkara 1995–1998*. Budapest: Százszorszép Kiadó és Nyomda.

– 2003. 'The ancient nest of Horus above Thebes: Hungarian excavations on Thoth Hill at the temple of King Sankhare Montuhotep III (1995–1998)'. In *Egyptology at the dawn of the twenty-first century: proceedings of the Eighth International Congress of Egyptologists, Cairo, 2000*, edited by Z. Hawass and L.P. Brock, I, 547–56. Cairo: American University in Cairo Press.

– 2007. *Egyptian Temple Architecture: 100 Years of Hungarian Excavations in Egypt, 1907–2007*. Budapest: Kairosz Press.

VÖRÖS, G. and R. PUDLEINER 1997. 'Preliminary Report of the Excavations at Thoth Hill, Thebes: The Temple of Montuhotep Sankhkara (Season 1995–1996)'. *MDAIK* 53: 283–87.

– 1998.   'Preliminary report of the excavations at Thoth Hill, Thebes: the pre-11th dynasty temple and the western building (seasons 1996–1997)'. *MDAIK* 54: 335–40.

WAHBA, A. 2015. 'Royal Musical Chairs: To Whom Does the New Pyramid in Saqqara Belong?' In *Egyptian Bioarchaeology: humans, animals, and the environment*, edited by S. Ikram, J. Kaiser and R. Walker, 143–55. Leiden: Sidestone Press.

WASEDA UNIVERSITY, INSTITUTE OF EGYPTOLOGY (ed.) 2001, 2006. アブ・シール南 [*Abusir South*], 2vv. Tokyo: Kakuzandō/Akhto.

WEEKS, K.R. 1983. 'The Berkeley Map of the Theban Necropolis: report of the fifth season, 1982'. *NARCE* 121: 41–58.

– 1998. *The Lost Tomb: the Greatest Discovery in the Valley of the Kings since Tutankhamun.* London: Wiedenfield and Nicholson, 1998.

– 2000.   *KV5: A Preliminary Report.* Cairo: American University in Cairo Press.

WEEKS, K.R. (ed.) 2000. *Atlas of the Valley of the Kings*. Cairo: American University in Cairo Press.

– 2001. *The Treasures of the Valley of the Kings: Tombs and Temples of the Theban West Bank in Luxor*. Cairo: American University in Cairo Press.

WEGNER, J. 1995. 'Old and New Excavations at the Abydene Complex of Senwosret III'. *Kmt* 6/2: 59–71.

– 2006a. 'The Archaeology of South Abydos'. *Expedition* 48/2: 6–10.

– 2006b. 'Beneath the Mountain-of-Anubis: Ancient Egypt's First Hidden Royal Tomb'. *Expedition* 48/2: 15–22.

– 2007a. 'Reopening the tomb of Senwosret III at Abydos'. *EgArch* 30: 38–41.

– 2007b. *The Mortuary Temple of Senwosret III at Abydos*. New Haven: Peabody Museum of Natural History of Yale University.

– 2009. 'The tomb of Senwosret III at Abydos: considerations on the origins and development of the royal *Amduat*-tomb'. In *Archaism and innovation: studies in the culture of Middle Kingdom Egypt*, edited by D.P. Silverman, W.K. Simpson and J. Wegner, 103–68. New Haven, CT: Department of Near Eastern languages and civilizations, Yale University/Philadelpia, PA: University of Pennsylvana Museum of Archaeology and Anthropology.

– 2013. 'Protection and Restoration of the Tomb of Senwosret III at South Abydos'. *BARCE* 230: 10–25.

– 2014. 'Kings of Abydos, solving an Ancient Egyptian Mystery'. *Current World Archaeology* 64: 20–27.

– 2016. 'Woseribre-Senebkay: a Newly Identified Upper Egyptian King of the Second Intermediate Period'. In *The Age of Khyan*, edited by I. Förstner-Muller and N. Moeller. Vienna: Österreiches Akadamie der Wissenschaften.

WEGNER, J. and K. CAHAIL 2015. 'Royal Funerary Equipment of a King Sobekhotep at South Abydos: Evidence for the Tombs of Sobekhotep IV and Neferhotep I?' *JARCE* 51: 123–64.

WEGNER, J. and M. ABU EL-YAZID 2006. 'The Mountain-of-Anubis: Necropolis Seal of the Senwosret III Tomb at Abydos'. In *Timelines: Studies in Honour of Manfred Bietak*, edited by E. Czerny, I. Hein, H. Hunger, D. Melman and A. Schwab, I, 399–415. Leuven: Peeters.

WEILL, R., Mme TONY-REVILLON and M. PILLET 1958. *Dara: campaignes de 1946–1948*. Cairo: Organisme Générale des Imprimeries Gouvernmentales.

WERNING, D.A. 2011. *Das Höhlenbuch: Textkritische und Textgrammatik*, 2vv. Wiesbaden: Otto Harrassowitz.

WILKINSON, R.H. 1995. 'Symbolic Orientation and Alignment in New Kingdom Royal Tombs'. In *Valley of the Sun Kings: New Explorations in the Tombs of the Pharaohs*, edited by Richard H. Wilkinson, 74–81. Tucson: The University of Arizona Egyptian Expedition.

– 2011. 'Controlled Damage: The Mechanics and Micro-History of the *Damnatio Memoriae* Carried Out in KV-23, the Tomb of Ay'. *JEH* 4: 129–47.

– 2012. 'The "Temple of Millions of Years" of Tausret'. In *Tausret: forgotten queen and pharaoh of Egypt*, edited by R.H. Wikinson, 67–91. New York: Oxford University Press.

WILKINSON, R.H. (ed.) 2011. *The Temple of Tausret: the University of Arizona Egyptian Expedition Tausret Temple Project, 2004–2011*. [Tucson, AZ]: University of Arizona Egyptian Expedition.

WILLIAMS, B. 1975–1976. 'The date of Senebtisi at Lisht and the chronology of major groups and deposits of the Middle Kingdom'. *Serapis* 3: 41–55.

WILSON, P. 2006. *The survey of Saïs (Sa el-Hagar) 1997–2002*. London: Egypt Exploration Society.

– 2016. 'A Psamtek Ushabti and a Granite Block from Sais (Sa el-Hagar)'. In *Mummies, Magic and Medicine: Multidisciplinary Essays in Egyptology for Rosalie David*, edited by C. Price, P. Nicholson, R. Morkot, J. Tyldesley, A. Chamberlain and R. Forshaw, 73–90. Manchester: Manchester University Press.

WILSON, R.S. 2010. *KV-63, The Untold Story of the New Tomb in Egypt's Valley of the Kings*. Florida: Ferniehirst Publishing.

WINLOCK, H.E. 1924. 'The Tombs of the Kings of the Seventeenth Dynasty at Thebes'. *JEA* 10: 217–77.

– 1947. *The Rise and Fall of the Middle Kingdom in Thebes*. New York: Macmillan.

WYSOCKI, Z. 1984. 'The results of research, architectonic studies and of protective work over the North Portico of the Middle Courtyard in the Hatshepsut Temple at Deir el Bahari'. *MDAIK* 40: 329–49.

– 1986. 'The Temple of Queen Hatshepsut at Deir el Bahari: Its Original Form'. *MDAIK* 42: 213–28.

YOSHIMURA, S. 2004. 'The Tomb of Amenophis III: Waseda University Excavations 1989–2000'. *ASAE* 78: 205–10.

YOSHIMURA, S. (ed.) 2008. *Research in the Western Valley of the Kings, Egypt – The Tomb of Amenophis III (KV22)*. Tokyo: Chuo Koron Bijutsu Shuppan.

YOSHIMURA, S. and J. KONDO 1995. 'Excavations at the tomb of Amenophis III', *EgArch* 7: 17–18.

YOSHIMURA, S. and H. KUROKOCHI 2013. 'Research report. Brief report of the project of the second boat of King Khufu'. *JAEI* 5/1: 85–89.

YOUSSEF, M. 2011. 'New scenes of hunting a hippopotamus from the burial chamber of Unas'. In *Abusir and Saqqara in the Year 2010*, edited by 2010, edited by M. Bárta, F. Coppens and J. Krejči, 820–22. Prague: Czech Insititute of Egyptology.

ZINK, A. and A. NERLICH 2003. 'Anthropologische und paläopathologische Untersuchungen des Skelettmaterials'. *MDAIK* 59: 124–36.

Sources of Images

All images are by the author, except as detailed below:

Maps

2.	Adapted from Chugg 2004/5: fig. 8.9.
3, top	Terrain adapted from Lepsius 1849–59: I, taf. 11.
3, bottom	Terrain adapted from Lepsius 1849–59: I, taf. 14.
4, top	Terrain adapted from Lepsius 1849–59: I, taf. 32.
4, bottom	Contours adapted from Ministère de l'Habitat et de la Reconstruction, *Le Caire*, sheet H21.
5.	Contours adapted from Ministère de l'Habitat et de la Reconstruction, *Le Caire*, sheets H21 & H22.
6.	Contours adapted from Ministère de l'Habitat et de la Reconstruction, *Le Caire*, sheets H23 & H24.
7.	Terrain adapted from Lepsius 1849–59: I, taf. 34–35.
8.	Contours adapted from Ministère de l'Habitat et de la Reconstruction, *Le Caire*, sheets H27.
9, top	Adapted from Arnold 1977: 89–90.
9, bottom	Terrain adapted from Lepsius 1849–59: I, taf. 44.
14.	Adapted from Weeks (ed.) 2000: sheet 3/72.
15.	Adapted from Leblanc 1989b: pl. xxxi.

]Figures

14c.	Adapted from De Morgan 1895: fig. 243.
27.	Adapted from Schmidt 1970: figs. 1, 6, 31, 33–36, 38.

Plates

Ia	Courtesy Renée Friedman.
IIa	Courtesy German Archaeological Institute, Cairo.
IIb	Courtesy German Archaeological Institute, Cairo.
IIIb	Reginald Clark.
IVd	Courtesy German Archaeological Institute, Cairo.
VIb	Courtesy German Archaeological Institute, Cairo.
VIIb	Courtesy Renée Friedman.
VIIIa	Courtesy German Archaeological Institute, Cairo.
Xb	Firth and Quibell 1935: pl. 15–17.
XIb	Goneim 1957: pl. lvii.
XIIa	Lepsius 1849–59: I, pl. 12.
XVa	Salima Ikram.
XVIIa	Leslie V. Grinsell, courtesy Department of Archaeology & Anthropology, University of Bristol.
XVIIb	Leslie V. Grinsell, courtesy Department of Archaeology & Anthropology, University of Bristol.

XIXa	Barsanti 1912: pl. iii.
XXb	Martin Davies.
XXVIIa	Adapted from Maspero 1901: 437.
XXXIb	Salima Ikram.
XXXIIb	Martin Davies.
XXXIIIa	Salima Ikram.
XXXIVa	John Ward and Maria Nilsson.
XXXIVb	John Ward and Maria Nilsson.
XXXVa	Courtesy Theban Mapping Project.
XXXVa, inset	John Ward and Maria Nilsson
XXXVb	Courtesy Theban Mapping Project.
XXXVIa	Adapted from Naville and Hall 1907–1913: II, pl. xiv-xvi.
XXXVIIIb	Petrie, Brunton and Murray 1923: pl. xxv[5].
XXXIXa	Dieter Arnold, Metropolitan Museum of Art.
XLIa	Petrie, Brunton and Murray 1923: pl. xxv[6].
XLIb	De Morgan 1903: fig. 98.
XLIc	Adapted from De Morgan 1903: fig. 97.
XLIIIb	Courtesy Josef Wegner, University of Pennsylvania.
XLIVa	Courtesy Josef Wegner, University of Pennsylvania.
XLVIa	Petrie 1909: pl. xxiii.
XLVIb	Stephen P. Harvey.
XLVIIa	Lepsius 1849–59: III, pl. 4b.
XLVIIIa	Francis Dzikowski, © and courtesy Theban Mapping Project.
XLVIIIb	Francis Dzikowski, © and courtesy Theban Mapping Project.
Lb	Naville 1895–1909: IV, pl. cx.
LIIa	Martin Davies.
LIIb	Francis Dzikowski, © and courtesy Theban Mapping Project.
LIVa	Francis Dzikowski, © and courtesy Theban Mapping Project.
LIVb	Lepsius 1849–59: III, pl. 79.
LVa	Courtesy Jiro Kondo.
LVIIa	Dyan Hilton.
LVIIb	Francis Dzikowski, © and courtesy Theban Mapping Project.
LIXa	Francis Dzikowski, © and courtesy Theban Mapping Project.
LIXb	Francis Dzikowski, © and courtesy Theban Mapping Project.
LXIb	Salima Ikram
LXIIa	Francis Dzikowski, © and courtesy Theban Mapping Project.
LXIIb	Adapted from Belzoni 1820: pl. 40.
LXIVa	Francis Dzikowski, © and courtesy Theban Mapping Project.
LXIVb	Francis Dzikowski, © and courtesy Theban Mapping Project.
LXVb	Francis Dzikowski, © and courtesy Theban Mapping Project.
LXVIa	Dyan Hilton.
LXVIIb	Martin Davies.
LXIXa	Francis Dzikowski, © and courtesy Theban Mapping Project.
LXIXb	Martin Davies.
LXXa	Martin Davies.
LXXIIa	Francis Dzikowski, © and courtesy Theban Mapping Project.
LXXIIb	Francis Dzikowski, © and courtesy Theban Mapping Project.

LXXIIIa	Horeau 1841: pl. xxi.
LXXIIIb	Martin Davies.
LXXIVa	Francis Dzikowski, © and courtesy Theban Mapping Project.
LXXVIa	Martin Davies.
LXXVIIa	Montet 1951: pl. xi.
LXXVIIb	Montet 1947: pl. xxvi.
LXXVIIIa	Dyan Hilton.
LXXIXa	Montet 1960: pl. xxvi.
LXXIXb	Montet 1960: pl. xxx.
LXXXb	Hölscher 1954: pl. 9A.
LXXXIIb	Dyan Hilton.
LXXXIVb	Dyan Hilton.
LXXXVa	Dyan Hilton.
XCIIIb	Nicholas J. Saunders.
XCVIa	Hébrard and Zeiller 1912: pl. X.
XCVIb	G. Dall'Orto, via Wikipedia Commons.

Index

Names of Egyptian rulers are given in
CAPITALS; non-rulers' tombs are
given as part of their entries, where
known.

DIOCLETIAN, 126
DJEDEFRE, 21, 22, 23, 24, 26, 28
Djedkhonsiufankh I (High Priest of
  Amun), 106, 109
Djedmutesankh A (wife of the High Priest
  of Amun; MMA60), 109
DJER, 4, 5, 6, 7
DJOSER (Netjerkhet), 9, 11, 12–3, 14,
  16, 17, 29, 30, 44–5, 46, 47, 129 n.49,
  130 n.1
DOMITIAN, 126
Dra Abu'l-Naga see Thebes-West, Dra
  Abu'l-Naga
Edinburgh
  National Museums Scotland
    A.1909.527.1ff, pl. XLVIa
El-Khor see Thebes-West, El-Khor
El-Kurru, 114, 115, 116
  Ku3 (Ñaparaye), 116
  Ku4 (Kheñsa), 116
  Ku5 (Qalhata), 116
  Ku6 (Arty), 116
  Ku8 (Kashta), 114
  Ku15 (Shabaka), 115
  Ku16 (Tanutamun), 116
  Ku17 (Piye), 114
  Ku18 (Shabataka), 115
  Ku52 (Neferukakashta)
  Ku53 (Tabiry), 116
El-Kula (Nag el-Miamariya, Edfu-North),
  130 n.25
El-Tarif see Thebes-West, El-Tarif
El-Zawayda see Nubt
Elephantine see Aswan

Fayyum, 17, 37, 43, 46,

GALBA, 126
Gebel Barkal, 114, 116
Giza, 19, 21, 23, 24
  L.IV/Great Pyramid (Khufu), 19–21,
    24
  L.V/GIa (Hetepheres I?), 24
  L.VI/GIb, 24
  L.VII/GIc, 24
  L.VIII/Second Pyramid (Khaefre), 22,
    23, 25, 119

L.IX/Third Pyramid (Menkaure), 21,
  22–23, 25, 36
L.X/GIIIa, 23, 25, 131 n.41
L.XI/GIIIb, 23, 25
L.XII/GIIIc, 23
LG83 (Nakhtsebastetru, Ahmose C &
  Tashentihet), 119
LG88 (Persenet), 25
LG100/GIV (Khentkawes I), 25
MQ1 (Khuenre), 25
Cemetery G7000, 24, 25
  G7000X (Hetepheres I), 24
Galarza Tomb (Khamerernebty I), 25
Gurob, 92

HAGAR, 123
Hanebu (owner of Abusir L.XXV/1 or
  2?), 31
HATSHEPSUT, 63–64, 65, 66–9, 70, 72,
  80, 91, 136 n.36
Hawara
  L.LXVII (Amenemhat III), 46–7, 51
  Labyrinth, 47
Hawara-South
  Pyramid of Neferuptah B, 52
Helwan
  175 H8 (Khnemetptah), 11
  964 H8 (Nysuheqat), 11
  1241 H9 (Satba), 11
Hemetre (daughter of Unas?; Saqqara
  D65), 32
Henhenet (wife of Montjuhotep II;
  DBXI.11), 41
Henttawy A (wife of Panedjem I), 106
Henttawy B (daughter of Panudjem I;
  MMA60), 109
Henttawy C (granddaughter of Panedjem
  I; MMA60), 109
Henutmire (wife of Rameses II; QV75),
  91, 112
Henutsen (daughter of Khufu?; Giza
  GIc?), 24
Herakleopolis (Ihnasiya el-Medina), 37,
  110
HERCALIUS, 127
HERIHOR, 103, 106
Herneith (wife of Den?), 6

L.LXI/9 (wife? of Senwosret I), 48
954, 47
956, 47
London, British Museum
  EA23, 136 n.40
  EA478, pl. XLVb
  EA683, pl. XLVIIb
  EA35597, pl. VIIa
  EA36635, 138 n.103
  Papyrus Abbott (pEA10221), 38, 39,
    58, 59, 60, 62

Maatkare A (God's Wife of Amun), 106
Mansions of Millions of Years *see*
  Memorial Temple
Masaharta (High Priest of Amun), 106
Mayet (DBXI.18), 41
Mazghuna, 53
  L.LIX/South Pyramid, 55, 56
  North Pyramid, 54
Mehaa (wife of Pepy I; Saqqara-South), 34
Mehytenweskhet C (wife of Psametik I),
  117, 119
Meidum
  L.LXV (Seneferu), 17–18, 19
  6 (Rahotep), 23–4
  9 (Ranefer), 23–4
  16 (Nefermaat), 23–4
  17 (unknown), 24
Melanaqeñ (King of Kush; Nu5), 116
Memorial temple, 63, 66, 67, 68, 70, 72,
  76, 77, 79, 83, 85, 89, 90, 94, 97, 104,
  112
Memphis, 7, 8, 17, 28, 92, 110, 113, 124,
  137 n.48, 143–4 n.31
  Kom Rabia
  Tombs of the High Priests, 113
Mendes (Tell el-Rub'a), 122–23
MENKAUHOR, 26, 28, 29, 31, 32, 37,
  132 n.73, 133 n.14
MENKAURE (MYKERINUS), 16, 21–2,
  23, 25, 26, 36, 131 n.39
Menkheperre (High Priest of Amun), 106,
  109, 113
MERENPTAH, 72, 86–7, 89, 96, 108
Mereruka (vizier; son-in-law of Teti;
  Saqqara), 34

Meresankh IV (wife of Menkauhor?;
  Saqqara 82), 31
Meroë, 116
Meryetamun B (wife of Amenhotep I;
  TT358), 62, 67, 79, 109, 136 n.23
Meryetamun E (daughter-wife of
  Rameses II; QV68), 91
Meryetamun G (princess), 117
Meryetneith, 4–5
Meryetre (wife of Thutmose III; KV42),
  64, 80, 136 n.25
Meryetyotes IV (wife of Pepy I; Saqqara-
  South), 34
MERYKARE, 37, 132 n.71
Merymontju (son of Thutmose IV?;
  KV40), 138 n.96
Montjuhirkopeshef B (son of Rameses
  III), 104
Montjuhirkopeshef C (son of Rameses
  IX; KV19), 105
MONTJUHOTEP II, 38, 39, 41, 42, 59,
  62, 66, 135 n.11
MONTJUHOTEP III, 40–41
MONTJUHOTEP IV, 40
Mortuary temple, 7, 15, 18, 19, 20, 21,
  22, 23, 24, 25, 26, 27, 28, 29, 30, 31,
  32, 36, 37, 41, 42, 43, 45, 47, 48, 55,
  56, 80, 88, 95, 97, 114
Mutemwia (wife of Thutmose IV), 81
Mutnedjmet A (wife of Horemheb), 82
Mutnedjmet B (sister-wife of
  Pasebkhanut I), 108

NAEFARUD I, 123
NAEFARUD II, 123
NAKHTHORHEB (NEKTANEBO II),
  123–24, 125
NAKHTNEBEF (NEKTANEBO I), 123
Nakhtsare (Abusir), 31
Nakhtsebastetru (wife of Ahmose II; Giza
  LG83), 119
Ñaparaye (wife of Taharqa; El-Kurru
  Ku3), 116
Napata, 114
Naqada, 6, 130 n.25; *see also* Nubt
Naqada I (Amratian) Culture, 1
Naqada II (Gerzian) Culture, 2

Naqada III Culture, 2
NARMER, 3
Nashq-e Rustam, 119, 120–22
Nauny (daughter of Panedjem I; TT358), 109
Nebet (wife of Unas; Saqqara), 31, 48
Nebet II (princess; Koptos), 35
NEBKA *see* SANAKHTE
NEBKARE *see* SETH?KA
Nebwenet (wife of Pepy I; Saqqara-South), 34
Nedjmet A (wife of Herihor), 106
NEFEREFRE, 27, 31
Neferet I (mother of Amenemhat I), 48
Neferethenut (wife of Senwosret III; Dahshur L.XLVII/II), 50
Neferhetepes A (wife of Userkaf; Saqqara), 31
NEFERHOTEP I, 57
NEFERIRKARE, 27, 28, 31, 32
Nefermaat (son of Seneferu, Meidum 16), 23
NEFERNEFERUATEN, 74, 75, 76
Nefertiry C (wife of Thutmose IV), 81
Nefertiry D (wife of Rameses II QV66), vi, 85, 91
Nefertiti (wife of Akhenaten), 74, 82, 137 n.59, 138 n.93; *see also* Neferneferuaten
Neferu II (wife of Montjuhotep II; TT319), 41
Neferu IV (wife of Senwosret I; Lisht L.LXI/1), 48
Neferukakashta (wife of Piye?; El-Kurru Ku52), 116
Neferuptah B (daughter of Amenemhat III; Hawara), 47, 51, 134 n.34
Neferure (daughter of Hatshepsut; Wadi el-Qurud[?]), 80
Neith (wife of Pepy II; Saqqara-South), 34
Neithhotep (wife of Hor-Aha), 6
Neitiqerti (Nitokris) I (God's Wife of Amun), 117, 119
NEKAU II, 118, 119
NEMTYEMSAF I (MERENRE), 33, 34
NEPHERITES *see* NAEFARUD

NERO, 126
NESIBANEBDJEDET I (SMENDES), 107, 110
Nesibanebdjedet II (High Priest of Amun), 106
Nesibanebdjedet III (High Priest of Amun), 112
Netjeraperef (son of Seneferu, Dahshur II/1), 24
NETJERKHET *see* DJOSER
Netjerykhethor (son of Pepy I and Mehaa; Saqqara-South), 34
New York
    Metropolitan Museum of Art
        47.60, 141 n.6
        60.144, 129 n.45
NINETJER, 7–8, 9, 29, 129 n.47
Nitokris *see* Neitiqerti
NIUSERRE, 27–8, 29, 30, 31, 32, 132 n.75
North chapel *see* Chapel, north
Nubheteptikhered (daughter of Hor?; Dahshur L.LVIII/2), 58
Nubkhaes B (wife of Sobekemsaf I; Dra Abu'l-Naga), 60
Nubkhesbed (wife of Rameses VI), 104
Nubt (El-Zawayda, Naqada), 130 n.25
Nuri, 116
    Nu1 (Taharqa), 115–16
Nymaathap A (Beit Khallaf K1?), 11
Nysuheqat (Helwan 964 H8), 11

Osireion *see* Abydos, Osireion
OSORKON THE ELDER, 108
OSORKON II, 107, 110–12, 113, 142 n.26
OSORKON III, 113, 117
Osorkon G (son of Takelot III; Ramesseum B27), 114
OTHO, 126

Paabtameri (Abydos D9), 117
PAMIU, 112
PANEDJEM I, 64, 103, 106, 109, 111
Panedjem II (High Priest of Amun; TT320), 79, 109

Parehirwenemef B (son of Rameses III; QV42), 104
Paris
  Louvre Museum
    A23, 131 n.36
    E.3019, 135 n.25
    E.3020, 135 n.26
    E.11007, pl. IVb
    E.32580, 143 n.2, pl. LXXXVIIIb
    N.491=E.2538, 135 n.27
Pasagardae, 119, 120
PASEBKHANUT (PSUSENNES) I, 87, 107–108, 109, 111, 112
PASEBKHANUT II, 108, 110
Pasebkhanut III/IV (High Priest of Amun), 106
Pasebkhanut A (grandson of Panedjem I; Abydos D22), 113
Pashereniset, son of Hori (general), 110, 142 n.26
Pedieset A (High Priest of Ptah), 113
Peksater (wife of Piye; Abydos), 117
PEPY I, 32–3, 34,
PEPY II, 30, 33, 34, 35, 36
Per-Rameses (Qantir), 92
PERIBSEN, 8–10, 11
Persenet (wife of king; Giza LG88), 25
Persepolis, 120, 121, 122
Philadelphia
  University Museum of Archaeology & Anthropology
    E6878, pl. IVc
PHILIP III ARRHIDAEUS, 124
PIYE, 114–15, 116, 117
PSAMETIK I, 117, 119
PSAMETIK II, 118, 119
Psametik (official; Saqqara), 124
Ptahshepses B (son-in-law of Niuserre; Abusir), 32
Ptahshepses D (son of Pepy II?; Saqqara-South), 35, 37
PTOLEMY I, 124
PTOLEMY II, 124
PTOLEMY IV, 125
PTOLEMY VIII EUERGETES II, 67
PTOLEMY X, 125
Pyramid Texts, ix, 13, 30, 32, 33, 34, 36, 91

QAA, 6
Qalhata (wife of Shabaka; El-Kurru Ku5), 116
Qantir see Per-Rameses

Rahotep (son of Seneferu; Meidum 6), 23–4
RAMESES I, 78, 82–3, 85, 92, 102, 136 n.46
RAMESES II, 67, 69, 72, 83, 84, 85, 86, 91, 92, 95, 96, 103, 104, 106, 112, 114, 136 n.36
RAMESES III, 94–6, 98, 103, 104, 105, 111, 112, 114, 139 n.128
RAMESES IV, 77, 96, 97–8, 99, 100, 103, 104
RAMESES V, 97, 98
RAMESES VI, 97, 98, 100, 104
RAMESES VII, 99–100, 101
RAMESES VIII, 100, 101, 108
RAMESES IX, 38, 59–60, 62, 97, 99, 100, 101–102, 104, 105
RAMESES X, 102, 103, 106
RAMESES XI, 102–103, 106
Rameses C (son of Rameses III: later Rameses IV; QV53), 104
Rameses-meryamun-Nebweben (son of Rameses II; Gurob), 92
Ramesesnakht (High Priest of Amun), 62
Ranefer (son of Seneferu; Meidum 9), 23
Re-use of material, 49, 50, 57, 64, 76, 77, 88, 104, 107, 108, 111, 117
RENEB, 8, 9
Rome, 125–26
RUDAMUN, 114

Sa el-Hagar see Sais (Sa el-Hagar)
Sadhe (wife of Montjuhotep II; DBXI.7), 41
Saff-tomb, 37–8
SAHURE, 26–7, 28, 30, 31
Sais (Sa el-Hagar), 118, 112, 143 n.2
Sammanud see Sebennytos
San el-Hagar see Tanis
SANAKHTE, 14, 130 n.1
Sandraulics, 55–6
Saqqara, 6, 7, 8, 10–12, 25, 26, 41, 91, 92

Table 1

Kings' Monument Dimensions of the Old and Middle Kingdoms

Owner/Name	Location	Base		Height		Angle
		(metres)	(cubits)	(m)	(cu)	
Djoser	Saqqara	121x109	230x208	60	114	Step pyr
Sanakhte(?)	Abu Rowash	20	38	?	?	?
Sekhemkhet	Saqqara	120	229	?	?	Step pyr
Khaba(?)	Zawiyet el-Aryan	84	160	?	?	Step pyr
Huni(?)	Abu Rowash	215	410	?	?	Step pyr?
Seneferu	Meidum	144	274	92	175	51.8°
Seneferu (Bent)	Dahshur	188	358	105	200	54.5/43.3°
Seneferu (Red)	Dahshur	220	419	105	200	43.3°
Khufu	Giza	230.3	439	146.6	279	51.8°
Djedefre	Abu Rowash	106	202	67	128	52°
Unfinished Pyr.	Zawiyet el-Aryan	200	381	?	?	?
Khaefre	Giza	215	410	143.5	273	53.2°
Menkaure	Giza	103.4	197	65	124	51.3°
Shepseskaf	Saqqara-South	99.6x74.4	190x142	18	34	Mastaba
Userkaf	Saqqara	73.3	140	49	93	53.1°
Sahure	Abusir	78.8	150	47	90	52°
Neferirkare	Abusir	105	200	~72	137	53.1°
Neferefre	Abusir	65	124	?	?	Mastaba
Niuserre	Abusir	78.9	150	51.7	98	51.8°
Menkauhor	Saqqara	~60	115	?	?	?
Isesi	Saqqara-South	78.8	150	52.5	100	52°
Unas	Saqqara	57.8	110	43	82	56.3°
Teti	Saqqara	78.8	150	52.5	100	53.2°
Pepy I	Saqqara-South	78.8	150	52.5	100	53.2°
Nemtyemsaf I	Saqqara-South	78.8	150	52.5	100	53.2°
Pepy II	Saqqara-South	78.8	150	52.5	100	53.2°
Ibi	Saqqara-South	31.5	60	21?	40	?
Khui(?)	Dara	130	248	?	?	Mastaba?
Amenemhat I	Lisht	84	160	55	105	54.4°
Senwosret I	Lisht	105	200	61.3	117	49.4°
Amenemhat II	Dahshur	~50	95	?	?	?
Senwosret II	Lahun	106	202	48.6	93	42.6°
Senwosret III	Dahshur	105	200	78	149	56.3°
Amenemhat III	Dahshur	105	200	75	143	57.2°
Amenemhat III	Hawara	105	200	~58	~110	48.7°
North Pyramid	Mazghuna	~60+	115+	?	?	?
South Pyramid	Mazghuna	52.5	100	?	?	?
Ameny-Qemau	Dahshur-South	~52	100	?	?	?
Khendjer	Saqqara-South	52.5	100	~37.4	71	55°
Unfinished	Saqqara-South	91	173	?	?	?
Iy	?	?	?	?	?	~60°
S9	Abydos-South	?	?	?	?	?
S10	Abydos-South	?	?	?	?	?
Inyotef VI	Dra Abu'l-Naga	10	19	9.9	19	67°
Ahmose I	Abydos-South	80	152	?	?	?
Piye	El-Kurru	8	15	?	?	?
Shabataka	El-Kurru	11	21	?	?	?
Shabaka	El-Kurru	11	21	?	?	?
Taharqa	Nuri	52	99	67	129	69°
Tanutamun	El-Kurru	8.3	16	?	?	?

195

Table 2

The distribution of books of the Underworld in representative kings' tombs of the New Kingdom

ELEMENT OF TOMB	TOMB					
	Thutmose III (KV34)	Amenhotep III (WV22)	Horemheb (KV57)	Sethy I (KV17)	Ramesses III (KV11)	Ramesses VI (KV9)
Burial chamber [J]	Book of Amduat; Litany of Re	Book of Amduat; the king and the gods	Book of Gates	Books of Gates; Amduat; astronomical ceiling; he king and the gods	Book of Gates; the king and the gods	Book of the Earth
Antechamber [I]			The king and the gods	The king and the gods	Book of the Dead; the king and the gods	Book of the Dead; the king and the gods
4th & 5th corridors [G, H]				Opening the Mouth	Opening the Mouth	Book of Amduat
Mid-length pillared hall [F]	List of divinities	The king and the gods	The king and the gods	Book of Gates	Book of Gates	Books of Gates; Caverns
Well-room [E]				The king and the gods	The king and the gods	Books of Gates; Caverns
3rd corridor [D]				Book of Amduat	Litany of Re; Amduat	Books of Gates; Caverns
2nd corridor [C]				Litany of Re	Litany of Re	Books of Gates; Caverns
1st corridor [B]				Litany of Re	Litany of Re	Books of Gates; Caverns

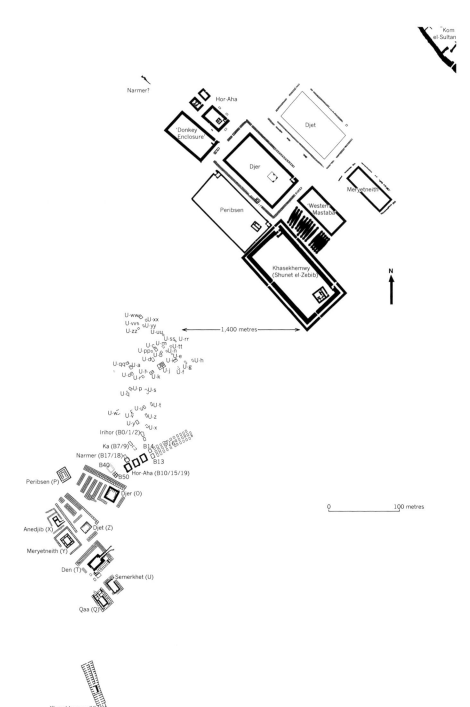

N

Kom
el-Sultan

Narmer?

Hor-Aha

'Donkey
Enclosure'

Djet

Djer

Meryetneith

Peribsen

'Western
Mastaba'

Khasekhemwy
(Shunet el-Zebib)

U·ww   ∘U·xx
U·vv∘ ∘U·yy
U·zz∘ ∘U·uu
              U·ss U·rr
        U·c U·m
        U·pp∘ ∘U·n
        U·d∘ ∘U·tt
              ∘U·e
U·qq∘ ∘U·a   ∘U·h
U·o∘   U·j   ∘U·g
    U·r∘ U·k   ∘U·f
       U·k

U·q ∘U·p ∘U·s

         ∘U·t
U·w⁓ U·f̃ ∘U·u∘
   U·y∘ ∘U·z
       ∘U·x

Irihor (B0/1/2)

Ka (B7/9)   B14
Narmer (B17/18)   B13
         B40
         B50 Hor-Aha (B10/15/19)
Peribsen (P)

Djer (O)

Anedjib (X)   Djet (Z)

Meryetneith (Y)

Den (T)   Semerkhet (U)

Qaa (Q)

Khasekhemwy (V)

←————— 1,400 metres —————→

0   100 metres

Figure 1

197

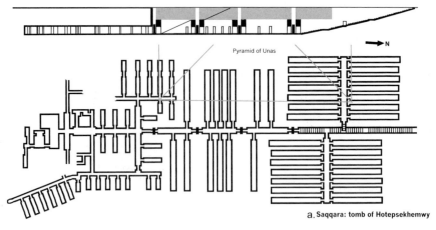

a. Saqqara: tomb of Hotepsekhemwy

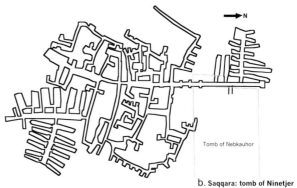

Tomb of Nebkauhor

b. Saqqara: tomb of Ninetjer

C. Abydos/Umm el-Qaab: tomb P (Peribsen)

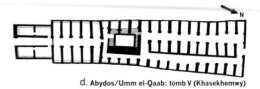

d. Abydos/Umm el-Qaab: tomb V (Khasekhemwy)

Figure 2

0   10m

198

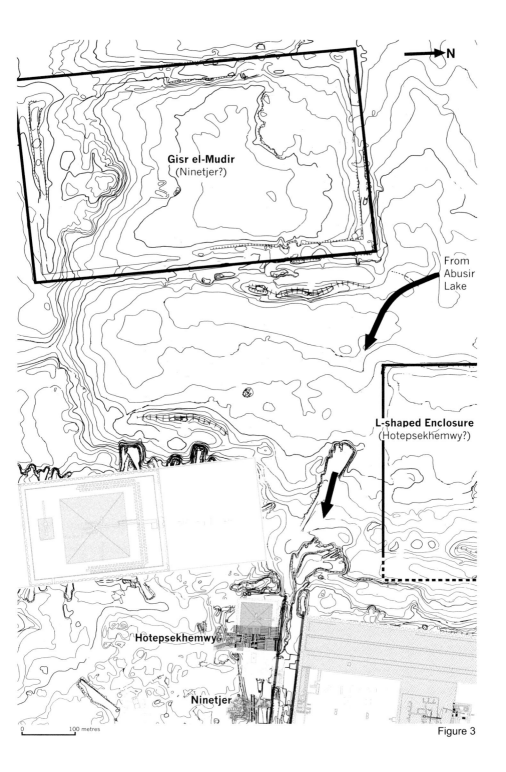

Gisr el-Mudir
(Ninetjer?)

From
Abusir
Lake

L-shaped Enclosure
(Hotepsekhemwy?)

Hotepsekhemwy

Ninetjer

N

0   100 metres

Figure 3

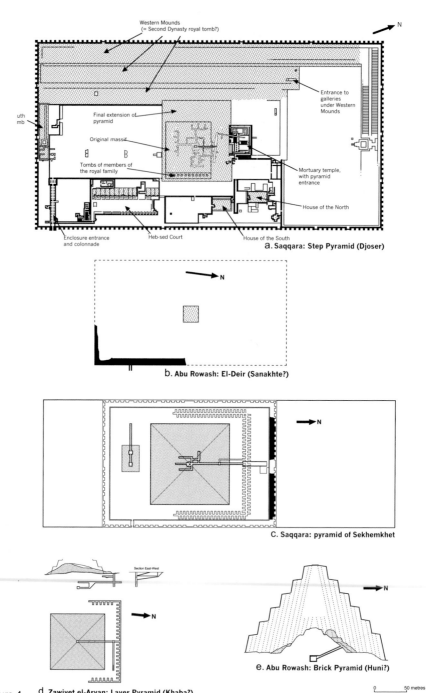

Western Mounds
(= Second Dynasty royal tomb?)

N

Entrance to
galleries
under Western
Mounds

uth
mb

Final extension of
pyramid

Original massif

Tombs of members of
the royal family

Mortuary temple,
with pyramid
entrance

House of the North

Enclosure entrance
and colonnade

Heb-sed Court

House of the South

a. Saqqara: Step Pyramid (Djoser)

N

b. Abu Rowash: El-Deir (Sanakhte?)

N

C. Saqqara: pyramid of Sekhemkhet

Section East-West

N

N

e. Abu Rowash: Brick Pyramid (Huni?)

0   50 metres

Figure 4   d. Zawiyet el-Aryan: Layer Pyramid (Khaba?)

200

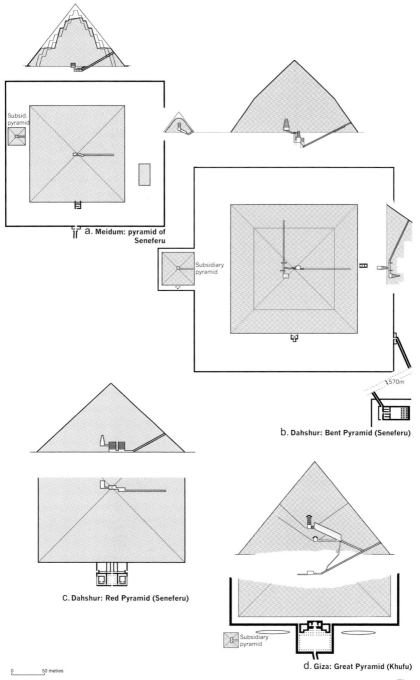

a. Meidum: pyramid of Seneferu

Subsid. pyramid

b. Dahshur: Bent Pyramid (Seneferu)

Subsidiary pyramid

570m

c. Dahshur: Red Pyramid (Seneferu)

d. Giza: Great Pyramid (Khufu)

Subsidiary pyramid

0   50 metres

Figure 5

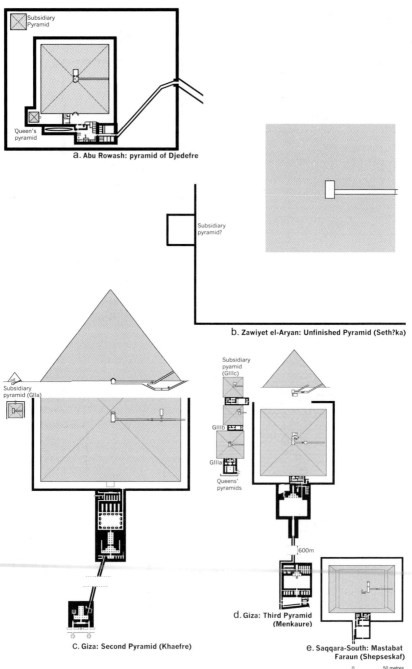

a. Abu Rowash: pyramid of Djedefre

b. Zawiyet el-Aryan: Unfinished Pyramid (Seth?ka)

c. Giza: Second Pyramid (Khaefre)

d. Giza: Third Pyramid (Menkaure)

e. Saqqara-South: Mastabat Faraun (Shepseskaf)

Figure 6

0   50 metres

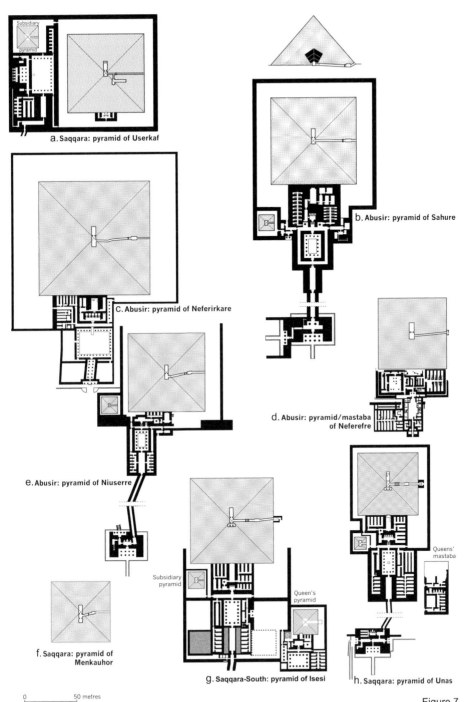

a. Saqqara: pyramid of Userkaf

b. Abusir: pyramid of Sahure

c. Abusir: pyramid of Neferirkare

d. Abusir: pyramid/mastaba of Neferefre

e. Abusir: pyramid of Niuserre

f. Saqqara: pyramid of Menkauhor

g. Saqqara-South: pyramid of Isesi

h. Saqqara: pyramid of Unas

Subsidiary pyramid

Queen's pyramid

Queens' mastaba

0   50 metres

Figure 7

203

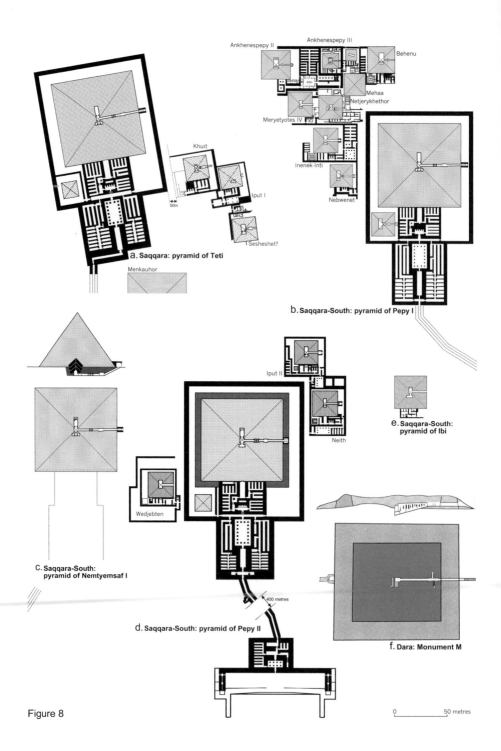

a. Saqqara: pyramid of Teti

Khuit

Iput I

Sesheshet?

Menkauhor

50m

Ankhenespepy II

Ankhenespepy III

Behenu

Mehaa

Netjerykhethor

Meryetyotes IV

Inenek-Inti

Nebwenet

b. Saqqara-South: pyramid of Pepy I

Iput II

Neith

e. Saqqara-South: pyramid of Ibi

Wedjebten

c. Saqqara-South: pyramid of Nemtyemsaf I

d. Saqqara-South: pyramid of Pepy II

400 metres

f. Dara: Monument M

Figure 8

0   50 metres

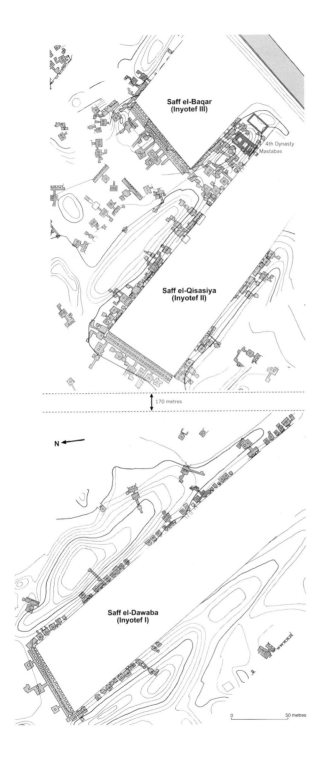

Saff el-Baqar
(Inyotef III)

4th Dynasty
Mastabas

Saff el-Qisasiya
(Inyotef II)

170 metres

N ←

Saff el-Dawaba
(Inyotef I)

0   50 metres

Figure 9

205

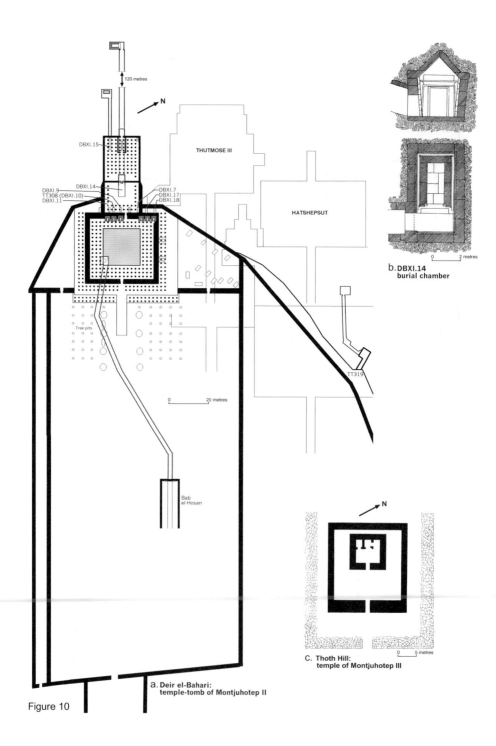

120 metres

N

DBXI.15

THUTMOSE III

DBXI.9
TT308 (DBXI.10)
DBXI.11

DBXI.14

DBXI.7
DBXI.17
DBXI.18

HATSHEPSUT

Tree pits

0   20 metres

TT319

Bab
el-Hosan

a. Deir el-Bahari:
temple-tomb of Montjuhotep II

Figure 10

b. DBXI.14
burial chamber

0   2 metres

N

C. Thoth Hill:
temple of Montjuhotep III

0   5 metres

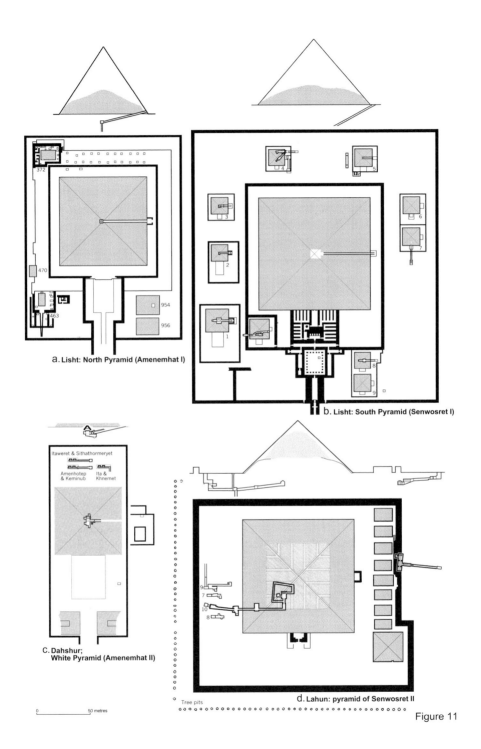

a. Lisht: North Pyramid (Amenemhat I)

372

470

463

954

956

b. Lisht: South Pyramid (Senwosret I)

1
2
3
4
5
6
7
8
9

c. Dahshur;
White Pyramid (Amenemhat II)

Itaweret & Sithathormeryet

Amenhotep
& Keminub

Ita &
Khnemet

0   50 metres

d. Lahun: pyramid of Senwosret II

Tree pits

Figure 11

207

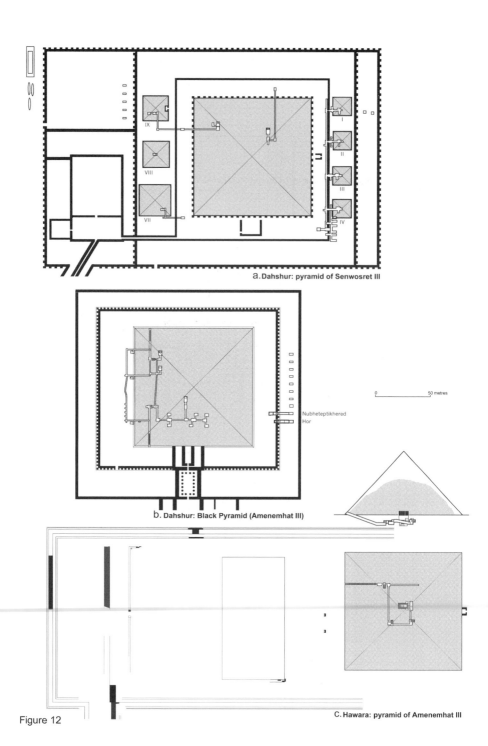

a. Dahshur: pyramid of Senwosret III

b. Dahshur: Black Pyramid (Amenemhat III)

Nubheteptikhered
Hor

0   50 metres

c. Hawara: pyramid of Amenemhat III

Figure 12

208

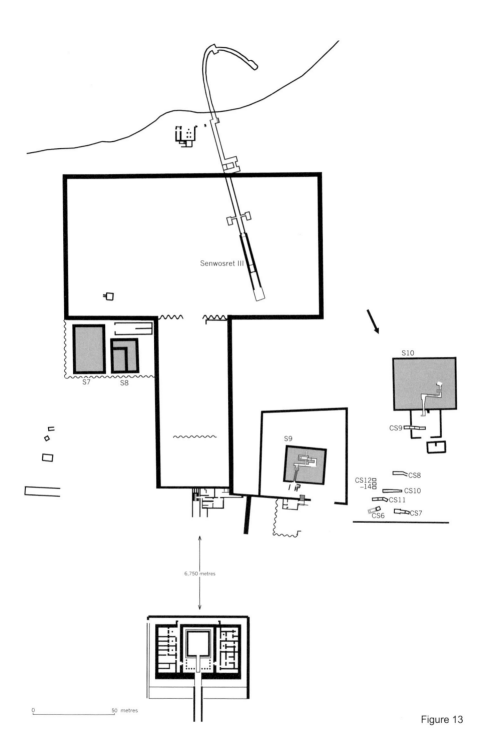

Senwosret III

S7   S8

S9

S10

CS9

CS12
–14

CS8

CS10

CS11

CS6   CS7

6,750 metres

0   50 metres

Figure 13

209

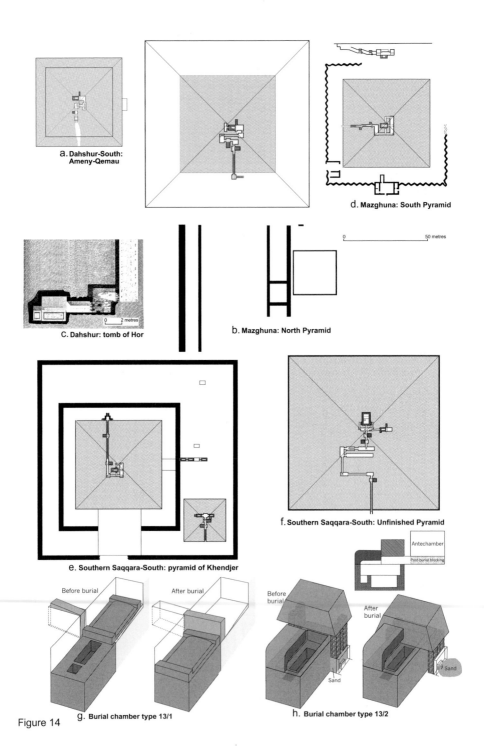

a. Dahshur-South: Ameny-Qemau

d. Mazghuna: South Pyramid

0   50 metres

C. Dahshur: tomb of Hor

0   2 metres

b. Mazghuna: North Pyramid

e. Southern Saqqara-South: pyramid of Khendjer

f. Southern Saqqara-South: Unfinished Pyramid

Antechamber

Post-burial blocking

Before burial   After burial

Before burial   After burial

Sand

Sand

g. Burial chamber type 13/1

h. Burial chamber type 13/2

Figure 14

210

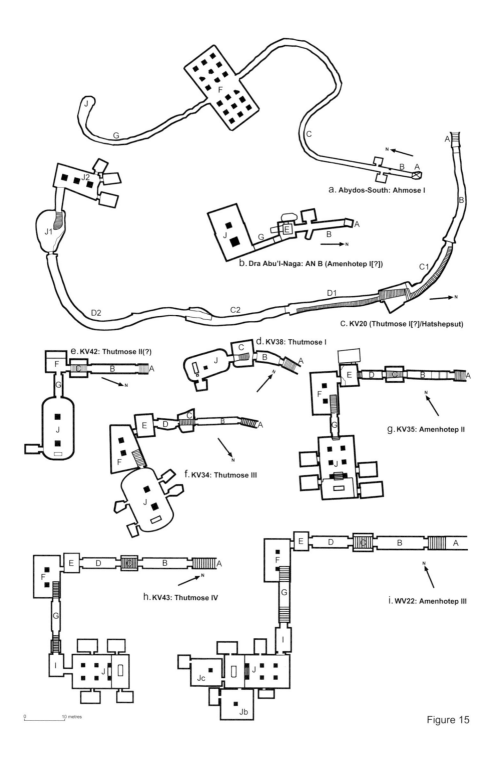

a. Abydos-South: Ahmose I

b. Dra Abu'l-Naga: AN B (Amenhotep I[?])

c. KV20 (Thutmose I[?]/Hatshepsut)

d. KV38: Thutmose I

e. KV42: Thutmose II(?)

f. KV34: Thutmose III

g. KV35: Amenhotep II

h. KV43: Thutmose IV

i. WV22: Amenhotep III

0   10 metres

Figure 15

211

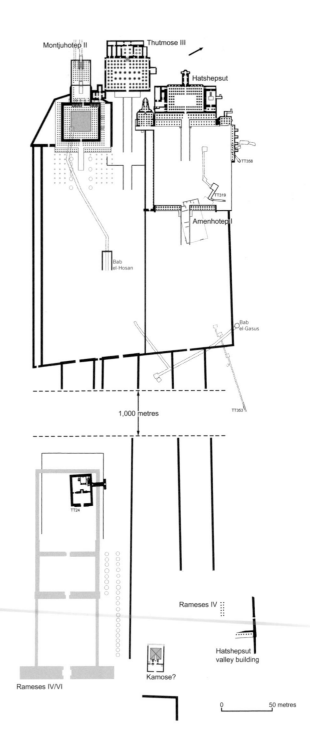

Montjuhotep II
Thutmose III
Hatshepsut
TT358
TT319
Amenhotep I
Bab
el-Hosan
Bab
el-Gasus
TT353
1,000 metres
TT24
Rameses IV
Hatshepsut
valley building
Kamose?
Rameses IV/VI
0   50 metres

Figure 16

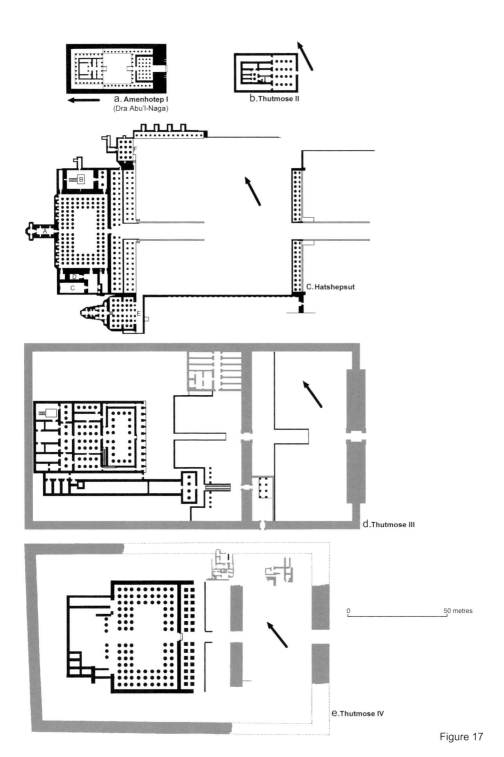

a. Amenhotep I
(Dra Abu'l-Naga)

b. Thutmose II

C. Hatshepsut

d. Thutmose III

0   50 metres

e. Thutmose IV

Figure 17

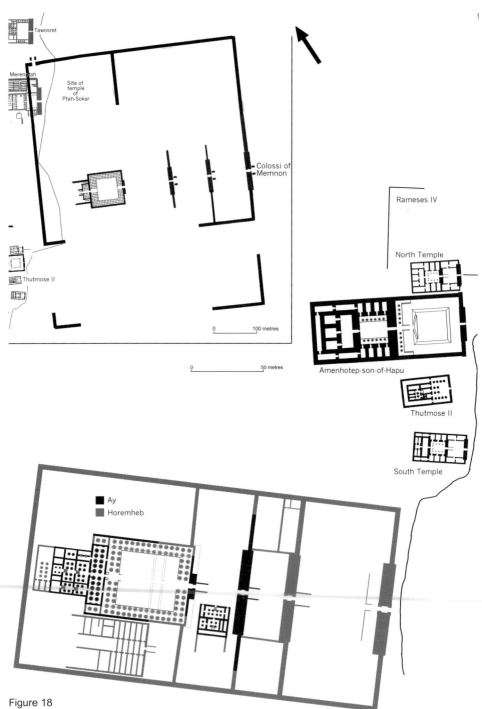

Tawosret

Merenptah

Site of
temple
of
Ptah-Sokar

Colossi of
Memnon

Thutmose II

0   100 metres

0   50 metres

Rameses IV

North Temple

Amenhotep-son-of-Hapu

Thutmose II

South Temple

Ay
Horemheb

Figure 18

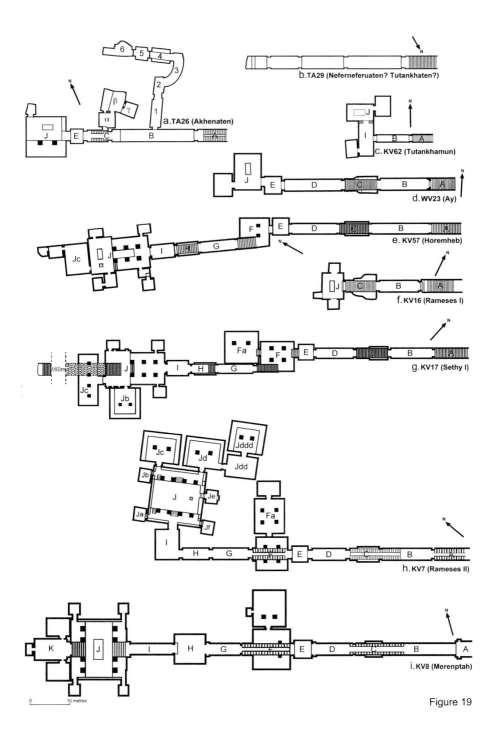

b.TA29 (Neferneferuaten? Tutankhaten?)

a.TA26 (Akhenaten)

c. KV62 (Tutankhamun)

d. WV23 (Ay)

e. KV57 (Horemheb)

f. KV16 (Rameses I)

g. KV17 (Sethy I)

h. KV7 (Rameses II)

i. KV8 (Merenptah)

Figure 19

0   10 metres

215

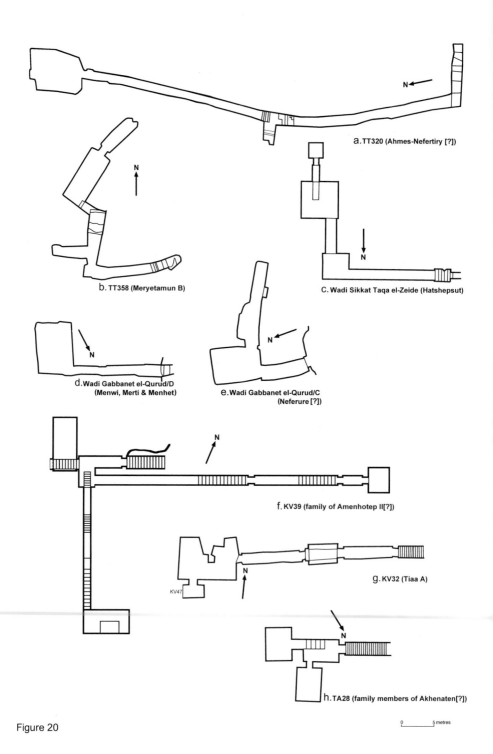

a. TT320 (Ahmes-Nefertiry [?])

b. TT358 (Meryetamun B)

c. Wadi Sikkat Taqa el-Zeide (Hatshepsut)

d. Wadi Gabbanet el-Qurud/D
(Menwi, Merti & Menhet)

e. Wadi Gabbanet el-Qurud/C
(Neferure [?])

f. KV39 (family of Amenhotep II[?])

g. KV32 (Tiaa A)

KV47

h. TA28 (family members of Akhenaten[?])

Figure 20

0   5 metres

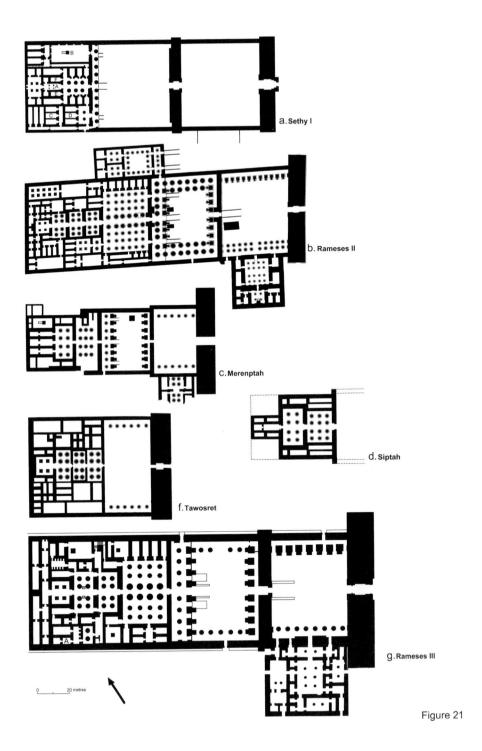

a. Sethy I

b. Rameses II

c. Merenptah

d. Siptah

f. Tawosret

g. Rameses III

0   20 metres

Figure 21

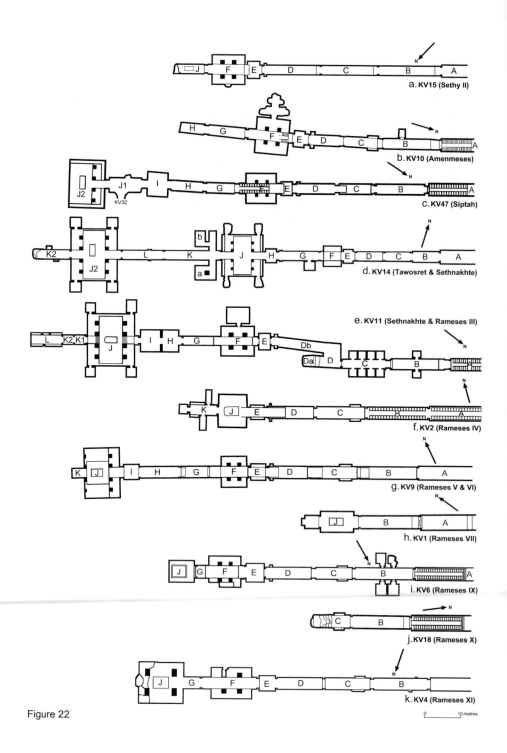

a. KV15 (Sethy II)

b. KV10 (Amenmeses)

c. KV47 (Siptah)

d. KV14 (Tawosret & Sethnakhte)

e. KV11 (Sethnakhte & Rameses III)

f. KV2 (Rameses IV)

g. KV9 (Rameses V & VI)

h. KV1 (Rameses VII)

i. KV6 (Rameses IX)

j. KV18 (Rameses X)

k. KV4 (Rameses XI)

Figure 22

0   10 metres

218

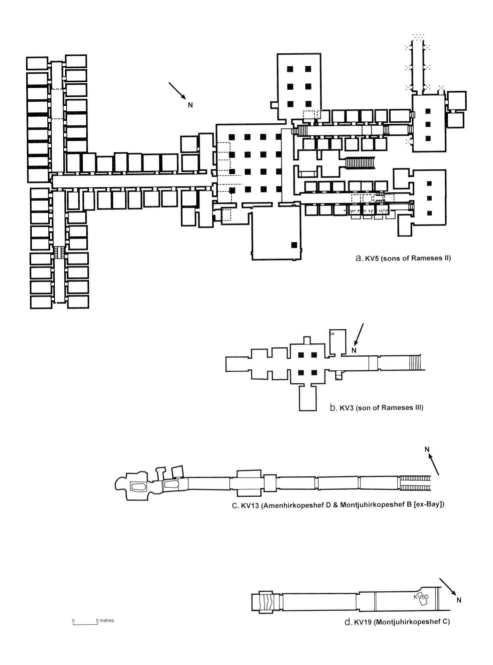

a. KV5 (sons of Rameses II)

b. KV3 (son of Rameses III)

C. KV13 (Amenhirkopeshef D & Montjuhirkopeshef B [ex-Bay])

d. KV19 (Montjuhirkopeshef C)

0   5 metres

Figure 23

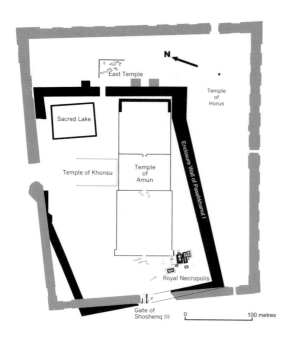

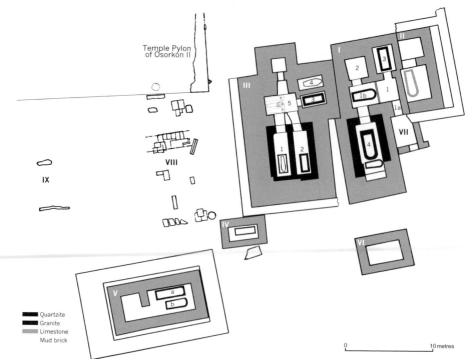

Figure 24

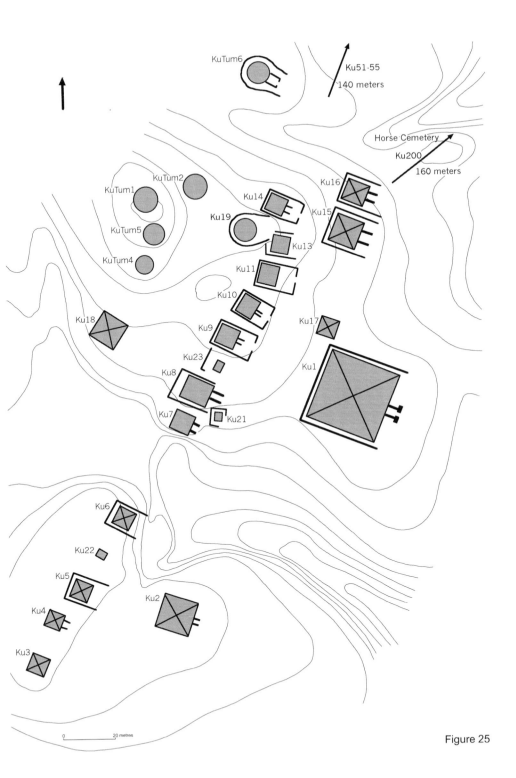

KuTum6

Ku51-55
140 meters

Horse Cemetery
Ku200
160 meters

Ku16

KuTum2
KuTum1   Ku14
Ku19   Ku15
KuTum5
Ku13
KuTum4
Ku11
Ku10
Ku18   Ku9   Ku17
Ku23
Ku8   Ku1
Ku7   Ku21

Ku6

Ku22

Ku5
Ku2
Ku4

Ku3

0   20 metres

Figure 25

221

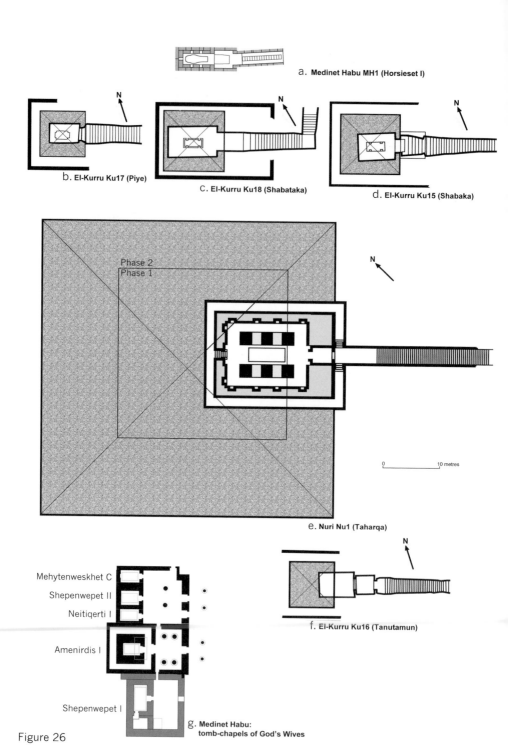

a. Medinet Habu MH1 (Horsieset I)

b. El-Kurru Ku17 (Piye)

c. El-Kurru Ku18 (Shabataka)

d. El-Kurru Ku15 (Shabaka)

Phase 2
Phase 1

0   10 metres

e. Nuri Nu1 (Taharqa)

f. El-Kurru Ku16 (Tanutamun)

Mehytenweskhet C
Shepenwepet II
Neitiqerti I

Amenirdis I

Shepenwepet I

g. Medinet Habu:
tomb-chapels of God's Wives

Figure 26

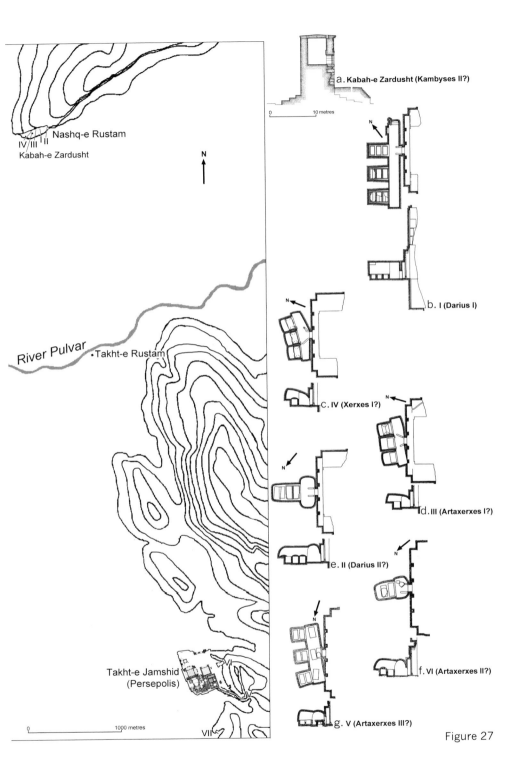

Nashq-e Rustam

IV/III II

Kabah-e Zardusht

N

River Pulvar •Takht-e Rustam

Takht-e Jamshid
(Persepolis)

0   1000 metres

VII

a. Kabah-e Zardusht (Kambyses II?)

0   10 metres

N

b. I (Darius I)

N

C. IV (Xerxes I?)

N

d. III (Artaxerxes I?)

N

e. II (Darius II?)

N

f. VI (Artaxerxes II?)

N

g. V (Artaxerxes III?)

Figure 27

223

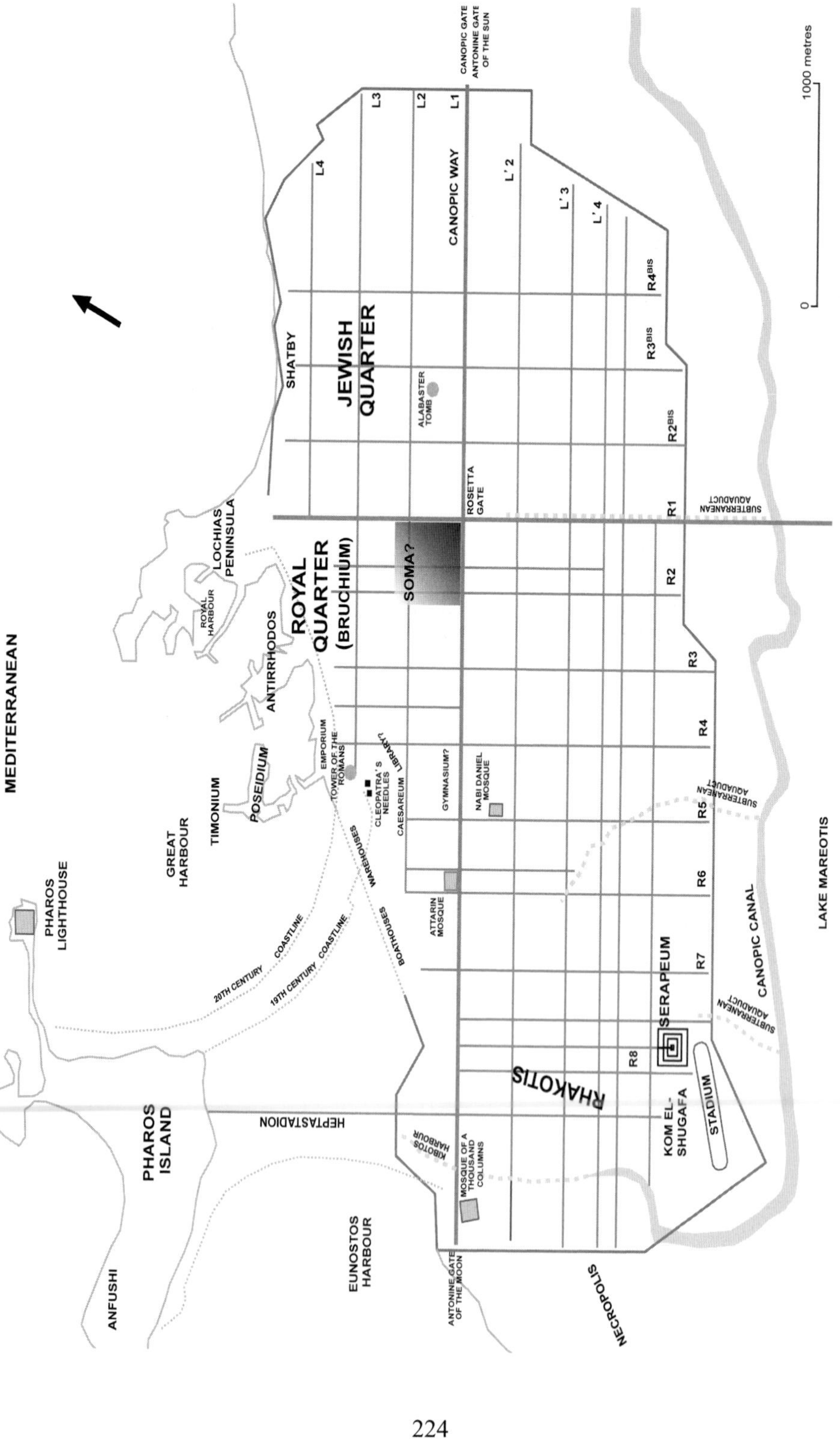

MEDITERRANEAN

PHAROS ISLAND

ANFUSHI

PHAROS LIGHTHOUSE

GREAT HARBOUR

TIMONIUM

POSEIDIUM

ANTIRRHODOS

ROYAL HARBOUR

LOCHIAS PENINSULA

ROYAL QUARTER (BRUCHIUM)

SOMA?

SHATBY

JEWISH QUARTER

ALABASTER TOMB

L4

L3

L2

L1

CANOPIC GATE
ANTONINE GATE
OF THE SUN

CANOPIC WAY

L' 2

L' 3

L' 4

R4BIS

R3BIS

R2BIS

R1

ROSETTA GATE

SUBTERRANEAN AQUADUCT

R2

R3

R4

R5

SUBTERRANEAN AQUADUCT

R6

R7

CANOPIC CANAL

LAKE MAREOTIS

SUBTERRANEAN AQUADUCT

R8

SERAPEUM

KOM EL-SHUGAFA

STADIUM

RHAKOTIS

NECROPOLIS

ATTARIN MOSQUE

NABI DANIEL MOSQUE

GYMNASIUM?

CAESAREUM

CLEOPATRA'S NEEDLES

LIBRARY?

EMPORIUM

TOWER OF THE ROMANS

WAREHOUSES

BOATHOUSES

20TH CENTURY COASTLINE

19TH CENTURY COASTLINE

KIBOTOS HARBOUR

MOSQUE OF A THOUSAND COLUMNS

HEPTASTADION

EUNOSTOS HARBOUR

ANTONINE GATE OF THE MOON

0

1000 metres

Figure 28

224

a. Hierakonpolis area HK23, tomb 6.

b. Abydos-Umm el-Qaab, looking west.

a. Abydos-Umm el-Qaab U-j (Scorpion?).

b. Abydos-Umm el-Qaab B10/B15/B19 (Hor-Aha).

II

a. Abydos: view of Shunet el-Zebib from the east.

b. Abydos-Umm el-Qaab O (Djer).

Stelae from the offering-places of Abydos-Umm el-Qaab tombs:
a. O (Djer: Cairo JE34992); b. Z (Djet: Louvre E.11007); c. Qaa (Q: UPMAA E6878).

d. Abydos-Umm el-Qaab B13/B14/B16 (family of Hor-Aha).

a. Saqqara, including a distant view of Dahshur; the pyramid in the foreground is that of Userkaf, with Djoser's behind, and Unas's beyond that.

b. View from above into the tomb of Hotepesekhemwy at Saqqara.

a. The cutting that defined the northern edge of the Second Dynasty royal funerary precinct at Saqqara; the railway marks the entrance to the tomb of Hetepsekhemwy.

b. Abydos-Umm el-Qaab P (Peribsen)

a. Stela from the offering-place of Abydos-Umm el-Qaab P (Peribsen). The Seth-animal atop the serekh has been erased. It is unclear whether this was done during the conflicts of the late Second Dynasty, or far later, during the Ptolemaic Period, when Seth became a devil-figure, and his images mutilated on ancient monuments (BM EA35597).

b. The 'fort' at Hierakonpolis.

a. Abydos-Umm el-Qaab V (Khasekhemwy).

b. Beit Khallaf K1 (Nimaathap?)

a. Saqqara: Djoser's Step Pyramid from the northwest.

b. Saqqara: *ḥb-sd* court of the Step Pyramid.

a. Saqqara: eastern end of the south face of the Step Pyramid, showing traces of earliest building phases.

b. Saqqara: reliefs of Djoser below the Step Pyramid.

a. Saqqara: remains of the pyramid of Sekhemkhet from the north.

b. Saqqara: burial chamber of Sekhemkhet.

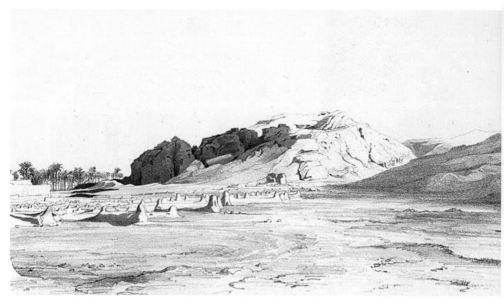

a. Abu Rowash: the remains of the Brick Pyramid as seen in the 1840s.

b. Meidum: pyramid from the east.

a. Meidum: burial chamber of pyramid.

b. Dahshur: stela from chapel of subsidiary pyramid of Bent Pyramid (Cairo JE89289c).

c. Dahshur: Bent Pyramid and its subsidiary from the south; the Red Pyramid is in the background.

a. Dahshur: mortuary temple of Bent Pyramid.

b. Dahshur: Red Pyramid.

a. Dahshur: antechamber
in Red Pyramid.

b. Aswan-Elephantine: miniature step pyramid.

a. Giza: view from the south.

b. Giza: Great Pyramid (Khufu), queens' pyramids and cemetery G7000 from the southeast.

a. Giza: Grand Gallery in the Great Pyramid.

b. Giza: King's Chamber in the Great Pyramid.

a. Abu Rowash: the denuded core of the pyramid of Djedefre.

b. Abu Rowash: the cutting for the substructure of the pyramid of Djedefre.

a. Zawiyet el-Aryan: view from the pit of the Unfinished Pyramid towards the descending cut, showing the stairway for the use of workmen.

b. Giza: Second Pyramid (Khaefre), from the east.

a. Giza: burial chamber
of Second Pyramid,
showing sarcophagus
and canopic chest.

b. Giza: valley building of Second Pyramid.

a. Giza: Third Pyramid (Menkaure) from the south, with subsidiary (left) and queens' pyramids in the foreground.

b. Saqqara-south: *Mastabat Faraun* (Shepseskaf).

a. Giza LG100/GIV (Khentkawes I) from the southeast.

b. Saqqara: pyramid of Userkaf from the south.

a. Abusir from the southeast.

b. Abusir: pyramid of Sahure from the top of the pyramid of Neferirkare.

a. Abusir: pyramid of Neferirkare from the east.

b. Abusir: pyramid/mastaba and mortuary temple of Neferefre.

a. Abusir: pyramid and mortuary temple of Niuserre.

b. Saqqara-South: pyramids of Isesi and his wife from the northeast.

a. Saqqara: pyramid and mortuary temple of Unas.

b. Saqqara: valley building of Unas.

a. Saqqara: burial chamber of Unas.

b. Saqqara: family cemetery of Unas. Left: double-mastaba of Queens Khenut and Nebet; right: mastabas of Princess Sesheshet and Prince Unasankh.

a. Saqqara: pyramid and mortuary temple of Teti.

b. Saqqara-south: pyramid and mortuary temple of Pepy I.

a. Saqqara-south: pyramid of Nemtyemsaf I, from the northeast.

b. Panorama of Saqqara-south, with the *Mastabat Faraun* and the pyramid of Pepy II in the middle distance and the Dahshur pyramids of Seneferu

c. Saqqara-south: pyramid and mortuary temple of Pepy II, with pyramid of Queen Wedjebten in foreground.

a. Saqqara-south: pyramids of wives of Pepy I, from the north.

b. Saqqara-south: pyramids of Queens (left) Iput II and (right) Neith.

c. Saqqara-south: pyramid of Ibi, from the north.

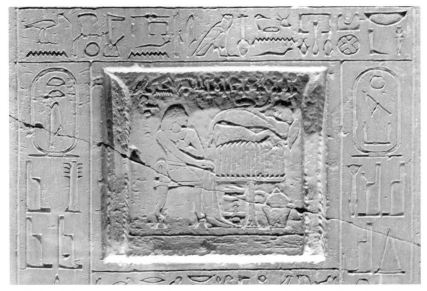

a. Stela of Gemeniemhat, a priest of the pyramids of Teti and Merykare; from Saqqara (Ny Carlsberg ÆIN1616).

b. Aerial view of El-Tarif and the road to the Valley of the Kings.

a. Fragmentary lower section of the 'dog-stela' from the tomb of Inyotef II (Cairo JE20512).

b. Deir el-Bahari: temple-tomb of Montjuhotep II from above.

a. Entrance to the burial-corridor of Montjuhotep II (DBXI 14), with the rock-cut sanctuary and the hypostyle hall of the temple in the background.

b. The unfinished mortuary temple behind the Sheikh Abd el-Qurna hill.

a. Thoth Hill, showing the location of the temple of Montjuhotep III.

b. Thoth Hill: temple of Montjuhotep III.

a. Thoth Hill, North Wadi: location of probable tomb of Montjuhotep III.

b. Thoth Hill, North Wadi: integral sarcophagus.

a. Reconstruction of funerary shrine of Queen Ashayet in temple of Montjuhotep II.

b. Lisht: pyramid of Amenemhat I, from the east.

a. Lisht: pyramid of Senwosret I, from the east.

b. Dahshur: White Pyramid (Amenemhat II), from the west.

a. Lahun: pyramid of Senwosret II, with mastabas of royal family on left.

b. Lahun: burial chamber of Senwosret II.

a. Dahshur: pyramid of Senwosret III.

b. Abydos-south: pyramidal hill with tomb of Senwosret III at its base.

a. Dahshur: Black Pyramid (Amenemhat III), with the Bent Pyramid in the background.

b. Hawara: pyramid and mortuary temple of Amenemhat III.

a. Dahshur: tomb of Ita and Khnemet, with the blocks above the burial chambers removed.

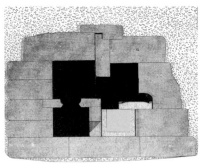

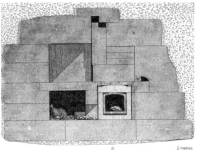

0   2 metres

b. Section through a burial chamber in the tomb of Ita and Khnemet, showing situation before and after burial.

c. Lahun: burial chamber of tomb 621.

a. Hawara: pyramid of Neferuptah.

b. Saqqara-south: remains of pyramid of Khendjer, with the pyramids of Seneferu at Dahshur in the background.

a. Pyramidion of Aya; from Kataana (EMC JE43267).

b. Abydos-south: cemetery of the Abydos Dynasty, with tomb CS6, incorporating the reused sarcophagus coffer from tomb S10, in the foreground.

a. Abydos-south: tomb of Senebkay, from the north.

b. Dra Abu'l-Naga: area of the Seventeenth Dynasty royal cemetery, with on the left the Khawi el-Almat, ultimately giving access to the probable tomb of Amenhotep I.

a. Dra Abu'l-Naga: Seventeenth Dynasty royal cemetery, with pyramid of Inyotef VI (in reconstructed outline) in centre.

b. Fragmentary pyramidion of Inyotef V (BM EA478).

a. Qurna–El-Khor: queenly burial of the Seventeenth Dynasty (NMS A.1909.527.1ff).

b. Abydos-south: pyramid of Ahmose I, from the east.

a. Brick from the chapel of Amenhotep I at Deir el-Bahari.

b. Osirid statue of Amenhotep I from his chapel at Deir el-Bahari (British Museum EA683).

c. The Valley of the Kings from the east.

a. Valley of the Kings: burial chamber of KV38 (Thutmose I).

b. Valley of the Kings: burial chamber of KV42 (Thutmose II?/Meryetre).

a. Block from the wall of KV20, with section of the Book of Amduat (EMC TR 10/12/14/13).

b. The Asasif and Birabi, looking towards Deir el-Bahari.

a. Deir el-Bahari: memorial temple of Hatshepsut, from the south.

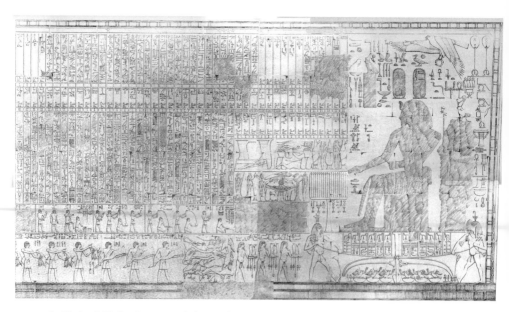

b. Deir el-Bahari: memorial temple of Hatshepsut, south wall of the offering-chapel of Hatshepsut.

a. Thebes-west: memorial temple of Thutmose III; the first pylon is separated from the rest of the building by the modern road.

b. False-door stela from memorial temple of Thutmose III (now at Medinet Habu).

a. Valley of the Kings: burial chamber of KV34 (Thutmose III).

b. Valley of the Kings: burial chamber of KV35 (Amenhotep II).

a. Thebes-west: memorial temple of Amenhotep II.

b. Thebes-west: memorial temple of Thutmose IV; the rear part of the temple is under and beyond the modern road.

a. Valley of the Kings: well-room (E) of KV43 (Thutmose IV).

b. Valley of the Kings: section of the Book of Amduat in the burial chamber of WV22 (Amenhotep III).

a. Valley of the Kings: wall of the antechamber (I) of WV22 (Amenhotep III).

b. The outer part of the memorial temple of Amenhotep III.

a. Kom el-Hetan: the western side of the peristyle court of the memorial temple of Amenhotep III.

b. The sarcophagus of Akhenaten, restored from fragments (EMC TR 3/3/70/2).

a. Tell el-Amarna: TA29 (Neferneferuaten or Tutankhaten[?])

b. Valley of the Kings: burial chamber of KV62 (Tutankhamun).

a. Valley of the Kings: burial chamber of WV23 (Ay).

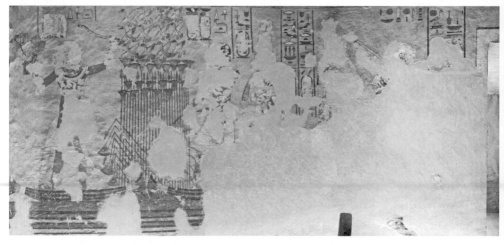

b. Valley of the Kings: hunting and fishing wall of burial chamber of WV23 (Ay).

a. Valley of the Kings: antechamber of KV57 (Horemheb).

b. Valley of the Kings: crypt of burial chamber of KV57 (Horemheb).

a. Valley of the Kings: unfinished decoration in burial chamber of KV57 (Horemheb).

b. Medinet Habu: remains of memorial temple of Ay and Horemheb, from the west.

a. The Valley of the Queens.

b. Wadi Sikka Taqa el-Zeide: the entrance to the tomb of Hatshepsut as regent lies at the bottom of the vertical cleft.

a. Valley of the Kings: burial chamber of KV16 (Rameses I). The columns are modern consolidation.

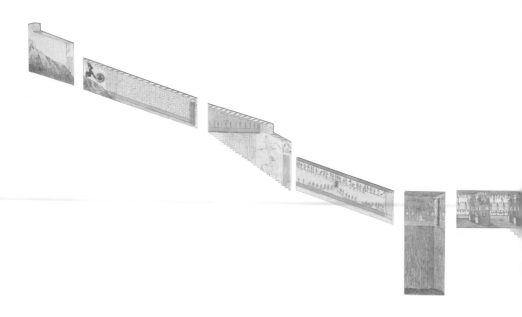

b. Section of KV17 (Sethy I), showing decoration.

a. The memorial temple of Sethy I at Qurna.

a. Valley of the Kings: burial chamber of KV17 (Sethy I).

b. Valley of the Kings: entrance left doorjamb of KV7 (Rameses II), showing the damaged state of the rock in the tomb.

c. The main hall of the Osireion of Sethy I at Abydos, showing infiltrated groundwater.

a. Thebes-west: the Ramesseum, the memorial temple of Rameses II.

b. Valley of the Kings: burial chamber of KV8 (Merenptah), showing the foot of his middle sarcophagus, set in the 20th century AD on the calcite base-block of the smashed outer sarcophagus. The latter was restored in the early 21st century.

a. Valley of the Kings: pillared hall and burial chamber of KV15 (Sethy II).

b. Valley of the Kings: entrance of KV10 (Amenmeses), showing the erased decoration.

a. Valley of the Kings: rear corridors (I and J1) and burial chamber of KV47 (Siptah), showing the damage caused by flooding.

b. Valley of the Kings: Litany of Re in corridor B of KV47, showing the erasure and reinstatement of the cartouches of Siptah.

a. Valley of the Kings: figure in corridor B of KV14, first carved to show Tawosret as queen, then modified to depict her as king, and finally recarved as Sethnakhte.

b. Model of the burial chamber of Valley of the Queens QV66 (Nefertiry D; Museo Egizio, Turin).

a. Valley of the Kings: burial chamber of Tawosret as queen in KV14.

b. Valley of the Kings: corridor C of KV11 (Sethnakhte, then Rameses III).

a. Valley of the Kings: lintel at entrance to corridor G of KV14, showing figures of Tawosret plastered over and replaced by the names and titles of Sethnakhte.

b. Medinet Habu: vignettes from the Book of the Dead showing Rameses III in the Fields of *Iaru*.

Medinet Habu.

a. Valley of the Kings: burial chamber of KV2 (Rameses IV).

b. Valley of the Kings: burial chamber of KV9 (Rameses VI).

a. Valley of the Kings: burial chamber of KV1 (Rameses VII).

b. Valley of the Kings: corridors C and D in KV6 (Rameses IX).

a. Valley of the Kings: burial chamber of KV6 (Rameses IX).

b. Valley of the Kings: entrances of (from the left) KV18 (Rameses X), KV17 (Sethy I) and KV16 (Rameses I).

a. Valley of the Kings:
view from the entrance
of KV4 (Rameses XI).

b. Valley of the Queens, showing the locations of QV42 (Prehirwenemef B),
QV43 (Sethhirkopeshef B), QV44 (Khaemwaset E) and QV45 (unfinished,
possibly a Queen Satefmire).

a. Valley of the Queens: scene in QV55 (Amenhirkopeshef B), showing Rameses III and the tomb owner.

b. Tanis (San el-Hagar): the royal necropolis (NRT-I: Osorkon II; NRT-II: Pamiu; NRT-III: Pasebkhanut I; NRT-IV: Amenemopet; NRT-VI: unknown), with the pylon of the temple of Amun at the top-left.

a. Tanis: south wall of antechamber of NRT-III (Pasebkhanut I), including the secondary addition of a figure of Amenemopet on the left, probably replacing an image of Queen Mutnedjmet B.

b. Tanis: north wall of antechamber of NRT-II, showing the judgement of Osorkon II.

a. Tanis: chamber 2 of NRT-I, with the sarcophagus reused for the burial of Takelot I.

b. Tanis: burial chamber of Osorkon II in NRT-I.

a. Tanis: NRT-V (Shoshenq III) as first uncovered.

b. Tanis: south wall of NRT-V.

a. Tanis: NRT-II
(Pamiu).

b. Medinet Habu
MH1 (Horsieset
I): view from the
burial chamber
towards entrance.

c. Memphis: tombs of the Twenty-second Dynasty high priests of Ptah.

a. Façade of burial chamber of Shoshenq D; from Memphis (EMC JE88131).

b. El-Kurru, from the south, with the (4th century?) pyramid Ku1 on the right.

a. El-Kurru: mastaba Ku8 (Kashta?)

b. El-Kurru: Ku17 (Piye), from the west.

a. El-Kurru: Ku18 (Shabataka), from the southeast.

b. El-Kurru: Ku15 (Shabaka) and Ku16 (Tanutamun).

a. Nuri: Nu1 (Taharqa), from the east, viewed from between Nu7 (Karkamani – late 6th century) and Nu8 (Aspelta – early 6th century), with Nu4 (Siaspiqa – mid 5th century) to the right.

b. El-Kurru: burial chamber of Ku16 (Tanutamun).

a. The pyramid-field of Nuri, the cemetery of most the later Napatan kings. From the left the monuments are: Nu2 (Amaniastabarqa – early 5th century); Nu1 (Taharqa); Nu3 (Senkamanisken – mid 7th century); Nu15 (Nastasen – later 4th century); Nu4 (Siaspiqa); Nu17 (Baskakereñ – late 5th century); Nu19 (Ñasakhma); Nu12 (Amanneteyerike); Nu11 (Malewiebamani – all 5th century); Nu10 (Amaninatakilebte – later 6th century); Nu9 (Amtalqa – mid 6th century); and Nu8 (Aspelta – early 6th century).

b. The pyramid-fields at Meroe, the Kushite royal cemetery from the end of the 4th century BC to the middle of the 4th century AD.

a. Gebel Barkal: Bar1–7 (1st century AD) and (left) 8 (4th century BC).

b. El-Kurru: burial chamber of Ku5 (Qalhata).

a. Medinet Habu: tomb-chapels of the God's Wives of Amun.

b. Medinet Habu: forecourt of tomb-chapel of Amenirdis I.

a. Sais (Sa el-Hagar).

b. Fragment of sarcophagus of Psametik II (Louvre E.32580).

LXXXVIII

a. The tomb of Kyrus II at Pasagardae.

b. The *Zendan-e Soleiman* at Pasagardae, possibly the original intended tomb of Kambyses II.

c. The *Kabah-e Zardusht* at Nashq-e Rustam, possibly the tomb of Kambyses II.

a. A distant view of the necropolis of Nashq-e Rustam.

b. The monuments of Nashq-e Rustam, with the *Kabah-e Zardusht* on the right and tombs IV, III, I and II, showing how the latter lies at right angles to the rest of the tombs.

a. Tomb I at Nashq-e Rustam, built by Darius I and the prototype for all subsequent Persian royal tombs. The reliefs at the bottom of the cliff date from the third century AD.

b. The terrace of Persepolis, with royal tombs VI and V in the hill behind.

a. Tomb VI, probably the sepulchre of Artaxerxes II.

b. Tomb V, probably the constructed for Artaxerxes III.

a. Tell Ruba (Mendes), with the sarcophagus and site of the tomb of Naefarud I.

b. Alexandria: antechamber of the Alabaster Tomb.

a. Alexandria waterfront: on the far left are the remnants of the Lochias Peninsula, while the Royal Quarter occupied most of the remainder of the area shown, and extended under what is now the sea.

b. Rome: the Mausoleum of Augustus.

a. Rome: the Forum of Trajan.

b. Rome: the Mausoleum of Hadrian (Castel Sant'Angelo).

a. Split: the Mausoleum of Diocletian, as incorporated into the Cathedral of St Domnius.

b. Istanbul: the sarcophagi of three of the earlier successors of Constantine, formerly in the Church of the Apostles (Archaeological Museum).